This excellent book, put together by Foss and Gibson, provides a unique and fresh perspective on entrepreneurial universities. The editors offer us insightful theoretical ideas whilst the empirical studies illustrate the variety of contexts entrepreneurial universities can operate in successfully.

Friederike Welter, *Institut für Mittelstandsforschung (IfM) Bonn and University Siegen, Germany*

This insightful book offers ideas, thoughts and research results on the role of context in the emergence and development of entrepreneurial universities through the lens of institutional theory. This is done mainly by examining a number of cases providing a great level of diversity. After reading the book, factors and strategies which could facilitate the transition to more entrepreneurial university behaviors appear in a wide variety of contexts and institutional conditions.

Alain Fayolle, *Professor, EMLYON Business School, France*

Lene Foss and David Gibson provide us with a splendid variety of new cases – from familiar locales of Austin and Cambridge UK to unfamiliar settings of the Arctic University and Lund University – where universities are an anchor tenant in burgeoning regional economies. The cases are enriched with a provocative analysis of the institutional changes and conflicts that are triggered by these enterprising efforts to make higher education an engine of economic growth.

Walter W. Powell, *Professor, Stanford University, USA*

The Entrepreneurial University

Global recessions and structural economic shifts are motivating government and business leaders worldwide to increasingly look to "their" universities to stimulate regional development and to contribute to national competiveness. The challenge is clear and the question is pressing: How will universities respond?

This book presents in-depth case narratives of ten universities from Norway, Finland, Sweden, the UK, and the US that have overcome significant challenges to develop programs and activities to commercialize scientific research, launch entrepreneurial degree programs, establish industry partnerships, and build entrepreneurial cultures and ecosystems. The universities are quite diverse: large and small; teaching and research focused; internationally recognized and relatively new; located in major cities and in emerging regions. Each case narrative describes challenges overcome, actions taken, and resulting accomplishments.

This volume will be of interest to policymakers and university administrators as well as researchers and students interested in how different programs and activities can promote university entrepreneurship while contributing to economic growth in developed and developing economies.

Lene Foss is a professor of innovation and entrepreneurship at the University of Tromsø (UiT) in Norway.

David V. Gibson is Associate Director and the Nadya Kozmetsky Scott Centennial Fellow, IC² (Innovation, Creativity, Capital) Institute, The University of Texas at Austin.

RIOT! Routledge Studies in Innovation, Organization and Technology

The Entrepreneurial University

Context and institutional change

Edited by
Lene Foss and
David V. Gibson

Routledge
Taylor & Francis Group

LONDON AND NEW YORK

First published 2015
by Routledge
2 Park Square, Milton Park, Abingdon, Oxfordshire OX14 4RN

Simultaneously published in the USA and Canada
by Routledge
711 Third Avenue, New York, NY 10017, USA

First issued in paperback 2017

Routledge is an imprint of the Taylor & Francis Group, an informa business

British Library Cataloguing in Publication Data
A catalogue record for this book is available from the British Library

Library of Congress Cataloging in Publication Data
The entrepreneurial university: context and institutional change / edited by Lene Foss and David V. Gibson.
    pages cm
    Includes bibliographical references and index.
    1. Academic-industrial collaboration. 2. Entrepreneurship.
    3. Economic development. I. Foss, Lene. II. Gibson, David V.
    LC1085.E57 2015
    378.1'035–dc23   2014048608

ISBN 13: 978-1-138-74354-0 (pbk)
ISBN 13: 978-1-138-83077-6 (hbk)

Typeset in Sabon
by Wearset Ltd, Boldon, Tyne and Wear

Dedicated to

W. Richard Scott
Professor of Sociology Emeritus
Stanford University

Contents

Figures

Tables

Contributors

Editors

Lene Foss is Professor in Innovation and Entrepreneurship at School of Business and Economics, UiT The Arctic University of Norway, and is currently a visiting fellow at the Judge Business School, University of Cambridge, UK. Her research concentrates on university entrepreneurship, entrepreneurial networks, entrepreneurial education and gender in innovation and entrepreneurship. She has published work in *International Small Business Journal*, *International Journal of Entrepreneurship and Innovation*, *International Journal of Entrepreneurial Behaviour and Research*, *International Journal of Entrepreneurship and Small Business*, *European Journal of Marketing*, *International Journal of Tourism Research*, *Systemic Practice and Action Research*, and *International Journal of Gender and Entrepreneurship*. Foss is associate editor of *Journal of Small Business Management* and editorial consultant and editorial board member of *International Journal of Gender and Entrepreneurship*.

David V. Gibson is Senior Research Scientist, Associate Director and The Nadya Kozmetsky Scott Centennial Fellow, IC² (Innovation, Creativity, Capital) Institute, at The University of Texas at Austin (USA). In 1983, he received a PhD from the Department of Sociology, Stanford University, concentrating on organizational behaviour and communication theory. He is a consultant to business, government, and academia worldwide and his research and publications have been translated into Mandarin, Japanese, Korean, Russian, Spanish, Italian, French, Greek, German, Portuguese, Finnish, and Norwegian. He was a Fulbright Scholar at Instituto Superior Tecnico, Lisbon, Portugal, 1999–2000, and a visiting Professor II at UiT The Arctic University of Norway, School of Business and Economics, 2012–2014.

Contributors

Christina Lea Butler is Senior Lecturer in the Department of Management at Kingston Business School. She holds an MBA from Ivey Business

School (Canada) and a PhD from London Business School (UK). Her research interests include innovation and creativity in culturally diverse teams and the leadership of global teams. She is a founding member of the international research network Leveraging Culture in Teams. Her work has been published in journals such as *Organizational Behavior and Human Decision Processes*, *Journal of World Business*, *Scandinavian Journal of Management*, and *International Journal of Human Resource Management*. She is also a co-author of *Leveraged Innovation*, a book that explores the relationship between manufacturers and suppliers in the new product development process.

John S. Butler is the J. Marion West Chair at the McCombs School of Business and Professor of Sociology and Management at The University of Texas at Austin (USA). He is the former Director of the Herb Kelleher Center for Entrepreneurship, Growth and Renewal at McCombs School of Business and former Director of the IC² Institute. He received his PhD from Northwestern University in Evanston, Illinois. He has published in the *American Sociological Review*, *Journal of Armed Forces and Society*, *Sociological Perspectives*, *Foresight-Russia*, and *Journal of Developmental Entrepreneurship*. His books include *Global Perspectives on Technology Transfer* (with David Gibson), *Entrepreneurship and Self-Help among Black Americans*, *An American Story: Mexican American Entrepreneurship and Wealth Creation* (with David Torres and Alfonse Morales), *All That We Can Be* (with Charles C. Moskos), and *Immigrant and Minority Entrepreneurship: Building American Communities and Economies* (with George Kozmetsky).

Steffen Farny is a doctoral candidate in the Entrepreneurship Discipline, Department of Management Studies at Aalto University School of Business in Helsinki, Finland. He holds an MSc in Corporate Development from the University of Cologne and an MSc in Entrepreneurship from Aalto University. His research interests include entrepreneurship and sustainable development, social entrepreneurship, entrepreneurship education, and post-disaster community development. Steffen's dissertation focus is on institutional work of entrepreneurs in post-disaster contexts.

Robert Hodgson is the Managing Director of Zernike (UK) which manages an ICT focused incubator and provides start-up capital for knowledge based firms. He has over 30 years' experience of international consulting and has worked in more than 30 countries on innovation policies and technology commercialization, half with international agencies like the World Bank and half with national, regional, and local agencies and the private sector. Prior to the launching of Zernike (UK), he was for 14 years an executive director of SQW Ltd which is best known for its path-breaking study, *The Cambridge Phenomenon*. He is a Senior Fellow at the Institute for Innovation, Creativity, and Capital at The University of Texas at Austin.

Tatiana Iakovleva is Associate Professor in Stavanger Business School, Stavanger Centre for Innovation Research, University of Stavanger. She received her PhD in management from Bode Graduate School of Business, Norway (2007). Her research interests include personal and organizational antecedents leading to innovation and superior entrepreneurial performance on enterprise and regional level, female entrepreneurship, as well as factors affecting entrepreneurial intentions. She has over 30 publications in international journals and books on the topic related to entrepreneurship, innovation, and transitional economies.

Tomas Karlsson attained his PhD in Business Administration from Jönköping International Business School in 2005. He was responsible for the master's program in entrepreneurship at Lund University 2009–2013. Since 2013 he has been employed as Associate Professor at Chalmers University of Technology, Department of Managing Organizational Renewal and Entrepreneurship. He is currently a reviewer for the Academy of Management Learning and Education, the *Journal of Business Venturing* and *Entrepreneurship Theory and Practice*. His research primarily focuses on new venture creation, entrepreneurship education, and business planning. He has published in journals such as *Journal of Business Venturing*, *Journal of Management*, and *Journal of Technology Transfer*.

Jill R. Kickul is the Director of New York University's social entrepreneurship program and teaches courses in entrepreneurship and social entrepreneurship and is the Faculty Chair and Academic Advisor for the 30-course MBA specialization in Social Innovation and Impact. Her primary research areas of interest include innovation and strategic processes within new ventures, micro-financing practices and wealth creation in transitioning economies, and social entrepreneurship. She is the co-author of numerous books and has more than 100 publications in entrepreneurship and management journals. Her work on entrepreneurship education development and curriculum design has been nationally recognized and supported through the National Science Foundation (NSF) and Coleman Foundation Entrepreneurship Excellence in Teaching Colleges Grant and was named by *Fortune Small Business* as one of the Top 10 Innovative Programs in Entrepreneurship Education.

Paula Kyrö (PhD Educ. and PhD Econ.) is Professor of Entrepreneurship Education at Aalto University School of Business. She has worked as a Research Professor of Entrepreneurship Education in the School of Economics and Business Administration at University of Tampere. She has held a position of Assistant Professor in education in the University of Helsinki, Professor in Entrepreneurship at the University of Jyväskylä, School of Business and Economics, and she has worked as a Visiting Professor in entrepreneurship in Jönköping International Business School in Sweden. Her research interests are in the dynamics of entrepreneurial and enterprising learning, entrepreneurial university, and sustainable development.

Hans Landström attained his PhD in Industrial Management at Lund Institute of Technology in Sweden. He holds a Chair in Entrepreneurship at Lund University. He is co-founder of two research centres on entrepreneurship and innovation at Lund University: Centre for Innovation, Research and Competence in the Learning Economy (CIRCLE), and the Sten K. Johnson Centre for Entrepreneurship (SKJCE). His research interests include entrepreneurial finance, informal and institutional venture capital, entrepreneurial learning and teaching, and the history of entrepreneurship research. He has published in journals such as *Research Policy, Journal of Business Venturing, Entrepreneurship Theory and Practice, Small Business Economics, Entrepreneurship and Regional Development,* and *Journal of Small Business Management.*

Ari Lindeman is Team Leader of Leadership and Entrepreneurship at Kymenlaakso University of Applied Sciences, Finland. He also coordinates interdisciplinary developments of the university's Master School. He has studied and taught philosophy as a Fulbright grantee at the University of South Florida, 2000–2003. In the 1990s, he worked as a management consultant after studies at Turku School of Economics, UMIST/ Manchester School of Management, WHU Koblenz, and University of Helsinki. His current research interests focus on interdisciplinarity in development work and education, wicked problems, and the entrepreneurial university. He is an honourable member of the editorial board of the scientific journal of St Petersburg State Polytechnical University.

Mats Lundqvist is Professor in Entrepreneurship at Chalmers University of Technology, in Gothenburg, Sweden. His research interests are in the area of university entrepreneurship, including academic entrepreneurship, incubation practice, action-based entrepreneurship education, as well as institutional transformations. He is the director and co-founder of Chalmers School of Entrepreneurship started in 1997 and top-ranked by the Swedish government in 2009. The school operates with the dual objectives of developing entrepreneurs and new technology ventures by arranging partnership with its students and inventors from Chalmers and beyond. As a direct result more than 50 technology ventures have been started since 1997, of which many now are high-growth companies. It is today the leading start-up environment in Sweden as regards technology venture revenue. The school's incubator, Encubator, was ranked number eight in the world in the 2014 University Business Incubator index (UBIindex.com). Mats is engaged in several boards dealing with incubation and technology transfer and has been the co-founder of the biotech start-up Ellen, publicly listed since 2003. His research appears in journals, such as *Research Policy, Science and Public Policy, R&D Management,* and *Technovation.*

Martha Mador is Associate Professor and Head of Enterprise Education at Kingston University London. She holds a DBA from Henley Management College and Brunel University. Her practical and research interests are in entrepreneurship promotion and practice dissemination across the higher education community. She is the Chair of the Higher Education Entrepreneurship Group, a national group of enterprise educators which works to share and develop practice. She is also Director of KnowledgeLondon, which supports the knowledge transfer community in London and beyond. She is the co-author with David Stokes and Nick Wilson of *Entrepreneurship* (2010), a best-selling textbook on the subject, and the co-designer of numerous educational games for entrepreneurship.

Bala Mulloth is Assistant Professor of Entrepreneurship and Innovation Management at Central European University (CEU) Business School. His main research interests are in entrepreneurship and innovation, particularly in the areas of social entrepreneurship and the development of global innovation ecosystems. He teaches courses on new venture development, social entrepreneurship, sustainability in business, India and south Asia, and business in a global city: New York City (a month-long MBA course that CEU runs in NYC). Prior to moving to Hungary and joining CEU Business School, He was the Senior Manager of Polytechnic Institute of New York University's Office of Innovation Development, Technology Transfer and Entrepreneurship. He holds a PhD in Technology Management from Polytechnic Institute of New York University.

Elin Oftedal wrote her PhD on the topic of entrepreneurship and innovation for the University of Nordland, Norway. She is currently Associate Professor at the Tromsø University School of Business and Economics (HHT), where she teaches, and also supervises and carries out research on commercialization, academic entrepreneurship, student entrepreneurship, regional development, and CSR issues. Her research interest is especially focused on projects concerning renewable energy and climate change.

Caroline Wigren-Kristoferson attained her PhD in Business Administration in 2003 at Jönköping International Business School, Jönköping University. She is currently Associate Professor in Entrepreneurship at the Centre for Innovation, Research and Competence in the Learning Economy (CIRCLE), and at the Sten K. Johnson Centre for Entrepreneurship (SKJCE), both at Lund University, Sweden. She carries out research on entrepreneurship in different contexts, e.g. the academic setting, the healthcare industry, and rural areas. She has a general interest in institutional entrepreneurship, regional development, and methodological issues. She has published in journals such as *Action Research Journal, Science and Public Policy, Journal of Technology Transfer, International Journal of Entrepreneurship and Small Business*, and *Journal of Developmental Entrepreneurship*.

Acknowledgements

The motivation for this volume, *The Entrepreneurial University: Context and Institutional Change*, emerged as a part of an international research project sponsored by the Norwegian Research Council and led by Professor Lene Foss at the School of Business and Economics at UiT, the Arctic University of Norway. The research programme known as "FORFI: Knowledge base for research and innovation policy" focuses principally on expanding and improving the knowledge base for research by conducting research of high international standard with a strong relevance to policy development. Furthermore, the programme aims to strengthen theory development and methodology within the field of innovation while promoting comparative studies and international cooperation across subject fields, disciplines, and research traditions. We gratefully acknowledge the funds provided for project 212290, "From university research to implementation and commercialisation: A comparative study" at UiT in Tromsø.

Dr David Gibson, IC^2 Institute, the University at Texas at Austin and Professor II at UiT, joined the research project and became co-editor of this book alongside Professor Foss. As editors, we are most appreciative for the assistance of our colleagues at New York University, Kingston University London, Chalmers Institute of Technology, Kymenlaakso University of Applied Sciences, the University of Stavanger, and the University of Nordland. Additional pieces fell into place after receiving an invitation to the "Entrepreneurial Learning Forum" at Chalmers University of Technology in the spring of 2012, where we had the opportunity to speak with Professor Hans Landstrøm from Lund University and doctoral candidate Steffen Farny from Aalto University. They also offered to contribute with their colleagues to the volume with perspectives on their own universities. The last important contribution was secured at "The Circumpolar Conference on High North Entrepreneurship and Innovation" at UiT in November 2012, when Bob Hodgson, a conference contributor, agreed to provide a chapter on the "Cambridge Phenomenon". As editors we requested narrative-based accounts of how various universities developed entrepreneurially over different periods of time. Our authors exceeded our expectations with insightful and informative case narratives. Contributing to this research project necessitated their attention through numerous review processes requiring their ongoing patience, for which we are eternally grateful. We thus acknowledge all our case authors and express our heartfelt "thank you" for their chapters and their enduring contributions throughout this two-year process.

Our theoretical slant on the content and our analyses was inspired and guided by Professor Emeritus Richard W. Scott, Department of Sociology, Stanford University, whom we had the pleasure of collaborating with as our mentor in this project. We visited with him at Stanford and benefited from his advice, most importantly on the theoretical framing and interpretation of the cases.

Editing a book with 12 chapters from an international collection of authors required administrative assistance. Margaret Cotrofeld of the IC^2 Institute at The University of Texas at Austin served as the master coordinator of this process – assisting chapter authors in shaping their content, preparing the manuscript to Routledge's guidelines, and providing an index for the volume. We thank Erin Newton Mulloth, Jessica Green, Uladzimir Kamovich, and Geir Mikalsen for providing statistics, searching for relevant literature as well as language cleaning. In addition, we are indebted to our four Routledge reviewers for improving our book proposal and resulting drafts of Chapters 1 and 12. We especially thank Associate Professor Einar Rasmussen of University of Nordland for his continually helpful comments and advice. The Visiting Fellowship of Professor Foss at the Judge Business School in Cambridge provided us with a network of scholars in the United Kingdom who contributed helpful comments. Accordingly we thank Dr Shai Vyarkarnam, Dr Nina Granqvist, Dr Tim Vorley, Dr Elvira Uyarra, and Dr Fumi Kitagawa for comments on book chapter drafts.

We sincerely hope that this publication makes a scholarly contribution to the field, proves useful in the classroom, and inspires scholars in the fields of entrepreneurship, organization, innovation, and higher education to build further on our research. As for policymakers and university administrators, this book is intended to provide useful insights into the structures and processes that are conducive to executing the university's third mission. In that regard we thank Special Advisor Ken Enoksen at Troms County Council, Senior Advisor Jan-Roger Iversen and Research Director of Research Pål Vegar Storeheier at UiT, Special Advisor Per Ramvi at University of Stavanger, Special Advisor at the Research Council of Norway, Elisabeth Bakkelund, and Bård Hall, previous CEO of Norinnova Technology Transfer in Tromsø for being a solid user group for policy implications in the project.

It has been a challenging endeavour for us to produce this volume of ten case studies covering considerably different regions in five countries, employing institutional theory and the entrepreneurial architecture framework to achieve a more profound understanding the entrepreneurial university, context, and institutional change. Finally, we are indebted to Jacqueline Curthoys, Commissioning Editor, and Sinead Waldron, Editorial Assistant, at Routledge for their patient support while we refined and completed this volume.

Lene Foss, Cambridge
David V. Gibson, Austin
1 December 2014

Foreword

The quest to understand the role and purpose of higher education institutions has existed since the reflections of Newman (1852) about the "idea of a university". Much of the debate initially focused on teaching and research, and such arguments about the relative merits of universities as research-led versus teaching-led institutions continue to persist. More recently, there has been growing academic and political interest in the wider socio-economic role of universities; perhaps more accurately embodying what Kerr (1963) referred to as the *multiversity*. The civic and economic role of universities are now at the fore, and while such roles are not new, this evolving focus has certainly become more explicit.

Universities around the world have sought to position and establish themselves in response to the new expectations of them. Far from being ivory towers, today universities have come to be regarded as important engines of economic growth and social change. Scholars and commentators alike have conceptualized and characterized this transformation, as universities have sought to forge and renew their identities. Of the various neologisms used to describe the contemporary university, it is that of the "entrepreneurial university" that is most apt. As well as reflecting the values of the entrepreneurial society of which it is a part, the term also embodies how universities have come to approach this new era.

The success of universities has been determined by their ability to function as autonomous institutions. Given that entrepreneurship confers a sense of autonomy, this is set to remain the case. The ability of entrepreneurial universities to act autonomously is shaped by their institutional environment, although universities are not passive actors as they in turn shape the institutional environment. While institutional arrangements differ university by university and region by region, the institutional lens provides an approach to explore these intra- and inter-institutional dynamics.

Much existing research either focuses on case studies of entrepreneurial universities as institutions, or examines the wider knowledge economy as the institutional environment. While both are worthwhile foci, the dynamic between entrepreneurial universities and the institutional environment remains under-researched. In this respect the challenge is to move beyond the idiosyncrasies of individual case studies to understand the dynamics that shape institutional arrangements. A contribution of this book is that it embraces this challenge.

The rich selection of case studies presented in this book provides insights into the entrepreneurial development of universities and the societies of which they are a part. The case studies present the experiences of a broad range of institutions drawn from different countries with different institutional systems. While the institutions and institutional systems considered have developed in different ways and at different rates, they are all testament to the entrepreneurial turn in society, and in universities in particular.

As the book concludes, it is neither possible nor desirable to generalize from the empirical cases presented, as this would be to oversimplify their institutional complexities. That said, there are a number of lessons that are highlighted about universities being, and becoming, entrepreneurial. The case studies serve to highlight the heterogeneity of what we understand to be the entrepreneurial university, a characteristic which is born from their own institutional autonomy. The different national and regional settings examined also highlight how the institutional environment can influence the increasingly diverse entrepreneurial behaviours of universities.

Universities have shown a variety of motivations in being entrepreneurial, a number of which are shared while others are more institutionally specific. Likewise, while the impetus of governments to leverage the entrepreneurial potential is increasingly common, the means by which this is achieved remain diverse. Indeed the phenomenon that is the entrepreneurial university is the product of institutional push factors coupled with a range of socio-economic pull factors. How theses factor play out is a balance, which will differ according to the both the institution and the institutional setting.

In advancing our understanding of entrepreneurial universities, the institutional lens assumed by the book offers a means to bridge micro institutional case studies and macro perspectives of the institutional environment. If entrepreneurial universities are to realize their potential as part of the institutional landscape, they need to become more established. This will only be achieved if they are able to develop their entrepreneurial capacity, a challenge which is about both the institution and its environment. For me, the book serves to emphasize that the entrepreneurial turn is about more than the creation of institutions and institutional environments; it is as much about redressing the institutional asymmetries that stymie entrepreneurialism.

Tim Vorley
University of Sheffield, UK

References

Kerr, C. (1963). *The Uses of the University*. Cambridge, MA: Harvard University Press.

Newman, J.H. (1852). *The Idea of a University*. London: Longmans Green and Co.

1 The entrepreneurial university
Context and institutional change

Lene Foss and David V. Gibson

Introduction

In the current globally competitive business environment, nations and regions are pressuring their universities to stimulate job and wealth creation. In addition to the key objectives of excelling in education and research, universities worldwide are increasingly tasked with fulfilling and enhancing the third mission of "service" with a concerted effort to help stimulate and sustain economic development. With this increased emphasis on commercializing research, licensing of technology, creating university spin-offs, introducing entrepreneurship programmes, and expanding university–industry relations, universities are being encouraged to take an *entrepreneurial turn*. We introduce this term to identify the transition that challenges universities as institutions, beyond their first mission (education) and second mission (research). Theoretically the entrepreneurial turn can be viewed as an institutional change (Scott, 2014) consisting of the roles, norms, and conventions that society has identified for how universities are expected to perform. We view the entrepreneurial turn as being heavily influenced by the institutional environment in which the university is embedded. Scott (2014: Chapters 1 and 2) devotes many pages to characterizing or defining institutions by drawing on, for example, Spencer (1876, 1896, 1910); Durkheim (1893/1949); Parsons (1934/1990), and Powell and DiMaggio (1991). In the end Scott (2014: 56) suggests using the omnibus conception that institutions comprise regulative, normative, and culture-cognitive elements that, together with associated activities and resources, provide stability and meaning to social life. Also well suited to our purposes, Storper (2013: 8, 9) considers institutions as being made up of rules, laws, and formal policies as well as the organization of key groups or communities from elite networks to civic associations and neighbourhood groups. In this regard, we are interested in how national and regional institutions interact to shape policies and attitudes and actions toward the entrepreneurial turn within and external to the university.

The term "entrepreneurial university" can be traced back to the highly cited book *Academic capitalism* (Slaughter and Leslie, 1997) that examines the changes of academic labour between 1970 and 1995, while identifying the term "academic capitalism" with the market effort to secure universities external finance. In a study of the transformation of five European universities, Clark (1998: 3–4) uses the term "entrepreneurial university" to mean a

> characteristic of social systems; that is, of entire universities and their internal departments, research centres, faculties and schools. The concept carries the overtone of "enterprise" – a wilful effort in institution-building that requires much special activity and energy. Taking risks when initiating new practices whose outcome is in doubt is a major factor. An entrepreneurial university, on its own, actively seeks to shift in organizational character so as to arrive at a more promising posture for the future. Entrepreneurial universities seek to become "stand-up" universities that are significant actors on their own terms. Institutional entrepreneurship can be seen as both process and outcome.[1]

According to recent literature, universities can be entrepreneurial in two main ways. First, *academic entrepreneurship* focuses on the commercialization of knowledge and research findings (Klofsten and Jones-Evans, 2000; Roessner *et al.*, 2013). In this way universities relate the third mission to research by becoming knowledge hubs (Youtie and Shapira, 2008) and are often concerned with the challenges and opportunities associated with technology transfer (Mowery *et al.*, 2002; Owen-Smith and Powell, 2003). Second, *entrepreneurial education* (Gibb and Hannon, 2006) links the third mission to the university's teaching mission and the building of entrepreneurial competency (Altmann and Ebersberger, 2013). In recognizing these two specific ways in which universities can develop entrepreneurially, this volume follows Clark's (1998) definition by viewing universities as institutional entrepreneurs when seeking to accommodate the entrepreneurial turn as a societal norm.

It is clear that governments, businesses, and societies differ in how they expect universities to contribute to knowledge-based growth, just as societal and institutional contexts differ in how they enhance or impede third-mission programmes and activities.[2] Despite an increasing number of edited books on university entrepreneurship (Morris *et al.*, 2013; Hoskinson and Kuratko, 2014; Fayolle and Redford, 2014; McKelvey and Holmén, 2009; Fetters *et al.*, 2010), scant attention has been given to the role of context in the emergence and development of entrepreneurial universities as institutions. Given the political and market context of universities worldwide, there is a clear need for a theoretical lens that addresses this multilevel phenomenon in a diverse range of environmental settings. We believe such theory should emphasize that organizations are both creatures of their institutional environments and active players in these processes (Scott, 2014). Thus the emerging entrepreneurial university is a result of complex recursive processes by which institutional forces both shape, and are shaped by, organizational actions. Accordingly, this volume focuses on the interrelationship between the university and its context through the lens of institutional theory as we seek to contribute theoretically, empirically, and methodologically to the area of university entrepreneurship.

Theoretical framework and research questions

This volume follows the call by Tolbert *et al.* (2011) that the mutual neglect of entrepreneurship research and institutional theory has limited the development of both traditions. We therefore aim to to integrate the entrepreneurial architecture concept at an organizational level in a larger institutional framework (Nelles and Vorley, 2010a, 2011; Vorley and Nelles, 2008). Theoretically, we employ a dual-level framework, focusing at both organizational and institutional levels of analysis, while exploring the entrepreneurial turn of universities embedded in different national and regional environments, meeting the need to also contextualize entrepreneurship theory (cf. Steyaert and Katz, 2004; Zahra, 2007; Welter, 2011). The two main research questions we address are: (1) What actors and forces are important in motivating institutional change in the development of a university's entrepreneurial architecture? (2) How do universities interact with institutional context in developing entrepreneurially? We aim to provide (1) new knowledge on actors and forces that motivate change in universities' entrepreneurial architecture, and (2) comparative examples of universities as they affect and are affected by institutional contexts in their entrepreneurial development.

Empirically, we sample universities from different national and regional contexts to develop in-depth comparative studies of emerging and well-developed entrepreneurial universities across institutional contexts. American universities have long been influenced by the Bayh–Dole Act of 1980, which accelerated the diffusion of new technology from universities and federal laboratories to firms (Lockett *et al.*, 2005). The United Kingdom was influenced in the mid-1980s by British business leaders collaborating with the Thatcher government to build an enterprise culture in tertiary education (Slaughter and Leslie, 1997). Legislation was enacted through three key programmes: the University Challenge, the Science Enterprise Challenge, and the Higher Education Innovation Fund, which stimulated the commercialization of university-based research, innovation in small firms, and the development of public–private partnerships (Lockett *et al.*, 2005). We selected two universities from the United States and two from the United Kingdom, as cases to better understand the perspective of these early adopters of third-mission activities and programmes. We have further selected universities from the northern European countries of Finland,

Sweden, and Norway as these universities have been embedded in different political and market contexts compared to the United States and the United Kingdom. In Finland, universities and the government have addressed the increased pressure to transform its higher education system by emphasizing greater institutional autonomy, and multidisciplinary teaching and research (Kyrö and Mattila, 2012; Ministry of Education Finland, 2007). Sweden has preserved the law of the university teacher's exemption, which allows researchers (as opposed to universities) to retain full rights to their discoveries (Wigren-Kristoferson *et al.*, 2011). Norwegian universities have only recently become formally involved in spin-off formation. Intellectual property ownership was previously assigned to the individual scholar, but transferred to universities as recently as 2003 (Rasmussen *et al.*, 2014). The universities vary from small to large, old to new, with varying histories of research contributions. Furthermore, some are embedded in rather small regions that may be either developed or developing, while others are in large and established cities.

Methodologically, this volume seeks to fill a third gap inasmuch as research on university entrepreneurship has been dominated by macro analysis and the use of indicators and surveys. We employ a narrative case study methodology to portray the intricate interrelationships between the university and its surrounding institutional environment – and allow the reader access to a complexity in models and a richness in data of interdependent processes across different actors, agents, and institutions involved in university entrepreneurship. Narratives have long traditions in organizational research as being appropriate to investigate actions and events (Van Maanen, 1988; Czarniawska, 1995), yet few such studies exist in the university entrepreneurship literature. The case narratives can be considered anthropological accounts as they were written by actors involved in their university's evolution of and engagement in third-mission activities – including commercializing scientific research, integrating entrepreneurship into courses and degree programmes, securing public financing, establishing industry partnerships, and impacting regional development.

Entrepreneurial architecture

In an extensive literature review, Rothaermel *et al.* (2007) concluded that current research in university entrepreneurship lacks a complexity in models and richness in data to understand the interdependent process across different actors, agents, and institutions. Recent empirical studies support the complex interrelationship between the university and an intricate institutional organization and its environment (Curi *et al.*, 2012; Howells *et al.*, 2012). Nelles and Vorley (2010b) claim that few contributions have attempted to establish a theoretical approach to conceptualize how universities can respond effectively to entrepreneurial imperatives. They propose that the third mission can and should reinforce the missions of teaching and research and that embedding the third mission and viewing the three missions as mutually constitutive are essential for the future coherence of the contemporary university (p. 342). Nelles and Vorley further (2011) identify a gap in previous studies as not seeking to theorize the process or dynamics of transformation in response to the pressure to become more entrepreneurial as institutions, nor encouraging entrepreneurship from within. They advocate that the concept of entrepreneurial architecture contributes to the literature by reconceptualizing the dynamic process of organizational change that accompanies university adaption of the third mission (p. 344). They introduce the concept of "entrepreneurial architecture" from the corporate entrepreneurship literature (Burns, 2005) as a lens through which the expanded mission of the universities can be better understood (Nelles and Vorley, 2010a). According to Vorley and Nelles (2008) the metaphor "entrepreneurial architecture" refers to the collection of internal factors that interact to shape entrepreneurial agendas at the universities. It comprises five dimensions that represent the institutional, communicative, coordinating, and cultural elements of an organization oriented towards the third mission:

1　*Structures* include technology transfer offices, incubators, technology parks, and business portals.
2　*Systems* focus on networks of communication and the configuration of linkages between structures and administration.
3　*Leadership* emphasizes the qualification and orientation of key influencers including administrators, board of directors, department heads, and "star scientists".
4　*Strategies* refer to institutional goals elaborated in institutional planning documents, incentive structures, and policy.
5　*Culture* refers to institutional, departmental, and individual attitudes, and norms.

Entrepreneurial architecture as an institutional change

Following Scott (2008), we view the university as constrained, shaped, penetrated, and renewed within a wider context or environment. Institutional Theory is concerned with the interplay of stability and change in different institutions and their agencies within organizational fields of activity (Scott, 2014). Within the institutional perspective, the organizational field is defined as "those organisations that, in aggregate, constitute a recognized area of institutional life: key suppliers, resource and product consumers, regulatory agencies, and other organisations that produce similar services or products" (DiMaggio and Powell, 1983: 148). This concept fulfils the vital role of connecting the university as an organization to its wider macrostructures – sectorial, societal, and even transnational. As DiMaggio (1986: 337) asserts, "the organisation field has emerged as a critical unit bridging the organisational and the societal levels in the study of social community and change". Institutional theory therefore allows for a structured analysis of the interaction between the various agents and the organizational field of concern as defined by those organizations, agencies, programs, and activities and relationships that enhance, or inhibit, the development of the entrepreneurial university which leads to our first research question: *What actors and forces are important in motivating institutional change in developing universities' entrepreneurial architecture?*

The dual framework, at the university and institutional levels, necessitates working across different units of analysis accommodating Welter's (2011: 174) argument "that contexts are intertwined and cut across levels of analysis – contextualizing theory thus needs to a apply a multi-context perspective". To assess institutional change at different levels of analysis we refer to Scott's regulative, normative, and cognitive pillars to better understand the forces that shape and constrain the entrepreneurial turn within universities embedded in different contexts (Scott, 2014: 59).

1   The *regulative pillar* concerns mandated specifications including laws, governance, and monitoring systems. This pillar, derived from economics, represents a rational actor model of behaviour including rules, sanctions, and conformity. How or to what degree do national or regional rules and regulations encourage or discourage entrepreneurship?
2   The *normative pillar* incorporates values, expectations, and standards, including roles, repertoires of action, conventions, and standards. As university cultures and their surrounding contexts may encourage or discourage entrepreneurship, this pillar is important in understanding motivation for, or resistance to, behavioural and institutional change toward the entrepreneurial turn.
3   The *cultural-cognitive pillar* encompasses predispositions and symbolic value as models for individual behaviour regarding the individual acceptance of entrepreneurship, or not, within universities and their contexts. Are professors of certain academic disciplines or professions or colleges more inclined to support the entrepreneurial turn?

Institutional theory encourages a structured analysis of the interaction between the various agents in an organizational field of concern and considers the interplay of stability and change in different institutions and their agencies. Scott's Institutional Pillars Model with its regulative, normative, and cognitive levels of analysis incorporates feedback and interactive loops of top-down influences (for example, changes in the broad national and regional policy environment) as well as bottom-up contributions from individual actors. Thus, the analysis of the cases draws on this model to discuss the pressures and influences to which organizations and institutions are subjected and the means through which these entities accommodate change, or not, in terms of the entrepreneurial turn. For example, in some cases the university's dominant influence is a top-down legal framework that is determined by national law. In others there is almost complete freedom within the university to determine its future as faculty and administrators have a large degree of independence from central control.

Our perspective in combining the entrepreneurial architecture framework and institutional theory is that the architecture can be viewed as an institutional change to help execute the third mission. Further, the institutional perspective allows analysis within the embedded contexts of universities. Finally, cross-case analysis will present how different organizational fields shape, constrain, and empower the university as well as how these fields of concern are influenced by the interests and activities of university participants. In agreement with institutional theory and the orientation of Nelles and Vorley (2010a), each of the five entrepreneurial dimensions is to be seen as interconnected with the other dimensions, both within the university and with external actors, well representing the multi-dimensional nature of the academy.

Embedding the entrepreneurial university

The notion of embeddedness stems from the seminal work of Granovetter (1985) who argues that most behaviour is closely embedded in interpersonal relations. Wright *et al.* (2008: 1222) also emphasize that universities cannot be seen as single isolated institutions in that they are embedded in regions that have an impact upon the intensity and nature of relationships. This leads us to the second research question: *How do universities interact with institutional context in developing entrepreneurially?*

There are four components of institutional theory that underpin our research methodology and discussion of the case narratives. First, in each case, the chapter authors emphasize the importance of the social context within which the university operates, supporting a main premise of Institutional Theory that the emphasis needs to be on the importance of the "ground" or environment in which the university is embedded (Scott and Christensen, 1995: 310). In this way, as institutional theorists do, we recognize the value of "attending to the larger drama, rather than to the individual player" (Scott, 2014: 262). This orientation encourages an emphasis on the importance of organization fields, which surround, "penetrate", and are "penetrated by" the entrepreneurial university. Vorley and Nelles (2008: 130; 2009: 288) advocate that the third mission is best integrated into an institutional strategy where inner connections link functions and goals while coordinating and embedding third-stream activities as fundamental to institutional development. Welter (2011) also calls for contextualizing the phenomena while Zahra (2007) states that contextualizing research effectively means linking theory, research objectives, and sites.

Second, in accordance with institutional theory, the case narratives provide many examples of how innovative actions make use of pre-existing activities and enter into existing contexts, which affect them and to which they must adjust. As Scott (2014: 263) states, institutionalists stress the continuing impact of the old on the new and the existing on the becoming. The case narratives highlight the importance of the types of effects occurring over time and provide a timeline of important changes related to the entrepreneurial turn. In accordance with institutional theory, there is also an emphasis on how things happen in addition to what happened as the authors attempt to uncover the sources of agency in the entrepreneurial university. Scott (2014: 264–265) elaborates that conceptualizing "over time" is a challenging task since institutional change is an unending process of learning about the imperfect enactment of social rules in interaction with a complex and unpredictable environment (Streeck, 2010: 665).

Third, institutionalists "rediscovered" the important role that ideas and symbolic elements play in the functioning of organizations – in addition to material resources, technological drivers, and exchange/power processes in the shaping of organizations. As Scott states (2014: 263), throughout much of the twentieth century, organizations have been treated as if they were "culture-free" systems driven by instrumental objectives and governed by "natural" economic laws. Accordingly, it is important to appreciate that universities are multifaceted and culturally complex and are best understood as organizations with multiple levels of control and loosely coupled activity where different components are likely to have a cultural identity that motivates normative and cognitive behaviour (Meyer and Rowan, 1977; Wright *et al.*, 2008).

Fourth, our analysis supports the interdependence of factors operating at multiple levels to affect the outcomes of interest. In many of the cases we see the interplay of top-down and bottom-up processes as they affected the formation and sustainability of the entrepreneurial university. As Scott (2014) emphasizes, organizations operate within fields that shape, constrain, and empower them, but they are also influenced by the interests and activities of their own participants. When placed in the context of an organizational field, there are forces at work between organizations and agencies that interact at the regional, national, and international levels and together may foster and sustain an entrepreneurial economy.

We conclude that a dual-level framework helps illuminate how universities execute their third-mission activities through entrepreneurial architecture, which in turn is conditioned by the institutional environment in which they are embedded and with which they interact. A main contribution of this approach is to offer a greater appreciation for the history and unique nature of the entrepreneurial university's development and operation in relation to its institutional context, and to learn from an enhanced understanding of these interrelationships and interdependences.

Sample of cases

A recent claim states that institutional research needs to ensure that the setting examined has a wide applicability and should include samples and investigations from multiple countries, otherwise it is difficult to be sure that institutional impact is applicable to a wide set of environments rather than merely represents an idiosyncratic result of the sample of a given country (Bruton *et al.*, 2010: 432–433) According to Uyarra (2010) there is a lack of accountability of the institutional diversity of universities both within and across national systems as there have been few in-depth attempts to collect and compare such empirical material in different national and regional contexts. Furthermore, as noted by Wright *et al.* (2013), much of the research on academic entrepreneurship has focused on universities that are "outliers" in terms of being atypical both in their own countries and worldwide.[3] Accordingly, the field needs knowledge from more mid-range universities and from other countries than the United States and the United Kingdom. Whereas central European universities have been sampled in earlier contributions (McKelvey and Holmén, 2009; West *et al.*, 2009), Scandinavian universities have received scant empirical investigation.

The interest of this volume lies primarily in examining universities that have embraced the entrepreneurial turn at various points in time. In order to control for a host of extraneous variables we limited our cases to universities in civil societies employing the rule of law. A further criterion was to select universities where entrepreneurship and innovation programs and activities were either working relatively well or were being challenged in interesting ways. Accordingly, the cases in this volume were sampled from two regions and different contexts within Sweden, Finland, and Norway and compared with two rather diverse regions and universities in the United States and the United Kingdom. This selection includes early adopters as well as universities that only recently began pursuit of the entrepreneurial turn.

The cases provide considerable diversity to compare and contrast on such characteristics as size of faculty, students enrolled, research budgets, historically renowned and newly formed institutions, and location in large, established cities as well as small, developing cities (Fetters *et al.*, 2010; Hoskinson and Kuratko, 2014; Fayolle and Redford, 2014), as shown in Table 1.1. Importantly, the entrepreneurial architecture dimensions are seen to be capable of being applied to diverse universities and contexts, as noted by Nelles and Vorley (2010a: 173):

> since institutional dynamism is central to entrepreneurial architecture, the framework can be applied to a wide variety of universities and can accommodate very different initial and policy contexts. As a result, entrepreneurial architecture is equally relevant to universities irrespective

Table 1.1 Select comparative statistics on universities and regions discussed

University (year established)	Total students	Undergraduate students	Graduate students	Faculty	Staff	Research budget (€ million)	Region population
Cambridge (1209)	18,812	11,878	6,934	3,175	6,648	332	200,000
Lund (1666)	48,000	36,000	12,000	5,200	2,300	649	700,000
Chalmers (1829)	10,107	6,415	3,692	2,012	826	205	1,000,000
New York University (NYU) (1831)	38,391	19,401	18,990	6,564	2,424	96	8,336,697
University of Texas (UT) at Austin (1883)	52,000	38,463	12,682	3,081	20,919	412	1,900,000
Arctic University of Norway (UiT) (1972)	11,759	7,885	3,874	1,448	1,164	159	70,000
Kingston University London (KUL) (1992)	20,668	16,658	4,010	807	2,146	3	8,416,535
Kymenlaakso University of Applied Sciences (Kyamk) (1996)	4,200	4,000	200	174	157	4	180,738
University of Stavanger (UiS) (2005)	10,148	6,940	3,208	632	419	37	460,000
Aalto (2010)	16,143	10,101	9,235	2,747	2,246	266	1,092,404

of the nature and stock of research within the institution, the characteristics of the regional economy, the power of and political status of the university, or the legacies of different institutional priorities regarding teaching and research agendas.

Case-based narrative approach

Among Scandinavian institutionalists there is strong interest in the practice of conducting field studies and taking the embeddedness of case examples seriously (Czarniawska, 2008). According to acknowledged organizational scholars, case narratives are most appropriate for representing actions and events (Van Maanen, 1988; Czarniawska, 1995). Therefore, a case-based narrative approach was selected for the present research. Each of the cases was written by participant-observers with an orientation that was clearly influenced by their individual histories and positions. The strength of each case is that it reflects each observer's autoethnographic account of "their" institution's effort to be more entrepreneurial. In an effort to enhance cross-case comparability, the authors were asked to consider the Nelles and Vorley (2010a) entrepreneurial architecture framework as it applied, or not, to their case narratives. However, we left it up to the authors to decide in which way they wanted to portray the development of this architecture.

This "insider characterization" of each case is a part of creating a reality from the viewpoint of the author, which is the strength of narratives. Golden-Biddle and Locke (1993) suggest that the narrative style appeals to the reader through authenticity and plausibility. We concede that different authors writing about the same case might well emphasize a different narrative; however, external expert observers were considered less likely to provide rich case narratives important to the research. Following Brannick and Coghlan (2007), insider research provides important knowledge that traditional descriptive approaches may not uncover, and is particularly relevant to an emphasis on contextualization. Indeed, the readers are invited to consider their own interpretations of the collected cases and to reflect on the challenges of establishing an entrepreneurial architecture at other universities and in other regions and nations. It is our intention that the case narratives in this book might provide useful teaching material in the fields of entrepreneurship, organization change, and regional development.

Contents

Two case studies from the United States present the challenges and opportunities of building an entrepreneurial architecture within established research universities located in extremely different environments. Chapter 2, "New York University: Nurturing entrepreneurship in New York City", by Mulloth and Kickul, provides an overview of how NYU is building a range of innovative academic and commercialization initiatives with collaboration across New York City's business, government, and academic sectors. Gibson and Butler, in Chapter 3, "Creating and sustaining high-technology development in Austin, Texas", tell the story of how influencers from academia, business, and government at the regional level catalysed the Austin Technopolis – which in turn provided the context for The University of Texas to launch and grow a broad range of entrepreneurial programmes and activities, and for the Austin region to be able to launch and grow globally successful technology-based companies.

In Chapter 4, we move to the United Kingdom where "High-technology entrepreneurship in a university city: The Cambridge story", by Hodgson, describes the transition of a renowned and ancient university and its surrounding agricultural region into one of the world's leading centres of technology entrepreneurship. In contrast, Chapter 5 "Kingston University London: Using entrepreneurship programmes to attract talent and to enhance educational and enterprise impact", by Butler and Mador, documents how a polytechnic university worked to transform itself into an entrepreneurial university to attract and educate students, many of whom are the first generation in their families to attend a university.

Chapter 6, "Chalmers: An entrepreneurial university institutionalizing the entrepreneurial?" by Lundqvist exemplifies how the region and industry played a major role in fostering the entrepreneurial architecture of the Swedish university. The case clarifies why and how Chalmers has become such a highly regarded and productive entrepreneurial university while at the same time highlighting the challenges of institutionalizing and sustaining these activities. In Chapter 7, "The evolution of Lund University's entrepreneurial ecosystem from 1980 to 2012", by Karlsson, Wigren-Kristoferson, and Landström, tells the story of a university in Sweden with strong academic traditions that made integrating the entrepreneurial turn more difficult.

Chapter 8 "Entrepreneurial Aalto: Where science and art meet technology and business" takes us to Finland where Farny and Kyrö explain how students took the lead at Aalto University to foster initiatives for building the university's entrepreneurial ecosystem while describing how policy interventions, with a local focus, created a positive spiral of self-reinforcing initiatives. Lindeman's Chapter 9, "Kymenlaakso University of Applied Sciences, Finland: In search of university-wide entrepreneurial action", tells the story of how the relatively small regional university responded to national policy changes and economic challenges by transforming itself from a provider of skilled labour for established industries into a provider of creative and entrepreneurial talent that supports small- and medium-sized Finnish companies.

Chapter 10 moves to northern Norway where Oftedal and Foss, in "UiT, the Arctic University of Norway: Challenges at the Arctic crossroads", describe the story of erecting the last of four classical universities in Norway in 1972. The chapter illuminates the challenges of being a public sector oriented university in a remote region that needs a strong private sector. The launch of the business school and evolution of a business creation and entrepreneurship program are an attempt to begin fulfilling the third mission. In the final case, Chapter 11, "Stavanger: From petroleum focus to diversified competence through crisis and consensus", we learn from Oftedal and Iakovleva how Stavanger University, one of Norway's newer universities, began as a regional college based on industry's need for competence in the petroleum sector, but shifted to a new focus on entrepreneurship and the challenges of the region's future.

Chapter 12, "The entrepreneurial university: Case analysis and implications" by Foss and Gibson is focused on answering the two research questions: (1) *What actors and forces are important in motivating institutional change in the development of a university's entrepreneurial architecture?* (2) *How do universities interact with institutional contexts in developing entrepreneurially?* Examples from the ten case narratives are used to analyze each of the five dimensions of the entrepreneurial framework in addressing these two research questions. The chapter concludes with research and policy implications.

Notes

1 Research on the entrepreneurial university began with higher education literature and received more attention within the fields of management, organization, entrepreneurship, and regional perspectives at a later stage. Whereas the current debate is highly multidisciplinary, this volume is limited to exploring the synergy between entrepreneurship and the organization field in studying entrepreneurial universities. Readers interested in further information on the entrepreneurial university within the higher education field will enjoy recent contributions in *Higher Education*, *Higher Education Policy*, and *Higher Education Quarterly*. Readers interested in university-driven entrepreneurship within the regional innovation system literature will find relevant publications in *European Planning Studies*, *Regional Studies*, *Cambridge Journal of Regions*, *Economics and Society* and *Environment and Planning C: Government and Policy*.
2 For an historical account of the university's role in supporting the third mission see Etzkowitz (2003).
3 Outliers like Stanford University and MIT (Shane, 2004; Hsu *et al.*, 2007) and Cambridge and Imperial College (Nicolaou and Birley, 2003) have a historical legacy of world-class research and regional infrastructure supporting technology-based ventures.

References

Altmann, A. and Ebersberger, B. (2013). Universities in change: a brief introduction. In *Managing higher education institutions in the age of globalization* (pp. 1–8). New York: Springer.
Brannick, T. and Coghlan, D. (2007). In defense of being "native": The case for insider academic research, *Organizational Research Methods*, 10(1), 59–74.

Bruton, G.D., Ahlstrom, D., and Li, H.L. (2010). Institutional theory and entrepreneurship: Where are we now and where do we need to move in the future? *Entrepreneurship Theory and Practice*, 34(3), 421–440.

Burns, P. (2005). *Corporate entrepreneurship: Building an entrepreneurial organisation*. Basingstoke: Palgrave Macmillan.

Clark, B.R. (1998). *Creating entrepreneurial universities: Organizational pathways of transformation*. Issues in Higher Education. New York: Elsevier.

Colyvas, J.A. (2007). From divergent meanings to common practices: The early institutionalization of technology transfer in the life sciences at Stanford University. *Research Policy*, 36(4), 456–476.

Colyvas, J.A. and Powell, W.W. (2006). Roads to institutionalization: The remaking of boundaries between public and private science. *Research in Organizational Behavior*, 27, 305–353.

Curi, C., Daraio, C., and Llerena, P. (2012). University technology transfer: How (in)efficient are French universities? *Cambridge Journal of Economics*, 36(3), 629–654.

Czarniawska, B. (1995). Narration or science? Collapsing the division in organization studies. *Organization*, 2(1), 11–33.

Czarniawska, B. (2008). How to misuse institutions and get away with it: Some reflections on institutional theory(ies). In R. Greenwood, C. Oliver, K. Sahlin, and R. Suddaby (eds), *The Sage handbook of organizational institutionalism* (pp. 769–782). Thousand Oaks, CA: Sage.

DiMaggio, P.J. (1986). Structural analysis of organizational fields: A block model approach. In Barry M. Staw and L.L. Cummings (eds), *Research in organizational behavior*, Vol. 8. (pp. 335–370). Greenwich, CT: JAI Press.

DiMaggio, P.J., and Powell, W.W. (1983). The iron cage revisited: Institutional isomorphism and collective rationality in organizational fields. *American Sociological Review*, 48(2), 147–160.

Durkheim, E. (1893/1949). *The division of labor in society*. Glencoe, Ill.: Free Press.

Etzkowitz, H. (2003). *MIT and the rise of entrepreneurial science*. London: Routledge.

Fayolle, A. and Redford, D.T. (eds) (2014). *Handbook on the entrepreneurial university*. Northampton, MA: Edward Elgar.

Fetters, M.L., Greene, P.G., Rice, M.P., and Butler, J.S. (eds) (2010). *The development of university-based entrepreneurship ecosystems: Global practices*. Cheltenham, UK: Edward Elgar.

Gibb, A., and Hannon, P. (2006). Towards the entrepreneurial university. *International Journal of Entrepreneurship Education*, 4(1), 73–110.

Golden-Biddle, K. and Locke, K. (1993). Appealing work: An investigation of how ethnographic texts convince. *Organization Science*, 4(4), 595–616.

Granovetter, M. (1985) Economic action and social structure: The problem of embeddedness, *American Journal of Sociology*, 91(3), 481–510.

Hoskinson, S. and Kuratko, D. (2014). *Innovative pathways for university entrepreneurship in the 21st century*. Bingley, UK: Emerald Group.

Howells, J., Ramlogan, R., and Cheng, S.L. (2012). Innovation and university collaboration: Paradox and complexity within the knowledge economy. *Cambridge Journal of Economics*, 36(3), 703–721.

Hsu, D.H., Roberts, E.B., and Eesley, C.E. (2007). Entrepreneurs from technology-based universities: Evidence from MIT. *Research Policy*, 36(5), 768–788.

Hughes, A. and Kitson, M. (2012). Pathways to impact and the strategic role of universities: New evidence on the breadth and depth of university knowledge exchange in the UK and the factors constraining its development. *Cambridge Journal of Economics*, 36, 723–50.

Klofsten, M. and Jones-Evans, D. (2000). Comparing academic entrepreneurship in Europe: The case of Sweden and Ireland. *Small Business Economics*, 14(4), 299–309.

Kyrö, P. and Mattila, J. (2012). Towards future university by integrating entrepreneurial and the third generation university concepts: Case Aalto University from Finland. Presentation at the 17th Nordic Conference on Small Business Research, Helsinki, Finland, 2012.

Lockett, A., Siegel, D., Wright, M., and Ensley, M.D. (2005). The creation of spin-off firms at public research institutions: Managerial and policy implications, *Research Policy*, 4, 981–993.

McKelvey, M. and Holmén, M. (2009). *European universities learning to compete: From social institution to knowledge business.* Northampton, MA: Edward Elgar.

Meyer, J.W. and Rowan, B. (1977). Institutionalized organizations: Formal structure as myth and ceremony. *American Journal of Sociology*, 83, 340–363.

Ministry of Education, Finland. (2007). *New university in the field of technology, Business studies and art and design (Teknillisen korkeakoulun, Helsingin kauppakorkeakoulun ja Taideteollisen korkeakoulun yhdistyminen uudeksi yliopistoksi).* Reports of the Ministry of Education, Finland, 2007: 16.

Morris, M.H., Kuratko, D.F., and Cornwall, J.R. (2013). *Entrepreneurship programs and the modern university.* Northampton, MA: Edward Elgar.

Mowery, D.C., Sampat, B.N., and Ziedonis, A.A. (2002). Learning to patent: Institutional experience, learning, and the characteristics of US university patents after the Bayh–Dole Act, 1981–1992. *Management Science*, 48(1), 73–89.

Nelles, J. and Vorley, T. (2010a). Constructing an entrepreneurial architecture: An emergent framework for studying the contemporary university beyond the entrepreneurial turn. *Innovation of Higher Education*, 35, 161–176.

Nelles, J. and Vorley, T. (2010b). From policy to practice: Engaging and embedding the third mission in contemporary universities, *International Journal of Sociology and Social Policy*, 30(7/8), 341–353.

Nelles, J. and Vorley, T. (2011). Entrepreneurial architecture: A blueprint for entrepreneurial universities. *Canadian Journal of Administrative Sciences*, 28, 341–353.

Nicolaou, N. and Birley, S. (2003). Social networks in organizational emergence: The university spinout phenomenon. *Management Science*, 49(12), 1702–1725.

Owen-Smith, J. and Powell, W.W. (2003). The expanding role of university patenting in the life sciences: Assessing the importance of experience and connectivity. *Research Policy*, 32(9), 1695–1711.

Parsons, T. (1934/1990). Prolegomena to a theory of social institutions. *American Sociological Review*, 55, 319–339.

Perkmann, M., Tartari, V., McKelvey, M., Autio, E., Brostroem, A., D'Este, P., *et al.* (2013). Academic engagement and commercialization: A review of the literature on university–industry relations, *Research Policy*, 42, 423–442.

Philpott, K., Dooley, L., O'Reilly, C., and Lupton, G. (2011). The entrepreneurial university: Examining the underlying academic tensions. *Technovation*, 31(4), 161–170.

Powell, W.W., Owen-Smith, J., and Colyvas, J.A. (2007). Innovation and emulation: Lessons from American universities in selling private rights to public knowledge. *Minerva*, 45(2), 121–142.
Powell, W.W. and DiMaggio, P.J. (eds) (1991). *The new institutionalism in organizational analysis*. Chicago: University of Chicago Press.
Rasmussen, E., Mosey, S. and Wright, M. (2014). The influence of university departments on the evolution of entrepreneurial competence in spin-off ventures. *Research Policy*, 43: 92–106.
Roessner, D., Bond, J., Okubo, S., and Planting, M. (2013). The economic impact of licensed commercialized inventions originating in university research. *Research Policy*, 42(1), 23–34.
Rothaermel, F.T., Agung, S.D., and Jiang, L. (2007). University entrepreneurship: A taxonomy of the literature. *Industrial and Corporate Change*, 16(4), 691–791.
Scott, W.R. (2008). Approaching adulthood: The maturing of Institutional Theory. *Theory and Society*, 37(5), 427–442.
Scott, W.R. (2014). *Institutions and organizations: Ideas, interests, and identities*, 4th edition. Thousand Oaks, CA: Sage.
Scott, W.R. and Christensen, S. (1995). *The institutional construction of organizations*. Thousand Oaks, CA: Sage.
Shane, S.A. (2004). *Academic entrepreneurship: University spinoffs and wealth creation*. Northampton, MA: Edward Elgar.
Slaughter, S. and Leslie, L.L. (1997). *Academic capitalism: Politics, policies, and the entrepreneurial university*. Baltimore: Johns Hopkins University Press.
Spencer, H. (1976, 1896, 1910). *The principles of sociology*, vols. 1–3. London: Appleton-Century-Crofts.
Steyaert, C. and Katz, J. (2004). Reclaiming the space of entrepreneurship in society: Geographical, discursive and social dimensions. *Entrepreneurship and Regional Development*, 16(3), 179–196.
Storper, Michael (2013). *Keys to the city: How economics, institutions, social interactions, and politics shape development*. Princeton, NJ: Princeton University Press.
Streeck, W. (2010). *Taking capitalism seriously: Towards an institutional approach to contemporary political economy*. Max Plank Institute for the Study of Societies (MPIfG) discussion paper (10/15).
Tolbert, P.S., David, R.J., and Sine, W.D. (2011). Studying choice and change: The intersection of institutional theory and entrepreneurship research. *Organization Science*, 22(5), 1332–1344.
Uyarra, E. (2010). Conceptualizing the regional roles of universities, implications and contradictions, *European Planning Studies*, 18(8), 122–124.
Van Maanen, J. (1988). *Tales of the field: On writing ethnography*. Chicago Guides to Writing, Editing, and Publishing. Chicago: University of Chicago Press.
Varga, A. (2009). *Universities, knowledge transfer and regional development: Geography, entrepreneurship and policy*. Northampton, MA: Edward Elgar.
Vorley, T. (2014), Interview with Tim Vorley November 18, 2014.
Vorley, T. and Nelles, J. (2008). (Re)conceptualizing the academy: Institutional development of and beyond the third mission. *Higher Education Management and Policy*, 20(3), 1–17.
Vorley, T. and Nelles, J. (2009). Building entrepreneurial architectures: A conceptual interpretation of the third mission. *Policy Futures in Education*, 7(3), 284–296.

Welter, F. (2011). Contextualizing entrepreneurship: Conceptual challenges and ways forward. *Entrepreneurship Theory and Practice*, 35(1), 165–184.

West III, G.P., Gatewood, E.J., and Shaver, K. (eds) (2009). *Handbook of university-wide entrepreneurship education*. Northampton, MA: Edward Elgar.

Wigren-Kristoferson, C., Gabrielsson, J., and Kitagawa, F. (2011). Mind the gap and bridge the gap: Research excellence and diffusion of academic knowledge in Sweden, *Science and Public Policy*, 38(6), 481–492.

Wright, M., Clarysse, B., Lockett, A., and Knockaert, M. (2008). Mid-range universities' linkages with industry: Knowledge types and the role of intermediaries. *Research Policy*, 37(8) 1205–1223.

Wright, M., Mosey, S. and Noke, H. (2013). Academic entrepreneurship and economic competitiveness: rethinking the role of the entrepreneur. *Economics of Innovation and New Technology*, 21(5–6), 439–444.

Youtie, J. and Shapira, P. (2008). Building an innovation hub: A case study of the transformation of university roles in regional technological and economic development. *Research Policy*, 37(8), 1188–1204.

Zahra, S.A. (2007). Contextualizing theory building in entrepreneurship research. *Journal of Business Venturing*, 22(3), 443–452.

2 New York University
Nurturing entrepreneurship in New York City

Bala Mulloth and Jill R. Kickul

Introduction

> The most complex problems will yield only to a combination of the
> deepest insights and the boldest willingness to act. So, entrepreneur-
> ship occupies a special place at universities: the span of higher educa-
> tion's research enterprise and the interests of its scholars to advance
> human knowledge not only through inquiry into the fundamental
> nature of things, but also through a desire to apply knowledge to solve
> the problems of the societies in which we live.
>
> (John Sexton, NYU President, 2012)

Historically, New York City has been a strong magnet for entrepreneurs
from all over the world, even following the 2008 global financial crisis.
Most recently, due to an influx of capital and other key resources, the Big
Apple has seen a rise of new ventures spanning a host of industries. Many
have been born as a result of entrepreneurship, including initiatives in the
city's universities, such as New York University (NYU). Founded in 1831,
NYU is now one of the largest private universities in the United States. Of
the more than 3,000 colleges and universities in America, NYU is one of
only 60 member institutions of the distinguished Association of American
Universities.

Enrolment has grown from a student body of 158 during NYU's very
first semester, to more than 40,000 students attending 18 schools and colleges at five major centers in Manhattan and in sites in Africa, Asia,
Europe, and South America. The faculty, which initially consisted of 14
professors and lecturers, now totals over 3,100 full-time members whose
research and teaching encompasses the humanities, the sciences, and the
social sciences; the law; medicine; business; education; the fine arts, studio
art, and the performing and cinematic arts; music; social work; public
administration; the ancient world; and continuing and professional studies.
These academic centers at NYU are home to four Nobel and Crafoord
Prize winners, three Abel Prize winners, 21 members of the National
Academy of Sciences, and seven Howard Hughes Medical Investigators,

among many other honors. Starting with Professor Samuel F.B. Morse (inventor of the electric telegraph and among the original 14 faculty members), NYU has been a major source of prolific inventors, scientists, and entrepreneurs. NYU alumni have founded and built industry-defining companies including Audible, Arista Records, Bloomberg, Burton, Def-Jam Records, Home Depot, Fairchild Semiconductor, Southwest Airlines, and Symbol Technologies, among many others. Offering more than 2,500 courses, the university awards more than 25 different degrees. Although the university is large overall, the individuals schools and colleges are small- to moderate-sized units (each with its own traditions, programs, and faculty), and within the larger NYU community, there are many smaller communities to be found, based on interests, activities, and shared experiences.

The center of NYU is its Washington Square campus in the heart of Greenwich Village. One of the city's most creative and energetic communities, the Village is a historic neighborhood that has attracted generations of writers, musicians, artists, and intellectuals. NYU, in keeping with its founder's vision, is "in and of the city." The university itself has no walls and no gates, and is purposely and deeply intertwined with New York City, drawing inspiration from its vitality. In addition to its Manhattan locations, the university is located in Brooklyn, with the second oldest school of engineering and technology in the country, and the university has research facilities in Sterling Forest, near Tuxedo, New York – notably the Nelson Institute of Environmental Medicine.

The university has also established itself as the first global network university, with a comprehensive liberal arts campus in Abu Dhabi – the first to be operated abroad by a major US research university – and other sites for study and research in Accra, Ghana; Berlin, Germany; Buenos Aires, Argentina; Florence, Italy; London, England; Madrid, Spain; Paris, France; Prague, the Czech Republic; Shanghai, China; and Tel Aviv, Israel, among other locations (New York University, 2013).

With its explicit focus on entrepreneurship, NYU has consistently ranked first among US universities in income from technology licensing (see Appendix 2.1). Compared to other US universities, NYU had 80 percent more new start-up companies created, per research dollar expended, than the national average in 2010 (New York University, 2011). Dozens of products have been commercialized, and more than 100 start-ups have been launched to bring NYU innovations to market. These and other activities have attracted millions of dollars from venture capitalists, the federal government, and the State of New York, have produced new ventures, licenses, and patents, and led to acquisitions by large corporations. Further, in recognition of the quality of the research, NYU received over $300 million in government research grants in 2010.

As Figure 2.1 shows, NYC's entrepreneurial ecology plays a vital part in fostering and driving NYU's entrepreneurial community, leading to several

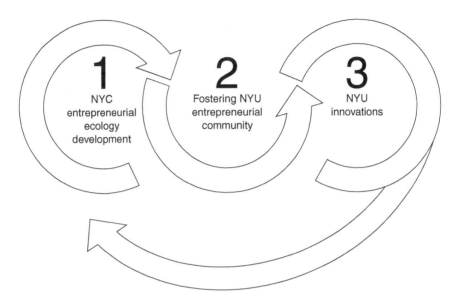

Figure 2.1 The self-reinforcing cycle linking New York City's entrepreneurial ecology with NYU innovation.

NYU innovations and start-up companies that positively impact the overall NYC entrepreneurial ecology, as a virtuous circle. This self-reinforcing relationship, as described in this chapter, between NYC and NYU is a critical component for the success of both the city and the university.

This chapter begins by setting NYU within the context and ecology of New York City and recent policy efforts to strengthen the city's entrepreneurial ecosystem. We then provide an overview of the key university initiatives including technology commercialization activities and describe the available entrepreneurship support resources at NYU. The economic impact of these initiatives and how they enhance the city's overall competitiveness are also presented.

NYC entrepreneurial ecology: an infrastructure for the creation of new innovations and enterprises

New York City, as many of the world's great metropolitan areas, has historically thrived on competition, innovative ideas, diversity, resilience, and determination – making it a breeding ground for entrepreneurial activity. Indeed, as a 2012 report by Manhattan Borough President Scott M. Stringer titled, *Start-up city: Growing New York City's entrepreneurial ecosystem for all* (Stringer, 2012), reminds us, "New York City's history of entrepreneurship dates back to its founding as New Amsterdam – a port of entry to the New World and a place of exchange for ideas and innovation." The report states that NYC has grown into "the entrepreneurial capital of the world – from finance and fashion to marketing and media" and has now "staked out a significant presence in the new entrepreneurial economy" as "tech-rich entrepreneurial businesses offer a gateway to the middle class for thousands of New Yorkers."

For example, "unlike other growth areas of the economy, an entry-level coding job at a start-up tech firm can pay as much as $65,000 a year." Another indicator of tech's growth is from an analysis of New York State Labor Department which found that the number of information technology jobs in the five boroughs rose from 33,000 in February 2003 to 52,900 in February 2012, a 60 percent increase; further, of the tech start-ups founded in New York since 2007, 15 have raised more than $50 million in investments, 27 have investments of at least $25 million, and 81 have raised at least $10 million (New York City, 2012a). Further still, venture capital (VC) deals increased by 32 percent from 2007 to 2011 in New York City, leading the state to leapfrog Massachusetts to become the #2 state in the country for technology-related VC (New York City, 2012b).

Some of Stringer's key recommendations in the *Start-up city* report were to:

- build a sophisticated curriculum based on developing real-world skills for New York City public school students;
- improve internet connectivity by investing in a municipal fiber broadband network;
- create a strong digital presence for NYC-based businesses;
- provide financial aid incentives for students who major in engineering;
- establish a cabinet for emerging business development made up of local entrepreneurs to advise the mayor's office on how city government can provide support to local business people;
- create a crowdsourcing mechanism for office space.

Tech entrepreneurs and start-ups at NYC universities such as New York University are in an excellent position to take advantage of the recent favorable policy recommendations encouraging the development of a robust entrepreneurial ecology. It is also important to note that the entrepreneurial economy isn't just being fuelled by small start-ups. Large fast-growth companies have flocked to New York in recent years, including Google, Facebook, and Twitter.

Important steps have been made by Mayor Michael Bloomberg's administration to solidify a strong present and future for NYC's entrepreneurial ecosystem throughout the five boroughs. In December 2011, Cornell University and Technion (Israel Institute of Technology) won a New York City contest to build an engineering and applied sciences campus with a grant of land on Roosevelt Island and $100 million for infrastructure improvements. The brainchild of Mayor Bloomberg, the project is intended to be instrumental in the renaissance of New York City following the 2008 financial crisis, by focusing on entrepreneurship and innovation in the city's technology sector. Further, in April 2012, NYU's Center for Urban Science and Progress (NYU CUSP) was launched as part of a historic partnership between universities, tech companies, and the City of New York. This is a graduate school and research center that combines big data to serve a very special mission: to make the world's cities better places to live, work, and thrive.

In addition to these historic initiatives, the Bloomberg administration and the city council have appointed the city's first Chief Digital Officer, provided financial support for tech incubators and workshare spaces, underwritten the BigApps and Next Idea competitions/hackathons, and helped create the New York City Entrepreneurial Fund – a $22 million fund to provide promising New York City-based technology start-up companies with early-stage capital (NYC EDC). Ultimately, however, as noted in *Start-up city*:

> Government is not going to build the entrepreneurial economy in New York City. The ingenuity of New Yorkers and the drive of people who come to the five boroughs from across the country and around the world are the keys to economic growth in the 21st century, just as they were when the City was a small port in Lower Manhattan in the 17th century. However, government is responsible for creating the environment and infrastructure to support robust economic growth.

Finally, in another important initiative highlighting the state/regional government support for building entrepreneurial growth firms, as of October 22, 2013, New York Governor Andrew M. Cuomo formally launched START-UP NY, a high-profile initiative that will create tax-free zones to attract and grow new businesses across the state. The primary purpose of this initiative is to accelerate entrepreneurialism and job creation across the city and state on a large scale (Governor's Press Office, 2013). Among other things, this means investing in education and infrastructure and supporting universities such as New York University that prepare New York City's youth for the industries of tomorrow.

University initiatives

As corporations have cut back on research, the government has increasingly encouraged universities to take a larger role in maintaining American economic competitiveness – as, for example, in the passage of the Bayh–Dole Act of 1980, which encouraged universities to commercialize inventions created with federal financing (Kunhardt, 2004). However, "academic entrepreneurship" (the patenting and licensing by universities and their faculty) has not become part of the academic mainstream, and is generally viewed within the ivory tower as conflicting with the mission of the university. That mission is now often captured by the phrase: *to teach and to research*. Universities such as NYU, as part of their long-range planning, have embarked on a series of undertakings to add a third element: *to invent*.

During the last four years, numerous new programs and resources have been developed to further support NYU entrepreneurs throughout the full life-cycle of start-up development – from ideation and inspiration, through business model validation and seed funding. Today, NYU's science and technology researchers increasingly bear in mind the importance of commercializing discoveries, helped by the 2008 addition of the Polytechnic Institute (NYU-Poly), NYU's school of engineering, where the motto is "i^2e" – invention, innovation, and entrepreneurship.[1] Figure 2.2 highlights the integration of its entrepreneurial initiatives and support activities. Educational activities centered on students and high-quality faculties are at the core of the NYU's activities. Specifically, the university seeks to foster innovation and entrepreneurship through a wide variety of offerings both inside and outside the classroom. (See Appendix 2.2 for a sample of NYU entrepreneurship-related course offerings.) Researchers are encouraged to move science to application, product, and service, and from there to let

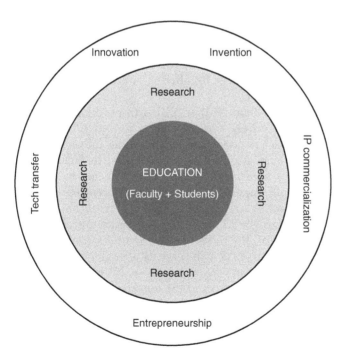

Figure 2.2 Integration of entrepreneurial initiatives and support activities.

their discoveries take flight as start-up companies. Further, the university has launched several new technology transfer and intellectual property (IP) commercialization initiatives bolstering and expanding existing programs to foster innovation, to bridge the gap between basic and applied science, and to look for opportunities to move discoveries from the laboratory to the marketplace. To quote Paul Horn, NYU's senior vice provost for research (New York University, 2011):

> Innovations born in NYU boost productivity, conserve energy and resources, and save lives – all while creating jobs. The university is committed to developing start-ups from student, faculty and researchers' ideas across a broad spectrum of fields, spanning information technology, the physical sciences, engineering, and medicine.

At NYU, student entrepreneurs come from many nations and virtually all colleges and departments, as evidenced by the recent NYU Entrepreneurs Festival, where the 45 entrepreneur/founder speakers were comprised of alumni, students, and faculty from 18 different schools within NYU. It is often stated that entrepreneurship requires a multi-disciplinary team to succeed; a team comprised of scientists, engineers, designers, marketers, financial professionals, and other discipline experts. According to Frank Rimalovski, executive director of the NYU Entrepreneurial Institute, although there were several entrepreneurially minded students at NYU, until recently there was a relatively lower proportion of entrepreneurial companies emerging from the university. In order to address this key challenge, the NYU Entrepreneurial Institute was created in 2010 to empower entrepreneurs from idea to impact by offering educational programming, events, resources, and funding.

Further, while no one school within NYU can produce students from all these disciplines, collectively as a university, it does. One of the challenges in doing so has been in coordinating the various university resources when they are spread across such a large university. In fact, it could be hard to find a place for students from all the 18 colleges to collaborate. Historically when people wanted to learn more about entrepreneurship at NYU, they were steered to a website or told to attend an event. As a response to this challenge, the Mark and Debra Leslie Entrepreneurs Lab was launched in the fall of 2014. The 5,900-square-foot lab space in the heart of Washington Square Park will serve as a single, central space for researchers, students, and faculty from across NYU's schools to get plugged into programs and resources at the university. In addition to connecting interested parties with programs within the university, the lab also aims to get entrepreneurs at NYU more woven into the New York innovation ecosystem. The center will also become the home for the NYU Entrepreneurial Institute that will offer facilities for co-working space, meeting and events, as well as a fabrication lab.

Commercialization activities

NYU has implemented several university-wide policies to increase its commercialization footprint. The Office of Industrial Liaison (OIL) provides commercial partners a contact point where mutually beneficial relationships may be built, often resulting in NYU inventions in a wide range of disciplines. Many products have come to market and start-ups have been built based on NYU technologies and intellectual property. The university has been awarded over 700 patents, two-thirds of which have been licensed to industry. This success rate puts NYU at the top of US universities in technology licensing income, providing funds for further research and education (Anderson *et al.*, 2007). Perhaps best known is the blockbuster drug Remicade, developed by researchers at NYU School of Medicine in collaboration with Centocor, which is now owned by Johnson & Johnson. Remicade alone represented $4.6 billion of Johnson & Johnson's 2010 sales, making it the company's best-selling drug. Likewise for NYU, this one main drug patent heavily accounted for its high licensing income. After this initial success, numerous additional life science products are in clinical trials or en route to market by NYU licensees and start-ups. In fact, over the past decade, the pace of invention at NYU has more than doubled in number each year and licensing agreements have tripled, earning NYU $1.3 billion to further its research efforts.

Another major effort on the part of NYU to support entrepreneurship has been through its support for various business incubator initiatives. In the wake of the 2008 financial crisis, NYU Poly President, Jerry Hultin, was one of the community leaders called upon by New York Mayor Michael Bloomberg as he envisioned and strategized the future direction for the city. It was clear that the city needed to diversify its economic base beyond Wall Street, and it was facing a shortage of young engineers and entrepreneurial talent to accomplish that. The university was prompt in embracing the call from the New York City Economic Development Corporation to become the city's first partner to create a start-up business incubator with space provided by Trinity Real Estate.

This public–private–academic partnership at the core of the NYU-Poly Incubator initiatives dates to 2009, when it launched the Varick Street Incubator in Manhattan's Hudson Square in partnership with New York City Economic Development Corporation (NYCEDC) and Trinity Real Estate. It also housed a second innovation center, the New York City Accelerator for a Clean and Resilient Economy (NYC ACRE), supported by the New York State Energy and Research Development Authority (NYSERDA) and focused on clean-tech and clean-energy start-ups. In 2012, NYU-Poly opened the DUMBO Incubator in Brooklyn in partnership with NYCEDC and Two Trees Management.

These business incubators form an integral component of NYU-Poly's i²e philosophy and the goal of each of them is to provide start-ups with the guidance, expertise, and resources to become successful ventures that bring economic growth to New York City. Together, the three incubators (Varick Street, DUMBO, and NYC ACRE) currently house almost 60 innovative start-ups, with more than 35 companies graduated to a larger space in New York City and several others acquired.

In an August 2013 global benchmark report released by UBI Index, a Sweden-based research initiative, NYU-Poly business incubators were cited among the 20 best university business incubators in the world (Strom, 2014). The researchers studied 150 university incubators in 22 countries and measured their performance on 50 indicators, including job creation capacity, ability to boost the economy, and level of success of graduated companies. The incubators at the top of the list were calculated to have generated almost three times as many jobs as the global average and graduated twice the number of clients receiving venture capital or angel funding. *Worth* magazine recently named the incubators – Varick Street Incubator, DUMBO Incubator, and NYC ACRE – among the Top 10 Idea Labs in the United States (see Appendix 2.3 for a sample list of start-ups housed at the incubators).

A recent focus on incubating: Cleantech

Cleantech is a sector that is just emerging into the NYU–NYC public sphere; it is rooted in long-standing practices of efficiency gains and more effective energy use (Gardett, 2013). (See Appendix 2.4 for a sample list of cleantech start-ups housed at the incubators.) In addition to the NYC ACRE incubator, NYU-Poly's newest incubator opened in the fall of 2013. In partnership with NYCEDC, the Brooklyn campus will house the 10,000-square-foot Clean Technology Entrepreneur Center, whose 20 start-up clients will focus on solving urban challenges related to energy efficiency, sustainability, climate adaptation, and resilience. This newest incubator will be located at 15 MetroTech Center in Brooklyn.

Overall economic impact of the incubator initiatives

In October 2012, NYU researchers assessed the economic impact of the university's incubators. They surveyed existing and graduated companies, analyzed available data, and applied standard economic formulae to determine the economic activity generated.[2] As can be seen from Figure 2.3, as of December 2012, through both direct and indirect job creation, taxes, and spending, the joint economic impact of the incubators has been $251.2 million. This figure is projected to be $719.8 million by 2015. In terms of job creation, since 2009 the NYU-Poly incubators have created 900 jobs and by 2015 the incubators are projected to create nearly 2,600 jobs. The average graduate of an NYU-Poly incubator makes $72,230 annually, and from 2009 to 2012, former and current members contributed roughly

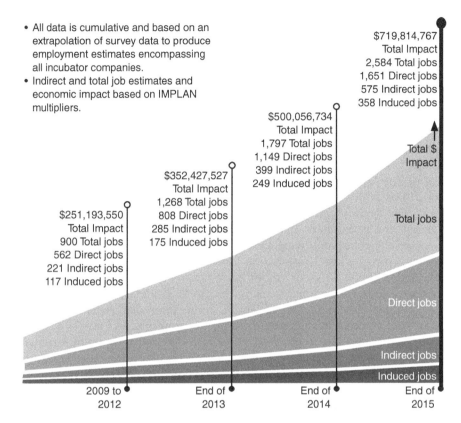

- All data is cumulative and based on an extrapolation of survey data to produce employment estimates encompassing all incubator companies.
- Indirect and total job estimates and economic impact based on IMPLAN multipliers.

$719,814,767
Total Impact
2,584 Total jobs
1,651 Direct jobs
575 Indirect jobs
358 Induced jobs

$500,056,734
Total Impact
1,797 Total jobs
1,149 Direct jobs
399 Indirect jobs
249 Induced jobs

$352,427,527
Total Impact
1,268 Total jobs
808 Direct jobs
285 Indirect jobs
175 Induced jobs

$251,193,550
Total Impact
900 Total jobs
562 Direct jobs
221 Indirect jobs
117 Induced jobs

Total $ Impact

Total jobs

Direct jobs

Indirect jobs

Induced jobs

2009 to 2012 | End of 2013 | End of 2014 | End of 2015

Figure 2.3 NYU Business Incubator economic impact.

$31.4 million in tax revenue. In terms of capital raised, current tenants could expect a funding growth rate of 147 percent from their entry to an incubator until graduation. It was noted that incubator graduates have substantially higher funding/revenue upon graduation. Further, incubator companies to date have raised more than $60 million in total.

Entrepreneurship support and resources

In its efforts to broaden the academic mission of the university with an emphasis on invention and to enrich the academic community through a new dimension of creative expression, NYU supports several competitions that help identify, nurture, and showcase entrepreneurial talent among its students. The Berkley Center for Entrepreneurship and Innovation at the Stern School of Business sponsors the $200k annual Entrepreneurs' Challenge in an effort to equip students, alumni, and researchers from across NYU's campus with the skills, know-how, and ability to launch and grow sustainable ventures. Now in its thirteenth year, the Entrepreneurs' Challenge awards a total of $200,000 in cash prizes for its three competitions. The New Venture Challenge ($75,000) includes all the for-profit venture ideas, the Social Venture Challenge ($50,000) is for ventures that have a social cause, and the newest addition, the Technology Venture Challenge ($75,000), focuses on the creation of new and the acceleration of existing early stage businesses based on technologies developed by NYU students, faculty, and researchers.

The Entrepreneurs' Challenge is an eight-month program during which participants benefit from team-building initiatives, entrepreneurial workshops, bootcamps, mentoring, and coaching, as they develop their business plans. The New Venture and Social Venture competitions are open to any individual with an idea and some sort of tie to the Stern School of Business. The Technology Venture competition is open to all NYU students, faculty, and researchers. A key goal of the challenge is to spur new business development, and many winners have gone on to lead thriving businesses. Over the last 12 years, the Entrepreneurs' Challenge has awarded over $1,500,000 in cash to 40 start-ups including ones now getting national and international attention such as Pinterest, Madecasse, and SocialBomb. The annual Inno/Vention competition challenges NYU-Poly and NYU students from across the globe to prototype and pitch commercially viable ideas for real-world problems. The goal is to build a robust culture of competition at NYU-Poly that drives innovation through ideation and entrepreneurship and ultimately encourages students to take part in the NYU Entrepreneurs' Challenge.

Additionally, the university has created and developed several platforms for students and would-be-entrepreneurs to explore and access their entrepreneurial interests. Some of the main resource offerings are as indicated in Table 2.1.

In 2010, NYU-Poly teamed up with NYCEDC and Columbia University to launch the NYC Media Lab. This public–private partnership was aimed at connecting companies seeking to advance new media technologies with academic institutions undertaking relevant research, in order to drive collaborative innovation. The Media Lab tackles the large questions facing the media industry today, with the goal of generating research, knowledge transfer, talent development, R&D, and new business models. In 2013, an annual summit of the NYC Media Lab focused on fostering open innovation. A snapshot of some of the best thinking across the media arena was presented, featuring talks from researchers and corporate innovators on data, technological change, networks, and talent development. An important question that the summit aimed to address was: How can companies learn from one another and engage with cutting-edge university partners to shape the future of media together? The summit also premiered the results of NYC Media Lab's first round of seed research projects.

Table 2.1 Entrepreneurship resources

Entrepreneurships platform	Purpose
NYU Entrepreneurs Speaker Series	To support, encourage, and inspire NYU students, faculty, and researchers in entrepreneurial pursuits and technology commercialization.
Himelberg Speaker Series	Bring high-profile entrepreneurs and pioneering thought leaders to campus to share their unique perspectives on start-up strategies and trends impacting business.
NYU Reynolds Speaker Series	Highlights social entrepreneurship as a meta-profession by presenting prominent social entrepreneurs and leaders from across the spectrum of public and professional sectors.
The Innovation Lab	Teaches students, researchers, and alumni from all majors and backgrounds how to generate unique business ideas, and how to generate revenue from new technology.
Invention to Venture Workshops	Teaches technology entrepreneurship basics, help build networks, and provide a framework for moving ideas and research forward.
Entrepreneurship and Innovation Association at NYU-Poly	Seeks to create an entrepreneurial and networking ecosystem that assists motivated students in transforming ideas into functional businesses.

Concluding thoughts

As described in this chapter, NYU has a robust infrastructure for entrepreneurial activities that have proved to be extremely successful. In many ways, it owes this success to its immediate environment: New York City, a city that is thriving, as it has throughout its history, as an entrepreneurial hotbed. As quoted by Frank Rimalovski, executive director of NYU Entrepreneurial Institute (New York University, 2010):

> Today, New York City is an exciting and fertile landscape for entrepreneurship. It possesses a compelling mix of angel and venture capital investors, entrepreneurs with a keen eye for the next great business opportunity, a dynamic and increasingly tight-knit ecosystem, and top commercial and research institutions, medical centers, and corporations. The intersection of that environment and a great research university dedicated to creating pioneering innovations holds extraordinary possibilities.

This favorable ecosystem coupled with NYU's explicit commitment and focus on entrepreneurship, and the extensive resources to foster and support entrepreneurial education and related activities have resulted in producing start-ups as well as generating economic activity within the university. Numerous products have been commercialized and several start-ups have been launched, with the support of the NYU business incubators. Further, as shown by the latest study of the economic impact of the incubator initiatives, the NYU innovations and start-up companies have generated economic activity in terms of capital raised, new jobs created, and financial contributions back to the city in the form of local, state, and federal tax revenue.

However, the possibilities are far greater, given the breadth and depth of NYU's research and incubators and the size of the university and of the city. NYU innovators and entrepreneurs sit poised to strengthen NYC as a global entrepreneurial hub and to bring valuable ideas to market with support from alumni, university leadership, and New York's entrepreneurial ecosystem of angel investors, venture capitalists, and business incubators. This virtuous circle and reinforcing relationship between NYC and NYU play a critical role in strengthening the competiveness and attractiveness of NYC as a magnet for entrepreneurs in the global economy.

Appendix 2.1

Table 2.A1 Top 10 US universities in license income (2004–2010)

University	License income
New York University	$1,568m
Northwestern University	$1,238m
Columbia University	$941m
University of California System	$786m
Stanford University	$741m
Emory University	$682m
Wake Forest	$487m
University of Minnesota	$473m
University on Washington	$385m
Massachusetts Institute of Technology	$382m

Source: Association of University Technology Managers.

Appendix 2.2. Sample entrepreneurship courses offered across campuses

- Accounting, tax, and legal issues for entrepreneurs
- Emerging technologies and business innovation
- Entrepreneurial selling
- Entrepreneurship for the new economy
- Foundations of entrepreneurship
- Innovation and design
- New product development

- New product marketing and design
- Operations for global entrepreneurs
- Social entrepreneurship
- Technology innovation and new product development
- Venture capital financing
- Equity investing
- Entrepreneurial finance

Appendix 2.3. A sample list of start-ups housed at the NYU business incubators

Anzenna

Based on the research of NYU-Poly Professor Kalle Levon, a team of NYU-Poly students and faculty are developing a diagnostic device to quickly detect hospital-acquired infection in patients. Although Anzenna has not yet sold a product, it has exclusively licensed six patents from NYU and is developing more advanced prototypes. Funding so far has come from institutional grants (federal, state, medical), not venture capitalists or private investors, but the company's goal was to raise private capital by the end of 2012.

Digital Assembly

Founded by NYU-Poly Professor Nasir Memon in 2006, Digital Assembly designs software products for digital forensics and data recovery. With a mission to help clients "recover more with less effort," Digital Assembly introduced its one-of-a-kind SmartCarving™ technology, which allows recovery of fragmented files from any media with or without a file system. Digital Assembly's first consumer product, Adroit Photo Recovery, retrieves and restores deleted or lost photos from a variety of digital media.

Synthezyme

A company commercializing technology developed by Professor Richard Gross, an NYU-Poly professor who holds 19 patents and has authored over 300 publications. One of SyntheZyme's most promising products is a bioplastic in which the monomer is produced by using SyntheZyme's genetically modified strain of the yeast Candida tropicalis. The engineered yeast is capable of converting fatty acids of plant oils into large quantities of omega-hydroxy fatty acids. When polymerized, the new material is a suitable substitute for petroleum-derived plastics such as polyethylene for uses such as disposable gloves, multilayer food packaging films, and films for ice, trash, garments, produce bags, and more.

Appendix 2.4. A sample list of cleantech start-ups housed at the NYU business incubators

Rentricity

One of the original start-up companies in the NYC ACRE, NYU-Poly cleantech support system, has been named a Later Stage Global Top 10 greentech company – chosen from a field of 4,000. The award by the Global Cleantech Cluster Association (GCCA) also named Rentricity as the winner of the "Best of Water" category for 2011 (AlaskaDispatch.com, 2011).

The firm recovers energy from excess water pressure in pipes to produce clean, renewable electricity. It targets water, wastewater, and industrial infrastructure to produce electricity that is then sold into the electric grid or used behind-the-meter. Established in 2003, the company is based in New York City with offices in New Jersey, Connecticut, and Pennsylvania.

GCCA recognized Rentricity for winning access to sources of growth capital and management guidance. The association also cited Rentricity for significant success in growing the cleantech industry in New York City and for its support of regional green job growth. Founder and President Frank Zammataro kept the young company self-financed, and in 2012 it generated $500,000 in revenue. Rentricity has completed two commercial projects and has four other projects in development. Among them is a project funded by NYSERDA to develop wastewater solutions for New York City. As Zammataro notes:

> This international recognition gives us inspiration, and we hope to use it as a springboard to find our first project outside of North America … NYC ACRE's nomination of Rentricity for the GCCA award has now expanded its support for us beyond New York City and the State of New York to the global cleantech community.
>
> (AlaskaDispatch.com, 2011)

ThinkEco

Founded in 2008, ThinkEco, Inc. is a NYC-based company developing easy-to-use energy-efficient technologies for the consumer market. The company's product is the modlet – i.e. the modern outlet – a best-in-class device for monitoring and managing electricity at the plug-load level. The modlet has an average payback period of six months, saving users approximately 10 percent on their electricity bill with no behavior change required. The product addresses the fact that power is consumed by appliances and electronic equipment even when not in use. Studies have shown this standby power use is responsible for up to 26 percent of the average electric bill, and is steadily rising annually as more appliances and gadgets are purchased for the home.

The modlet is a patent-pending electricity conservation solution for homes and offices that eliminates wasteful energy use by automatically turning off power to appliances when not needed. Appliances are plugged into the modlet which in turn is plugged into an existing electric outlet. The modlet creates a schedule of on and off times, shutting off power at the plug and thus eliminating wasteful electricity use. These money-saving schedules can be viewed and modified through a computer's web browser. The firm recently announced that the Association of Energy Service Professionals (AESP) has recognized the coolNYC program with two energy awards: (1) Outstanding Achievement in Residential Program Design and Implementation; (2) Outstanding Achievement in Pricing and Demand Response.

Notes

1 The Polytechnic Institute of New York University (formerly the Brooklyn Polytechnic Institute and the Polytechnic University, now widely known as NYU-Poly) is an affiliated institute of New York University, soon to be its School of Engineering.
2 The economic impact of NYU-Poly Incubator clients was estimated using IMPLAN, in industry-leading input/output model. The IMPLAN model was used to estimate the economic impact of these new businesses. In our case, IMPLAN takes the full-time equivalents by industry as inputs and uses an "output per worker" figure to calculate the final economic impact as an output. Additionally, to quantify the economic impact of a new business in the marketplace, economists measure three types of economic impacts: direct, indirect, and induced. The direct economic impacts are generated as new businesses make purchases and hire workers to fill new positions. IMPLAN expresses its output in a number of ways, including direct output, jobs, labor income, and taxes. Direct output is the dollar amount spent by new firms. Jobs are the full-time equivalent increases in employment due to hiring and spending by the new firms. Labor income is defined as the sum of salaries and wages, other labor income, and proprietors' income less transfer payments, dividends, and rent. Tax impacts are the governmental fiscal impacts created by incubator clients. The IMPLAN model relies on multipliers to determine indirect and induced effects of industry segments or firms. Multipliers represent the relationship between direct effects and the sum of the direct, indirect, and induced effects.

References

Anderson, T.R., Daim, T.U. and Lavoie, F.F. (2007). Measuring the efficiency of university technology transfer. *Technovation*, 27(5), 306–318.
Gardett, P. (2013, June 24). Cleantech leaders of New York Top Ten. *Breaking Energy*.
Governor's Press Office (2013). Governor Cuomo launches START-UP NY program at int'l conference in New York City. www.governor.ny.gov/press/10222013-governor-launches-start-up-ny-program.
Kunhardt, E. (2004, December 14). Necessity as the mother of tenure? *New York Times*.

New York City (2012a). New tech city, center for an urban future. http://nycfuture.org/pdf/New_Tech_ City.pdf.

New York City (2012b). NYC digital roadmap 2012. www.nyc.gov/html/digital/downloads/pdf/digitalroadmap2012.pdf, p. 34.

New York University (2010, June 28). NYU to launch venture fund to spur commercialization of NYU innovations and discoveries, www.nyu.edu/about/news-publications/news/2010/06/28/nyu-to-launch-venture-fund-to-spur commercialization-of-innovations-and-discoveries.html.

New York University (2011, September 16). In Pasteur's Quadrant: Innovation and research at NYU. States News Service. www.highbeam.com.doc/1G1-267214076.

New York University (2013). New York University website. www.nyu.edu/.

Stringer, S.M. (2012). *Start-up city: Growing New York City's entrepreneurial eco-system for all*. A Report of the Manhattan Borough.

Strom, B. (2014). *Global benchmark report, 2013*. UBI Index. http://ubiindex.com/?s=The+Global+Benchmark+Report+2013.

3 Creating and sustaining high-technology development in Austin, Texas

David V. Gibson and John S. Butler

Background and introduction

The following background serves to highlight Texas's and Austin's relatively recent and fast development from a traditional ranching and agriculture economy to a major globally competitive technology and entrepreneurial region. Texas, located in the southwestern United States, is the second most populous state with a growing population of 26 million residents, and the second-largest state with an area of 268,820 square miles (696,200 square kilometers). Texas shares US borders with four states and an international border with Mexico. The term "six flags over Texas" came from the six nations that ruled the territory. Spain twice claimed sovereignty over "Texas" from 1519 to 1685 and from 1690 to 1821. France occupied a Texas colony from 1685 to 1689. Mexico controlled the territory from 1821 through 1836, after which Texas won its independence and became an independent republic. In the 1830s, pioneers began to settle central Texas along the Colorado River and in 1839, the region was officially chosen as the republic's capital and was named Austin in honor of Stephen F. Austin, the "Father of Texas."

In 1845 Texas became the 28th state of the United States, which set off a chain of events that led to the Mexican–American War in 1846. Texas is called the Lone Star State to emphasize that it was an independent republic. As a slave state, Texas joined the Confederate states of America during the Civil War. Into the early 1900s, Texas was predominantly rural, with an economy based largely on cattle ranching, cotton farming, and lumber. Due to its long history as a center of the cattle industry (and more recently as portrayed on TV and in the movies), Texas is identified worldwide as representing the Wild West, with cowboys riding the range.

The state's economic fortunes changed significantly when the "Gusher Age" began with the discovery of a large petroleum reserve near Beaumont, Texas, in 1901. The find was unprecedented in size and was followed by rapid development and industrialization. Texas quickly became a leading oil-producing state along with Oklahoma and California, and by 1940 was dominating US production. Along with a pro-business philosophy and investments in the state's universities, Texas developed a diversified economy, and as of 2012 was home to the headquarters of 57 Fortune 500 companies. Texas leads the United States in agriculture, petrochemicals, energy, computers and electronics, aerospace, and biomedical sciences. The Lone Star state has also led the nation in export revenue since 2002 and, after California, has the second-highest gross state product. Houston, with a population of about two million, is the largest city in Texas and the fourth-largest in the United States. San Antonio with 1.5 million is the second largest city in the state, followed by Dallas with a population of about one million, followed by Austin with a population of about 842,600.

Austin's emergence as a technology hot spot

The Texas constitution of 1876 mandated that the state establish a "university of the first class." In 1881 Austin was chosen as the main location for The University of Texas, and began admitting students in September 1883. The state's constitution also established the Permanent University Fund (PUF) which initially benefited from land donated by the Pacific Railroad. The million acres (4,000 km^2) was considered too worthless to survey, while it did earn modest revenue from grazing leases. However, on May 28, 1923, Santa Rita No. 1 struck oil, giving The University of Texas access to an important and continuing source of revenue. As a result, as of 2014, The University of Texas at Austin is among the wealthiest universities in the United States with a PUF endowment of about $15 billion that yearly contributes to the university's endowment of about $3 billion.

Up until the mid-1980s, Austin was not known as a center of entrepreneurship or innovation. A major shift in the city's economic landscape came in 1983, when to the surprise of public and private leaders in the east and west coasts, Austin won a major national competition for the country's first for-profit R&D consortium: the Microelectronics and Computer Technology Corporation (MCC). Three key reasons for Austin's unexpected win centered on the belief by the MCC site selection committee (Gibson and Rogers, 1994):

- that UT Austin was on its way to becoming one of the nation's top US public research and teaching universities in science and technology and the consortium wanted to be on the receiving end of pipeline of highly educated talent;
- Austin's high quality of life would enable MCC to recruit and retain the most qualified talent from the east and west coasts as the R&D consortium was all about increasing US competitive strength in computer and information technology;
- Austin's recruitment effort demonstrated that key influencers from The University of Texas at Austin, the city and state, and regional business were known to each other and could work effectively together on

"the Austin Model" for accelerating technology-based growth (Smilor *et al.*, 1988).

City leaders promoting the "Austin Model" had additional success in 1984 with the recruitment of major R&D divisions from 3M Corporation head-quartered in Minnesota and in winning a second major national competition in 1988 for Sematech which was to focus on advancing US semiconductor research and manufacturing. The impact of these events gave a significant boost to Austin's emergence as a technology city as well as The University of Texas's pursuit of research and education excellence in science and technology during the latter part of the twentieth century. During the same time period, technology firms such as IBM, Motorola, AMD, and Applied Materials expanded their Austin-based R&D operations. In addition, local entrepreneurs launched ventures that were to become global corporations based in Austin: In 1976, four UT Austin professors left the university's Applied Research Labs to form National Instruments; a UT undergraduate student and his girlfriend dropped out in 1978 to found SaferWay later known as Whole Foods; and in 1984 Michael Dell, an undergraduate business major, launched PC Limited in his UT Austin dorm room. More recently, additional *Fortune 500* companies have established major regional divisions in Austin including Intel, Apple, eBay, and Google. Richard Florida (2002) and many other observers list Austin as a leading US region in creativity and innovation, entrepreneurship and business start-ups, and the creation of wealth and jobs.[1]

The University of Texas at Austin[2]

Although UT Austin is considered the keystone institution in fostering and sustaining Austin's technology-based growth it is important to also recognize the key role played by the region's other colleges and universities.[3] According to regional industry leaders, UT's most important contribution for industry is to graduate well-educated students. And, indeed, with an enrolment of about 38,000 undergraduate and 11,500 graduate students, UT Austin is a major supplier of educated talent for regional, national, and global industry, as well as the public sector. Following in order of relative importance, after the number one priority of graduating educated students, Austin's industry's top needs from the university are continuing education opportunities; consortia and research centers; consulting; and sponsored research followed by, and in last place, intellectual property (IP) and technology licensing (Mulcahy, 2007). In this chapter, we present an overview of three factors that have been central to UT Austin's emergence as a highly ranked teaching, research, and entrepreneurial university: (1) the recruitment and retention of outstanding faculty and students; (2) maintaining high levels of research funding; and (3) the founding and evolution of key entrepreneurial support programs, activities, policies, and structures.[4]

The recruitment and retention of outstanding faculty and students

Competition is intense among research universities worldwide to recruit the best and the brightest professors and students. In the United States, endowed professor chairs help attract "star" researchers who are key to winning competitive state, federal, and international research grants that fund fellowships and attract superior graduate students. The result is a clustering of established and emerging talent in centers of research and education excellence and rising prestige for a university. This clustering of talent is important for generating new knowledge that can change the world through science, technology, and innovation.

There was a dramatic rise in the number of endowed chairs at UT Austin in 1982 (32 chairs) and 1983 (41 chairs) which was directly linked to Austin's winning the Microelectronics and Computer Technology Corporation (MCC) in 1983. This increase from fewer than 50 endowed professors pre-1982 to more than 300 in 2013 was possible, in large part, because of private sector financial donations that were enhanced by matching contributions from the PUF.[5] These endowed professorships enhanced the university's ability to hire "star" faculty which had an immediate impact on student recruitment and on winning competitive research grants from government and the private sector. For example, by 1986 UT Austin's Department of Computer Science was receiving three times as many graduate student applications (about 700 per year) as they had prior to 1983 and was admitting candidates with substantially higher Graduate Record Exam (GRE) scores (Gibson and Rogers, 1994). The vast majority of UT endowed chairs exist in the College of Engineering (19 percent); School of Law (16 percent); College of Natural Sciences (15 percent); College of Liberal Arts (12 percent); College of Business (11 percent); and Geosciences (4 percent).

In August 2004, the Board of Regents of the University of Texas System approved $32 million funding from the PUF to be awarded to UT System Institutions to help attract and retain highly qualified faculty. The resulting STAR (Science and Technology Acquisition and Retention) program provides funding to help purchase state-of-the-art research equipment and laboratory renovations to help retain star faculty. The program evolved and expanded in 2005 to include additional support for faculty retention, research, and teaching. As a research-to-commercialization oriented example, two UT Austin STAR faculty founded Molecular Imprints with $3 million support from State of Texas Emerging Technology Research Fund. This research built on UT Austin's Cockrell School of Engineering patented ink-jet technology with a revamped manufacturing process known as ink-jet roll-to-roll nano-patterning to produce large, inexpensive manufacturing tools needed for electronic devices and photovoltaics.

The Texas Advanced Computing Center (TACC) includes high-performance computing, visualization, data analysis, storage systems, software, and portal interfaces. TACC launched a Science and Technology

Affiliates for Research (TACC-STAR) program to work with non-UT researchers and businesses on supercomputing, advanced visualization, grid computing, and massive scientific data management. TACC experts work with researchers on over 3,000 projects per year to help answer complex research questions using TACC's advanced computing resources. For example, Aramco Services Company, a Houston-based affiliate of the Saudi Arabian state oil company, used STAR to remotely execute a billion-cell mesh visualization of an oil reservoir. The TACC-STAR program is currently expanding into undergraduate and PhD-level computational education to better fulfil growing industry needs.

Research funding

Underpinned by the recruitment of highly ranked faculty, UT Austin research expenditures grew from $120 million in 1986 to $376 million dollars (financial year 2002–2003) and to $589 million (financial year 2010–2011). During 2010–2011, federal government funding to UT Austin totalled $355.5 million and the main funding agencies were Department of Defense (DoD) at $122 million; National Science Foundation (NSF) at $76.5 million; Health and Human Services (HHS) at $72 million; Department of Energy (DoE) at $42.5 million; and National Aeronautics and Space Administration (NASA) at $13 million. For the same time period, corporate funding to UT Austin was about $58 million; state and local research funding totalled about $41 million; non-profits about $31 million; and institutional funding at about $88 million (Figure 3.1).

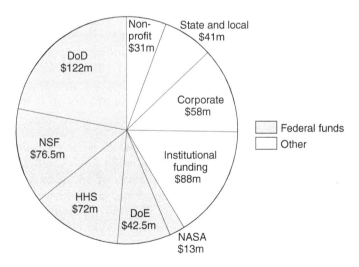

Figure 3.1 UT Austin research expenditures, 2010–2011 (total $355.5 million) (source: the University of Texas at Austin).

As of 2010–2011, research expenditures by academic unit were $158 million for the Vice-president (VP) for Research,[6] $146 million for the College of Natural Sciences, $130 million for the College of Engineering, $56 million for Geology, and $30 million for the College of Education. In 2012, UT Austin's College of Natural Sciences had 27 science and technology (S&T) research units with annual budgets greater than $1 million followed by the Cockrell School of Engineering with 21 such research units; UT Austin's VP Research with eight; and the Jackson School of Geology with four. Twenty-eight of these UT Austin research units have annual budgets of greater than $5 million.

The Office of Sponsored Projects (OSP) serves as the coordinating office for externally funded research and sponsored projects at UT Austin. OSP works to assist faculty and professional research staff in their effort to secure external funding and to ensure proper stewardship of this funding. As of 2014, federal research funding reductions were taking their toll on UT Austin researchers and students in the form of grant cancellations, delayed projects, and diminished assistance from federal agencies. For example, NSF accepted nearly 1,000 fewer grant applications for 2013–2014 and the National Institutes of Health (NIH) cut its 2013 fiscal year budget by 5 percent or $1.55 billion (Heise, 2013). The university is continually working to increase industry-sponsored research to help offset decreased federal research support. Industry-sponsored research includes gifts and unrestricted grants, industry affiliate programs, research cooperation, and other industry–university agreements. The Office of Industry Engagement (OIE), under the Office of the Vice-president for Research, works to enhance the university's industry research enterprise by coordinating with other campus units to facilitate research alliances with industrial sponsors and by establishing collaborative research around strategic technology initiatives. OIE also helps to mitigate questions about the university's policies regarding interactions with industry sponsors and industry constraints on research conducted in university labs. Conflict of interest issues are of high concern at the university and submission of "financial interest disclosures" is required to assure compliance with federal regulations and UT policy.

An example of successful UT Austin research–industry collaboration is the Cockrell School of Engineering's Wireless Networking and Communications Group (WNCG). WNCG's research funding has exceeded $20 million since its formation in 2002 with the support of 13 industry affiliates and sponsors.[7] In 2012 WNCG was named an NSF Industry/University Collaborative Research Center (I/UCRC). The award provides WNCG with about $400,000 in funding over a five-year period. The funding is renewable up to 15 years. The I/UCRC program is an annual competition created by NSF to reward university research centers that demonstrate great promise for research breakthroughs while exhibiting a strong track record of collaboration with companies and other universities. As a further example of WNCG academic–business cooperation, the 12th Annual Texas Wireless Summit was held in November 2014, co-hosted with the Austin Technology Incubator, to provide a forum for entrepreneurs and start-ups, established industry representatives, venture capitalists and corporate investors, and academic and corporate researchers, to discuss emerging technologies and business models that are expected to impact the wireless industry. As noted by Dean Gregory L. Fenves, Cockrell School of Engineering,

> WNCG is one of the world's leading wireless research centers, involving more than 16 faculty and 120 graduate students in electrical engineering, aerospace engineering and computer science. The crucial support provided by NSF will allow WNCG to accelerate its research on the greatest wireless challenges that society needs to solve in the next several decades.
> (UT web site, "WNCG awarded NSF Industry Collaboration Center," Wednesday, February 2, 2011)

UT Austin's growing entrepreneurial fever

Starting in 1977 with the founding of the IC² (Innovation, Creativity, Capital) Institute at UT Austin, entrepreneurship teaching, competitions, and other related activities have grown campus-wide from the Moot Corp Business Plan Competition launched in 1984 by two MBA students at UT's Business School and the Chair of Free Enterprise established in the College of Engineering in 1985, the founding of the Austin Technology Incubator in 1989, to an explosion of campus-wide programs and classes on entrepreneurship (Table 3.1).

The Austin Technology Incubator

Beginning operations in 1989, the Austin Technology Incubator (ATI) at UT Austin has been a key catalyst in developing Austin's entrepreneurial and innovation ecosystems continuing into 2015. In 1989, Austin was in an economic slump and "see through" (vacant) buildings were prevalent. Led by the IC² Institute at UT Austin, the Austin Technology Incubator "experiment" secured modest three-year funding of $50,000 per year from the City of Austin and $25,000 per year from the Greater Austin Chamber of Commerce (GACC) and a onetime donation of $70,000 from Travis County plus $50,000 from a private donor. ATI was launched, near the epicenter of Austin's emerging software cluster, in 4,000 square feet of "borrowed" office space with office furniture donated from university storage and Austin retail stores.[8] University administration was not entirely comfortable with the idea of a state-supported educational institution hosting a business incubator, even if it was not-for-profit, so the concept

Table 3.1 Timeline of select entrepreneurial and technology transfer initiatives at The University of Texas at Austin

1977	• IC² Institute established
1984	• Moot Corp Business Plan Competition
1985	• Chair of Free Enterprise Center for Technology Entrepreneurship
1988	• First US Technopolis Conference (IC² Institute)
1989	• Austin Technology Incubator (ATI) (of IC² Institute)
	• Texas Capital Network (with assistance of IC² Institute)
1991	• Office of Technology Licensing (OTL)
1992	• McCombs Entrepreneur Society
	• Austin Entrepreneurs Council (with assistance of IC² Institute)
1993	• Austin Software Council (ASC) (with assistance of IC² Institute)
1996	• MS in Technology Commercialization Degree (of IC² Institute)
1997	• Intellectual Entrepreneurship (IE) Consortium
1999	• Venture fellows
2000	• RGK Center for Social Innovation
	• Austin Technology Council
2001	• Herb Kelleher Center for Entrepreneurship
	• ATI Clean Energy
	• Idea-to-Product (I2P) competition
2003	• OTL becomes Office of Technology Commercialization (OTC)
2005	• IC² Institute Global Commercialization Group
2006	• ATI Wireless
2007	• Dell Social Innovation Challenge
2008	• 3 Day Start-up program
	• ATI Biosciences
	• Bridging Disciplines Program: Innovation, Creativity and Entrepreneurship
	• Entrepreneur in Residence program (School of Engineering)
2009	• Entrepreneur in Residence program (Herb Kelleher Center)
	• Start-up Meet-up Conference
	• Student Entrepreneur Acceleration and Launch (SEAL) program
2010	• Texas Venture Labs
	• Entrepreneur in Residence program (OTC)
2011	• UT Austin Inventor of the Year Awards (OTC)
	• UThink Tank
	• 1 Semester Start-up Course
	• Student Entrepreneurship Symposium
2012	• Longhorn Start-up Programs
	• Selig Center of Excellence in Entrepreneurship
	• Novel Programs in Education for Innovation and Entrepreneurship (UT System)
2014	• Southwest Alliance Innovations Corps (I-Corps) (NSF)

Source: IC² Institute and The University of Texas at Austin.

was presented as a technology venturing laboratory for UT students and professors – much like a chemistry or physics lab.

The lack of venture or angel capital was a noted challenge for the successful operation of ATI and the growth of a regional entrepreneurial culture. Recognizing this need, IC² Institute and key community influencers launched the Texas Capital Network (TCN) in 1989, as a non-profit angel fund that matched promising ventures to potential investors. TCN was built with the participation of wealthy influencers state-wide who agreed, with expert assistance, to review business plans in specific technology sectors and (if they so desired), provide seed funding to a particular entrepreneurial venture.[9] In 1992 the Austin Entrepreneur's Council (AEC) was formed to network the region's entrepreneurs and to provide support for start-up companies. By 1994 the focus was on Austin's growing software start-ups and the AEC morphed into The Austin Software Council (ASC). ATI, TCN, and ASC were key early programs that helped build Austin's emerging innovation ecosystem by conducting training seminars on business plan development, deal structuring, managing the investment process, and organizing venture competitions.

Over the years, as Austin's regional innovation and entrepreneurial ecosystems have grown and matured, so has ATI (Figure 3.2). Austin in 2015 has a broad range of private and public support structures and associations

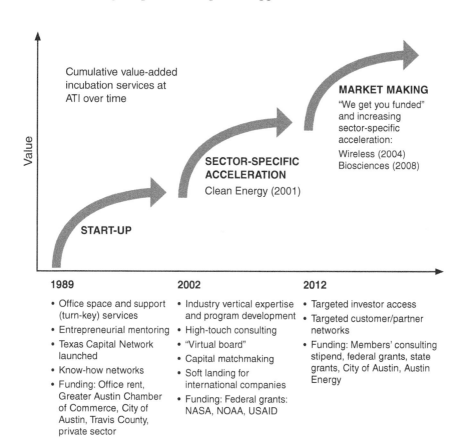

Figure 3.2 ATI evolved as did Austin's technology venturing ecosystem (source: Austin Technology Incubator).

supporting technology venturing; consequently, ATI incubation activities have focused on providing high-value mentoring in four IP-based technology verticals: IT, clean energy, wireless, and biosciences. ATI brings to its portfolio of companies, in each industry sector, deep domain management expertise and investor network access and helps to meet the increasing challenge of locating and hiring needed talent. It is important to note that each of these industry verticals has important formal and informal links to UT Austin research and education assets as well as to city and chamber of commerce economic development objectives.

Since its inception, ATI has had a dual purpose: to serve the university as an education and research laboratory for entrepreneurship and technology venturing, and to be a regional catalyst for economic development. For example, ATI's SEAL (Student Entrepreneur Acceleration and Launch) program identifies highly prospective student entrepreneurial teams from across UT colleges and departments and engages them in an intensive 12-week program, involving community and industry mentors and subject matter experts, to get the team members to a "go or no-go" decision. For example, in 2014, 140 student ventures were identified as SEAL candidates, from a broad range of UT Austin colleges and departments. From these candidates, 30 were selected for additional screening resulting in a final selection of ten ventures. It is emphasized that a "no-go" decision is as important and respected as a "go" decision, on the theory that it is better to "fail quickly" and move on than invest time and resources in a flawed business proposition. This "freedom to fail" helps invest SEAL students with an entrepreneurial mind-set that is independent of the success or failure of a single business concept. Over the past six years, about one third of the SEAL companies have either quit or failed, another third have bootstrapped successfully, and the remaining third have collectively raised about $12 million in private capital markets.

In brief, for over 25 years, ATI has been central to:

- assisting university-based entrepreneurs with building successful business teams;
- supporting technology ventures and facilitating access to angel, VC, and state funding;
- mentoring students from across campus;
- working with the city, chamber, and regional business community to help strengthen emerging technology sectors;
- graduating high-growth ventures into the Austin community.

With financial and other support from the university, the City of Austin, Austin Energy, and local business professionals, ATI has maintained a well-earned reputation as of one of the nation's finest examples or models for technology business incubation.[10] Table 3.2 shows the employment and economic impact of ATI from 2003 to 2012.

Table 3.2 Total economic impact of ATI graduate survey respondents, 2003–2012 cohort

Impact type	Employment (job years)	Labor income ($m)	Value added ($m)	Output ($m)
Direct effect	2,572	$240.9	$347.4	$411.7
Indirect effect	1,205	$60.1	$95.7	$148.8
Induced effect	1,782	$76.0	$136.3	$211.7
Total effect	5,558	$377.0	$579.4	$772.2

Source: Bureau of Business Research, The University of Texas at Austin.

Notes
Direct effect: Spending directly undertaken by the companies being studied.
Indirect effect (also known as the multiplier effect): Captures the rippling impacts of spending throughout a community. This refers to the increase (or decrease) in economic activity generated in the supply chain of the direct industry.
Induced effect (included under indirect impact) refers to changes in household expenditures impacted by spending or employment in the study industry or firm.
Employment: The number of workers, provided by companies in job years.
Labor income: Includes employee compensation as well as proprietor income.
Value added: Total sales (output) minus intermediate inputs.
Output: Total production value of goods and services, including intermediate goods purchased and value added.

The Office of Technology Commercialization

UT Austin's Office of Technology Licensing (OTL) was launched in September 1991. Reflecting university concerns of the time, the office was staffed by lawyers who emphasised the protection of UT's IP. As a result of increased state and Austin-based political and societal pressure calling for greater economic impact of UT Austin research, more emphasis has been placed on transferring knowledge and technology out of the university and into the marketplace. In brief, the transition to third-mission activities with increased emphasis on S&T commercialization has been a difficult challenge, given the established norms and values of a state university funded, in large part, by public money. As part of this transition, in September 2003, the OTL was renamed the Office of Technology Commercialization (OTC) with the objective of speeding the transfer of university R&D to commercial applications. In evolving toward a more proactive role in third-mission activities, OTC endured difficult institutional and personnel changes. Current staffing includes four physical science and four life science specialists; three patent specialists; one software and copyright specialist; two marketing and public relations staff, and about 11 administrative and finance staff. OTC activities and programs focus on:

- evaluating, protecting, marketing, and licensing university inventions and software;
- assisting in the formation of start-ups;

- promoting collaboration with industry, investors, and other stake-holders in technology commercialization;
- informing UT Austin faculty on appropriate and updated patent protection and commercialization processes.

Two interesting policies of UT Austin that help recruit and retain outstanding entrepreneurial-minded faculty and researchers are (1) comparatively high royalty payments to inventors, and (2) no forced retirement. OTC awards 50 percent of royalties, after expenses, to the research and 50 percent to UT Austin. Many other US universities present royalty awards of 20–30 percent. The no forced retirement policy has benefitted UT Austin by attracting and retaining outstanding faculty such as Professor John Goodenough and Dr Adam Heller. Dr Goodenough joined the Cockrell School of Engineering in 1986 after retirement from the University of Oxford. In 2012 Professor Goodenough won the National Medal of Science, the highest honor bestowed by the United States government upon scientists, engineers, and inventors. Professor Adam Heller received his PhD from Hebrew University in 1961 and in 1988 was named the Ernest Cockrell Sr. Chair (now Emeritus) in Engineering, Department of Chemical Engineering. To date, Heller has been named as inventor or co-inventor on 215 US patents; half of those have been registered since 2010. As an indicator of the changing culture of UT Austin toward third-stream activities, in 2011, Professors John Goodenough and Adam Heller were the first two professors to be awarded as UT Austin Inventors of the Year.

In 2014, another two well-respected UT Austin professors, Dr George Georgiou and Dr James W. McGinity, were recognized were recognized at UT Austin's Inventor of the Year Award Ceremony. Representatives from UT Austin and business and technology leaders from the Austin community joined the celebration. UT Austin researchers with US patents issued in the past fiscal year were also recognized for their achievements. This program was part of the 2014 Commercialization Series which was designed for UT faculty who are interested in exploring the discovery and commercialization process.

Table 3.3 shows the number of UT Austin IP-based located start-ups per year (Texas and non-Texas) from 1990 to 2011. There have been 58 spin-offs based on UT Austin research since 2003 with a high of 12 spin-offs in 2010.[11] Between 2004 and 2013, UT Austin was issued 392 US and 354 foreign patents. Annual tallies of license agreements at UT Austin have ranged from the mid-twenties to a high of 58 in FY 2008 for a total of 306 license agreements over the past nine years. Licensing revenue has increased from about $5.4 million in 1994 to over $25 million in 2011. However, as is common in most university royalty streams, a few patents provide the great percentage of financial rewards to UT Austin.

We believe it is also important and correct to include non-IP spin-offs in any assessment of the economic development impact of a research

Table 3.3 UT Austin patents, start-ups, licenses, disclosures, revenue (FY 2004–FY 2013)

Patents	FY 2004	FY 2005	FY 2006	FY 2007	FY 2008	FY 2009	FY 2010	FY 2011	FY 2012	FY 2013	TOTAL
US patents filed	110	104	78	133	143	161	183	125	113	150	1,300
Foreign patents filed	87	96	103	77	78	113	130	186	112	84	1,066
US patents issued	44	32	42	30	31	32	39	38	54	55	397
Foreign patents issued	55	29	17	25	33	43	27	31	43	51	354
Start-ups											
Texas start-ups	4	3	5	2	6	8	12	3	1	3	47
Non-Texas start-ups	3	4	2	1	4	1	0	1	1	2	19
Licenses											
Options	12	10	26	1	6	4	17	10	7	3	48
Non-exclusive licenses	11	13	16	11	20	11	10	9	2	7	118
Exclusive licenses	93	129	99	12	32	24	22	9	8	10	157
Disclosures filed				139	154	188	179	157	168	161	1,467
Licensing revenues ($m)	5.4	6.7	8.4	6.8	11.6	10.9	14.3	25.6	20.3	18.3	128.3

Source: Office of Technology Commercialization, The University of Texas at Austin.

university. For example, in Austin, it is important to include university connected companies such as National Instruments and Dell Corporation in the UT affiliated spin-off category, as it was UT Austin that attracted the founding entrepreneurs to Austin: Jim Truchard and colleagues launched National Instruments while working at UT's Applied Research Labs (ARL) in 1976; and Michael Dell launched his entrepreneurial effort as an undergraduate business student in 1984. It is also noteworthy that these entrepreneurs chose to grow their companies in Austin, in part, because of the region's quality of life which they and their colleagues, employees, and families enjoyed – and because of the critical importance of having a continuing supply of qualified talent graduating from UT Austin and other regional education institutions. In addition, we argue that UT Austin also deserves considerable credit for the founding of non-technology Austin-based entrepreneurial enterprises such as Whole Foods, Inc. and the SXSW Music, Film, and Interactive Festival, as both were founded by former UT Austin students and have been supported in their growth by UT students and graduates as employees, volunteer support staff, and as customers.

Entrepreneurial fever, current examples: UT Austin, state-wide, and nationwide

Launched in 1996 by the IC^2 Institute, the McCombs School of Business offers a one-year Master of Science in Technology Commercialization (MSTC) degree. The program is unique in that it is offered to students through class-based or Internet-based instruction and the emphasis is on building entrepreneurial teams that evaluate and launch a technology venture (often based on technologies from UT Austin research). Commercialization teams include professionals of varied technology, business, and educational backgrounds work together in class and taking virtual courses in converting technology to wealth and assessing technologies for commercial viability, marketing technology innovations, financing new ventures, commercialization strategies and venture planning, managing product development and production, and technology transfer in the global economy.

Housed in UT Austin's AT&T Executive Education and Conference Center, Jon Brumley Texas Venture Labs (TVL) provides networking links to the entrepreneurial, business, technology, and legal resources available across The University of Texas at Austin campus and the greater Austin entrepreneurial ecosystem. TVL provides mentoring, team-building, marketing and business plan validation, technology commercialization, and domain knowledge needed to start and grow innovative ventures. In semester-long consulting projects, the TVL accelerator connects Austin-based start-up companies with entrepreneurial graduate students from business, law, engineering, pharmacy, and natural sciences. Team mentoring objectives in New Venture Creation I and II include idea market validation, business model assessment, financial analysis and funding guidance, and competitive analyses. A competitively awarded TVL Partner position provides funding for graduate students to work on their start-ups for the first year after graduation. With about 400 investors, entrepreneurs, faculty, and students, Venture Expo is a semi-annual showcase of "Investor Ready" start-ups from UT Austin's ATI, OTC, TVL, and also Central Texas. Since its founding in 2010, TVL has worked with over 100 start-ups and raised over $235 million in a wide range of industry sectors.

The 3 Day Start-up (3DS) challenge is about launching technology companies over the course of a three-day weekend. The student participants represent a wide range of academic backgrounds including software engineering, business, graphic design, and others. The 3 Day Start-up event provides food and beverages while experienced entrepreneurs and investors mentor students as they brainstorm on Friday and vote to pick the top ideas to be developed over the rest of the weekend. The program culminates with a pitch and demonstration to a panel of VCs, entrepreneurs, and investors. Over the course of the weekend, students create a business model and prototypes, make contact with potential customers, and take advantage of networking opportunities to build professional and personal relationships. Founded by UT Austin graduate students with assistance from ATI, 3DS incorporated as a non-profit in 2010 and began presenting 3DS programs to universities across the globe.

The Longhorn Start-up programs of the College of Engineering are designed to cultivate entrepreneurship at UT Austin and with the community of Austin. Longhorn Start-up Lab is a semester-long class where students learn from faculty, practitioners, guest speakers, and mentors as they form interdisciplinary teams to start real companies. Longhorn Start-up Studios serve professors seeking to commercialize university technology, as well as leaders of growing tech companies that are beyond early start-up stage and are learning to scale. The Faculty Studio includes dinner-and-discussion programs to foster collaboration and mentorship. Facilitated by the university's OTC, each month, during an informal gathering, the regional business and entrepreneurial community gets to hear about new ideas and inventions coming out of the university.

It is important to remember that entrepreneurship is not all about IP and technology as liberal arts and humanities students also are involved in the entrepreneurial turn. For example, the Ronya and George Kozmetsky (RGK) Center for Philanthropy and Community Service, at UT Austin's LBJ School of Public Affairs focuses on non-profit organizations, philanthropy and volunteerism, non-profit management, and social entrepreneurship. Graduate portfolio programs provide opportunities for students to obtain credentials in an academic area of inquiry while completing a master's or doctoral degree in social work, business, communication, community and regional planning, sociology, and information. The Curtis W. Meadows, Jr. Social Enterprise Fellows program offers teams of graduate students in business and public affairs an opportunity to serve as non-profit consultants with NGOs in Latin America and the Caribbean. The RGK Center launched a Social Innovation Competition in fall 2006 to give undergraduate and graduate students from UT Austin as well as national and international participants the opportunity to turn their social innovation ideas into sustainable business or non-profit organizations. In 2011, Dell Corporation made a $5 million donation to the RGK Center to help support the Dell Social Innovation Challenge international competition that attracts more than 1,700 student venture plan submissions worldwide.

At the state level, to highlight the increasing importance of fostering the entrepreneurial experience in university environments, in February 2012, the UT System issued a call for proposals for novel programs in education for innovation and entrepreneurship. As stated,

> There is an emerging call for research universities to serve as entrepreneurial centres that drive research breakthroughs and discover solutions to large-scale scientific and social problems.... Many argue that innovation and entrepreneurial activity must grow exponentially if we are to continue to advance American science and technology. The institutions of the UT System are an ideal ground from which to advance a highly-visible, cross-institutional culture that fosters entrepreneurship rather than entrenched "silo" thinking. To accomplish such goals, fresh, new methodologies must be developed that will advance the education of established and budding scientists and train research leaders who are facile in forming academic-industry partnerships and creating companies and enterprises.

At the national level, in 2011, the NSF created the Innovation Corps (I-Corps) Program as a national network of public–private partnerships to transition fundamental science and engineering discoveries to the marketplace by training NSF-funded researchers to evaluate their scientific discoveries for commercial potential. In August 2014, NSF expanded the I-Corps program with the Southwest Alliance for Entrepreneurial Innovation Node that includes The University of Texas at Austin, Rice University, and Texas A&M University. In addition to the Southwest Alliance I-Corps, other regional nodes are located in Washington, DC; New York City; Michigan; northern and southern California; and Atlanta. Each node administers an I-Corps curriculum and activities to help support I-Corp teams as they evolve their technologies beyond the lab and into the marketplace. As designed, each node is expected to bring its own unique contribution and expertise, strengthening the National Innovation Network of mentors, researchers, entrepreneurs, and investors. To date, more than 167 institutions have participated and 319 three-person teams have completed the intensive seven-week training to launch more than 163 small businesses based on university R&D.

While the focus of this chapter is on UT Austin's emergence as an entre-preneurial university and its impact on the Austin region, it is also important to present a brief overview of important industry and govern-ment policies and activities that have impacted the university in this regard.

The industry sector

Successfully recruiting, retaining, growing, and creating globally com-petitive firms in one or more globally competitive industry sectors or clus-ters is perhaps the most important indicator of a successful innovation ecosystem. As noted, in 1983, public–private collaboration led by the Austin-based "MCC location team" of government, business, and aca-demic influencers also successfully recruited 3M R&D operations from Minnesota to Austin; followed by the successful bid for Sematech R&D consortium; the recruitment of Applied Materials in 1992; and Samsung in 2005.

TRACOR, founded in 1955 by UT Austin professors and researchers at Balcones Research Park (now the Pickle Research Center), was the region's first technology "mother company" as employees left TRACOR to found more than 20 tech-based companies in Austin (Smilor *et al.*, 1988). Other examples include Tivoli, founded in Austin in 1989, which had an initial public offering (IPO) of $35.5 million in 1995 and was acquired by IBM in 1996. Former Tivoli employees launched Austin-based start-ups such as Sailpoint (2005), Spiceworks (2006), and WhiteGlove Health (2007). Trilogy was launched in California in 1989 but moved to Austin in 1992 and former Trilogy employees started Convio in 1999, Broadway Techno-logy in 2003, and Otherinbox in 2008.

In addition to firm relocation and technology venturing, firm retention and growth are also important to regional economic development and sustainability. Initially attracted by Texas's lack of corporate and personal income tax, its cheap land, and a relatively low cost of living, IBM came to Austin in 1966 to manufacture the Selectric Typewriter. More importantly, IBM elected to stay in Austin and transition into a major research center. From the creation of the world's fastest UNIX servers and the ground breaking cell processor, IBM Austin has evolved as a critical component of the company's globally integrated enterprise as one of IBM's eight main research laboratories worldwide. IBM Austin's research facility focuses on software and hardware systems, high-speed communication chips, formal verification, distributed systems software, innovative cooling technologies, low power microprocessors, systems management, and performance evalu-ation. IBM and UT Austin have partnered to build substantial education and research programs while working with the city and the Greater Austin Chamber of Commerce to help shape the region's technology landscape.[12] With more than 6,239 employees and an annual payroll of about $600 million, IBM Austin is the largest corporate R&D operation in Texas. In 2008, IBM received 4,186 US patents, the most of any US company. IBM-Austin contributed 825 patents to the total, more than any other IBM location worldwide. As noted by Ben Streetman, former dean of UT Austin's Cockrell School of Engineering,

> Through the sharing of technology, resources, and talent, IBM and The University of Texas have enjoyed mutually beneficial relationship that goes back many years. IBM is a top hirer of UT engineering graduates year after year. We consider IBM and invaluable partner.
>
> (IBM press release, October 3, 2007)

Meeting a regional challenge for sustainability

In 2007, given the considerable downsizing of Austin-based semiconductor manufacturing as a result of the region's aging fabrication facilities and of increased global competition, it was clear to business and community leaders that the region could not base its future job and wealth creation so heavily on this one industry sector. Furthermore it was also clear that Austin's PC industry, i.e. Dell Corporation, would not be the main accelerator for job and wealth creation that it had been in the 1990s. The regional challenge was how to leverage Central Texas's considerable assets in fabrication facilities, experienced talent, and trained workers to the benefit of emerging industry sectors. In response to these challenges, the city and the Greater Austin Chamber of Commerce worked together to target the following seven industries for recruitment and entrepreneurial support: IT related automotive and aerospace research and components manufacturing; convergent technology; data centres; life sciences; wireless; clean energy; and creative industries and multimedia (Figure 3.3). It is important to note that this was not a "blue sky," list in that each of these industry sectors had an established and growing Austin presence including relevant research, education, and training programs at The University of Texas and other regional universities and colleges.

Austin-based inventors are granted 3,000 patents annually. UT Austin is the fourth most patent-earning university in the United States. Austin was #2 on the *Forbes* 2010 list of "America's most innovative cities" (based on per capita patent activity and VC investment). However, in terms of VC investment – while Austin ($620 million investment) made the top ten in the United States in 2012 – it is important to compare this with Silicon Valley, California, at the top rank with $10,868 million; New England second, with $3,208 million, and New York Metro area at third, with $2,343 million.

Figure 3.4 shows the number of jobs created by Austin's new and expanding hi-tech and non-hi-tech companies from 1994 to 2011. Over

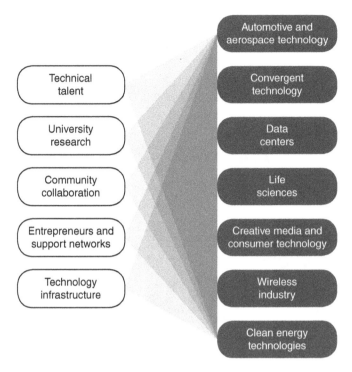

Figure 3.3 Leveraging Austin's assets to support emerging tech industries (source: Powers, 2007).

this 17 year period, hi-tech company growth created the most jobs in Austin (56,101 or 49 percent) followed by the growth of non-hi-tech companies (26,470 or 23 percent), followed by new hi-tech company formations (17,775 or 16 percent) followed by new non-hi-tech companies (13,775 or 12 percent).[13] Clearly, while start-up and entrepreneurial ventures are very important, the retention and expansion of existing firms are also a key regional job and wealth creation strategy.

As of 2012 Austin's technology employment is about 110,000, mostly represented in the following industry sectors: hi-tech information and other IT, 35,900; hi-tech manufacturing, 29,656; hi-tech trade, 23,613; creative media, 26,000; computers and electronics, 25,278; engineering, R&D and labs/testing, 20,000; and semiconductors, 13,441. As of 2014, Dell, with 14,000 employees, tops the list of Austin's largest technology company employer, followed by IBM with 6,000; Freescale Semiconductor with 5,000; Apple, 4,000; AT&T and AT&T Labs, 3,750; National Instruments, 2,800; Samsung Semiconductor, 2,600; Advanced Micro Devices, 2,500; Applied Materials, 2,500; Flextronics, 2,500.

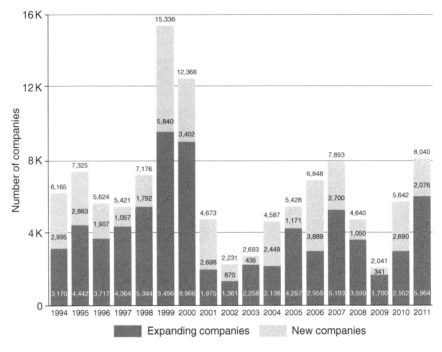

Figure 3.4 Austin jobs created by new company creation and company expansion (source: Greater Austin Chamber of Commerce data compiled by IC² Institute).

Government sectors

In the United States the government segment can best be understood at three levels: federal, state, and local. Each of these levels has contributed to and frustrated Austin's strategies for technology-based growth. When asked about the government's role in US business, casual observers often state, "The least government involvement the better," but clearly federal, state, and local government has played, and continues to play, an important role in the growth and competitiveness of both established and entrepreneurial firms in Austin.

Federal government: the good and the bad

The influence of the federal government on Austin as well as other technology-based regions in the United States has been largely manifested in policy initiatives such as the Bayh–Dole Act of 1980, the Small Business Innovation Research (SBIR) program that was founded in 1982, and national R&D initiatives such as NASA's program to land a man on the moon – and more recently, national energy, cyber security, and health policies. Other examples, for good or bad, include corporate tax levels, environmental regulations, infrastructure development and maintenance, and legislation concerning immigration and visa issues affecting a firm's ability to recruit and retain international talent. Federal government funding for university-based research (e.g. NSF, NIH, DoD, and DoE) has been crucial to US universities' prominence in discovery and invention, and such funding has indeed been crucial to UT Austin research and education contributions.

In addition, federal government actions have had major indirect impacts on Austin's development as a globally competitive technology region. One key example is the transition of a World War II magnesium plant in North Austin to a university research park. In 1949, with the assistance of then-Congressman Lyndon B. Johnson, UT Austin purchased the site for an off-campus research center that in 1953 became the university's Balcones Research Center and home to Applied Research Laboratories. In 1994 the center was renamed the J.J. Pickle Research Campus (PRC) in fond memory and recognition of US Congressman and UT alumnus, J.J. Pickle. The PRC is a collaborative effort of government, industry, and academia in science and engineering research and development. The PRC is home to 19 UT Austin affiliated research centers including Applied Research Laboratories, the Bureau of Economic Geology, the Center for Energy and Environmental Resources, the Microelectronics Research Center, the Robotics Research Group, Texas Advanced Computing Center (TACC), and the Institute for Geophysics. All of these research units are largely sustained by federal R&D funding.

State government: the good, the bad, and the fractured

Texas state government has had major and varied good, bad, and "fractured" impacts on the state's economic development and education quality. For example, the Texas governor appoints representatives who serve on the Board of Regents for The University of Texas System; and the influence of the governor and the regents on the UT System in general (and The University of Texas at Austin in particular) is significant.[14] Funding for higher education is one key area of influence that has been an especially contentious issue, as state funding for UT Austin has steadily decreased from about 52 percent in 1981 to about 12 percent by 2013. The most recent decreases have resulted in tight operating budgets for UT Austin, increasing the importance of other sources of funding including research, tuition, alumni support, gift giving, and endowments. This is most certainly not the vision of state-supported education excellence that the state's founding fathers called for with a "university of the first class" – nor does it well reflect the public–private collaboration that motivated the MCC site selection team to select Austin and UT Austin in 1983 as the home for the nation's first for-profit R&D consortium for enhanced US competiveness.

Low corporate taxes; no personal income tax; major oil, gas, and alternative energy resources; and pro-business policies have long been touted as key to Texas economic development. But Texas state government has also initiated specific programs to facilitate business growth and recruitment. For example, the 78th Legislature of 2003 enacted an economic development plan that included taking $390 million from the state's Economic Stabilization Fund (also known as the Rainy Day Account) to create a Texas Enterprise Fund (TEF), to help attract businesses to Texas and to create jobs. TEF projects must be approved by the governor, lieutenant governor, and speaker of the house.[15] As of 2013, $506 million has been awarded to 115 projects. On the downside, a 2013 audit questioned lax application and selection processes, undue political influence, and inflated claims of job creation, and suggested that companies "play government officials" for greater concessions – leading to bidding wars between states and a general lack of accountability for taxpayer money. As one state senator stated in late 2014, "before we give away one more taxpayer dollar, we need to enact serious legislative oversight, a strong independent review process, and verification that they work. Otherwise, we should just get rid of it" (AAS, 2014). On the upside, TEF funds have assisted Austin's recruitment of such high profile companies as Facebook in 2010, e-Bay in 2011, and Apple's major expansion in Austin that began in 2013.

Also under critical review is the companion Emerging Technology Fund (ETF) created by the Texas legislature in 2005 to provide funding for research, development, and commercialization of emerging technologies in the following three areas:

- Commercialization Awards to help companies take ideas from concept to market;
- Matching Awards to create public–private partnerships leveraging the strengths of universities, federal government grant programs, and industry;
- Research Superiority Acquisition Awards for Texas higher education institutions to recruit the best research talent worldwide.

By 2012 the ETF had invested $192 million in 133 companies which made it the largest seed investor in the state. Outside investors put three times this amount in the ETF start-ups which attracted almost $1.3 billion in investment. The state also awarded $178 million in research grants and other assistance to Texas universities including assistance in the recruitment of world-class researchers and their colleagues. In Central Texas (the Austin region), the TEF has invested $34,993,000 in 25 companies across 11 technology sectors. As required by the TEF, each of these companies has an affiliation with a Texas university; 23 ETF funded companies are linked to UT Austin research.

City government: where "the rubber hits the road"

Austin is the cultural and economic center of the Austin–Round Rock–San Marcos metropolitan area, with an estimated population 1,783,519, making it the 34th largest metropolitan area in the United States. Austin's public and private talent includes a diverse mix of government employees (e.g. university faculty and staff, law enforcement, politicians and administrative jobs); undergraduate and graduate students; industry employees; service and creative industries, healthcare, construction workers, and entrepreneurs. The city adopted the "Silicon Hills" label in the 1990s; however, the city also promotes Austin as "The Live Music Capital of the World." In recent years, Austinites have also adopted the "Keep Austin Weird" tag, proudly referring to Austin's brand of inclusive, eclectic, liberal lifestyles, and a preference for home-grown (non-franchised) local businesses and restaurants.

The importance of Austin's creative industry

The 1976 launch of *Austin City Limits* (*ACL*) at UT Austin's College of Communication TV studio was a seminal event. The pilot episode featured Willie Nelson and set fundraising records for the Public Broadcasting System (PBS). Following episodes showcased Texas blues, western swing, progressive country, and Tejano music – and over time included an increasingly diverse array of genres including jazz, alternative rock, folk music, and jam bands. In 2003, *ACL* was awarded the institutional Peabody Award and is the only TV series to receive the National Medal of Arts as the longest running music show in the history of American television. 2011 began *ACL*'s 37th season with its first live performance in the Moody Theater and Studio located in Austin's new W Hotel next to Willie Nelson Boulevard and the Willie Nelson statue in downtown Austin. Gibson and Rogers (1994) credit Austin's historic music venues and icons for inspiring the free and creative spirit and "Keep Austin Weird" culture.[16]

The city's Parks and Recreation Department lends support to the live music industry by regularly sponsoring public music performances, seasonal events, and outdoor concerts that showcase emerging and well-established musicians. One prominent example is *ACL*'s Music Festival which every October hosts over 130 artists and 225,000 patrons at Austin's Zilker Park. Another internationally known Austin-based music event is South by Southwest (SXSW) that was founded in 1987 by former UT Austin students. This annual March music festival hosts more than 2,500 local, national, and international performers in about 100 city venues. SXSW Film was added in 1994 and focuses on new directing talent and SXSW Interactive and Multimedia was added in 1999. The nine-day annual SXSW festival had an estimated regional economic impact of $190 million in 2012 and $218 million in 2013.

The Austin Film Society founded Austin Studios in 2000 through a partnership with the City of Austin, with the lease of 10,000 square feet of production office space in airplane hangars and office facilities at the recently closed Robert Mueller Airport. With the objective of strengthening the local film industry, the city's voters passed a $5-million bond initiative to upgrade the hangars to state-of-the-art soundproof, air-conditioned studios with expanded bandwidth and access for digital film production. In terms of the gaming and digital entertainment industries, the city and the Greater Austin Chamber of Commerce have worked with local educational and workforce development organizations to educate and train a highly skilled workforce for careers in gaming and film. As of 2011 Austin's digital media industry is the third largest in the United States and is a hub for game development across casual, social media, mobile, and online platforms. Austin-based IBM, AMD, Freescale, AT&T, Apple, Facebook, and Google develop hardware and software, products, and services for next generation entertainment and media technologies. Employment in Austin's video game industry grew from 2,848 employees in 2005 to 7,274 employees in 2010, with an annual economic impact of about $1 billion.

Austin's emerging and "game changing" challenges

A key ongoing challenge to Austin's sustainability as an important technology innovation and entrepreneurial region is striking an effective balance between fostering economic development and protecting the quality of life and natural and cultural assets so prized by Austin residents that attract and retain entrepreneurial and creative talent. City government and Austin citizens are especially concerned with seemingly ever-increasing traffic congestion, increasing utility rates and property taxes, and the lack of affordable housing. These issues complicate how best to maintain, if not grow, Austin's creative culture in a rapidly developing and increasingly expensive real estate market. In short, what constitutes "smart" growth? In 1983 when Austin's key influencers crafted the public–private strategy to gain MCC and other key technology wins, general public awareness and concern surrounding such efforts were considerably less than in 2015. As the number of stakeholder groups have proliferated so have the challenges to achieving a unified regional vision and development strategy. Numerous (and at times overlapping and conflicting) citizen and community groups frustrate the development and implementation of action specific strategies. For example, Austin's growth has outstripped the capacity of existing roads and public transport, yet citizens are conflicted over options promoted to supposedly improve the traffic situation such as light rail.[17] As an indicator of such concerns, several winning candidates in the November 2014 city council elections suggested that Austin's transformation into a rapidly growing metropolis had been accelerated by City Hall mistakes made at the expense of long-time residents (Toohey, 2014).

Support groups sector

The support groups sector (e.g. venture and angel capital, chamber of commerce, business professionals and associations, non-government organizations) has been critically important to the launch, growth, and sustainability of Austin's innovation ecosystem. Business-based support groups include professional services such as law, finance, accounting, and related professional associations that foster and mentor regional entrepreneurship and innovation. A key contribution of these groups is providing the business know-how for Austin-based ventures to scale so that they become major employers with national and international headquarters based in Austin. While Austin does not have a technology or science park, it is often noted that the greater Austin area is itself a creativity and business incubator. In terms of regional entrepreneurial support structures, the Greater Austin Chamber of Commerce lists 11 technology accelerators (in addition to the Austin Technology Incubator), eight co-working locations, and 11 resource organizations such as the IBM Innovation Center, UT Advance Dell Pediatric Research Institute, the Pike Powers Lab and Center for Commercialization, and the UT Austin Office of Technology Commercialization.

During the latter part of the twentieth century and into 2015, the Greater Austin Chamber of Commerce (GACC) has been an important regional actor for Austin's growth as an international technology center. The GACC's Greater Austin Technology Partnership includes business, academic, and public officials focused on specific targets of opportunity or technology sectors in mature and emerging companies. As of 2015, key chamber initiatives are: to leverage the new UT Austin medical school for biotech, medical device, and healthcare IT; to encourage greater investment in Austin-based companies; to enhance collaboration with UT Austin key research areas, entrepreneurship, and advanced manufacturing initiatives; and to develop and implement a sustainable talent recruitment and development pipeline for the greater Austin region.

Other groups of stakeholders include those representing minority issues, environmental concerns, non-profits, and a range of community lifestyles. Such groups proliferated as Austin grew and welcomed new residents. For example, *in addition* to the formal and informal entrepreneurial support activities resident at UT Austin and other regional colleges, the city of Austin, and the GACC, a 2010 survey found 24 community-based organizations and associations focused on supporting entrepreneurs with four of these focused on women entrepreneurs and three representing minority groups; 16 groups (not including Austin's established VC and angel organizations) providing venture funding advice including bootstrapping; 12 community-based education groups; 12 regularly scheduled entrepreneurial events; six incubators in addition to the Austin Technology Incubator; and six blogs focused on fostering regional entrepreneurship.

Civic and social entrepreneurs: giving back

An important category of community-based support groups concerns civic and social entrepreneurship including philanthropic foundations which are crucial to the development and sustainability of quality-of-life institutions and activities in Austin. A good deal of Austin's current philanthropy comes from the wealth of successful regional entrepreneurs who reinvest in their community in terms of social, cultural, and educational initiatives, as well as new business ventures.

One prominent example, the Michael and Susan Dell Foundation, was established in 1999 and is currently one of the largest family foundations in the United States. Over the years the foundation has committed $450 million to education, health, and financial programs with the goal of improving the lives of children living in poverty worldwide. The foundation gave Austin United Way its first $1 million contribution; $1.9 million to Austin's Seton Healthcare Network's Insure-a-Kid program to enroll uninsured local children in state and federally subsidised health insurance plans; $25 million to the Dell Children's Medical Center; $38 million to the Dell Pediatric Research Institute; $3.3 million to the Austin Independent School District; $5 million to the Ronya and George Kozmetsky (RGK) Center for Philanthropy and Community Service; and in early 2013, $50 million toward establishing a medical school at The University of Texas at Austin. In addition, Dell Corporation's spectacular growth built and enhanced the wealth of many former Dell employees, commonly called "dellionaires," who continue to give back to Austin with time, effort, and money with important community projects such as the Dell Children's Medical Center, the Long Center for the Performing Arts, and the Zachery Scott Theater.

Summary and conclusion

This chapter highlights several instances where a few regional influencers worked effectively across Austin's academic, business, government, and support group sectors to:

• win the national competition for MCC in 1983, 3M corporate research in 1984, and Sematech in 1988 – all events that helped launch Austin as a nationally and globally competitive technology region;
• leverage private sector funds with the university's Permanent University Fund to establish endowed professorships that were key to attracting top-quality faculty and students, winning competitive research grants, and launching research centers of excellence;
• launch the entrepreneurial laboratories or "experiments" called Austin Technology Incubator (ATI) and The Capital Network (TCN) in 1989 and more recently Technology Venture Labs, Longhorn Start-up Programs, and the RGK Center for Philanthropy and Community Service;

- transform UT Austin's Office of Technology Licensing to a more market-oriented Office of Technology Commercialization; and
- link economic development efforts of the City of Austin with those of the Greater Austin Chamber of Commerce and University research and teaching assets to create and sustain emerging technology-based industry clusters.

Across the United States at federal, state, and local levels there are vocal and diverse views and considerable conflict concerning the most effective strategies for fostering and accelerating technology-based growth. This chapter has stressed the importance of higher education institutions to a state's creative and innovative economy. Yet in Texas, as well as many other states, funding for higher education has continually decreased as tuition costs have increased. Public and private leaders in Texas are concerned about how to maintain and hopefully enhance the research and education excellence at the state's two flagship research universities as well as accelerate the growth of additional tier one research institutions throughout the state. At a more fundamental level, how will the Great State of Texas compete in a global knowledge economy when high school dropout rates reach 20 to 30 percent in the very population that is becoming the state's dominant demographic?

Another challenge is the heightened awareness of cities and regions throughout the state who are developing their own strategies to spur regional technology/knowledge-based growth and to attract and retain educated talent. For example, it was a path-breaking "experiment" in 1989 when IC² Institute working with university, city, chamber, and county leaders launched the Austin Technology Incubator (ATI). As of 2010, there were 47 business incubators throughout Texas and the number has increased into 2015, as has the competition for talent, technology, and capital. At UT Austin, as of early 2015, in addition to the Austin Technology Incubator there are other incubation and acceleration programs for students including Longhorn Startup Studios, Texas Venture Labs, 3 Day Start-up, and MBA+Leadership Program. Greater Austin has ten incubators and seven co-working spaces to support entrepreneurs and emerging technology ventures.

Entrepreneurial forethought by academia, business, and government in fostering innovative environments is seen as a good thing. But one should be careful of the metrics used to measure the success of such programs. In the end, the successful growth of any entrepreneurial venture depends heavily on the innovation ecosystem in which the venture is embedded. Many of Austin's current role models (such as Michael Dell; Jim Truchard of National Instruments; or John Mackey of Whole Foods Inc.) launched their enterprises without winning an entrepreneurial competition or benefitting from institutionalized support, but these entrepreneurs did clearly benefit from critically important mentoring and financial support from experienced Austin-based academic and business talent.

Despite considerable regional and national public and private sector challenges, this chapter suggests that two main cultural assets of Austin's DNA will continue to set the region apart from other technology regions in Texas and the United States. One is the high level of open and accepting "live and let live" or "keep Austin Weird" culture that we suggest is sustained by Austin's music, cultural, and creative environment. Additionally, it is important to emphasize that the city of Austin and UT Austin, plus the region's other universities and colleges, attract a never-ending flow of talent which continually energizes Austin's creative, innovative, and entrepreneurial culture as does the region's immigrant talent from across the United States and worldwide.

Austin's second defining asset has been the cooperative "can do" attitude that key academic, business, and government influencers exhibit when coming together at important moments to implement regional action strategies or to assist civic, social, or technology entrepreneurship. More recently this cooperative ethic has been challenged if not shattered at the city, state, and federal level concerning education financial support and management oversight, healthcare cost and delivery, infrastructure support, immigration and border challenges, and more. However, despite increasingly strident political conflict on these issues, it is still a common occurrence within the Austin region to hear discussion characterized by, "How can we make this work?" rather than, "You're not going to try that are you?" Over the years, openness to new ideas and talent and cooperative support to grow assets and opportunities has given a major boost to key regional initiatives despite increasingly vocal and strident challenges.

Perhaps at the launch of a technology-based entrepreneurial region a unifying vision with close public–private cooperation is more important than after the region has built a brand and gained momentum. Once a region has established itself can it perhaps withstand a certain amount of challenge and lack of cooperation as Austin and UT Austin has most recently endured? However, as we look to the future, an important concern is whether current regional influencers and emerging leaders will provide the needed level of visionary and inclusive leadership that launched and sustained the Austin Technopolis from the 1980s into 2015. We conclude that a key dimension of a sustainable regional strategy is the ability to grow and attract visionary and effective influences from the academic, business, government, and support sectors. It is important to stress that regional collaborations are based on building win–win scenarios and relationships of trust and not enhanced private sector wealth accumulation, or public demonstrations, or broadband Internet access and high volumes of tweets. Over 25 years of successful and not-so-successful public–private collaborations have confirmed the observation that the more collaborative the relationships across key public–private sectors, the more likely it is that effective economic and other regional activities can and will take place.

Acknowledgments

The authors would like to thank the following for reviewing and otherwise contributing to this research paper: Jim Butler, Manager, Creative Industries, City of Austin; and Beverly Kerr, VP Research, Greater Austin Chamber of Commerce; as well as those from The University of Texas at Austin including Dr James Jarrett, Senior Research Scientist, IC² Institute; Betsy Merrick, Associate Director, Marketing/Public Relations, Office of Technology Commercialization; Dr Juan Sanchez, VP for Research; and Dr Robert A. Peterson, Associate VP for Research and Director of the IC² Institute.

Notes

1 *Newsweek* (November, 2010) described Austin as having the nation's strongest job growth, in 2009 and over the previous decade. "(Austin) enjoys good private-sector growth, both from an expanding roster of home-grown firms and outside companies, including an increasing array of multinationals such as Samsung, Nokia, Siemens and Fujitsu." Austin was named the "Best city for finding employment" (*Forbes*, 2011) and "Among top 10 US brain magnets" (*Forbes*, 2011). In May 2012 Austin's unemployment dropped to 5.5 percent after being at 6 percent since 2008.
2 Established in 1883, UT Austin is the flagship institution of The University of Texas System which includes nine universities and six health institutions. UT Austin has the fifth-largest single-campus enrolment in the nation, with over 52,000 undergraduate and graduate students and over 24,000 faculty and staff. The university has 18 colleges and schools and 86 doctoral programs. The Cockrell School of Engineering has 267 faculty and more than 7,800 students enrolled in nine undergraduate and 13 graduate degree programs. The College of Natural Sciences has 370 faculty, 10,800 students, and 37 research units.
3 For technology company growth and sustainability in the Austin region, it is important to emphasize the key role played by regional universities, colleges and community colleges, and technical education in contributing to the education and training of the managers and workers crucial to the growth and sustainability of public and private sectors. For example, Austin's Community College (ACC) industry training programs have been key to attracting technology-based manufacturing to the Austin region, including semiconductor manufacturing firms in the late 1980s and the currently emerging digital media and gaming firms. ACC's Game Developing Institute is a two-year training program that has become a key source of talent for the region's growing gaming industry. Austin's gaming community provides guest lectures and judges for ACC productions while providing opportunities for "real-life" training, internships, and employment.
4 The 2013 Center for World University Rankings ranked The University of Texas at Austin as 26th among the world's top 100 universities; and the university stands seventh among other public US universities that made the list. The World University Rankings are based on several criteria including publications by faculty, influence, citations of faculty research, faculty quality, number of patents, and employment of graduates. Among these criteria, the university ranked highest in patents (20th) and quality of faculty (24th). UT Austin's McCombs School of Business was ranked seventh in the United States in terms of entrepreneurship by *US News and World Report* in 2014.

5 Winning the MCC provides an excellent example of public and private sector synergy at the regional level while strengthening UT Austin as a top research university. Peter O'Donnell, a successful Dallas businessman, arranged with UT administrators to leverage his $8-million gift for endowed chairs with an additional $8 million from the private sector which was matched with $16 million from the University of Texas Permanent University Fund (PUF) to create, in 1983, 32 million-dollar chairs in computer science and engineering. The PUF is a sovereign wealth fund with total assets of $14.9 billion as of December 2013. A portion of the returns from the PUF are annually directed towards UT Austin's Available University Fund.

6 VP for Research funding includes university activities and programs such as UT Austin's Applied Research Labs (APL), Center for Electromechanics, the Center for Computational Engineering and Sciences, the Texas Advanced Computing Center, and the IC^2 Institute.

7 These sponsors are: AT&T, Cisco Systems, US Department of Defense, Panasonic, Yokogawa, Powerwave Technologies, Commscope Corp., Samsung, National Instruments, Dell, Qualcomm, Texas Instruments, and Huawei, who participate as industrial affiliate members, as well as major government support from the Army Research Laboratory, NSF and the Defense Advanced Research Projects Agency.

8 As one of the wealthiest Texans, the founding Director of IC^2 Institute, Dr George Kozmetsky, could have simply underwritten the start-up expenses of ATI; however, he wanted to secure buy-in and commitment from key public and private stakeholders and he wanted to emphasize building an entrepreneurial start-up culture as being most important to the launch and sustained success in the management and operation of the Austin Technology Incubator. As an additional challenge to the launch of ATI, a previously launched and well-funded Austin-based technology incubator called Rubicon had closed its doors with no successful graduate companies and millions in lost investment.

9 The Capital Network (TCN) grew to be the largest angel fund in the southwest US, facilitating more than $150 million in total investments with 2,000 registered entrepreneurs. TCN's annual Venture Capital Conference regularly attracted upwards of 300–500 investors and entrepreneurs who came from across the nation and internationally to hear venture pitches from Texas start-ups. As VC and business angel groups became more prevalent in the Austin region, TCN terminated operations in 2001.

10 Since its founding in 1989, ATI has graduated over 150 companies; raised more than $720 million; had four IPOs; 25 acquisitions; created an estimate of over 10,000 direct and indirect jobs; and trained hundreds of UT Austin students from a range of UT colleges and departments. Capital raised by ATI member companies and alumni in recent years totalled $111,571.000 in 2011 and $103,918,000 in 2012. Overall the estimate of capital raised by ATI since 1989 is $1,081,186,000. ATI received the Randall M. Whaley Incubator of the Year award in 1994 from the National Business Incubator Association (NBIA). In 1996 ATI company, Evolutionary Technologies, Inc. (ETI) won the Graduate of the Year NBIA award for technology start-ups and CEO and founder Kay Hammer appeared on the cover of *Forbes* (August, 1996).

11 A university spin-off is considered to be a company that licenses a university technology in order to function; that is, the company did not exist until the time the university technology was licensed. A company is considered a spin-off regardless of whether or not the company founders were involved in the creation of the licensed technology.

12 *Forbes*, in their first-ever ranking, dubbed "the Silicon Hills" of Austin as America's second most innovative city after Silicon Valley, CA. The ranking was based on the 100 largest metropolitan statistical areas in the United States using data from the US Patent and Trademark Office combined with venture capital investment per capita along with ratios of hi-tech science and "creative" jobs (Greenburg, 2010).

13 Data were extrapolated from longitudinal datasets provided by the Greater Austin Chamber of Commerce. High-technology companies were selected according to the following parameters: R&D and manufacturing in IT, software, and semiconductors; precision parts and applications (i.e. semiconductors and medical devices); clean energy companies (but not fossil fuel energy companies); business-to-business hi-tech products and services; b2b and b2c Internet or technology infrastructure services. Default, and therefore error margin, falls toward the non-technical or "other" categories.

14 Wallace L. Hall is a member of the University of Texas System's Board of Regents. Hall was appointed to a six-year term as a member of the UT System Board of Regents by Governor Rick Perry. Shortly after his appointment, Hall began making frequent open records requests for high volumes of UT Austin records and emails, to examine favouritism in student admissions and forgivable loan programs at the university. In response to what some characterize as overzealous requests, state legislators initiated an impeachment process for a university regent, the first of its kind. As stated in *Texas Monthly*,

> Wallace Hall has been a one-man wrecking crew in his attempt to bring down the president of The University of Texas at Austin. Is he an out-of-control regent who deserves to be impeached or is he a selfless hero who is interested only in the truth? An unprecedented battle of ego, money, and power engulfs the Capitol.
>
> (Hollandsworth, 2014)

15 The fund grants discretion to the Governor of Texas when it comes to awards and this has drawn criticism from Texans for Public Justice among others while advocates call the fund "a deal closer". Companies that pass the state's selection criteria are also usually approved for tax and other incentives from city and county levels and school districts if applicable (Gaar, 2012).

16 Threadgill's garage of the 1950 and 1960s, in addition to gas and an oil change, also served beer and music while welcoming local and emerging guest artists including yet-to-be-discovered icons such as Janis Joplin, as well as a wide sampling of local musicians. Austin's Armadillo World Headquarters (1970–1980), located in an old National Guard Armory, was the iconic venue for established and yet-to-be-established music talent – as well as an occasional ballet, poetry reading, and other performing artists. The "dress as you want and come as you are" audience included university professors, students, bikers, cowboys, and rednecks, and hippies all sharing the music, Shiner and Lonestar, guacamole, and occasional marijuana.

17 "Austin America's fastest growing city" (*Forbes*, web, May 2012). Austin's MSA population grew 37 percent from 2000 to 2010 as the population growth for Texas was 20.5 percent and for the United States, 8.7 percent (US Bureau of the Census). As of 2012 Austin was the second fastest growing US metr and o area (at 3.9 percent) between April 2010 and July 2011. Austin Metro area's population is at 1.8 million. Austin's projected growth rate is 2.8 percent per year, almost triple the national rate and is projected to be two million by 2015 and to double every 20 years.

References

AAS (2014, 30 September). Viewpoints: Incentive fund oversight long overdue, *Austin* American Statesman, A6.

Florida, R. (2002). *The rise of the creative class and how it's transforming work, leisure, community and everyday life.* New York: Basic Books.

Gaar, B. (2012, April 22). Fund called a "deal closer," *Austin American Statesman*, A10–11.

Gibson, D.V. and Rogers, E. (1994). *R&D collaboration on trial.* Boston, MA: Harvard Business School Press.

Greenburg, A. (2010, April 24). Americas most innovative cities. *Forbes.com.*

Heise, T. (2013, December 1), UT Austin researchers feel the toll of federal research funding reductions. www.utexas.edu.

Hollandsworth, S. (2014, August). Is this the most dangerous man in Texas? *Texas Monthly.*

Mulcahy, T. (2007). *Corporate relations functions at the nation's leading research universities.* Minneapolis: University of Minnesota Press.

Powers, P. (2007). *Building the Austin technology cluster: The role of government and community collaboration in the human capital.* Unpublished paper.

Smilor, R.W., Gibson, D.V. and Kozmetsky, G. (1988). Creating the technopolis: High-technology development in Austin, Texas. *Journal of Business Venturing*, 4, 49–67.

Toohey, M. (2014, November 17). *Austin American Statesman*, A1.

4 High-technology entrepreneurship in a university town

The Cambridge story

Robert Hodgson

The region around Cambridge changed markedly during the 30 years spanning roughly from the 1960s to the 1990s and continues to change to the present day. There were seeds of change that can be traced to earlier times, but in the 1960s Cambridge was a relatively quiet agricultural service centre distinguished by a renowned and ancient university. By the 1990s Cambridge had become recognized as one of the leading centres of technological entrepreneurship at a European level, with technology-based business the dominant economic sector in a vibrant and fast-growing region. Indeed, during the 1990s, managing growth became a strong preoccupation of policymakers looking to mitigate the negative consequences of congestion and rising property prices while continuing to harness the vibrancy of the rapid business growth.

Unlike many of the cases in this book, the Cambridge Phenomenon, as it became known, was not a consequence of strategic initiatives taken by public authorities nor of the senior management of the University of Cambridge setting out to achieve something different. Both university and public authorities made vital contributions, but in essence the story is of a bottom-up drive from a group of agents who took on responsibility for making change happen. The university and public authorities were represented through individuals in this driver group, but they joined the group in their personal capacity as residents of Cambridge rather than as representatives of the bodies by whom they were employed.

The driver group was made up of 25 leaders who began meeting regularly, yet informally, in a pub. They had no constitution, they had no elected representation, they had no organization or political legitimacy in any formal sense, but over time they formed a shared view of what they wanted Cambridge to become – a centre for high-technology business – and each did their day jobs differently in order eventually to make their vision reality. Several had travelled to California and had seen the vibrancy of Silicon Valley and had recognized that many of the same ingredients that had come together there were also present in Cambridge, and they were motivated to utilize these ingredients to create a similar momentum.

This group of 25 had among its members someone from all the agencies needed to come together in Cambridge – in more modern terms they represented all the agencies of a modern innovation ecosystem and, more specifically, of the triple helix of business, government, and academia (Etzkowitz, 1993). So one member was a bursar with responsibility for managing the finances of one of the larger colleges of the University of Cambridge; one worked in the local authority planning department responsible for advising on the granting of permissions for land zoning; one was the regional manager of the largest bank in the region; and several were entrepreneurs of whom a few also had academic positions.

In the following case study, the organization is partly thematic, following elements of the entrepreneurial ecosystem through the full period which leads to a potential confusion of the sequence of events. So Table 4.1 sets out a timeline of some of the major events.

Key players

Looking in more formal institutional terms at the three key players – university, government, and business – the early stages were very different from what can be found today.

University of Cambridge

The University of Cambridge in important ways defines the town and is crucial to everything that goes on in the region, but at the time the momentum was gathering it was not a driving force in the creation of the new technology businesses. Its contribution was described as "benign neglect" in the path-breaking book, *The Cambridge Phenomenon* (SQW, 1985). By benign neglect is meant a permissive attitude to faculty and to intellectual property emerging from research activity at the university. The implications of this attitude are elaborated below. Over the 30 years of change in Cambridge there were also significant changes at the university and some of these are also described later.

One of the key milestones in the changes at the university was the 1969 report of the Mott Committee, a special Cambridge University committee set up under the chairmanship of Sir Nevill Mott (then Cavendish Professor of Experimental Physics and a Nobel laureate) to consider an appropriate response from Cambridge to an initiative of the Labour government following its election in 1964. That government had urged UK universities to expand their contact with industry with the objective of technology transfer and also to increase the payback from investment in basic research and an expansion in higher education, in the form of new technologies. The committee concluded that the university was already doing a great deal as one of the major national research centres, with an entrepreneurial

Table 4.1 Timeline of important events in and around Cambridge

	1960s	1970s	1980s	1990s	2000s
University	Management Studies (incl. technology transfer)	Wolfson Industrial Unit		Full-time Vice-Chancellor M. Thatcher, Chair of Entrepreneurial Studies Judge Institute	Judge Business School New IP rules Cambridge Enterprise
Research centres	CAD-Centre Laboratory of Molecular Biology			Genome Campus Babraham Campus	Cambridge Biomedical Campus
Technology consultancy	Cambridge Consultants	PA Technology	TTP Scientific Generics		
S&T parks		Trinity Science Park	St John's Innovation Centre	Granta Park	
Network initiatives				ERBI Cambridge Network	GEIF
Publications	Mott Committee Report		Cambridge Phenomenon		Biotech Cluster Report

attitude to applications; in one of its recommendations it identified the need to develop a facility to cluster technically advanced industry close to research, in a science and technology park.

In addition to the substantial knowledge contribution, there were two key cultural characteristics of the university that shaped the effectiveness of the Cambridge entrepreneurial ecosystem. The first, mentioned earlier, was an enabling culture that permitted faculty to pursue external interests, which was deeply embedded in the university's extensive history. As long as an academic carried out their allotted teaching load, undertook research or scholarship that resulted in frequent high-quality academic publications, and fulfilled their pastoral and social duties around their colleges,[1] whatever additional legally proper activity any academic chose to pursue was deemed acceptable. If this additional activity involved being an entrepreneur, then fine – it was neither encouraged nor discouraged but it was permitted.

Another key element of this permissiveness extended to any research findings that the academic chose to exploit in any potential business venture. Until relatively recently (the current position to be described later), the university choose not to exercise its rights with regard to intellectual property (IP) emerging from research activity. The default legal position in the United Kingdom is that the party who pays the wages of the researcher, typically the university, owns the rights to any IP emerging from the research – so this permissive part of the culture at Cambridge was distinctive.[2] Arguably, this was one of the main aspects of the "benign neglect" that fostered the Cambridge Phenomenon.

The second key cultural characteristic emerged from the historic position of the colleges in the running of the university. One of the social duties of fellows of the colleges (academic staff of the university were referred to as fellows in relation to their membership of colleges of the university) was to attend a minimum number of dinners, each term, where they would join other fellows of the college at high table. Typically around the dinner table were represented the major academic subjects of the university, and the consequence of this practice was development of very rich horizontal networks across the faculties of the university, rather than the more frequently found academic subject silos of universities organized on a predominantly faculty basis.

Such connectivity to different bodies of knowledge was a normal condition which enabled an ease of assembly of distinct knowledge sets that are often found necessary to launch a successful enterprise. Alumni of the university also frequently remained in Cambridge after graduating, being employed in professional careers in the city, or resident but working in London – an easy commutable distance away. So these horizontal networks are a common feature even of those residents of Cambridge who no longer retained any formal connection to the university.

Public authorities

In England (as opposed to the United Kingdom, with Scottish, Welsh, and Northern Irish regional agencies) there is little of a regional government tradition so public authorities fall into two categories: those at a local level including municipal and county authorities; and those of the central government with its predominantly national perspective. With the risk of simplification, the stance of the local government bodies was, in development planning terms, restrictive of growth with a tight "green belt" to stop development's spread into the rural edges of towns and cities. This was practised widely across much of southern England where development pressures were strongest. Additionally, the administrative geography of Cambridge acted as a stronger than normal restriction because the city of Cambridge is entirely surrounded by its neighbouring district of South Cambridgeshire and this neighbour was vigorous in its defence of encroachment by the expansion of the town into its territory.

From the national government level, there were early initiatives to harness new technologies, for example, the Wedgwood-Benn inspired "white heat of technological revolution"[3] in the 1960s out of which one initiative – the CadCentre – was established in Cambridge and was very influential, as much for indirect reasons as well as its direct activities. But there was, at this stage, little of the emphasis now given to innovation, technology transfer, and entrepreneurship in economic development policy. Again, it would be too simplistic to say that central government did not make significant contributions, as they were the source of much of the funding for the university sector,[4] and central funding also provided the resource for the very considerable presence of national research council R&D centres located in and around Cambridge.

Business

While Cambridge was not a major business centre, there were some important ingredients that helped initiate the growth of hi-technology companies. The first was the presence of Marshalls, which was a high-value engineering business and the largest private employer in the city where it had a wide range of interests – most notably an aircraft maintenance business based at the Cambridge Airport site. The second was the presence of Pye, a local firm producing radios which had developed the UK's first transistor radio in the late 1950s and subsequently conducted research on new television technology.

Business services were slightly more sophisticated than normal for a small agricultural service centre (the town had a little over 100,000 population) because of the distinctive demands of the university and its colleges, some of whom were and remain major landowners in their own right. This meant that the local estates professions and legal services were more sophisticated than would otherwise have been expected.

On the negative side there were no businesses related to venture funding, to international marketing, or to IP legal services, that are now regarded as essential to a vibrant innovation and technology entrepreneurship eco-system. Nor was there a cadre of middle and senior managers who had the experience to take a small new business through a fast growth path to address international markets, which are often an inevitable consequence of specialist niche technology businesses. As the phenomenon gathered pace, these service elements did arrive, grow, and become foundational to the current vibrancy; but they needed the demand to be established first, rather than being an ingredient present from the start.

The CadCentre[5] – the first wave

During the 1940s and 1950s a small number of businesses were established in Cambridge that were based on knowledge originating from R&D in the city's university and research centres. However in the 1960s the momentum accelerated, which was in significant part due to the arrival in Cambridge of the CadCentre. It was a national government initiative to harness new developments in the IT field as part of a competitiveness drive for British industry. In spite of its distance from industrial centres, Cambridge was selected as the best location for this government initiative. Its main novelty, in addition to the technology, was that the management of the centre was contracted to a private company rather than being managed by a research council or university. This introduced a commercial perspective into both the selection of staff and the agenda for research and operations, which differentiated it from the more academic orientation of other units in the Cambridge area. It was an early form of the public/private partnership model, which has become more widely used as innovation initiatives seek to benefit from a blend of public and private interests and motivations.

The effect on Cambridge was felt in both the short and long term. In the short term, a cadre of specialists was attracted to the town, several of whom – after working at the centre – subsequently set up the first wave of hi-technology companies in the 1970s. This wave was not the start of technology company formation, but it significantly accelerated the pace of growth and helped to create the critical mass of businesses needed to create the conditions for a specialist market for advanced business services and advanced labour skills to emerge in Cambridge (SQW, 2000).[6]

The second and longer-term effect was to reinforce the linkage between the academic research community and the emerging technology business community. Smart young scientists could do interesting work and could do this in companies as well as in the more traditional academic settings. The subsequent growth of the major new business engines – private technology research and development businesses – that have been the major source of new technology businesses in Cambridge emerged from this linked world and are described below.

Technology consultancies

One of the most distinctive features of the Cambridge innovation ecosystems emerged slowly from private companies set up to harness the new technologies and to offer a service to private businesses to utilize better the opportunities flowing from these new technologies. The first, created in 1960 by two academics at the university, quickly attracted a broader team under the name Cambridge Consultants Ltd (CCL). An early member of the team, Gordon Edge, had come to Cambridge to work with Pye and saw the potential of the new technology services consultancy which he joined in 1962, and where he became managing director in 1968. When in 1972 CCL became part of Arthur D. Little, Edge left and became the founding leader of PA Technology, the second of the technology consultancies to emerge in Cambridge. By 1986 he had left and set up another group called Scientific Generics, but not before a fourth consultancy had emerged from a spin-out from PA Technology to form the Technology Partnership, now usually known as TTP.

Each of these four has their differences, but as a set of businesses they became the source of many of the next wave of new technology businesses to emerge in Cambridge and were certainly more significant than the direct spin-outs from the university R&D groups. In part this was because of the different orientations of the consultancies – they were dealing with advanced technologies but were oriented to practical challenges in application rather than blue sky research for its academic interest. It was also, in part, because of their position as links between the business world and the advanced scientific world – but it also flowed from the culture that emerged from how they managed their intellectual property.

Again there are differences, but in general, an R&D contract with a client business would typically provide for any IP that emerged from the R&D to be owned by the commissioning firm – but only in the area of application related to the existing business of the firm. The rights to use the IP in other applications not related to the commissioning firm's market were retained by the consultancy, which meant they had a private reservoir of potential IP that was available for exploitation.

The internal cultures of the consultancies then encouraged staff to explore how these potential IP assets could be used in novel or different markets and encouraged teams of staff to develop their ideas to the point that they could spin out and form a new business using the IP. This culture was taken a step further when the parent companies set up risk capital arms to provide some of the early stage funds to launch the new businesses. So they had evolved into new business-generating engines with very positive impacts on incubation in the Cambridge area.

It is also worth noting that the first formal early stage risk capital fund based in Cambridge, called Prelude, was set up on the initiative of CCL and staffed by CCL personnel. So even the financing sector of the Cambridge innovation ecosystem owes a debt to the innovation engines of the technology consultancies.

Development of infrastructure

To accommodate the growth of hi-tech companies, the Cambridge group again looked to emulate the model of Silicon Valley, and more specifically the Stanford Research Park, which several of the group of 25 had visited independently. So it was no surprise that, with the support of the Mott Committee, the science park model was adopted in the Cambridge area for the first time in Europe. The science park also became an important flagship for the new direction Cambridge was taking: the city was open for business. From the beginning of the 1970s, as many as eight followers replicated the model within the larger Cambridge area.

The Trinity Science Park

The first science park in Europe was an investment by Trinity College[7] in 1973 on land it had owned for some time on the northern fringe of the town. The model was of a specialist property development where new technology businesses would locate in a cluster of business activity linked to the University of Cambridge and its advanced research activities through a panel of researchers and scholars who were fellows of the college.

Permission was granted by the local planning authorities to rezone the land from agricultural use to light industrial use with a special condition that all occupants on the site would have an explicit link to the work of the University of Cambridge and be non-polluting. The infrastructure for the site was funded by Trinity College and the management of the scheme was handed over to the private estate agents who already managed the other properties of the college. The target market was medium-sized firms, or the technology centres of larger firms, with links to Cambridge research. The park developed slowly by commercial infrastructure norms, but established and retained its image as a selective development at the premium end of the property market.

While there was the offer of connections to the academic community through the group of college fellows mentioned above, most of the firms who chose to locate on the Cambridge Science Park, as the scheme became known, were already well established and had links that were important to the conduct of their business. So the service content of Cambridge Science Park was at the lower end of the normal S&T park model.[8]

St John's Innovation Centre

Almost immediately opposite the Trinity Park site on the northern fringe of the town, a second college (St John's) also owned land, and the next major piece of infrastructure to be developed in 1987 was the St John's Innovation Centre. Wisely the property development was differentiated from the Trinity scheme in that it targeted small and medium-sized businesses that wished to rent property, rather than the bigger established firms who were looking for an independent and permanent presence offered by the Trinity Science Park. Again this investment carried risks as these new small firms did not have the strong financial covenants which are normally sought by commercial property developers. So the first multi-occupancy buildings of the Innovation Centre were filled with small firms, many of whom had their first business addresses in the building. The centre then became the nearest thing that Cambridge offered to an incubator of new firms and the manager of the centre, Walter Herriot[9] became one of the most important nodes in the networks around Cambridge for potential entrepreneurs looking to commercialize technologies.

Subsequent expansion of the Innovation Centre first offered additional accommodation for similar small firms, but then developed larger premises for specific tenants, so the sharp contrast with the Trinity Cambridge Science Park became less clear. The Innovation Centre became an important initiator and host to several additional initiatives, such as the EU Relay Centre[10] for the wider region, which increased it as a crucial node of the town's technology ecosystem.

Granta Park

Granta Park was another later development; the ground-breaking ceremony took place in 1997, in one of the villages to the south of Cambridge. It was significant in signalling the willingness of the surrounding South Cambridgeshire District Council to envisage breaches in its tight green belt policy. The developers were the Welding Institute Ltd (now known as TWI[11]), one of the most significant industrial technology research institutes in South Cambridgeshire, in alliance with a private property developer, MEPC Plc. The planning authority was persuaded to grant the development permission in order to enable technology firms to locate close to the research institute and to encourage spin-outs of technology and start-up firms from research carried out at TWI.

In actuality the park became home for a growing cluster of biotechnology companies that had only the loosest connection with TWI, if any at all. Some of the firms had been spin-outs from the biotechnology research base of Cambridge, but many were incomers hoping to benefit from the growing specialized labour market created by the clustering of the largest concentration of commercial biotechnology companies in Europe – but more of that later.

Peterhouse Technology Park

Later still, in 1998, a long-established industrial area owned by the smaller Peterhouse College had a make-over and was upgraded to a technology park signalling the move of the S&T park model to mainstream premier property provision in the town. The move was not of particular significance except that it eventually became the home of ARM, one of the stars of the Cambridge technology business firmament.

The Cheshire cat's grin

By the late 1980s Cambridge was becoming noticed as an emerging centre for technology business, particularly following the publication of *The Cambridge Phenomenon* book, and attracted interest from academics and commentators who made up a good part of the growing "enterprise tourism" who visited the town to explore what lessons could be learned from the experience of technology spin-outs from academia. If a small but high-quality university in a relatively small city could achieve so much, there might be hope that the experience could be replicated.

The growing pride that achievements were being noticed may have given rise to a degree of complacency; so it was no surprise that Anna Lee Saxenian, a well-known academic commentator with a background in Route 128 Boston and Silicon Valley, should be less than impressed by the smaller scale of what had been achieved than what she was used to at home. Saxenian (1989) wrote about the Cambridge area having a Cheshire cat's grin,[12] which was a less than complementary allusion to Lewis Carroll's literary creature that appeared in the air without a body and was thus insubstantial. The response to this slight was to point out how long it took from the start of a recognizable Silicon Valley for the first corporation with a billion-dollar valuation to be achieved and that the age of the Cambridge Phenomenon was still within that timeframe, so patience might be appropriate. There have since been several companies that have emerged from Cambridge of this scale, including ARM technologies and Autonomy. Further, while in pure economic terms Silicon Valley may have produced higher valuations and bigger companies, what has happened in Cambridge is different, inasmuch as it has produced Nobel Prize winners, then translated their descendants' work into companies and lit the way toward new industries.

Emergence of biotechnology

While the first wave of technology companies were related to IT, a second substantial wave of business growth emerged in the biotechnology field. Unlike the first wave, this biotechnology wave had a significant element of inward moving firms as well as a significant number of new starts emerging from the extensive high-quality research base. In the 1999 *Report on Biotechnology Clusters* published by Lord Sainsbury, then Minister for Science and Innovation in the UK government,[13] Cambridge was identified as a fully operating cluster and one in which investments should be concentrated for national competitiveness.

The biotechnology research base

This research base includes the University of Cambridge but also several units of national research councils (the Medical Research Council (MRC) and the Biotechnology and Biological Sciences Research Council (BBSRC)), units funded by medical charities (for example, Wellcome Trust and Cancer Research UK) and companies located on the Cambridge Biomedical Campus which is located adjacent to the region's major hospital, Granta Park, the Babraham Research Campus, and the Genome Campus. Within the network culture of Cambridge and the multi-source funding model, the formal and informal networks between all these bodies ensures that there is a flow of knowledge between them. It also means that the Cambridge area has developed a specialist labour market which makes it an attractive place for talented biotechnologists to pursue their careers.

The Laboratory of Molecular Biology

The Laboratory of Molecular Biology (LMB) is a Medical Research Council unit that was first established in 1962 although it was based on an earlier unit that had worked in Cambridge since 1947. In its inaugural year it was awarded two Nobel Prizes, for work done in its predecessor unit, and has since gone on to be awarded a further eight Nobel Prizes. It is also a major source of commercialization of technology, and in the five years till 2010 earned some £330 million from royalties and licences of IP and through sales of shares in companies it had been responsible for establishing with the efforts of its in-house technology transfer unit, the Research Office. In 2013 the LMB moved into a new, purpose-built building costing £212million which was part funded by its royalty income.

Sanger[14] Institute and the Genome Campus

The Genome Campus is a 55-acre estate south of Cambridge in the grounds of Hinxton Hall, which includes two world-class research facilities: the Sanger Institute and the European Bioinformatics Institute (EBI). The Wellcome Trust bought the site as a home for the new Sanger Centre which was a jointly funded facility with the Medical Research Council. Since then the site has developed to become one of the main British hubs of biomedical science. The campus is also home to the Wellcome Trust Advanced Courses and Scientific Conferences programme and the Wellcome Trust Conference Centre.

The Human Genome Project was launched in the USA in 1990, through funding from the US National Institutes of Health (NIH) and Department of Energy, and looked for international collaborators to sequence 95 per cent of the DNA in human cells in just 15 years. In 1992, John Sulston submitted a grant application for over £40 million to fund a new centre – the

Sanger Centre – which was to form the British arm of the Human Genome Project's sequencing efforts. By 1999 over 500 staff worked at the Sanger Institute and by 2009 this had risen to more than 800.

The European Bioinformatics Institute is part of EMBL, Europe's flagship laboratory for the life sciences. EMBL-EBI provides freely available data from life science experiments covering the full spectrum of molecular biology. While it is best known for its bioinformatics services, about 20 per cent of the institute is devoted to basic research. Extensive training programmes help researchers in academia and industry to make the most of the incredible amount of data being produced every day in life science experiments. EMBI-EBI is a non-profit, intergovernmental organization funded by EMBL member states. Its 500 staff are drawn from 43 nationalities, who are supplemented by a regular stream of visiting scientists throughout the year

Babraham Institute and Babraham Research Campus

The Babraham Institute is an independent charitable life sciences institute funded by BBSRC and involved in biomedical research, set in an extensive parkland estate just south of Cambridge and about three miles to the north of the Genome Campus and an equal distance north from Granta Park and south from the Cambridge Biomedical Campus.

Babraham Institute has the status of a recognized postgraduate institution within the University of Cambridge; all the PhD students are registered within the Faculty of Biology for their degrees and the institute's group leaders are full university supervisors. The Babraham Institute is involved with the Graduate School of Biological, Medical and Veterinary Sciences within the university, which co-ordinates and provides training, network, and career support for all postgraduate students in the biological sciences in Cambridge. It also links to business through its trading arm, Babraham Institute Enterprise Ltd.

On the Babraham Research Campus basic bioscience researchers are co-located with growing biotechnology enterprises. This ensures that newly established and growing spin-out companies and SMEs have access to world-leading researchers and facilities, and drives excellent research into application. Babraham's Bioincubator was established in 1998 and now provides around 100,000 square feet of serviced facilities and expertise to support new bioventures, and catalyses the commercial exploitation of bio-medical research. In 2011, the government awarded BBSRC £44 million to invest in the campus, including a fifth new bioincubator building, two follow-on laboratory/office buildings (one chemistry, one biology) and a new central scientific services building.

Babraham Bioscience Technologies (BBT) is the company that manages and develops the Babraham Research Campus, supporting and promoting the regional and UK bioscience ecosystem. The campus provides companies with laboratory and office space together with access to outstanding scientific facilities in an ideal geographical location at the core of the Cambridge cluster.

The Babraham Research Campus illustrates the linkages among the active and integrated biotech networking community in Cambridge, making this a vibrant and stimulating environment in which to develop new bio-ventures. Several Eastern Region Biotechnology Initiative (ERBI) events (see below for a fuller description of ERBI) have been hosted there. Babraham is represented on the board of the Cambridge Network and has board membership of the University of Cambridge Challenge Fund (an early stage proof of concept and seed fund) and is committed to supporting innovation and knowledge transfer to stimulate the economic development of the greater Cambridgeshire region.

Collaborative research projects with the institute may be eligible for a number of funding schemes: for examples, from BBSRC there are industrial partnership awards, flexible interchange programme (FLIP) and CASE studentships, while from the Technology Strategy Board, a public body, there are funds for collaborative research and development, for knowledge transfer partnerships, and smart awards. Even with all of these initiatives there was still need to improve the game in terms of biotechnology's contribution to regional economic development.

Eastern Region Biotechnology Initiative (ERBI)

The region around Cambridge developed into one of Europe's major centres for commercial biotechnology with both home-grown companies coming out of the research base and inward investment from companies looking to link and benefit from the quality and depth of research and development activity in the Cambridge area. However, in spite of the concentration, it was noticed that the companies were not acting according to the expected pattern from Porter's Cluster Theory (Porter, 1990) in that there were few linkages evident between the companies nor was there a rich array of support companies offering specialist services to the biotechnology cluster.

ERBI was launched in 1997 with the support of a small government seed grant and some matching funds from one of the major accounting firms who were keen to promote linkages and to be seen to be the partner of choice for the firms in the cluster. The programme followed by ERBI over the first couple of years of its operation was what has become a conventional mix of face-to-face events plus the creation of a web-based portal through which firms could link and events could be publicized. So there were breakfast meetings where firms could make a short pitch of work in which they were involved and where they saw their strengths; at other events, industry leaders were brought in to discuss selected topics of a mix of science and technology advances, market development initiatives, or shared problem areas affecting a range of firms in the region. Buyer/seller meets were arranged and a web portal developed where news, both local and from wider afield, and events could be publicized, as well as commentaries on the topical events that made up the breakfast programmes.

Public funding was designed to kick-start the initiative and the objective was to have demonstrated, within the usual window of a couple of years, sufficient added value that the firms in the cluster would be prepared to take on the relatively modest costs of maintaining the programme and web portal. In contrast to many such programmes that did not manage to survive much beyond the period of public funding support, ERBI did manage to survive and prosper. The killer application that caused the firms to value the effort and fund its continuation through annual membership fees was the development of the web portal of a virtual labour market exchange. Individuals with particular specialist skills registered their availability on the site and firms with particular skill needs advertised these needs at the same location. This virtual exchange is still active and the support programme continues to the present day.[15]

Great Eastern Investment Forum (GEIF)

In common with many other areas, Cambridge suffered from the problem of getting those with innovative early stage ideas for new businesses to meet those with capital seeking to invest in just such businesses. There were by this stage (the early 2000s) a number of venture funds active in the Cambridge area but they were interested largely in those opportunities that had already achieved some early market sales and had the potential to grow quickly to reach a wider market. The networks that had been an essential part of the early success were still working to fill the gap but more was needed to organize those that were attracted to Cambridge but did not have the benefit of active membership of the local networks.

With a small public sector grant a programme was established to set up a network event that would bring together the two interested parties – technology entrepreneurs and those with capital to invest. The management of the GEIF was won through competitive tender by N.W. Brown, a local financial services group that was part of the inner circle of Cambridge networks. GEIF had a remit wider than just Cambridge, hence the name Great Eastern which refers to the wider region, but it was the magnet and image of the centre of technology entrepreneurship that Cambridge had become that added to its momentum.

The GEIF model worked on both sides of the challenge because it was recognized that it was often necessary to prepare the entrepreneur to present their ideas successfully and for the investor to improve their knowledge of what constituted a successful early-stage venture funding deal. A monthly meeting cycle was established around investment breakfasts with potential investors invited to hear pitches of early-stage business ideas from potential entrepreneurs. The entrepreneurs were first screened to identify ideas with the best prospects of attracting investors, then gaps in information about the potential business's prospects were identified and addressed by the entrepreneur before being presented to the meeting. Coaching was given in how to pitch successfully to potential investors.

The target potential investors were a mix of high net worth individuals, the so-called business angels, and early stage funds that had some appetite for investing in new technology businesses. Meetings were open to all and charges levelled to cover the cost of the events so that the majority of the public funds were targeted at the work of preparing the early-stage entrepreneurs. As a consequence, a much wider audience of attendees was attracted than initially envisaged, with regular attendance from international fund managers from as far afield as Singapore as well as national and a smaller number of European funds.

The meetings followed a format of, first, a presentation by a successful local technology business during breakfast. This was designed to shape the thinking of the investors about the range of participation that might be envisaged and the roles that early-stage investors might play in early-stage business start-up and growth. This was followed by short pitches by the prepared entrepreneurs, usually four, of their business ideas and the range of investment participation in which they were interested. Any investor interested in one of the businesses was then encouraged to meet and talk with the entrepreneur to learn more about their business idea and to register their interest in taking the matter further.

These conversations were encouraged to continue directly between the entrepreneur and the potential investors, with both parties advised to have the support of legal and financial advisors as appropriate, but this lay outside the programme which was designed to create the forum not to complete the deals. Over the years the programme ran many investments in new technology businesses were successfully concluded and a much higher level of accelerated businesses created. It helped to establish a marketplace in the Cambridge area and from there a number of business angel networks emerged, and the city became a home for a larger than could be expected number of early-stage technology venture funds. The extent of business services linked to these early-stage investments also flowered, to the broader benefit of the innovation ecosystem.

The Cambridge Network

During the 1990s there was a growing volume of visitors to Cambridge with a special interest in learning what secrets lay behind the successful growth of hi-tech businesses, plus a growing number of businesses decided to relocate to Cambridge to participate in the technology buzz. As a consequence, pressure was put on the open network approach, as calls from the visitors for time and explanations fell disproportionately on those at the centre of the momentum, and the integration of the larger number of new businesses which did not have the network connections from their birth became an equal strain. Networks prosper if participants put in as much effort and energy to the common good as they get out, and this balance was being lost.

These pressures gave rise to the Cambridge Network, which was formed as a private company whose shareholders are among the most frequently called-on agents in Cambridge. It offered members access to network activities and visitors a service that planned their visits for a fee. It was established to bring people together – from business and academia – to meet each other and share ideas, encouraging collaboration and partnership for shared success. It currently has over 1,200 corporate and 300 individual members. The services and events it orchestrates include:

- the Cambridge Corporate Gateway, a service dedicated to matching external organization's technological requirement to companies in the Cambridge area
- open meetings and lectures intended to bring together business and academic interests
- the Learning Collaboration, encouraging local companies to pool training resources
- the Recruitment Gateway, a service designed to attract and retain the best and most talented people to work in Cambridge.

A number of special interest groups have arisen from Cambridge Network activities and Cambridge has a vibrant community of networks.

Adaptions at the university

While an ancient institution, and often opaque in its decision processes, the University of Cambridge has made great changes through the period covered by the emergence of the hi-tech sector in the town. Among the most significant to the story is the increasing professionalization of the technology transfer and IP management system, the continued investment in specialist infrastructure, and the various developments around the Engineering Department and Judge Business School, with related subjects that interact with the local hi-tech business base. What has continued has been the emphasis on excellence in all aspects of its work, especially in relation to its academic standing as one of the top universities of the world.

Perhaps the most significant change over the period has been in the central direction and management of the university, which has taken on a stronger strategic role and changed the balance of power between the university and its constituent colleges. Most evident here is the creation of a full-time position as Vice-Chancellor or Chief Executive of the University of Cambridge. For 400 years prior to this change, the post had been filled on a rotating basis by the masters of one of the constituent colleges of the university. The transition was achieved by David Williams who, in 1992, as the 342nd post-holder, became the first full-time incumbent following on from the prior arrangement under which he took the post in 1989. The appointment is now made for a maximum of seven years and so provides the continuity to lead strategic changes in the institution.

Of the many additional changes at the university over the period, three are highlighted because of their significance to the continuation of the growth of hi-tech enterprises. They are:

- the treatment of intellectual property
- entrepreneurship in theory and in practice
- developments at and around the Department of Engineering and the emergence of the Judge Business School.

Intellectual property regime[16]

The major change at the university of relevance to the creation of new technology based businesses was in the regime for IP. Historically, the university had allowed individual academics to use their research findings without reference to the default UK legal position which would have normally given the university ownership of any IP. From 1970, with the founding of the Wolfson Industrial Liaison Office (WILO) with an endowment from the Wolfson Foundation, a voluntary arrangement was in place to help those who aspired to use IP from their work to find the right commercial outlet, either by forming a new firm or by establishing an IP asset and licensing its use.

In 2000 WILO merged with the then Research Grants and Contracts Office to form the Research Services Division, now the Research Office. This created a single organization dealing with technology transfer and the university's external research funding from industry, research councils, the European Union, and charitable trusts and foundations. In 2001 WILO was renamed the Technology Transfer Office to reflect its main activities. The Technology Transfer Office became part of Cambridge Enterprise after its formation in 2006.

Cambridge Enterprise is a wholly owned company of the University of Cambridge and offers the full array of contract and commercialization services, including having its own proof of concept and early-stage technology investment funds. Its services are offered to all university academics and to several of the related research entities of the wider Cambridge area (for example, the Babraham Institute and the health service staff of the main teaching hospital). The company generates a surplus, but in view of the leading edge nature of much of the academic research, it is still not a major source of additional finance for the university.

Within the university there is still a degree of freedom relating to the path chosen to exploit IP and a reward system that reflects differential use of the assistance of Cambridge Enterprise, but in all cases the intention to exploit now has to be registered. The scheme followed extended negotiations with the academic staff and reflects the reality of IP exploitation where remarkably few of the IP assets generate meaningful streams of revenue.

Where Cambridge Enterprise is involved in exploitation, the share of revenues from net royalties is distributed as shown in Table 4.2.

Where Cambridge Enterprise is not involved in exploitation, the share of revenues from net royalties is distributed as shown in Table 4.3.

The share of equity in new businesses is negotiated on a case-by-case basis having due regard of the contribution of creators to the business beyond the creation of IP and of any funding that is made available by the university or Cambridge Enterprise. Where a company is formed without the involvement of Cambridge Enterprise, the starting point for negotiations is a stake of 15 per cent to reflect the university's contribution.

Entrepreneurship

Entrepreneurship has also begun to feature more strongly through the university in both academic and extra-curricular activities. In 1998, following a £2 million donation, the Margaret Thatcher Chair in Entrepreneurial Studies was founded at the Judge Business School. When its present incumbent was appointed in 2013, the name was changed to the Margaret Thatcher Chair of Enterprise Studies in Innovation and Growth. Also, in the late 1990s, there emerged student-focused business plan competitions, now run by Cambridge University Entrepreneurs (CUE).

Table 4.2 Share of revenues from net royalties (with Cambridge Enterprise involvement) (%)

Net income	Inventors (jointly)	Department	Cambridge Enterprise
First £100,000	90	5	5
Next £100,000	60	20	20
Above £200,000	34	33	33

Table 4.3 Share of revenues from net royalties (without Cambridge Enterprise involvement) (%)

Net income	Inventors (jointly)	Department	Cambridge Enterprise
First £50,000	100	0	0
Above £50,000	85	7.5	7.5

In 1999 the Judge Business School also became the home for the Centre for Entrepreneurial Learning with a range of programs including:

- Ignite, an intensive, one-week training programme for aspiring entrepreneurs and corporate innovators to trial and prepare business ideas for the commercial environment. It consists of a blend of practical teaching sessions, expert clinics, mentor sessions, and experienced advice and support from leading entrepreneurs and innovators
- Postgraduate Diploma in Entrepreneurship, which consists of courses in entrepreneurial awareness and skills; opportunity recognition and idea evaluation; preparing and implementing the business case; managing the early stage venture
- Enterprise Tuesday: a series of free evening lectures and networking sessions open to all University of Cambridge staff and students, members of other universities, and the local business community, which aims to introduce participants to the world of business, as well as to encourage and inspire individuals to pursue their entrepreneurial ambition
- ETECH projects: these accelerate entrepreneurship and diffusion of innovations based on early-stage and potentially disruptive technologies from the University of Cambridge. Credit-bearing courses are delivered across natural sciences, technology, and biological sciences departments of the university to approximately 500 undergraduate and postgraduate students
- Enterprisers: the Enterprisers programme, established by the Cambridge–MIT Institute in 2002, is an educational experience that builds self-confidence and self-belief so that participants can begin to apply their knowledge and skills in entrepreneurial ways to create new ventures or support existing ones through being more proactive and innovative.

The Hauser[17] Forum

The Hauser Forum opened in 2010 as a focal point for entrepreneurship in the east of England. The Forum was made possible by an £8 million donation to the University of Cambridge by the Hauser–Raspe Foundation on behalf of Hermann Hauser and his wife Pamela Raspe, and a £2 million grant from the East of England Development Agency. The centre is managed and operated by the University of Cambridge. The forum is situated on the university's West Cambridge Research and Development Park which also includes many notable buildings at the forefront of science research including the Microsoft Research Centre, the Schlumberger Research Centre, and the Cavendish Laboratory.

Featuring two landmark buildings, the Broers Building and the Entrepreneurship Centre, the Hauser Forum is stimulating innovative collaboration between clusters of academics, start-ups, and established businesses.

The Entrepreneurship Centre is a state-of-the-art, multi-purpose installation featuring a modular seminar and meeting space, a café and atrium social meeting area, office units, and landscaped gardens. The centre already has five tenants including Cambridge Enterprise and ideaSpace, a pioneering initiative to support emerging innovations and link them with entrepreneurial activities in the East of England.

The Broers Building is adjacent to the Entrepreneurship Centre and offers state-of-the-art office space and resources in which small to medium-sized enterprises can lease space to work in closer partnership with university researchers and commercialization activities.

Additional development at the Department of Engineering and the Judge Business School

Manufacturing Group

Within the Engineering Department of the university there was a long-standing research team (led by Professor Mike Gregory) who were interested in the effects of technology on the manufacturing process, and some of this group became interested in the local technology manufacturing sector. This group – together with another team in the Department of Applied Economics who were interested in the entrepreneurial role of SMEs in new technology and innovation (led by Professor Alan Hughes who eventually became the first occupant of the Margaret Thatcher Chair in Entrepreneurial Studies) – ensured that the local technology business community were studied and their progress reported in academic and specialist literature.

Again there were two effects here. First was the rise in legitimacy of the study of business, which prepared the ground for the eventual emergence of the university's Judge Business School. Second, it added to the spread of the distinctive character of the new technology business phenomenon in Cambridge, which helped to attract others interested in just such activities to come and participate.

Institute for Manufacturing (IfM)

In 1998 the manufacturing group mentioned above formed a new Institute for Manufacturing which is located on the university's expansion site to the west of the city. It is in new premises close to the university's enterprise development team in the Alan Reece Building, a purpose-built building on the university's West Cambridge site, which was opened in November 2009. Part of the university's Department of Engineering, it takes a distinctive, cross-disciplinary approach, bringing together expertise in management, technology, and policy, to address the full spectrum of industrial issues. The IfM integrates research and education with practical application in industry.

It disseminates its research findings via a university-owned knowledge transfer company, IfM Education and Consultancy Services Ltd.

Research is clustered into a number of research centres. Some of the areas of expertise include industrial and innovation policy; the integration of technology considerations into business decisions; international manufacturing and supply networks; distributed information and automation systems; and industrial photonics. Various interdisciplinary, cross-centre programmes have been established to address such issues as service and support engineering, industrial sustainability, emerging industries, and high-value production.

Judge Business School

Cambridge Judge Business School is the business school of the University of Cambridge. Established in 1954 as Management Studies in the Engineering Department, it developed in 1990 into Judge Institute for Management Studies, and in 2005 as the Judge Business School.

The Judge Business School was funded by a significant donation and brings together several existing teams in the university as well as introducing some additional activities. One of the most significant of these new activities was the first UK academic chair of entrepreneurship that has been a major player in the adoption of entrepreneurship through the university, and particularly in the student community, with a variety of programmes.

Management of growth – new towns

Finally, from the 1990s, the dominant policy concerns balanced the need to maintain the vibrancy of the entrepreneurial growth around the Cambridge region and to manage the consequences to ensure a high quality of life was maintained. Many of the developments to continue the vibrancy have already been covered. To manage the effect on the urban environment, a number of initiatives have been taken to spread the growth (especially of housing and supporting urban services) away from the core medieval city of Cambridge.

This has been achieved in part by the more dense development of sites away from the centre of Cambridge but much of the development pressure has been channelled into the development of new towns in the hinterland to the north and west of the main town. Key for the provision of affordable housing, Cambourne is the most developed of the current settlements – with a planned final population expected to be around 10,000 – in 2009 it had reached approximately 7,600 population. In the longer term there has also been much discussion about the potential for the redevelopment of the current Cambridge Airport site which is capable of accommodating as least as many again as Cambourne in a new district.

Notes

1 The University of Cambridge began in the twelfth century as a monastic establishment and in modern times is a collegiate system where the colleges have historically had greater weight in university matters than the central university administration. Colleges are the social and residential units each with a fellowship that represents the spread of subjects across the university rather than being tied to any particular faculty.

2 Only UMIST (University of Manchester Institute of Science and Technology) among the English universities had a similar policy with regard to IP. This has also more recently changed on the merger of UMIST to create the University of Manchester which has adopted the default norm of university ownership of IP.

3 Wedgwood-Benn was a minister in the 1960s UK government administration of Prime Minister Harold Wilson.

4 Universities in the United Kingdom at the time received funding for undergraduate teaching and some core funding for faculty to do research from a central government university funding body, they also hosted research centres from national research councils and academics at the universities competed for research funds for specific projects from the same research councils. In some fields, most notably medicine, charitable funding for research was also significant and so too was industrial funding, either for specific contract research or through untied endowments or strategic alliances of broader scope or longer duration than the typically project-related contract research. For a more recent picture see the description of changes to the university scene.

5 CADCentre became a private company in 1983, was the subject of a management buyout in 1994, and became a publicly quoted company in 1996. It changed its name to AVEVA in 2001.

6 An elegant model that describes a similar staged emergence of the conditions for such support services in Israel around the Yosa Program is set out in various publications by Morris Teubal and colleagues (Avnimelech and Teubal, 2004).

7 The colleges at the University of Cambridge are registered educational charities whose trustees have the legal duty to maximize the income from their assets to the benefit of their charitable purpose. So while not strictly commercial investors, they were required to invest where returns would be good so were to some degree taking a risk with an unproven real-estate model. The Bursar of Trinity was one of the group of 25.

8 Professor John Allen, *Third generation science parks – a vision for the future.* Report of a two-day workshop. Manchester Science Park/International Association of Science Parks.

9 Walter Herriot was also one of the group of 25, and at that time worked as a credit officer in the main commercial bank in the town, Barclays. He and his boss Matthew Bullock (also one of the group of 25) are credited with funding several of the first wave of technology start-ups and eventually earned their bank the image as "the technology bank". He managed the Innovation Centre for 18 years until his retirement in 2008.

10 Relay centres were established across the EU to promote the commercial use of findings from EU-funded research projects. They additionally help connect researchers and businesses across the EU to form consortia to bid for EU Framework research programmes.

11 TWI was originally a sponsored research unit of the Department of Trade and Industry but was, by the time Granta Park was developed, no longer in receipt of public funds and had become a successful independent body funded by member firms plus competitively won research contracts. It is one of several non-university research units in the wider Cambridge area.

12 Saxenian, 1989.
13 *Biotechnology Clusters*, report of a team led by Lord Sainsbury, Minister for Science, August 1999, DTI/Pub 4306/1.5k/08/99. URN 99/1027.
14 Named after Fred Sanger, who, while working at the LMB, was awarded the 1958 Nobel Prize in Chemistry for developing methods to determine the order of the building blocks of the protein insulin. In 1980 Sanger was awarded his second Nobel Prize developing a technique still used today: "dideoxy" or "Sanger" sequencing.
15 In 2010 ERBI merged with the London Biotechnology Network to form One Nucleus, a single association with the critical mass to support life sciences on a global scale.
16 This is a simplified version of a very complex area. The main case described is where there is no external party involved (contract research, for example) and where a patentable product or service has been developed by university-employed staff. For other circumstances complex rules apply, (for example, concerning background and foreground status of IP and the use rights of different parties) to govern a very complex area of legal practice.
17 Hermann Hauser is one of the long-standing Cambridge serial entrepreneurs who also got into venture funding early with Amadeus Capital Partners which he helped to found in 1997.

References

Avnimelech, G. and Teubal, M. (2004). Venture capital start-up co-evolution and the emergence and development of Israel's new hi-tech cluster. *Economics of Innovation and New Technology*, 13(1), 33–60.
Etzkowitz, H. (1993). Enterprises from science: The origins of science-based regional economic development. *Minerva* 31(3), 326–360.
Minister for Science (1999). *Biotechnology Clusters*. Report of a team led by Lord Sainsbury DTI/Pub 4306/1.5k/08/99. URN 99/1027.
Porter, M.E. (1990). *The competitive advantage of nations*. New York: Free Press.
Saxenian, A.L. (1989). The Cheshire cat's grin: Innovation, regional development and the Cambridge case. *Economy and Society*, 18 (4), 448–477.
SQW (1985). *The Cambridge phenomenon: The growth of hi-technology industry in a university town*. Cambridge: Segal Quince Wicksteed.
SQW (2000). *The Cambridge phenomenon revisited: Parts one and two*. Cambridge: Segal Quince Wicksteed.

5 Kingston University London

Using entrepreneurship programmes to attract talent and to enhance educational impact

Christina Lea Butler and Martha Mador

Regional context

Kingston University London (KUL) is located in south-west London in Kingston-upon-Thames (Kingston), a pretty and historic market town with origins extending back as far as Roman times. One of only four royal boroughs in England, the town has a rich Anglo-Saxon history. A church has stood on the site of All Saints Church in the central market square for over 1,000 years; seven Anglo-Saxon monarchs were crowned here during the tenth century. This royal connection re-emerged during Tudor times when Henry VIII made his home at Hampton Court Palace, directly across the Thames from Kingston. Now rated as one of the happiest and safest boroughs in Greater London, Kingston boasts a university, a hospital, local government, and a department store as major employers, and continues as a thriving retail centre jostling up against central London, a mere 12 miles away. Kingston is thus an integral part of Greater London's intensely competitive metropolitan region. Greater London is the first of several important ecosystems within which KUL is embedded. Later in the chapter, three other important ecosystems will be discussed: (1) the higher education sector in London and the United Kingdom; (2) the innovation systems promoted by government agencies; (3) the student entrepreneurship base that KUL has developed over recent years (Almirall and Casadesus-Masanell, 2010).

Greater London now has a population of eight million, with the metropolitan region home to some 18 million. According to A.T. Kearney's *2012 Global Cities Index*, London again ranked as one of the top two global cities across 25 metrics alongside New York City. London is not just a big city: it is an economic and financial powerhouse, a social and cultural leader, and intense, crowded, and expensive. In recent decades the city, with its leading role in the world's financial sector, has been the UK's engine for growth. Beginning with the UK banking crisis of 2008, however, London's financial sector and the UK economy has shrunk. In November 2012, Dr Vince Cable, the UK's Business Secretary, compared the effects of the banking crisis and subsequent economic recession to the country having had a "heart attack" from which it was taking considerable time to recover. In 2012, Boris Johnson, Mayor of London, noted that "while the rest of the United Kingdom struggles to return to prosperity, London continues to be a place of great (if currently somewhat reduced) economic activity, and so now needs to move into the age of enterprise" (Johnson, 2012).

London: a world-leading higher education city

While London is well known for its leading role in the world's financial sector, it also attracts some of the world's best talent into other fields including higher education. The city has one of the largest concentrations of universities and higher education institutions (HEIs) in the world with 42 domestic HEIs and a student population of more than 400,000. Collectively, and in some cases individually, the London HEIs are major actors within the United Kingdom and London economies, providing employment, international opportunity, and research and innovation, among other benefits. Some of these older world-famous colleges today make up the federal University of London (e.g. Imperial College, London School of Economics, King's College, and University College); the modern universities (e.g. KUL and City University London) often have origins dating back some 100 to 150 years; and a number of smaller universities and colleges are often highly specialized (e.g. Central School of Speech and Drama, and Ravensbourne). The city's top HEIs are among the best in the world. Three of the top 20 universities (QS Ltd, 2013a) are in London: Imperial College, University College, and King's College. The only other city in the world that rivals this record is Boston, with two in the top ten: Harvard and Massachusetts Institute of Technology (MIT). London is also rated one of the three best cities worldwide for student life, alongside Boston and Paris (QS Ltd, 2013b).

Kingston University London (KUL): a rapidly changing modern university

KUL, one of the city's modern universities, has a history dating back over 100 years to what was then called Kingston Technical Institute. Opening in 1899, the institute offered applied courses in subjects ranging from chemistry, electrical wiring, and building construction, to nursing, dressmaking, and clay modelling. Over the decades, the institute evolved and merged with other institutions, acquiring new names and disciplines along the way, but always remaining true to its applied heritage. In 1992 the institution acquired university status in an act of parliament, alongside more than 30 other polytechnics. Today KUL employs nearly 3,000 staff across the following five faculties offering undergraduate and postgraduate courses, and undertaking research in related areas: art, design, and architecture; arts and social sciences; business and law; health, education, and social care sciences; science, engineering, and computing.

Across these five faculties 21,000 students are enrolled, about twice as many as in 1992 when KUL became a university. This increase reflects growth across the sector as a whole. With growth has come greater competition between universities to recruit and retain students. About 80 to 90 per cent of students at KUL are full-time undergraduates from the United Kingdom or the European Union, with the remainder coming from around the world.

Two-thirds of KUL students are first generation British, from an ethnic minority background, from lower socio-economic classes, and/or the first in their family to engage with higher education, and so the university is one of the more diverse institutions in the United Kingdom. Government policy aimed at widening participation in higher education in the United Kingdom, freedom of movement within the European Union, and the advent of a more dynamic international market for students, have all increased the diversity of students accessing the UK higher education system.

To survive and prosper, KUL has needed to increase its awareness of its own actions in addition to the higher educational institutional forces in Greater London, the United Kingdom, and the wider world. While formerly a local polytechnic drawing primarily "home" students from the south-west London and Surrey region, the institution has sought to develop a new identity as a modern institution, relevant at home and abroad, that helps students achieve their potential regardless of their background. The university benefited from the UK government's "widening participation" programme (HEFCE, 2013a) which rewarded universities that attracted "non-traditional" students to university education. Entry requirements were reduced and student numbers rose. However, since the onset of the global financial crisis, slower economic growth, and a change of government in the United Kingdom, spending cuts have brought into question the sustainability of this approach. A demographic trough in the number of 18-year-olds means that the number of UK students in higher education is set to fall; competition for students has become more international; the cost of education is being pushed increasingly onto the students themselves. There has been a growing realization, both at KUL and within the country at large, that the higher education landscape has changed.

For many institutions, developing commercialization, knowledge transfer, and entrepreneurship activities – together known as the "third mission" – is one part of this new approach. Within the tightly controlled government system of UK's higher education, KUL tackled this third mission first by focusing on knowledge transfer (now known as knowledge exchange), and then leveraging the increasing knowledge exchange expertise, to sow the first seeds of entrepreneurship activity in the form of new structures.

The UK's higher education and knowledge exchange landscape: a highly regulated system

The United Kingdom now has 165 HEIs, of which 115 are universities, serving a domestic population of about 63 million. Higher education in the United Kingdom is still largely state funded. In England, the Higher Education Funding Council for England (HEFCE) is the government agency responsible for distributing educational funds, including those for third-stream activity. In 2001, HEFCE announced a new third-stream funding programme, the Higher Education Innovation Fund (HEIF), to act as the core mechanism "to support and develop a broad range of knowledge-based interactions between universities and colleges and the wider world, which result in economic and social benefit to the United Kingdom" (HEFCE 2013b). The first round of funding (HEIF 1) was distributed in October 2002 with about £78 million allocated to fund 89 bids (out of 136 applications for funding from 128 HEIs and including 34 proposals from consortia). The largest awards were for consortia bids: a consortium bid led by University of Southampton was funded to a total of £5,000,000; one led by Cambridge University received £4,500,000; and one led by London Business School, £4,000,000. Ancient, modern, and specialist institutions all featured among the recipients. Although most UK HEIs submitted an application in this first round, KUL did not and so, de facto, became a late entrant to the third mission game.

The second round (HEIF 2) was allocated in summer 2004. This round also incorporated future activities based on the Science Enterprise Challenge and University Challenge initiatives in England. HEIF 2 was therefore the start of the consolidation of knowledge transfer funding into the core mechanism it now is. A total of £186 million was awarded across 124 bids, 46 of which involved collaboration between higher education institutions. Around £16 million of funding went to support a network of 22 new Centres for Knowledge Exchange. The awards ranged from £250,000 for a single institution to £12.9 million for a large-scale strategic collaboration led by University of Bristol that shared the funding among four partner HEIs. A consortium led by Cambridge University was once again funded and this time received about £3,000,000. KUL joined the bidding process as part of a consortium, a Centre for Knowledge Exchange to be called WestFocus led by Brunel University (see Table 5.1). West Focus was awarded £10,500,000, the second-largest grant of the round.

The third round of the programme (HEIF 3) started in academic year 2006/2007 and saw significant changes. As part of the government's commitment to a permanent third stream of funding, the majority of HEIF 3 funds (£164 million) was allocated by a funding formula which ensured a guaranteed allocation to every HEI that submitted an application outlining its third sector strategy. HEFCE received 133 applications. KUL received £1,000,000 to continue the WestFocus Knowledge Exchange and

Table 5.1 KUL timeline of third-stream activity: knowledge exchange and entrepreneurship

1899	• Kingston Technical Institute opens
1992	• University status is conferred upon KUL
2001	• HEFCE announces "third stream"
2004	• As part of a consortium, KUL wins £10.5 million GEIF 2 funding for WestFocus
	• WestFocus business portal established
	• WestFocus Knowledge Exchange activity begins, including Entrepreneurship Centre, University Talent
	• KUL Enterprise Education Unit established
2005	• HEIF 3: KUL wins additional funds
2006	• HEIF 4: Yet more funding awarded to KUL
2008	• WestFocus Knowledge Exchange activity ends but KUL Entrepreneurship Centre and Business Creation (now Park Fund) both continue
2009	• Professor Allan Gibb reviews KUL's Enterprise Education
2010	• KUL new Vice-Chancellor appointed
2011	• "Led-by-Learning" initiated
	• HEIF 5: KUL funding cut by 50%
	• KUL continues as UK university with highest number of graduate start-ups
2012	• KUL undertakes review of its academic framework (RAF)
2013	• Bright Futures runs at Dalian Nationalities University (China)
2014	• KUL reports more graduate start-us than other UK universities for sixth year
	• KUL achieves Small Business Charter for SME support
	• KUL shortlisted for *Times Higher Education* "Entrepreneurial University of the Year"

£1,500,000 per annum for other third-stream activities. There was a smaller competitive element designed to support high-impact innovative projects: 11 projects received £53 million.

HEIF 4 awarded £396,000,000 over three years from 2008 to 2010. Allocations were based partly on institutional size as an indicator of potential (40 per cent), and partly (60 per cent) on performance in terms of income generation from third-stream activities. A minimum guarantee of £100,000 allocation per institution was made. In addition, no institution lost more than 20 per cent of its previous year's funding. Kingston's final year allocation under this regime was £1,822,000, which was 80 per cent of its previous funding. Kingston thus benefited from its previous large awards under the WestFocus Knowledge Exchange umbrella.

Following a Comprehensive Spending Review, the UK government announced that HEIF 5, to be awarded in 2010/2011, would have an annual budget of £150 million and employ a more formulaic allocation, building on the formula used for HEIF 4. This increased rewards to institutions with higher third stream income, with an absolute cut-off in place. Despite a guarantee that no single institution would lose more than half its

HEIF 4 allocation, the result was a concentration of funds into a smaller number of institutions. Some institutions lost all funding; KUL's funding was halved to £911,000 per annum over the five-year period.

The UK government thus has acted initially through competitively awarded financial incentives and then through performance-related awards to encourage institutions of higher education to embed knowledge exchange and develop new income streams. However, the financial value of knowledge exchange to an institution varies with institutional legitimacy and credibility, as indicated by the depth and specific nature of the expertise it holds, as well as with institutional attitudes and embedded routines. The unintended consequence is that actors with less ecosystem legitimacy, such as KUL, will need to find very innovative ways to enhance knowledge exchange. In particular, KUL has less normative credibility (Scott, 2014) than many others. In contrast, an institution like Cambridge University can use its normative credibility to strengthen its innovation ecosystem. KUL's initial forays into knowledge transfer were generously rewarded by the UK government as it worked to encourage experimentation, build capacity, and thereby level the playing field. However, the playing field has of late become uneven once again, and the constellation of strong "organizations, institutions, and individuals that impact" the institution (Teece, 2009: 16) means that opportunities to shape the landscape in KUL's favour have reduced.

The WestFocus consortium: KUL takes a leading role

Through HEIF 2, WestFocus was founded as a collaboration between seven universities based in south and west London and the Thames Valley: Brunel, KUL, Roehampton, Royal Holloway, St George's, West London (formerly Thames Valley), and Westminster. The WestFocus initiative was set up to leverage the individual strengths of the seven quite different institutions. They varied in size from approximately 2,500 (St George's) students to 45,000 (UWL); from high (Royal Holloway) to low (UWL) research intensity; in location from the inner city (Westminster) to the country (Royal Holloway); in physical facilities from multi-campus (Westminster, KUL, UWL) to single campus (Brunel, Royal Holloway, Roehampton); in focus from medical sciences (St George's) to primarily arts and social science (Roehampton). The overall aim was to act as a knowledge transfer mechanism among entrepreneurs, community groups, academics, students, alumni, and local businesses through many projects, competitions, and events. Seeding these networks and activities was intended to lead to cultural change in the universities, as well as cultural and economic change across the region more generally (WestFocus, 2013).

The WestFocus consortium was successful in creating one important structure: the business portal (WestFocus) which has now been running for ten years. This portal has changed and developed over the years, its many elements having reflected the diverse nature of the WestFocus programme. The WestFocus initiative originally had four main strands of activity generating systems across the partner institutions: (1) academic knowledge and business development networks (KBDNs); (2) business creation; (3) University Talent; and (4) entrepreneurship (see Table 5.2).

First, the KBDNs drew together academic expertise across the institutions into collaborative, themed networks of academics and practitioners to work together on knowledge transfer. They included (for instance) advanced manufacturing, health and well-being, and sustainability in practice and design. The objectives were to build capacity and skills among academics, pump-prime activities, and create regional momentum and economic benefit by sharing resources and expertise in a geographically contiguous area. Each of these networks had its own web presence to promote expertise and the many ways in which enterprises could engage with universities. The networks ran events and sponsored projects with SMEs.

Second, business creation was a seed and proof of concept fund which was available to invest in academic-led projects across the universities. This was one of several established across the region, and had approximately £3,000,000 to invest. While the expectation was that most projects would be scientific in origin, in practice a wider variety of projects were funded, to include social enterprises based in social sciences. Similarly, while it was initially envisaged that projects would be driven by staff research, it became clear that some universities (including KUL) that were less research intensive had little opportunity to benefit. Student projects – which the universities would take a stake in – were brought into the pool.

Third, University Talent was an initiative founded by the careers services of the universities, specifically to encourage SMEs – the vast majority of businesses in the United Kingdom – to hire students for projects, placements, and long-term employment. Through this part of the portal SMEs

Table 5.2 The WestFocus collaboration's key activity areas

Activity area	Main purpose
Knowledge and business development networks	Academic/SME engagement on themes, e.g. advanced manufacturing; design; sustainability; creativity; ICT
Business creation	Proof of concept funding for potential university spin-out businesses
University Talent	A portal and service for SMEs to connect with universities, their students and graduates for jobs and placements
Entrepreneurship Centre	Developing and supporting entrepreneurship in the universities and the wider regions
Knowledge exchange	Collaboration governance mechanism

Source: Drawn from WestFocus Business Plan, 2004.

could advertise their requirements for free, while students could search for opportunities. Over the five-year period of the WestFocus Knowledge Exchange, 1,555 SMEs were engaged by University Talent, and 1,244 jobs advertised to students. At the end of the funded period, each university decided to take ownership of their own SME interactions, in order to manage their own relationships. This decision was driven by a variety of factors, including the competitive stance of each university's careers group, and a sense within the universities that each one needed to "join up the dots" on their varying interactions with employers.

The WestFocus Entrepreneurship Centre: supporting the fourth strand

KUL was the lead member of the WestFocus consortium from its inception, running the organization's governance on behalf of members, and developing entrepreneurship activities within and beyond the consortium. The Entrepreneurship Centre was initially conceptualized as a means of supporting regional SMEs to grow. Targeted growth programmes and new connections into the universities for technical help were envisaged. Once WestFocus began operating, however, this remit was quickly expanded to include developing new enterprises and in particular encouraging students to value their own ideas and develop them into new enterprises. This represented a completely new strand of activities at all of the collaborating universities. The educational activities and the pedagogic tools underlying them were developed by KUL.

The Entrepreneurship Centre focused on developing co-curricular activities (for instance competitions, intensive programmes, workshops) designed to foster entrepreneurship and encourage enterprising young people to become involved in business. Two of the notable and ongoing successes are the Bright Ideas competitions (KUL, 2013b) and the Bright Futures workshops. Bright Ideas runs annually between September and February. (See Table 5.3 for the list of 2010 winning and runner-up projects.) Applications number about 175 per year and, as joint applications are possible, involve about 290 students. KUL students account for about 60 per cent of the applications, some of whom also participate in Bright Futures, an intense workshop that aims to develop enterprise skills and enhance networking capabilities. Bright Futures runs several times per year with more than 100 in annual attendance. These workshops may be held at consortium members other than KUL, but KUL leads workshop delivery in cooperation with partner faculty (see Table 5.4 for an example of a workshop programme).

In terms of supporting staff enterprise and the push to increase enterprise education more generally, KUL helps lead (and sometimes establish) regional networks, e.g. KnowledgeLondon, supporting academic entrepreneurship; HEEG, supporting entrepreneurship education initiatives; and the STEM UEN, focusing on entrepreneurship in STEM subjects. In this

Table 5.3 Bright Ideas winning projects 2010

The annual student ideas competition attracted a wide range of students to present their ever more diverse ideas. Winners included students from all levels and backgrounds

First prize winners	Summary
Royal Holloway	BioLUX: an eco-friendly blend of enzymes that can replace up to 65% of the toxic chemicals used in paper mills
Kingston University	A prototype small-scale unit for recycling plastic in schools and universities to promote recycling with demos
KU/St George's joint faculty	A vital aid for healthcare providers in the prevention of deep vein thrombosis
Royal Holloway	The Hill Assistant: device to radically improve the ability of wheelchair users to negotiate steep slopes and hills
Kingston University	The social enterprise to supplement London's food base w/local fruits/veggies grown in vertical urban spaces
KU/St.Geo. joint faculty	A bright, single-use product to provide comfort/support to children undergoing intravenous (IV) therapy
Kingston University	New distribution channels for disadvantaged craftsmen/women in an EU territory for unique, handmade shoes
Second Prize Winners	**Summary**
Kingston University	Provide UK households w/biometric door-locks to eradicate the needs for keys via security firm technologies
Kingston University	Green Wash: eco waterless carwash company that offers customers innovative products successful in USA
Roehampton university	Safe and easy payment online using biometric recognition technology
Kingston University	Tinaye Crystals provide 3D laser crystal-engraved products via website and 3D retail booth; B2C and B2B markets
Thames Valley Univ.	Volunteer annual workshops to develop entrepreneurial/new media skills of St. Lucia Secondary School students
KU/St.Geo. joint faculty	Stethwipe: a quick, hygienic, cheap, safe way to decontaminate stethoscopes between patients
Kingston University	StudyKit Pro: mobile phone app that helps college and university students with their writing and referencing skills

Source: Centre for Knowledge Exchange Final Report 2009.

Table 5.4 Bright Futures example programme

The programme was developed to encourage enterprising skills and attitudes, and is run several times per year in boot camp format.

	Major content	*Main outcomes*
Day 1: Me and My Ideas		
9:15	Arrivals and registration	• Shared commitment to programme – student and facilitator participants
		• Identify self as a resource and active participant
9:45	Line out exercise: D. Reid	• Identify diversity of student community as a resource
10:15	Welcome	
10:30	Entrepreneurial behaviours and skills.	• Awareness of entrepreneurial behaviours and role models
11:30	Networking	• Understand the relevance of networking skills, identify and practice key skills
12:30	Working lunch/Myspace	• Establish a marketplace for your skills and resources
1:30	Creativity – Innovate!	• Acquire techniques for idea generation individually and in groups
	Introduction to creativity, ideas and innovation in entrepreneurship	• Discuss ideas and work in a group to select ideas for further development
		• Self-confidence in presenting ideas creatively
		• Increase capability in building small group interactions, trust, and reciprocity
4:00	Pitch your idea	• Communicating your solutions/questioning assumptions/teamwork
5:00	Meet the entrepreneurs:	• Expand group of role models: Understand various entrepreneurs' paths
6:30	Networking supper: business school	• Appreciate the value of failure as well as success
8:30	Group task: organize lifts for tomorrow	• Practise networking skills and build your network
Day 2: Markets and projects		
9:00	Arrival: tea and coffee available	• Awareness of different approaches to designing an enterprise
9:30	Business models: M. Mador	• Opportunity-seeking behaviour relating to revenues, resources, skills
10:00	*From Idea to Enterprise*	• Knowledge of different parts to a successful enterprise
12:00	Building block/lunch	• Critical influence of external factors
1:00	Marketplace features and benefits	• Ability to identify features/benefits for products/services to different groups
		• Understand customer needs and how to meet them
	How to communicate with customers	• Communications and negotiations skills
	Basics of negotiating	
3:00	Me and My Bright Future: soapbox pitching event/ letters home	• Communicate an idea or about yourself/give and receive feedback
		• Understand the value of practice
4:30	The last session: Martha Mador	• Reflection on learning
5:30	Close	• Establish objectives

Source: Course Materials, Bright Futures 2011.

way, KUL leverages various actors within WestFocus and beyond, initiating systems to develop a leading role in student and staff entrepreneurship in London and England's south-east region.

The success of the WestFocus Knowledge Exchange is reflected in the performance summary shown in Table 5.5: the programme exceeded targets across all measures. It demonstrated the appetite among companies to engage with universities, and also provided evidence to university staff that third stream activity could find partners. The entrepreneurship arena in particular revealed appetite among students. By the end of the funding period in 2009 each university had developed its own programmes and activities in knowledge exchange, building on their own experience and understanding of their particular institutional needs. Two collaborative systems, however, have remained – the Entrepreneurship Centre and Business Creation (now known as the Park Fund). Both continue in operation in the 2013/2014 academic year, evidence of the value placed on them by the partner universities. Within KUL, the WestFocus initiative also led to further structural developments in the form of an Enterprise Education unit, a hub for such systems within the university.

The Enterprise Education unit: working for change inside KUL

Established in 2004 as a result of the HEIF 2/WestFocus award, KUL's Enterprise Education unit is located in a central department known as Enterprise Support, and reports to the university's pro-Vice-Chancellor for research and enterprise. Enterprise Support is a structure which provides developmental, promotional, and brokerage roles between academics and the wider community, offering commercial services, knowledge transfer activities, and internal support for strategic projects. The Enterprise Education unit runs the WestFocus Entrepreneurship Centre as well as the regional networks that it leads, but its main focus is on KUL itself developing systems to engender cultural change.

The overarching aim of the Enterprise Education unit is "to embed the entrepreneurial spirit amongst students, alumni, and staff, and encourage entrepreneurs to develop their business in a learning environment" with the following specific objectives:

1   to ensure that all undergraduate and postgraduate students have opportunities to engage in non-assessed entrepreneurship activities (such as competitions, master classes, etc.);
2   to ensure that a high percentage of students (especially outside of the business school) have opportunities to take assessed modules in entrepreneurship;
3   to support undergraduate and postgraduate students and graduates who wish to develop an enterprise in a learning environment;

Table 5.5 WestFocus Centre for Knowledge Exchange: measures of performance 2004–2009

This shows actual performance against targets initially set for WestFocus. The five-year programme outperformed target across almost all dimensions. In most cases the targets were targets for engagement (for instance number attending events), as metrics for outcomes were more complex to evaluate, and took more time to achieve.

2004/2006 (2 years)		2006/2007		2007/2008	2008/2009	Total	2004–2009 target
Additional income (excluding CKE funding)	£250k		£343k	£125k	£81k	£799k	£450k
Attendance at events	unrecorded		1,399	3,767	3,506	8,672	7,500
Unique visitors to WestFocus web portal	45,000		70,000	60,100	64,700	239,800	120,000
SMEs engaged by University Talent	917		160	327	151	1,555	1,180
SME graduate/student job placement adverts	50		512	453	229	1,244	1,325
STEP and UTP applicants	437		432	300	340	1,509	1,300
STEP and UTP placements	39		75	53	43	210	189
Students educated or trained in entrepreneurship	2,840		1,354	5,066	3,423	12,683	5,800
Staff educated and trained in entrepreneurship	443		392	753	634	2,222	775
SMEs/start-ups receiving enterprise training/support	377		139	892	302	1,710	760
Project fund awards			3	9	6	18	
Value of awards			£31k	£96k	£130k	£257k	

Source: WestFocus Centre for Knowledge Exchange final report, 2009.

4   to provide opportunities for entrepreneurs and business owners to develop their enterprise in a learning environment;
5   to support staff in developing entrepreneurial outcomes for modules and fields across the university;
6   to develop and deliver learning opportunities for staff in the field of enterprise education;
7   to develop, publish, and disseminate learning materials in entrepreneurship education; to undertake research and publish articles in the field of entrepreneurship;
8   to develop regional, national, and international relationships that encourage and facilitate entrepreneurship education;
9   to respond to government bids and other entrepreneurship initiatives – regionally, nationally, and internationally.

A review of how these objectives have been pursued, and the corresponding results, is presented in Table 5.6.

In addition to the WestFocus evidence noted above, there are other achievements of student entrepreneurship that demonstrate the strides KUL has made in the last decade. KUL has reported the highest number of graduate start-ups of all UK universities over the last six years (2009 to 2014) (Higher Education Business and Community Interaction Survey). KUL is justified in being proud of its achievements in student entrepreneurship over the last decade (see Table 5.7).

One result of the structure and subsequent systems provided by WestFocus has been the impact beyond KUL. Higher education institutions in Europe, and beyond, regularly seek expertise from KUL staff within the WestFocus consortium. For instance, Danish entrepreneurship educators from Copenhagen Business School have repeatedly come to KUL to experience demonstrations of learning games developed there on behalf of West-Focus; Turkish students have experienced Bright Futures as part of a national innovation prize awarded there; Bright Futures was presented at Dalian Nationalities University in China in 2013; an NGO has used Bright Futures in Ethiopia to train some 2,000 educators, incubator managers, and prospective entrepreneurs.

In 2010, Allan Gibb, professor emeritus at Durham University, was commissioned to review Enterprise Education at KUL. He noted that, at a high level, Enterprise Education was entirely consonant with and supportive of the university's strategy, and showed how to embed it in strategic thinking. He applied his model of the entrepreneurial person at a more detailed level, observing the potential and the need for enterprise education to address a wide range of skills, knowledge, attitudes, and capabilities (Gibb, 2002) through the following objectives:

• entrepreneurial behaviours, skills, and attributes, including emotional intelligence;

- preparation for the "way of life" of the entrepreneur;
- entrepreneurial values and ways of doing things, feeling things, organizing things, communicating things, and learning things experientially;
- entrepreneurial behaviour and management in different contexts – not just business;
- harvesting ideas, and grasping and realizing opportunity;
- managing entrepreneurially, holistically, and strategically (know how); and
- managing and learning from relationships (know who).

KUL had been pursuing many of these objectives through both in-curriculum and co-curricular activities – systems – that bring entrepreneurs into the university for regular networking events, thus providing role models and insight into the aspirations and motivations of entrepreneurs. The university has also encouraged students to experience entrepreneurship through micro-businesses and projects that provide them with highly personalized learning practicums, including failures as well as successes. The approach had always been to situate entrepreneurship beyond the scope of commercial enterprises – across social, artistic, scientific, for-profit, and not-for-profit activities. The objective was to encourage and support student aspirations, rather than to teach a subject-specific syllabus.

Gibb noted, however, that the reach of Enterprise Education in the university curriculum remained limited compared to the institution's strategic objectives for enterprise. While many business school students studied entrepreneurship, some of that teaching was still linked to business planning and entrepreneurial theory, rather than engaging in entrepreneurship. This meant internal systems were still relatively underdeveloped. Modules in entrepreneurship were available for non-business students, but these reached only approximately 300 to 400 students per year. While the extra-curricular programme offered opportunities that student feedback showed was highly valued, its reach was again limited. It appeared that, culturally, the university had not yet integrated enterprise education into its wider thinking.

Since 2010, Dr Martha Mador, Head of Enterprise Education, has led work to increase the reach of extra-curricular programmes in particular, and to raise awareness of the need for enterprise education not just in modules labelled Entrepreneurship, but embedded across modules and disciplines. In addition, KUL has developed a virtual incubator, the Enterprising Business Awards, to offer students and staff the opportunity to meet on a weekly basis to learn new skills, find mentors, and apply for funding donated by a Kingston graduate entrepreneur. (See Table 5.8 for the list of grants awarded.) By the spring of 2013, registration in the programme topped 250, many more than previously, but still a relatively small proportion of the university as a whole.

Table 5.6 KUL entrepreneurship objectives and implementation, 2004–2011

The objectives and implementations reflected KU needs and structures; and required diverse activities within and alongside curriculum.

Main objectives	Implementation	Results
Ensure that undergraduate and postgraduate students have opportunities in non-assessed entrepreneurship activities	• Enterprising Business Awards, the virtual incubator • Bright Ideas competition • Bright Futures intensives • Mentoring • Talks from entrepreneurs	• Year-on-year increases in number of activities and in participation • 250 students w/incubator 2012/2013 • 175 entries to Bright Ideas • Additional mentors added to programme
Ensure that a high%age of students (esp. outside of the business school) have opportunities to take assessed modules in entrepreneurship	• Modules available in business school • Modules available on cross-faculty programmes "with business"; "management studies" • Some in-faculty modules, e.g. IT and entrepreneurship	• c.500 business school students study some form of entrepreneurship p.a. • Cross-faculty c.350 p.a. • c.100 students enrolled p.a.
Support under- and post-graduate students and graduates to develop enterprises in learning environment	• Virtual incubator • Financial support • Mentoring	• c.250 engaged with incubator p.a. • c.15 financial awards made p.a. • additional mentors added to programme
Provide entrepreneurs and business owners opportunities to develop enterprises in learning environment	• Business growth programme: Enterprising Business Awards (2005 to 2009) • Green Growth (2011 to 12)	• c.100 enterprises external to the university mentored and supported over the period

Objective	Activities	Outputs
Support staff in developing entrepreneurial outcomes for modules and fields across the university	• HEEG network, regular conferences • Talks at staff conferences • Mentoring/advice to individuals, schools, and depts.	• Module developments in nursing, physiotherapy, social work, bioscience, engineering
Develop/deliver learning opportunities for staff in Enterprise Education	• HEEG network, regular conferences • Knowledge Exchange Fellows programme	• KUL attendances at network meetings • 20 KUL staff involved as fellows
Develop, publish, and disseminate research and learning materials in entrepreneurship education	• Textbook, entrepreneurship, conference papers • Learning games • Dissemination through HEEG, ISBE, EEUK conferences	• Tabletop games sold to 15 universities • Publications and conference papers
Develop regional, national, and international relationships that encourage and facilitate entrepreneurship education	• KT programmes and joint university events in Hong Kong, China, Turkey, Denmark, and Ethiopia	• Shared experiences across universities • Trained facilitators in several countries • 2,000 people trained in Ethiopia
Respond: government/other entrepreneurship initiatives/bids: regional, national, international	• HEEG and KnowledgeLondon originate in regional bids • Green Growth a Capital Enterprise project	• Income to KU from bids, regional networks and projects over the period: £240,000

Source: Annual report on Enterprise Education, Kingston University 2011.

Table 5.7 Summary of enrolment in entrepreneurship activities 2006–2010

Engagement in activities varied from year to year. Intervening factors related to changes in personnel and system changes which either enabled or reduced attendances and enrolments.

Modules	2006/2007	2007/2008	2008/2009	2009/2010
Young Enterprise module	85	89	37	90
Entrepreneurship (long-thin version of module)	53	32	17	61
Entrepreneurship (short-fat version of module)	50	70	22	n/a
Entrepreneurship and New Venture Development	43	28	54	80
IT and entrepreneurship (estimates)	60	85	100	100
PG, BSM 113 Entrepreneurship in Context				60
Programmes				
MA Creative Economy (estimates)	n/a	30	40	30
Enterprising Graduate Awards	n/a	n/a	7	28
Enterprising Student Awards	n/a	n/a	n/a	8
Enterprising Business Awards	18	10	10	n/a
Bright Ideas, KU entries	84	31	64	78
Bright Ideas, KU students involved	102	47	43	176
Bright Futures, KU students	36	35	23	30
Entrepreneurship/Enterprise for Staff				
HEEG events (KU attendees)			Since January 2009	13
KnowledgeLondon events (KU attendees)			Since March 2007	27
Academic Enterprise (KU only)			Program run 2010 only	16

Source: Gibb, 2010.

Table 5.8 Enterprising Business Awards, semester 1, 2011

The action learning programme, initially devised as an SME growth programme, was turned to supporting student and graduate star-ups. The students were supported with mentoring and through facilitated action learning sets. They also were able to bid for funding to enable the next development step in their start-up process. Ideas were again diverse, including social and more commercial enterprises, web start-ups, and a football agency.

Name	Business/website	Description	Grant
A. Campbell	http://enfuseyouth.com	Not available	£817
A. O.-Thomas	www.emergingstudents.com/	Creative Suite 5 and website build	£750
C. Robert-Green	http://bornwithagift.com	Not available	£750
J. Hirani	http://saferminicabs.com	Not available	£750
J. Peach	http://thisbigcity.net	Facebook/Adwords campaigns, small competition	£750
J. Bucknell	http://upbeatagency.com	Not available	£750
N. Sechere	http://ballerzleague.com	Intellectual property and PR campaign	£750
R. Somauroo	Property Flock	Website design	£750
T. Munonyara	Study Kit Pro	Not available	£750
T. Harrington	Fancy dress via an Ebay store	Expansion/testing the hair extension market	£250
Y. Sadeghi	The Work Shop	Timber and machinery for Horney Coat Hook	£738
	Total awarded to date:		£7,805

Source: Kingston University internal records.

A further objective of the Enterprise Education Unit, and one of the reasons for it being located within Enterprise Support, is to support academic enterprise and the development of knowledge exchange across the university through (nascent) internal systems. Workshops and information sessions are run to encourage and educate staff. HEEG and KnowledgeLondon are also part of this picture, as they run monthly experience-sharing and knowledge-development conferences focused on academic enterprise and embedding enterprise education. In addition, Enterprise Education runs growth programmes for SMEs in the region, to further increase interaction between the university and its neighbours. This last activity brings SMEs into the university to benefit from resources such as students and graduates, staff expertise, equipment, and facilities.

Looking to the future: moving from a student-focused entrepreneurship agenda to an academic entrepreneurship and research agenda

A new Vice-Chancellor joined KUL in April 2011. One year later, KUL launched a new organizational strategy, "Led by Learning", aimed at building the university's reputation across a range of domains. The university defines "Led by Learning" as "enabling others to learn, continually learning ourselves, and pushing the boundaries of learning through teaching, research and enterprise, and professional practice to develop potential, transform lives, and improve the world around us" (KUL 2013a). The university has also declared its commitment to the dissemination of new ideas and discoveries through research, knowledge transfer, and support for learning in the region. Awareness of the larger ecosystems is apparent, as is awareness of the need to act within an innovation ecosystem that encompasses a wide range of actors.

"Led by Learning" is a strategic cultural change:

> At Kingston we believe that learning is the most powerful way to improve societies and communities; it is vital to address global transformation and achieve economic development. The university is, and will continue to be, highly international as well as closely linked to our local community; and will continue to provide courses that are relevant to business and the workplace, and to conduct high quality research because all these things lead to better learning. The university is also proud to encourage and support those who have hitherto been excluded from higher education. Our students will want to learn, to change, and to be challenged. Our systems, our estate, and our processes are all there to support better learning.
>
> (KUL, 2013a)

That knowledge exchange remains an important strand of the university's activity is not due to the university acting in isolation, but to the changing higher education landscape within which it is embedded. The UK government is increasingly concerned with the societal impact of its HEIs and so is seeking ways to measure that impact by linking academic research and third-stream activity. In December 2013, the current national round of academic research assessment, known as Research Excellence Framework 2014 (REF 2014), closed. One new feature of this round of research assessment is that of "impact".

Impact assessments are based on expert review of case studies submitted by higher education institutions. Case studies may include any social, economic, or cultural impact (or benefit beyond academia) that has taken place during the assessment period, and was underpinned by excellent research produced by the submitting institution within a given timeframe. Submissions also include information about how the unit has supported and enabled impact during the assessment period (HEFCE, 2013d).

Considered developmental in this first inclusion, "impact" counts for 20 per cent in REF 2014 (together with 20 per cent for environment and 60 per cent for outputs). It is expected that impact will rise to 25 per cent of the total score in the next REF. Institutions of higher education are now clearly being pushed to connect third-stream activity with research outputs in an unprecedented way, as government funding depends on strengths demonstrated by way of REF scores.

KUL has had tremendous success in developing student entrepreneurship in the highly competitive environment of higher education in Greater London, the United Kingdom, and beyond. As recommended by Professor Allan Gibb, the university is moving toward more of a focus on the entrepreneurial person, and to embedding in-curriculum by the various structures and systems previously identified. To meet future challenges, though, the institution will need to expand its academic research and "impact" bases significantly. Student entrepreneurship has led to some changes in faculty perceptions, but further cultural change from the top of the organization will be needed to drive future success. Careful consideration of how to do so is needed. A swing of the pendulum toward developing research is necessary but insufficient. Of greater need is for KUL's strategies-in-practice to reward faculty involvement in enterprise.

In 2012/2013, the Vice-Chancellor initiated two major strategic changes that will reward academic enterprise activity and lead to overall cultural change. The first of these is the Academic Progression and Promotion (AP&P) initiative implemented in 2013/2014 that, for the first time, rewards academics with career progression through to a professorship on the basis of their international reputation and expertise in one of four specialisms, one of which is enterprise and knowledge transfer. The second of these changes, the Review of the Academic Framework (RAF), was also implemented in 2013/2014. One of the major strands of the RAF is the embedding of employability, of which entrepreneurship should ultimately become a significant element, given KUL's significant track record in this area. At the same time, implementation of strategies such as these are subject to shaping by leadership throughout the organization and existing structures and systems, and so outcomes will not be apparent for some time yet.

Conclusions

External factors – such as changing attitudes to entrepreneurship across society and the changing policy landscape – are challenging UK universities and KUL in particular. Government incentives have driven growth in student numbers and pump-primed knowledge exchange activities. Universities increasingly need to embed new institutional attitudes, skills, and knowledge to support their students, faculty, and the many other actors within their reach who face a rapidly transforming world. In particular, universities need to prepare students for the portfolio careers that increasingly are their expectation.

Through leadership of the WestFocus initiative to deliver structures and systems to support the development of the entrepreneurial university, KUL has acquired considerable normative credibility within the Greater London higher education community and across the United Kingdom more generally. The building of the WestFocus portal, together with the creation of networks such as HEEG and initiatives such as Bright Ideas, has contributed to the university's prominence which continues to grow through new projects such as the Make It Global business growth programme for female-led businesses. Acclaim is growing internationally as well, with advice sought from other HEIs in Europe and farther afield. Viewed through the lens of external actors, especially newer and/or smaller HEIs, KUL's approach to its "third mission" is a success story to be emulated.

Alongside this positive external profile, KUL has achieved considerable success in developing and embedding structures and systems to support student enterprise and entrepreneurship. The creation of the Enterprise Unit, the appointment of a Head of Enterprise Education, and comprehensive, multi-faceted support for student enterprise initiatives are the tangible evidence of enduring internal structures, leadership, and systems. Key influencers like the Vice-Chancellor and Pro-Vice-Chancellor support these efforts both through their public presence at key events and behind the scenes in the day-to-day running of the institution. There are institutional goals in place for entrepreneurship, and it is an area of success which is celebrated internally by increasing numbers of involved students and academics alike.

Higher levels of engagement of faculty with enterprise and entrepreneurship are a precursor to both widening student participation and widening impact on society as a whole. Commercialization, the financial impact strand of the third mission, also depends on wider involvement of staff in opportunity seeking and development. Engagement by a significant proportion of academics within the university is necessary for financial sustainability.

The recent implementation of a series of inter-related strategic and cultural initiatives (i.e. "Led by Learning", AP&P, and RAF) provides the broad underpinning required for wider engagement in the future, but is not necessarily sufficient. While much progress has been made over the past decade with KUL exhibiting (to a greater or lesser extent) all five components of entrepreneurial architecture, none is yet robustly and comprehensively embedded within the wider university. In an increasingly competitive higher education sector within the United Kingdom and beyond, it is critical that KUL leverage its strengths in enterprise and entrepreneurship by attracting, supporting, and developing talent to create for itself a sustainable strategic niche.

References

Almirall, E. and Casadesus-Masanell, R. (2010). Open vs. closed innovation: A model of discovery and divergence, *The Academy of Management Review*, 35, 1, 27–47.

A.T. Kearney and the Chicago Council on Global Affairs (TCCGA) (2012). *2012 Global Cities Index*. www.atkearney.com/en_ GB/gbpc/global-cities-index/full-report/-/asset_publisher/yAl1OgZpc1DO/content/2012-global-cities-index/10192 (accessed 28 September 2013).

Cable, V. (2012, 18 November). Television interview by Andrew Marr, *The Andrew Marr Show*, BBC 1.

Gibb, A.A. (2002). In pursuit of a new "enterprise" and "entrepreneurship" paradigm for learning: Creative destruction, new values, new ways of doing things and new combinations of knowledge. *International Journal of Management Review*, 4(3), 213–233.

Gibb A.A. (2010). *A review of enterprise education at Kingston University*. Kingston University.

Higher Education Funding Council for England (HEFCE) (2013a). Available at: www.hefce.ac.uk/ (accessed: 28 September 2013).

Higher Education Funding Council for England (HEFCE) (2013b). Higher Education Fund round 3. Available at: http://webarchive.nationalarchives.gov.uk/20100202100434/http://hefce.ac.uk/pubs/hefce/2005/05_46/ (accessed 28 September 2013).

Higher Education Funding Council for England (HEFCE) (2013c). *Higher Education: Business and community interaction survey*. Available at: www.hefce.ac.uk/whatwedo/kes/measureke/hebci/ (accessed 28 September 2013).

Higher Education Funding Council for England (HEFCE) (2013d). *REF 2014: Research excellence framework*. Available at: www.ref.ac.uk/ (accessed: 28 September 2013).

Johnson, B. (2012). Speech to Confederation of Business Industry (CBI), 20 November, 2012. Viewed on *BBC TV News*, 21 November 2012.

Kingston University London (KUL) (2013a). *Led by Learning*. Kingston University London. Available at: www.kingston.ac.uk/aboutkingstonuniversity/howtheuniversityworks/universityplan/ (accessed 28 September 2013).

Kingston University London (KUL) (2013b). *Students dominate with their bright ideas*. Available at: www.kingston.ac.uk/services-for-business/news/bright-ideas/ (accessed 30 September 2013).

Kingston University London (KUL) (2013c). Available at: www.kingston. ac.uk/ (accessed 28 September 2013).

Quacquarelli Symonds Limited (QS Ltd) (2013a). *QS top universities: Worldwide university rankings, guides and events*. Available at: www.topuniversities.com/ university-rankings/ (accessed 28 September 2013).

Quacquarelli Symonds Limited (QS Ltd) (2013b). *QS best student cities: QS top universities: Worldwide university rankings, guides and events*. Available at: www.topuniversities.com/best-student-cities/ (accessed 28 September 2013).

Scott, W.R. (2014). *Institutions and organizations: Ideas, interests and identities*, 4th edn. Palo Alto, CA: Sage.

Teece, D.J. (2009). *Dynamic capabilities and strategic management: Organizing for innovation and growth*. Oxford: Oxford University Press.

WestFocus (2013). Available at: www.westfocus.org.uk/ (accessed 28 September 2013).

6 Chalmers

An entrepreneurial university institutionalizing the entrepreneurial?

Mats Lundqvist

Introduction

Chalmers University of Technology is the second oldest and second largest university of technology in Sweden, located in Gothenburg, the second largest city, which has strong traditions in trade and industry. Founded in 1829 on a donation from William Chalmers, a director of the Swedish East India Company, Chalmers has since then had entrepreneurship and industrial development as part of its identity. Today, Chalmers is widely recognized as an entrepreneurial university (Clark, 1998; Jacob *et al.*, 2003; Wright *et al.*, 2007; Berggren, 2011; Philpott *et al.*, 2011). Among other things, the university ranked number three in the world in the 2013 Leiden ranking as regards university–industry collaboration (CWTS, 2013). However, much of entrepreneurship at and around Chalmers has happened without any organized effort from the university. As at most recognized entrepreneurial universities (such as Stanford, Massachusetts Institute of Technology, and Cambridge), entrepreneurship at Chalmers, to a large extent, has occurred in the ecosystem and not through the governance system of the university. It is not as obvious how to institutionalize this third mission of *innovation and entrepreneurship* as compared to the established missions of *education* and *research*. If one does not settle with centralized technology transfer offices (TTOs) or peripheral incubators, the questions of why and how to institutionalize innovation and entrepreneurship are, to a large extent, open for experimentation.

This chapter will offer a historical case of innovation and entrepreneurship at Chalmers (bringing us to the present day), followed by a case analysis in regard to Swedish policy developments and related to the entrepreneurial architecture framework (Vorley and Nelles, 2009).

While Chalmers has a helf-century history of developments around the third mission, the thrust of the case is on the last 20 years of developments enabled by the Swedish government in 1994, when transforming Chalmers from a state university to a "private," foundation-based university. The freedom to operate caused by this structural shift enabled Chalmers to form new structures and mechanisms for innovation and entrepreneurship, including co-founding the first Swedish US-type venture capital firm (1994), and starting its own seed investor (1998), incubator (1999), and a school of entrepreneurship (1997). This last pioneered a new standard for how master's students engage in venture creation as student surrogate entrepreneurs to commercialize intellectual property (IP) from R&D as a main part of their program (Lackeus *et al.*, 2011; Åstebro *et al.*, 2012; Lindholm-Dahlstrand and Berggren, 2010).

With these activities focusing on venture creation at hand, Chalmers has, since the turn of millennium, primarily directed its efforts at how to consolidate and increasingly integrate the third mission with research and education. Such an ambition is not without challenge and controversy, as this chapter wishes to highlight. Institutionalizing innovation and entrepreneurship at Chalmers holds promise of broadly instilling entrepreneurial learning into educational programs, as well as offering tools and collaboration opportunities to research groups to increase their impact – not only through research but also through innovation. Even more importantly, institutionalization at Chalmers has meant organizational innovation and hybrid activities spanning education, innovation, and research (the three missions), while then also impacting how education and research are carried out.

This case will first offer a historical account of these developments aimed at increasing the institutionalization of innovation and entrepreneurship. Thereafter, the case will be put in perspective through a wider view of Swedish developments. Finally, the five-element entrepreneurial architecture framework of *structures*, *systems*, *leadership*, *strategies*, and *culture* (Vorley and Nelles, 2009) will be applied to the case to conclude the question: how might an entrepreneurial university institutionalize the entrepreneurial?

Pre-1994 developments

While Chalmers was founded upon a donation from an entrepreneur – and its first president, Carl Palmstedt, was also an entrepreneur – the main modern developments resulting in Chalmers being recognized as an entrepreneurial university started in the 1960s (See Table 6.1 for a timeline of these events.) In 1964, Torkel Wallmark was appointed Professor in Solid State Electronics at Chalmers. Prior to that he had spent 14 years at RCA Laboratories in Princeton, and was inspired by the emerging microelectronics revolution and the opportunities this meant for academic entrepreneurship through university spin-outs. At Chalmers, Wallmark increasingly supported innovation and entrepreneurship. As a result, Chalmers was relatively early in having an innovation center where advice and courses were given to professors and students who were interested in starting technology-based ventures. Even though Chalmers' main expansion into a full-fledged university of technology occurred as late as the

Table 6.1 Timeline of third-mission milestones at Chalmers University

1964	• Torkel Wallmark, with extensive experience from the US, is appointed Professor in Microelectronics at Chalmers
1969	• Holger Bohlin, the industrialist and entrepreneur, appointed as first Professor in Industrial Management
1979	• Innovation Center initiated by Wallmark
1983	• Wallmark named as first Professor in Innovation Engineering
1984	• Foundation established: Chalmers Industrial Technologies (CIT)
1986	• CIT initiates minor incubation and seed-investment activities
1991	• School of Technology Management and Economics started, based upon, e.g. the chair in industrial management
1993	• Sören Sjölander succeeds Wallmark as Professor in Innovation Engineering
	• Innovation Center and chair in Innovation Engineering transferred from School of Electronics to School of Technology Management and Economics
1994	• Chalmers transforms from state to "private," foundation-owned university
	• Chalmers co-founds Innovationskapital, Swedish US-type venture capital firm
1997	• Chalmers School of Entrepreneurship established
1998	• Chalmersinvest is formed, expanding on CIT activities with seed investment
1999	• Business incubator Chalmers Innovation established with €5 million donation
2001	• Chalmers School of Entrepreneurship together with Chalmersinvest starts Encubator – dedicated to surrogate entrepreneurship ventures at the school
2005	• Chalmers School of Entrepreneurship starts a bioentrepreneurship track in collaboration with the medical school of University of Gothenburg – Sahlgrenska Academy
2007	• Chalmers is granted one of five VINNOVA key actor projects – GoINN – in collaboration with University of Gothenburg
	• Chalmers School of Entrepreneurship students start development activities into social entrepreneurship, primarily in Eastern Africa
2009	• Innovation Office West formed by one of eight Innovation Office grants by government
	• Chalmers School of Entrepreneurship is top-ranked by Swedish government after international peer review, subsequently to receive annual extraordinary educational grants
2013	• Chalmers enacts its first strategy for innovation, entrepreneurship, and utilization
	• Chalmers School of Entrepreneurship starts track in corporate entrepreneurship with MS degree

1960s, the university spin-off rate per employee 1964–1981 was only slightly lower than at MIT, and was ten times higher than at Stanford (McQueen and Wallmark, 1982). However, in the comparison, Chalmers spin-offs on average had fewer employees and thus less growth.

In the early 1980s, US universities set up technology transfer offices based upon the 1980 Bayh–Dole Act, stipulating that universities should own patents and license inventions stemming from federally funded research. In 1983, Chalmers pursued the alternative model of instituting an academic chair with a professorship in innovation engineering appointed to Wallmark. The chair has been responsible for undergraduate and graduate teaching and research, but also for offering university support to inventive activities in general. This solution contrasts to what is now customary in most countries of the world having adopted Bayh–Dole inspired legislation. Many universities worldwide have created TTOs manned by administrative and business personnel. The Chalmers model, however, has been built around the chair and the innovation center. The chair had similar goals and working methods as other chairs at the university, and it was therefore easily accepted by the faculty (Wallmark, 1997).

Today, discussions in the United States and elsewhere are increasingly looking beyond the TTO IP licensing model, thereby pointing at the benefits of delegating IP ownership rights and encouraging academic entrepreneurship at the level of the employee, rather than employer (Merrill and Mazza, 2010). Not having spent time and energy on a TTO model, Chalmers developments should thus offer insights into how innovation and entrepreneurship can be encouraged on the level of individuals rather than institutions. Such an analysis is presented at the end of this chapter. However, one must then bear in mind that Chalmers, being a Swedish university, is still operating under a professor's privilege regime, which implies a bottom-up environment. Today, basically only one Swedish university – Uppsala University – upholds IP licensing based upon professors voluntarily transferring their IP to a university holding structure. That is, a minor portion of faculty patenting at Uppsala University is institutionally owned by the university holding company, whereas almost no such capabilities are in place at other Swedish universities. As a result, the otherwise widespread third-mission model of IP licensing is almost non-existent in Sweden. The Swedish model instead diffuses inventions through faculty offering patent ownership to industry partners and occasionally founding or co-founding ventures around their IP. From an institutional point of view, this implies that universities have no IP ownership role to play, other than when its faculty voluntarily asks for such ownership engagement.

Parallel to the development of Wallmark's innovation center, Chalmers also made investments in a Department of Industrial Management and Economics, conducting education and research into innovation and entrepreneurship among other things. In 1969, Chalmers appointed the industrialist and entrepreneur, Holger Bohlin, as its first Professor in Industrial

Management. Chalmers then started building educational and research activities relevant for innovation and entrepreneurship. In 1984, a strong tradition of informal collaboration between researchers and industry was leveraged by the forming of Chalmers Industrial Technologies (CIT), a Chalmers foundation conducting commercial R&D to which strong industrial networks were linked. Apart from conducting industry collaboration, CIT also set up early versions of an incubator and a seed-financier, thereby connecting industrial networks with the more science-oriented networks of the innovation center.

Becoming a "private" university focusing on venture creation

In the early 1990s, the then right-wing government invited state universities to apply for an opportunity to become foundation based. Chalmers, with its strong industrial track record, applied and was chosen by the government. In 1994 the university transformed from a state university into an incorporated firm owned by a foundation with a substantial capital base. The intention from the government was to increase the autonomy of Chalmers to shape its own destiny. In 1998, however, the then social democratic government forced Chalmers to sign the same law for higher education as state universities were operating under. In essence, Chalmers has had to adhere to the same routines as state universities, as regards research and education. However, as initially intended, it was still possible to seize opportunities as regards structures for innovation and entrepreneurship. Building upon its track record of venture creation, Chalmers now took steps into venture capital, seed-financing, incubation, and action-based entrepreneurship education.

In the mid-1990s, the innovation center as well as the Department of Industrial Management and Economics had become integrated into a School of Technology Management and Economics. Sören Sjölander had succeeded the retired professor Torkel Wallmark. Utilizing industrial networks around CIT, he co-founded the structures (seed-financier, venture capitalist, incubator, and School of Entrepreneurship) aimed at enabling more and higher-growth-oriented venture creation. Notable was a donation of more than €5 million from the Stena Foundation towards starting an incubator – Chalmers Innovation – formed as a foundation. Chalmersinvest Inc. was founded in 1998 as a fully owned daughter company to Chalmers that placed up to €200,000 lead seed-investment into start-ups, thereby becoming central in attracting other private and public venture capital to Chalmers and the region.

In 1997, based upon the analysis that entrepreneurial competence was the main bottleneck for venture growth, Chalmers School of Entrepreneurship was started by Sören Sjölander and Mat Lundqvist. Hence, the school has since then enabled its entrepreneurial master's students to work with promising intellectual property from the university and elsewhere, as a vehicle for both entrepreneurial learning and new venture creation. Multiple versions of the educational program have been launched over the years and today Chalmers School of Entrepreneurship is the leading Swedish start-up environment in Sweden. Of all technology ventures at Sweden's 21 leading incubators, more than 60 ventures started at the school and its incubator accounts for 27 percent of all venture revenue (Lundqvist, 2014). Ventures started at Chalmers Innovation represent 15 percent, thus positioning Chalmers with 42 percent of the total incubated technology venture revenue – far ahead of other university venture creation environments in Sweden. The incubators at Uppsala University (IUC), Royal Institute of Technology (STING), Linköping University (LEAD) and Malmö University (MINC) follow, each with approximately 10 percent of incubated technology venture revenue in Sweden. Thus Chalmers, along with this second echelon of incubators, stands behind more than 80 percent of the Swedish incubated venture revenue – a highly skewed distribution, indicating large differences in local venture creation capabilities in Sweden.

Critical in the Chalmers approach to venture creation is the use of surrogate entrepreneurs (most of them actually being young unproven students at Chalmers School of Entrepreneurship) while allowing venture ideas to originate from any type of environment – not only from Chalmers or other universities but also from corporations and the entrepreneurial ecosystem. Added to this, the development of an action-based venture creation pedagogy (Ollila and Williams-Middleton, 2011; Lundqvist and Williams-Middleton, 2008) at the School of Entrepreneurship has been critical not only in enabling the identity development of individual nascent entrepreneurs, but also for the formation of strongly knit multi-competent entrepreneurial teams able to span the institutional, financial, and cultural gap often labeled the Valley of Death (Lundqvist, 2014).

Adding innovation and entrepreneurship into the Chalmers leadership

In the wake of the new century, the Chalmers top management – as well as key persons involved in the above-mentioned venture creation activities – began formulating strategies to shape Chalmers as an entrepreneurial university. Up to then, innovation and entrepreneurship had translated into educational activities run by the former innovation center, now integrated into the Department of Technology Management and Economics, and including Chalmers School of Entrepreneurship. Innovation and entrepreneurship had also translated into the more peripheral innovation system structures run as foundations (CIT and Chalmers Innovation) or Chalmers daughter companies (Chalmersinvest and Encubator serving the School of Entrepreneurship). These actors were highly connected through physical vicinity and regular informal coordination meetings. With Chalmers management, they shared the aspiration to institutionalize and diffuse innovation and entrepreneurship beyond this relatively small venture-creating community.

Scholarly work (Jacob *et al.*, 2003) along with workshops and policy work resulted in the gradual formulation of a strategy for Chalmers. The Swedish national agency for innovation systems, VINNOVA, played a large role in sponsoring as well as expanding discussions carried out in the Gothenburg setting by Chalmers and other regional stakeholders (from the Region Västra Götaland, University of Gothenburg, etc.). A central analysis was that universities – from having been treated as black boxes as regards innovation and entrepreneurship – instead needed to become key actors. In the case of Chalmers, the analysis was also that its innovation system was uncoordinated and overly focused on downstream venture creation. Based upon insights from Chalmers and elsewhere, VINNOVA in 2006 launched an eight-year program – the Key Actor Program – aimed at helping seven selected universities to professionalize and institutionalize their approach to dealing with innovation or entrepreneurship. In collaboration with University of Gothenburg in 2007, Chalmers was granted one of five key actor projects, GoINN, with an eight-year budget totalling more than €6 million. Four other key actor projects were given to the universities of Linköping, Uppsala, Karlstad, and Umeå/Luleå (joint). As regards how Chalmers institutionalizes innovation and entrepreneurship, it is fair to say that GoINN has been a main source of mobilization and transformation at Chalmers since 2007, including key operative actors as well as the president and vice-presidents. Special interest will therefore be given to developments in this project.

The GoINN project

The GoINN project focuses on early-stage innovation and embraces two "logics" for institutionalizing the third mission: one focused on improving early stages of a more linear innovation process, and one aimed at helping research groups to build intellectual assets around their ongoing research. A main concern regarding the "innovation processing logic" was a lack of coordination among incubation and seed-financing actors, especially in the early stages prior to the establishment of a commercialization strategy for an invention. As regards the "intellectual asset creation logic," several different paths were undertaken. One was to attract more innovation advisors. Another was to include legal advisors at the university into innovation support. A third aim was to develop and apply intellectual asset assessment tools into research groups and enable university decision-making around innovation. Finally, as part of an "asset building logic," the two universities created research centers where IP-ownership transferred from individual researchers into structures owned partly or fully by the hosting university. In short, the project focused on early-stage innovation: either engaging advisors and commercial actors to process innovations around specific disclosures, or enabling research groups to build intellectual assets to expand their innovative capabilities.

Early stage innovation processing

If innovation processing was nothing new for Chalmers, what was to be developed through GoINN? There were several answers to this question, some of which would change over time. One ambition was to simplify navigation for researchers in a complex environment. The idea was to create one entrance point for researchers seeking advice regarding innovation activity. Many efforts were made to communicate this entrance point, called the "GoINN door." However, over time, it became apparent that this ambition was not only difficult to achieve, it was also deemed to be ineffective. "GoINN" was experienced as yet another actor and not as the joint door. The "GoINN" door was thus abandoned, and in its place, a "no wrong door" perspective evolved.

Another ambition was to increase coordination among actors to utilize appropriate competence and occasionally even have handovers from one actor to another. Such ambitions might seem obvious when one considers that they all have been mostly financed by the same public money. Even so, university incubators and seed-financiers in Sweden have had a long history of being measured on their own venture creation success, not necessarily stimulating coordination (and especially not handovers) between actors. Many incubators also take ownership in ventures, just like seed-financiers, which further complicates the question. Thus it was something new when Chalmers asked managers of different incubators to meet and exchange experiences and ideas under GoINN.

After more than five years of such exchange around early-stage innovation processing, it became apparent that a strong community facilitating informal collaboration in early stage ventures had developed among the actors. This was largely due to the relationship building among individuals sharing their experiences while engaging into the process. However, an ambition to register disclosures and their developments into a shared database did not work out. Among other things, the Swedish "principle of public" made it difficult to store sensitive information, as this legislation basically prohibits universities from upholding any secrecy except around aspects agreed upon in industry collaborations. Another ambition was to have more handovers between commercial actors. However, very few occurred (and mostly then from innovation advisors to a commercial actor). Given the Swedish professor's privilege entitling the faculty inventor to IP ownership, this lack of handovers is perhaps not so surprising. Judging from the actors themselves, researchers were able to connect with relevant actors.

A final innovation-processing ambition was, initially, the least articulated: to improve methods and tools for early-stage advice. At the outset of GoINN, the first national program for verification grants was just being launched by VINNOVA. Gothenburg actors involved in GoINN had also been instrumental for the start of this national program. However, agency-driven verification programs could only satisfy some of the large needs. Rather than merely await the next national call and then have to name the inventor as main applicant, university advisors and commercialization actors needed to initiate their own verification and gap-funding. Issues such as novelty and freedom to operate were seen as critical and needing to be resolved quickly and economically. Also, idea evaluations and market studies carried out by entrepreneurship students were identified as key activities in these early stages. As a consequence, the ambition to develop tools and methods has become a main focus area among the early-stage innovation processing actors.

Intellectual asset building

Intellectual asset building around research has opened more genuinely new territory as compared to innovation processing. The theorizing around intellectual asset building began as a discussion between IP and entrepreneurship scholars involving university vice-presidents. The first marks of such a discussion can be traced to Chalmers policy documents from 2001. However, real experimentation around intellectual asset building did not take off until 2007 and onwards. Not surprisingly, it did so in a variety of ways.

In the GoINN project, intellectual asset building in research groups was primarily approached through a focus on the role of university innovation advisors. The University of Gothenburg had pioneered a central research and innovation service function for a decade before the start of GoINN. However, with GoINN, this role became a strategic concern, and systematized efforts were made to recruit three new innovation advisors. From visits at research groups, and seminars with researchers, the innovation advisors developed an approach that was less about bringing innovation out to the world, and more about creating new synergies to spur innovative thinking into daily research efforts. In short, innovation through intellectual asset building was offered to research groups as a tool to expand research ambitions and attract new financing.

There were also contractual experiments with selected research centers, stipulating IP ownership responsibilities to universities (and not only to individual researchers as specified by the Swedish professor's privilege). IP holding entities of Chalmers and the University of Gothenburg thus became responsible for innovation developments in two and six centers, respectively. This contractual change allowed for increased engagement of university- and centre-directed management into innovation. However, it soon became apparent that a formal contractual change around IP ownership going to universities was not always appreciated in practice by individual researchers or industry partners. The norm that industry partners at the centers were always eligible for a free and simple license has also not helped the university to gain authority as regards licensing. IP licensing still remains somewhat rare in Sweden, where the normal practice is for inventing university researchers to sign over patent ownership rights to their industry partners.

It is still early to evaluate the intellectual asset building ambitions, especially in regards to any societal effects. However, some early comments can be made. First, research groups receiving innovation advice and/or having intellectual asset assessments carried out for them generally appreciate this new attention. Judging from much science policy research, this is in itself a surprising result. The integration of a more commercially oriented language and of advisors imposing a more commercial approach is sometimes seen as breaking with fundamental distinctions between public and private R&D, which can result in criticism and interrogation (Tuunainen, 2005). One explanation why this has not been an issue at Chalmers might be due to the careful crafting of an approach focusing on utilization and intellectual assets rather than on commercialization alone. A success factor thus might be that the approach emphasizes not one mode but many modes, of creating utility – such as through the public domain, collaboration, licensing, and/or venture creation – as well as emphasizing societal utility as much as any commercial utility.

Second, it seems to be relevant for innovation advisors and/or students to apply different intellectual asset tools on research groups, regardless of IP ownership regime or any changes in governance system of universities. This is promising, since changes in Swedish governance and ownership structures of universities are not possible to foresee, despite many such changes in surrounding national environments. However, it is also fair to say that the Swedish university system is not accustomed to having activities and policies institutionalized around the "third mission of innovation," other than through "peripheral" commercialization actors. Nevertheless, recent developments at Chalmers have been encouraging. In 2013 Chalmers enacted its first utilization-strategy as regards how innovation activities can be managed. If this recent development is well received, then perhaps a more university-wide development might commence around innovation and entrepreneurship also including aspects such as more general involvement of students in innovation and entrepreneurship.

Reflecting on the situation in 2013

In many ways, the situation around university innovation and entrepreneurship was dramatically different in 2013 than it was in 2007 when the GoINN key actor project was started. Then, early-stage innovation lacked resources. By 2013, early-stage innovation was well financed, not only through GoINN, but also through the government initiative in 2009 to grant eight innovation offices in Sweden – one located at Chalmers and called "Innovation Office West." The Chalmers office was built around the early-stage innovation processing as well as intellectual asset building logics of GoINN, while inviting all universities and university colleges in the region to partake. Since 2013, the University of Gothenburg has also been granted an innovation office by the Swedish government.

In 2007 there was concern about a lack of coordination and consolidation among commercialization actors. Today, coordination has improved especially around early-stage innovation. However, any opportunities from increased consolidation have yet to be seized. From the experiences around innovation processing, among other things, it has become increasingly apparent that any such consolidation should be related to a mother university and not necessarily as a joint concern between Chalmers and the University of Gothenburg. Informal collaboration between the two universities is probably thriving better than ever before. However, complexities within each university seem to be more than enough to deal with, making it questionable to go further on any joint structural consolidation. VINNOVA, as initiator of the GoINN project being joint between Chalmers and the University of Gothenburg, has reached similar conclusions.

In 2013, Chalmers as well as the University of Gothenburg had reached almost symmetrical structures for innovation. Both now have an office for innovation advice that increasingly serves as the operative coordination hub for commercialization actors at the respective universities. Both have engaged innovation and entrepreneurship scholars who have contributed to developments and enabled graduate students to leverage innovation, in collaboration with the offices and commercialization actors. Students today contribute to and learn from assessing intellectual assets, verifying early-stage ideas, and creating new ventures. In 2007, the entrepreneurship students were mostly engaged only in venture creation.

Both universities also have spent considerable time and effort to integrate the third mission of innovation into governance structures. At Chalmers this has been related to its eight "areas of advance":

- built environment;
- energy;
- information and communication technology;
- life science engineering;
- nanoscience and nanotechnology;
- materials science;
- production;
- transport.

However, there is still a large open question as regards how the third mission of innovation might become more institutionalized into a university-wide governance system, comparable to how education and research are conducted. A concern today is how to proceed. Can operative bottom-up processes – whether innovation processing or intellectual asset building – be sufficient? If so, what learning can be spread beyond those actors involved, and how can such an approach be legitimized and sustainable? And if not, what systemic processes can actually accomplish the institutional change of integrating the third mission into the heartland and managerial core of the university?

Contextualizing the Chalmers experience

One way of framing Chalmers developments is to appreciate the relatively dramatic changes in Swedish knowledge transfer models that have occurred during the last 20 years, primarily due to globalization (see Table 6.2). For decades, fields such as engineering, materials, and life sciences, had researchers informally collaborating with R&D departments of larger Swedish firms, in which they shared their knowledge but where researchers rarely took any direct responsibility for innovation. However, in the 1990s dramatic shifts occurred in how R&D departments of increasingly globalized and foreign-owned firms engaged in research collaboration. Many university researchers lost the informal exchange with industry, and policymakers started asking universities and researchers to engage more directly with innovation.

As already indicated, all EU countries except Sweden have national regimes consisting of university ownership of intellectual property. Sweden still has its professor's privilege. Partly because of this, the Swedish response

Table 6.2 Swedish university knowledge transfer paradigms from the point of view of nanotechnology research

Knowledge transfer model	Characteristics
Institutional separation model (to 1995)	University research is embedded with industrial R&D Researchers have an indirect role for innovation
TTO model and quasi-firm model (1995–2005)	Research becomes decoupled from industrial contexts Research groups are expected to start doing entrepreneurial work University and policy begin to develop innovation support functions (e.g. TTO and incubators) Direct role for innovation is expected from researchers but it remains weak
Network model (2005–present)	Deepening of the integration of research and innovation Entrepreneurial tasks start to become part of the networking activities of research groups and part of their "ordinary" roles, more or less supported by university innovation advisors

Source: Adapted from Fogelberg and Lundqvist (2013).

to globalization has emphasized stimulating academic entrepreneurship through incubation of new ventures, rather than developing technology transfer offices. Building on strong traditions around industry collaboration, venture creation, and entrepreneurship training – while having no patenting and licensing – Chalmers thus can offer unconventional insights around university innovation and entrepreneurship becoming more integrated with research.

Since the 1960s, Chalmers has maintained a leadership position as regards venture creation. Today Chalmers ventures account for almost half of all revenue generated by incubated Swedish technology ventures (Lundqvist, 2014). Because of this, the focus in recent years has been on taking further steps in integrating innovation into the daily work of research groups, while developing tools and methods to support such early-stage innovation. Relating to Figure 6.1, Chalmers' recent institutional developments have not been limited to building innovation support through TTOs, incubators, or similar "add-on" functions; nor have they been limited to stimulating more entrepreneurship into research groups becoming like "quasi firms." They have been committed to combining both these aspects into what can be called a "network model," allowing research groups to build on existing innovation even while increasing internal innovation capacities through relevant support and tools offered by support functions.

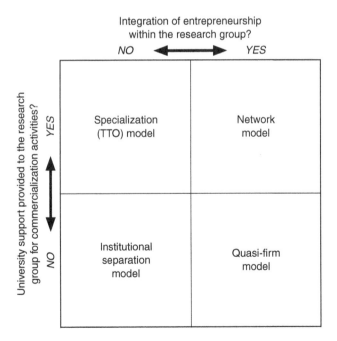

Figure 6.1 Analytical views on entrepreneurship roles within the university (Fogelberg and Lundqvist, 2013).

It should be noted that a movement towards a network model is in no way obvious. In fact, research is divided between those appreciating academic entrepreneurship and research groups becoming quasi-firms (Etzkowitz, 1983; Etzkowitz, 2003) and those questioning such developments and advocating an institutional separation model (Tuunainen, 2005) or a specialization (TTO) model (Vestergaard, 2007). Regardless of this, most research into university entrepreneurship has focused on the policy level or on the "university periphery" (i.e. the TTO or incubator) when it comes to innovation, and not really entered into the "academic heartland" of universities when it comes to innovation and entrepreneurship (Rothaermel *et al.*, 2007). As has been described, Chalmers's modern history of innovation and entrepreneurship dates back to the 1960s but has had more institutional ambitions since the 1980s and onwards. Relating to Clark's (1998) view of entrepreneurial universities following five pathways, Chalmers has put considerable effort into: (1) an enhanced developmental periphery and (2) a stimulated academic heartland, while only recently taking steps around (3) a strengthened managerial core, (4) the rise of a generally entrepreneurial culture inside the university, and (5) a diversified funding base. This last factor has been achieved through the dramatic exogenous changes in research and innovation financing occurring in Sweden since the 1980s. Chalmers in the early 1980s had 80 percent fixed funding and only 20 percent competitive grants while conditions today are the opposite (20:80 instead of 80:20).

Is Chalmers institutionalizing the entrepreneurial?

The main question in this case (how Chalmers institutionalizes innovation and entrepreneurship) can be analyzed through the entrepreneurial architecture framework encompassing structures, systems, leadership, strategies, and culture (Vorley and Nelles, 2009).

Structurally, Chalmers, from an innovation and entrepreneurship point of view, can be captured in the three phases illustrated in Table 6.2. From the 1960s up until the mid-1990s, the main structures were internal academic structures such as the Innovation Center and the Department of Industrial Management and Economics. These two structures operated in parallel until 1993 when they were merged into the same school. A focus at Chalmers was to offer informal support and advice to professors interested in doing spin-offs from their research. Instituting the first chair in Innovation Engineering in 1982 marked a distinctively different strategy to innovation and entrepreneurship at Chalmers, as compared to the international comparison of the time – the IP licensing regime enacted through the US Bayh–Dole Act.

Even when most of the developed world has adopted a Bayh–Dole-oriented regime of university ownership of IP, Sweden has kept its professor's privilege. Structurally, Chalmers, along with other Swedish universities, invested into a developmental periphery 1995–2005, focusing primarily on incubators and seed-financing. Chalmers also, in 1997, started a School of Entrepreneurship, pioneering student surrogate entrepreneurship linked to technology transfer. All these structures have had to attract and compete for researchers and other idea providers, since inventors have been free to choose partners to develop their innovations.

The current phase of structural change requires Chalmers to take larger responsibilities with early innovation and then, in particular, around the activities of innovation processing and intellectual asset-building at researcher groups. This phase also includes having more of a mother-company governance of its relatively autonomous peripheral structures. As this case has indicated, the initial structural idea of a "one-stop shop" for researchers has been abandoned. Instead a "no wrong door" policy has been adopted, whereby incubators and others increasingly operate within a strong, informally coordinated community. The new innovation office has become the hub for this overall coordination; while the School of Entrepreneurship is seen as a more Chalmers-central entity that is responsible for entrepreneurial competence development, not only for venture creators but for all types of innovation processing. Hence, a transformational institutional shift is pre-eminent. Research groups are expected to deal more proactively with innovation as part of their research strategies – and all students are expected to experience some sort of hands-on learning-by-doing in their batchelor's, master's, and PhD programs (albeit not to the extreme extent incorporated in the full-time venture-creating MSc program at the School of Entrepreneurship). Chalmers School of Entrepreneurship is playing an important role in this university-wide transformation. Its students are, since 2007, engaging into social entrepreneurship projects, primarily in eastern Africa (Gawell *et al.*, 2009; Henricson-Briggs, 2013). They are also attracting increasing student numbers from other educational programs to base their batchelor's or master's theses on the ventures at the school. Starting with the bio-entrepreneurship track in 2005, the school (with its student and courses) now expands into all Chalmers's Areas of Advance.

As the case has illustrated, entrepreneurial "*systems*," or more specifically entrepreneurial "networks," have been a continuous concern at Chalmers since the 1960s. Informal networks into the science base, as well as into industry, were the reasons behind starting the Innovation Center in the 1970s and CIT in the 1980s. With the foundation of incubators and seed-financiers, the networking increasingly also focused on venture capital and angel investors. Today, network building is much more about leveraging an entrepreneurial ecosystem, and in having alumni from Chalmers School of Entrepreneurship and others in the Chalmers network to act as trustees who contribute to innovation and entrepreneurship.

University *leadership* around innovation and entrepreneurship has been a key concern since the 1980s and onward. As the case illustrates, there is currently a situation at Chalmers where bottom-up advice and support are functioning in networked interaction with innovative research groups. This results in what is called the "network model" in Figure 6.1. Much innovation and entrepreneurship can probably occur without upper management involvement and without elaborate third-mission governance systems. However – as some research groups thrive through innovation success, while others operate more traditionally – there is reason to expect that leadership at Chalmers will increasingly be dealing with innovation and entrepreneurship in the daily work routine. The changes this implies are difficult to assess. Plans focus on developing yet stronger collaborative environments.

Chalmers University can trace explicit *strategies* for innovation and entrepreneurship from 2001 forward. These strategies, among other things, clarify that the role of Chalmers as an entrepreneurial university is to maximize the responsible utilization of new knowledge in society. They also stipulate that utilization can and should happen through multiple mechanisms often used in combination, such as venture creation, licensing, open innovation, and research collaborations. However, although these strategies have been formulated and even decided upon, most faculty members probably experience low actual insights regarding them. Only with the inception of the innovation office in 2010 did more systematic work with research groups and departments begin. The first elaborate utilization strategy at Chalmers was decided in 2013, which indicates that a large portion of the university is still without a clarified vision for innovation and entrepreneurship. However, there are now responsibilities depicted for departments and educational areas, as well as for direct innovation support and development actors – potentially preparing the university for an institutional and transformational change in which innovation and entrepreneurship soon can be part of both the curricula and the daily workflow of most research groups.

Culture, being the fifth element of the entrepreneurial architecture framework, is probably also the most difficult to analyze with the current case study. Perhaps most important is the university's consistency – since the inception of Chalmers and its industrial origin, to its pioneering into venture creation in the 1960s, and onwards. Clearly not all universities have this kind of history. Nor are they located in a town so focused on trade, entrepreneurship, and industry (for more than 200 years), and currently having firms such as Volvo, Ericsson, SKF, and AstraZeneca that propel the region to be among the most R&D intense per capita in the EU. Evidently, there has also been a conscious effort since the mid-1990s at Chalmers to build more growth-oriented venture creation capabilities (Jacob *et al.*, 2003; Berggren, 2011). Based on the McQueen and Wallmark (1982) study that Chalmers ventures were plentiful but did not grow as much as MIT or Stanford ventures, key persons at Chalmers in the 1990s emphasized venture growth. However, since the beginning of the millennium, many of the same persons have also been advocating the need for a more broad-based innovation strategy. Culturally, Chalmers can expect there to be challenges in how to combine a high-growth venture creation ambition with the need for research groups to build different types of intellectual assets while performing both research and education.

In conclusion, by emphasizing a view that not many researchers are interested in being lead venture creators – and by building successful complementing structures allowing surrogate entrepreneurs to take the main responsibilities (Franklin *et al.*, 2001) – Chalmers hopefully has created the fundamentals needed for a fruitful coexistence of broad-based as well as high-growth oriented approaches to innovation and entrepreneurship when relevant. So, addressing the initial question asked in the title of this chapter – perhaps Chalmers (in integrating innovation into its education and core research) is at the wake of a university-wide institutionalization of innovation and entrepreneurship, whereby it may eventually realize a vast potential. This implies that capabilities for the "third mission" of innovation and entrepreneurship perhaps are best utilized when strongly integrated with the first two: education and research.

References

Åstebro, T., Bazzazian, N., and Braguinsky, S. (2012). Startups by recent university graduates and their faculty: Implications for university entrepreneurship policy. *Research Policy*, 41, 663–677.

Berggren, E. (2011). The entrepreneurial university's influence on commercialisation of academic research: The illustrative case of Chalmers University of Technology. *International Journal of Entrepreneurship and Small Business*, 12, 429–444.

Clark, B.R. (1998). *Creating entrepreneurial universities: Organisational pathways of transformation.* New York: Pergamon Press.

CWTS (Center for Science and Technology Studies) (2013). *Leiden ranking 2013.* Leiden University. www.leidenranking.com/ranking.

Etzkowitz, H. (1983). Entrepreneurial scientists and entrepreneurial universities in American academic science. *Minerva*, 21, 198–233.

Etzkowitz, H. (2003). Research groups as "quasi-firms": The invention of the entrepreneurial university. *Research Policy*, 32, 109–121.

Fogelberg, H. and Lundqvist, M.A. (2013). Integration of academic and entrepreneurial roles: The case of nanotechnology research at Chalmers University of Technology. *Science and Public Policy*, 40, 127–139.

Franklin, S.J., Wright, M., and Lockett, A. (2001). Academic and surrogate entrepreneurs in university spin-out companies. *Journal of Technology Transfer*, 26, 127–141.

Gawell, M., Johannisson, B., and Lundqvist, M. (eds) (2009). *Samhällets entreprenörer – en forskarantologi om samhällsentreprenörskap.* Stockholm: KK Stiftelsen.

Henricson-Briggs, K. (2013). Entrepreneurship as a tool for economic development – experiences from Eastern Africa (thesis for Licentiate of Eng., Chalmers University of Technology, Gothenburg).

Jacob, M., Lundqvist, M., and Hellsmark, H. (2003). Entrepreneurial transformations in the Swedish university system: The case of Chalmers University of Technology. *Research Policy*, 32, 1555–1568.

Lackeus, M., Lundqvist, M.A., and Williams-Middleton, K.L. (2011). Obstacles to establishing venture creation based entrepreneurship education programs. Paper presented at the Nordic Academy of Management Meeting, August 22–24, 2011. Stockholm.

Lindholm-Dahlstrand, A. and Berggren, E. (2010). Linking innovation and entrepreneurship in higher education: A study of Swedish schools of entrepreneurship, in R. Oakey, A. Groen, G. Cook, and P. van der Sijde (eds), *New technology based firms in the new millennium*, Vol. VIII. Bingley, UK: Emerald Group Publishing.

Lundqvist, M.A. (2014). The importance of surrogate entrepreneurship for incubated Swedish technology ventures. *Technovation*, 34(2), 93–100.

Lundqvist, M. and Williams-Middleton, K. (2008). Sustainable wealth creation beyond shareholder value, in C. Wankel and J. Stoner (eds), *Innovative approaches to global sustainability* (pp. 39–62). New York: Palgrave Macmillan.

McQueen, D.H. and Wallmark, J.T. (1982). Spin-off companies from Chalmers University of Technology. *Technovation*, 1, 305–315.

Merrill, S.A. and Mazza, A. (2010). *Managing university intellectual property in the public interest*. Washington, DC: National Academies Press.

Ollila, S. and Williams-Middleton, K. (2011). The venture creation approach: Integrating entrepreneurial education and incubation at the university. *International Journal of Entrepreneurship and Innovation Management*, 13, 161–178.

Philpott, K., Dooley, L., O'Reilly, C., and Lupton, G. (2011). The entrepreneurial university: Examining the underlying academic tensions. *Technovation*, 31, 161–170.

Rothaermel, F.T., Agung, D.S., and Jiang, L. (2007). University entrepreneurship: A taxonomy of the literature. *Industrial and Corporate Change*, 16, 691–791.

Tuunainen, J. (2005). Contesting a hybrid firm at a traditional university. *Social Studies of Science*, 35, 173–210.

Wallmark, J.T. (1997). Inventions and patents at universities: The case of Chalmers University of Technology. *Technovation*, 17, 127–139.

Vestergaard, J. (2007). The entrepreneurial university revisited: Conflicts and the importance of role separation. *Social Epistemology*, 21, 41–54.

Vorley, T. and Nelles, J. (2009). Building entrepreneurial architectures: A conceptual interpretation of the third mission. *Policy Futures in Education*, 7, 284–296.

Wright, M., Clarysse, B., Mustar, P., and Lockett, A. (2007). *Academic entrepreneurship in Europe*. Cheltenham, UK: Edward Elgar.

7 The evolution of Lund University's entrepreneurial ecosystem from 1980 to 2012

Tomas Karlsson, Caroline Wigren-Kristoferson and Hans Landström

The university system in Sweden

Universities in Sweden are primarily state owned and controlled. Out of 39 universities and university-colleges in Sweden, 36 are state owned; exceptions are Chalmers University of Technology, Jönköping University, and Stockholm School of Economics. All higher education comes under the ordinance of higher education and the Swedish Higher Education Authority. The Swedish state is a major funder of university research. University education is almost exclusively financed by the Swedish state. University studies in Sweden have, until recently, been free of charge for all students. As a result, the number of international students at Swedish universities has steadily increased in number. In 2011, fees were introduced for non EU-ESS students, who are now subjected to a market-priced fee. Education at Swedish universities is still free of charge for all Swedish residents, EU residents, and ESS students.

Sweden has a "university teacher's exemption" which grants university researchers (not the universities as organizations) retention of full ownership rights to inventions stemming from their education and research (Law 1949: 345 on the right to employee intervention). Since the exemption is rare in relation to other EU countries, the exemption has been investigated and exhaustively scrutinized in three governmental investigations (1977, 1980, and 2005). At all of these investigations, the exemption has been upheld, and it now seems fairly cemented. Nonetheless, the exemption is still subject to critique, and has been blamed for a relatively low utilization of patents and commercialization of technology in Sweden. Arguments have been made that, due to the teacher's exemption, there is relatively little transfer of knowledge from individual researchers into the creation of companies (Acs *et al.*, 2009). The exemption also gives the universities limited financial value for supporting commercialization of technology from individual researchers. However, evidence is inconclusive whether removing the exemption would alleviate the problem. Many European countries struggle to commercialize university research. There are still large symbolic values for universities to support technology commercialization of university researchers, such as competitive advantages when applying for research funding from the state.

Beside the missions of producing scientific knowledge and raising the level of advanced knowledge among students, a "third mission" was added in 1997 in the Higher Education Act. The third mission stated that the university also should collaborate and cooperate with the surrounding society and inform about its actions. As a consequence, Swedish universities have enlarged their visions to formally include industry–university collaboration and/or stimulation of knowledge-intensive entrepreneurship. Since then, the third mission has been both criticized and integrated into the Swedish university system. The critique arises from a "pure" academic perspective which laments that the new mission detracts focus from free and independent research. At the same time, it is clear that universities, since 1997, have gradually become strong, salient, and active actors in forming regional entrepreneurial ecosystems.

Another consequence is that applications for research funding from the Swedish state in many cases include a requirement for industry collaboration. For example, a call for applications to the Swedish Council for Strategic Research had the following evaluation criteria: (1) research that, in the long term, has the prerequisites to be of the highest international quality; (2) research that can contribute towards fulfilling major needs and solving important problems in society; and (3) research in areas that have a connection to the Swedish business sector.

Swedish universities have, in recent decades, significantly increased focus on the "third mission," and issues such as entrepreneurship and technology commercialization have become more salient. This is likely due to both an increasing focus on these issues by universities all over the industrialized world (Foss and Gibson, 2014), and to the active interventions by the Swedish state, forcing universities to pay increased attention to putting education and research to socio-economic use.

The city of Lund

Lund is situated in the southern part of Sweden in the region of Scania. Scania is the second most densely populated region in Sweden, and has a population of 1.2 million inhabitants. A bridge spanning the Strait of Öresund connects the city of Malmö in Scania with Copenhagen. The land area was contested from the tenth century until the seventeenth century, and often formed the central point of dispute between Sweden and Denmark. Since the seventeenth century, the region has belonged to Sweden. The region has been associated with fertile agricultural soils, and retained a lingual accent and some cultural traits reminiscent of Denmark. The municipality of Lund has the oldest city privileges in the region, founded in the year 990 by the Danes. Its location was likely chosen for strategic military reasons, located on a hill, surrounded by swamps and a river. From its founding, Lund has held significant religious and scholarly importance. The church and burial ground were probably established at the founding of the city, and in 1060 became one of ten Danish dioceses. In 1085, the cathedral school was founded by the Danish King Knut, and is one of the oldest schools in Scandinavia, if not the oldest. Lund has never been a large city but has retained its position as a central city for Swedish education and theology.

Lund University in context

Lund University was established in 1666, by the Swedish King Karl X Gustav. As stated above, the region was Danish for a long period of time. Prior to the establishment of the "Swedish" version of Lund University, the Danes had established a school of general study in Lund in 1425 which had closed in 1536. The university was founded shortly after the treaty of Roskilde in 1658, when the most southern region of current Sweden, the county of Scania, was conquered by Sweden from the Danes. Arguably the university was built to educate teachers in the Swedish language and to culturally integrate the Scania region into Sweden. It was the second university established in Sweden, and at its inauguration it had four faculties: theology, law, medicine, and philosophy. In the years 1676 and 1709, the city of Lund and the university were again conquered by the Danes, only to be reconquered in 1682 and 1710 by the Swedes. Despite its distant location from the capital city of Stockholm, alumni from Lund University have played a significant part in central Swedish society and politics from the seventeenth century onwards. Throughout the eighteenth century, the university produced a number of prominent researchers and significant research results.

However, key commercial activities based on Lund University research did not arise until around the Second World War. In 1944 the tetrahedron milk carton was patented by Ruben Rausing and launched by the firm Tetra Pak in 1951, producing the first large-scale success in commercializing scientific research from Lund. Not too long after, researchers from Lund University developed a clinically viable artificial kidney. The kidney was invented by Nils Alwall, Professor of Medicine; together with industrialist Holger Crafoord he founded the global company Gambro. Since then Lund has introduced innovations such as the asthma drug Bricanyl, the tobacco addiction-breaking method of Nicorette, the oat-based milk products of Oatley, the lactobacillus of Proviva, and Bluetooth – all science-based breakthroughs with strong commercial applications. More recent examples of commercial success from Lund include Qliktech, and Axis. With these commercial successes, Lund University has recently landed very significant research funds for the European Spallation Source (ESS) and MaxLab 4, involving EU funding in the billion euro range, over a number of years.

Today, with approximately 47,700 students and 7,500 employees, Lund University is one of the largest, oldest, and most prestigious universities in Sweden and Scandinavia (76th in the *Times Higher Education* world university rankings, 2012/13). The university has around 285 educational programs and 2,200 independent courses. One hundred programs and 600 independent courses are run entirely in English. It is a full, comprehensive university that conducts world-class research in a broad range of research fields.

University strategy

The strategy of Lund University is complex in several dimensions. It has a long heritage and strengths in a diverse set of faculties, in teaching, research, as well as outreach activities. It also has an overall reputation in Europe in general and Sweden in specific to protect. The formal strategy document from the university consequently tends to stress the importance of excellence in teaching, research, and collaboration activities.

Reviewing four publicly available strategic plans of the university from 1995–2001, 2002–2006, 2007–2011, and 2012–2016, innovation occurred briefly in the strategic plan for the university 2007–2011. Entrepreneurship as a concept is largely absent from these strategy documents.

Lund University and its entrepreneurial ecosystem

In general, the entrepreneurial ecosystem in the Scania region could be regarded as rather fragmented. Altogether, the southwestern part of Scania (Lund and Malmö) was found to have around 35 organizations "officially" engaged in entrepreneurial ecosystem-related activities in the mid-2000s (Hallencreutz and Bjerkesjö, 2009), although the actual number was probably much higher. Many of these organizations have a close collaboration with Lund University and/or Malmö University College, and the number of collaborative organizations has probably increased slightly over the last few years. In Lund, specifically, there have been several recent layoffs of staff from large employers such as Sony Ericsson and AstraZeneca that, in turn, initiated new university activities. For example, in the wake of the AstraZeneca move from Lund to Gothenburg in spring 2010, 114,000 square meters of office space were left vacant. These premises have been converted to "Medicon Village," a new science park. Together with Ideon, the biomedical center, and the recent large science infrastructural investments, Max IV and ESS, Lund has one of the largest science parks in Europe, if not the largest.

The building of an entrepreneurial ecosystem in Lund is not a new occurrence. Notable constructions of the current ecosystems began in the 1980s. The first initiatives were taken to increase collaboration between academia and industry through the establishment of Ideon Science Park. Since then the entrepreneurship ecosystem has grown steadily and fairly rapidly.

Table 7.1 presents a timeline describing the evolution of entrepreneurial and tech transfer initiatives at Lund University. The early historical description is dedicated to major milestones in the overall development of the university, while the period after the 1940s puts an additional focus on commercialization of science and the construction of the entrepreneurial ecosystem we see today.

Many actors are associated with the entrepreneurial ecosystem at Lund University, which fall roughly into four categories: financiers, student initiatives, special topic support actors, and key university support actors. These are not distinct categories, so actors often house several of these activities. We will first briefly describe financiers, student initiatives, and special topic support actors, and then describe the key university support actors in more detail.

Financiers

Almi is the government's primary support organization for new and small businesses. They have around 50 employees in the region, and provide advice on ideation, business creation, acquisitions, and small firm growth. TechnoSeed AB is a seed-stage investor owned by Almi.

VINNOVA is a government institution to support effective innovation systems and create societal value from research results. Primarily funding research commercialization collaborations, VINNOVA has a budget on a Swedish level of more than SEK 2 billion per year.

There are a small number of private investors such as venture capitalists and business angels in the region. Connect is one such network. Many new hi-tech firms use the Connect network to pitch their first idea. However, all in all, regional private investors and venture capital are not the most significant actors in the entrepreneurial ecosystem of Lund.

Student-related activities

University students have initiated several organizations, such as the association for entrepreneurship and start-up spirit (FENA), a not-for-profit entrepreneurship network for students. Another student-initiated activity is Venture Lab, now a university-funded support organization that provides advice, seminars, and incubator space for student ventures. Another activity directly targeting students is the Ideon innovation-based Black Pearl, inspired by ideas of open innovation – a creative space open for anyone with an idea.

Table 7.1 Lund University timeline: evolution of entrepreneurship

1666	Founding letter for Lund University signed by King Karl X Gustaf of Sweden
1668	First classes were given at Lund University
1700s	Education in theology, law, philosophy, and medicine
1800s	Chairs introduced in mathematics, chemistry, physics, political sciences, geography
1880	First female students are allowed to study
1944	Invention of the tetrahedron milk carton, by LU lab assistant Erik Wallenberg
1946	Invention of the artificial kidney by Professor Nils Alwall
1951	Incorporation and patenting of Tetra Pak
1953	Invention of ultrasound diagnostics at Lund University
1961	The foundation of the Faculty of Engineering, and the Faculty of Business
1964	Incorporation of Gambro, the manufacturer of the first artificial kidney
1971	Development of the modern respirator by medical researchers Jonson and Ingelstedt
1981	The foundation of Ideon is laid
1983	Ericson radio systems (later Ericson mobile) moves into Ideon
1984	The foundation of Axis communication
1989–1999	Johansson becomes first Professor in Entrepreneurship in Sweden at Lund University and Växjö
1990	The Department for Industry Collaboration was established at Lund University
	Professor Öste replaces milk with an oat-derived product and founds Oatley, a company that creates oat-based beverages
1993	Company Qliktech was founded by researchers Berg, Gestrelius, and Wolge, based on an algorithm that analyzes information from various databases quickly and simply
1998	Mattisson and Hartsens invention wireless Bluetooth communication introduced to market
1998–2004	Business administration temporarily runs its first course in entrepreneurship
1999	LU innovation, donation for two chairs: one in innovation and one for entrepreneurship: Landström and Enqvist are employed
2001	Venture Lab, Lund University Student Lab is founded
2004	FENA, a student association for entrepreneurship is founded from Lund University
2005	Restart of entrepreneurship education at Lund University, on its current platform
2007	The master's programme in entrepreneurship is established
2010	MAX IV construction begins, a scientific infrastructural investment, at SEK 3 billion
	Qliktech made an IPO at Nasdaq at about US$200 million
	Applications for master's program in entrepreneurship reaches ~1,500 for ~40 places
2011	ESS construction begins, European spallation source, at SEK 14 billion
	Sten K. Johnsson Center for Entrepreneurship is established
2012	Lund University Social Innovation Center is established
	Medicon village is established

Special topic support actors

There are many actors supporting start-ups in different industries, or individuals with interests in specific topics. For example the private actors Colloidal Resources and QNano, were formed to assist and support researchers in the disciplines of chemistry and physics to commercialize their research. Lund University Social Innovation Center (LUSIC) supports individuals who engage in social entrepreneurship. Other actors focused on specific topics and industries are Sweden Cleantech Incubators, Medicon Valley Alliance, Mobile Heights Business Center (mobile phone technology), Öresund Food Network, Öresund Logistics, Öresund IT, Lund Bio Incubator, Medeon (medical science park), Ideon Agro Food, Öresund IT, Skånes Livsmedelsakademi (food). Coompanion is an economic association counselling entrepreneurship and innovation in the social economy. Medical Village could also be categorized in this category, although it is significantly larger than any of the other actors.

Key university-connected ecosystem actors

Generally speaking, the large number of actors makes the ecosystem complex, dynamic, and difficult to overview. One reason for the size and dynamism of the system is the funding model for support organizations. Central funding organizations have a preference for funding new project initiatives, rather than established organizations. As a result, many new

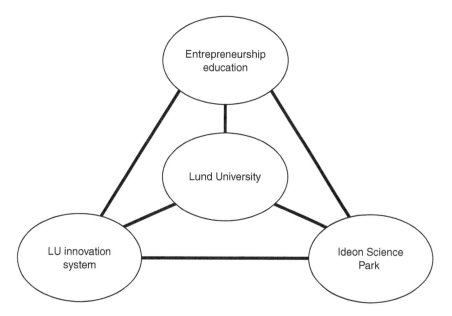

Figure 7.1 Three main actors in the entrepreneurial ecosystem at Lund University.

support organizations are continuously created and disbanded. Some continuously innovate and change in order to develop new project ideas and to implement the projects that receive funding. This funding model makes coordination between actors on a continuous basis difficult, and it also presents a challenge to stay current with the many actors in order to provide correct information to entrepreneurs.

We now bring focus on three key institutional settings at Lund University: Ideon Science Park, Lund University Innovation System (the internal technology transfer office), and Entrepreneurship Education at Lund University. We believe that these three settings illustrate how academic entrepreneurship is supported at Lund University.

Ideon Science Park

Ideon Science Park is one of the oldest and largest science parks in Scandinavia, with its 120,000 square meters of office space. Together with its sister, Medicon Village (started in 2012), the science parks consists of 200,000 square meters of office space. Ideon houses about 2,700 employees in about 350 companies. Companies such as Oatley, Probi, Nvidia, and Scalado benefit from being located close to the university, as do hi-tech companies such as Gambro, Ericsson Telecom, and Axis. While Ideon Science Park is open to any industry, most companies located in the park are in the biotech sector, followed by the IT sector. Ideon is owned and run by Lund University, the municipality of Lund, and a real estate company.

The idea to launch a science park in Lund originated in 1981, inspired by an article about a new science park in England to be established close to Manchester (Westling, 2001). A Lund University professor in chemistry, Sture Forsén, read the article on a return flight from the United States. High-status universities such as Stanford and Cambridge had established their own business parks years earlier; this probably made adoption of this idea easier for all three key stakeholders – the Lund University management, the city of Lund, and the Swedish state. The potential for the science park to create new sources for employment was of high importance. Structural problems of unemployment in the shipping sector in the region were also conducive to the establishment of a science park. Professor Sture Forsén first brought the idea to Lund, and without him, Lund University might not have been central in the founding of the first science park in Sweden.

The primary directive for the Swedish government at that time was to reduce unemployment. Southwestern Scania, and primarily the coastal cities of Malmö and Landskrona, had suffered a heavy crisis in the shipping industry, and the whole region was experiencing high levels of unemployment. Competition from countries with lower wage levels than Sweden led to reduced profitability and sales. The political understanding was that Sweden needed to structurally change its labor market for a greater focus on skilled labor. One key argument for establishing Ideon was therefore its promise to create jobs of the kind that the region needed. The establishment of Ideon also triggered Lund University's involvement with regional industries (Melander, 2006).

The Swedish state had previously invested heavily in the establishment of a new, large engineering school at Lund University, and was therefore not interested in investing more in Lund. One concern of the government was not to treat Lund preferentially over other universities. Instead, the project management team of Ideon approached the company IKEA. Ingvar Kamprad, founder and owner of IKEA, had recently been awarded an honorary doctorate at Lund University. Rules and regulations with respect to funding and city planning were fairly easily bypassed. Funding from IKEA was accessed by convincing the Swedish state that IKEA would be able to use its investment funds for "extraordinary," non-IKEA oriented investment, namely a science park for Lund University. The land used for Ideon was originally planned for university use – but would now serve as site for a for-profit science park. Working together, the university, city, and local industry enabled Ideon to circumnavigate bureaucracy and generally facilitate the construction of Ideon in many ways that would not have been possible without all three types of organizations working together.

Contrary to these positive aspects of establishing Ideon were a number of negative aspects as well. Many viewed the alliance between state, business, and university in a negative light. A vivid debate arose, regarding the potential threats to the independence of university. Would corporate interests start to influence the independence of university research and researchers? At the university itself, there was concern expressed regarding brain drain – that the sharpest minds would no longer take a research position at the university, but would be attracted by higher salaries in business (Melander, 2006). Farmers were critical of the use of fertile farming lands for the construction of Ideon.

While initially subjected to significant criticism, Ideon has grown to become part of the regional ecosystem and is now generally considered as a success story. One contributing factor to this acceptance was that Ericsson established its R&D activities in mobile telephony at Ideon, far away from the company's headquarters in Stockholm (Benneworth *et al.*, 2009). Ericsson had years of extraordinary success with their NMT phones during the late 1980s and early 1990s. Ericsson Mobile had long been important to the university as an employer of their graduates – and the university now became a research partner to Ericsson Mobile, and a chair in radio technology was established at Lund University (Löwegren, 2003).

Benneworth *et al.* (2009) point out a second phase in the development of Ideon with the activities that took place in the 1990s, when several organizations were established to support spin-offs. A dominant actor during this phase was the Technology Bridge Foundation; others included the business advice firm Teknopol, the seed capital firm Teknoseed, and the technology-transfer unit Forskarpatent Syd AB. Toward the end of the 1990s the Lund municipality invested in Ideon to establish Ideon Innovation. Ideon faced a financial crisis in the late 1990s and the regional savings bank stepped in – on the condition that Lund University was to more actively promote and run Ideon, which they did (Benneworth *et al.*, 2009).

Over time, Ideon began to be well established as companies emerging from the university started to move in. Having been a park dominated by Ericsson with 750 employees, the science park currently houses around 350 companies on the premises, with an average of fewer than ten employees per company. As a sign of the times, Ideon Open was founded in 2012 with the idea of further stimulating collaboration and generation of new ideas in open office spaces accessible to anyone with a great idea. Looking back, it can be concluded that Ideon has evolved from being a science park to becoming a campus that houses "a regional innovation community" (Benneworth *et al.*, 2009: 1653). Jonsson (2002) and Löwegren (2003) stress that the firms located at Ideon, primarily the small ones, consider it an advantage to be located there as Ideon is perceived to be a prestigious milieu, which gives the company a positive image to the outside world. Further, over time, the involved partners have extended their work to strengthen the innovation systems across the region.

The positive reputation of the park, the many jobs it has helped create, and the fact that it was the first science park in Sweden have all helped Ideon to be a success and a role model for the other university-connected science parks in Sweden that have followed.

Lund University Innovation System (LUIS)

Several departments and organizations at Lund University work with activities to strengthen the interaction with the surrounding society. We now focus on commercialization of research activities and the organizational unit Lund University Innovation System (LUIS), the university's technology transfer office. They have a quite broad agenda, more extensive than a traditional technology transfer office. LUIS serves employees and students who want to commercialize ideas; they work with business development and start-ups, patenting, financing, intellectual property rights, licensing, and different types of contracts related to the start-up process.

Over the past 15 years, LUIS (in its different forms as we shall describe) has contributed to approximately 60 start-ups, to 2,000 years of employment, and generated SEK 600 million in tax income (according to its own statistics). The organization now employs a staff of 22 members, including business developers, lawyers, administrative staff, and management. Clearly, the university strongly supports innovation activity among both students and employees, in terms of both moral support and substantial funding. In 2011 LUIS supported 79 ideas, 55 commercialization projects, 23 patent applications, formed 16 companies, and invested in another eight companies.

Historically, Lund University was resistant to participation in regional engagement (Benneworth *et al.*, 2009). It should not, however, be forgotten that at the Faculty of Medicine as well as at the Faculty of Engineering, researchers had worked with external actors for decades – and, as mentioned above, some of the first innovations derived from those faculties, such as Tetra Pak (1944), the artificial kidney (1946), ultrasound (1953), the asthma medication Bricanyl (1966), and the modern respirator (1971).

Generally speaking, there was a change in attitude during the 1980s. Lund University started to see itself as an important actor in society, and it was emphasized that collaborations with business society should be developed (Melander, 2006). In 1983, Lund University established a counselling agency and a unit for research collaboration tasked to increase university collaboration with external actors (Melander, 2006). The change in attitude was also influenced by the establishment of Ideon in 1983, as Ideon first made it possible to exploit knowledge from the university (Benneworth *et al.*, 2009).

In 1994 a holding company, the Lund University Limited Company (LUAB), was established to support university innovations and to ensure that knowledge from Lund University was utilized and commercialized. Research from the university should become profitable products and ventures. Through this process, incomes should be generated that should feed back into Lund University to strengthen education and research. Initially LUAB invested in a few ventures, in which they became principal owners; later they changed this strategy and began to invest in a broad portfolio of companies and limit their ownership to 5–10 percent (Melander, 2006).

Successful spin-offs began to serve the university as examples of how to promote commercialization of knowledge. In 2003, a new organization within the institutional boundaries of the university, Lund University Innovation (LUI), was established to encourage staff members to commercially exploit their knowledge. LUI could be seen as the first technology transfer office at Lund University. LUI's success in generating commercial deals between academics at the university and actors in the support system resulted in increased interactions between Lund University and external actors (Benneworth *et al.*, 2009).

LUI served as the interface between the university and the surrounding society, focusing on commercialization activities. They also worked with scouting, to find ideas that researchers could commercialize. The scouting took place primarily with the assistance of external consultants. As the organization continued to expand its activities over time, it became known as the LUI System, or LUIS.

From the perspective of LUIS there had, for a long time, been an attitude at the university that cooperation with the surrounding society was not necessary. This has gradually changed. An important occasion was when Per Eriksson took over as the Vice-Chancellor of the university in 2009, coming from the position of general director of VINNOVA, the Swedish governmental agency for innovation systems. It is said that when he was asked which areas Lund University should develop to support innovation, he answered that it was much dependent on what society needed. It is also said that he has expressed the idea that social scientists should dare to be involved in societal development, not to act only as evaluating and critical scientists.

LUIS was given the responsibility to make certain that university research funding applications would emphasize the utility of the research for society. This process made the role of LUIS visible to Lund University researchers, and applications became greatly successful. In 2009 the university received strategic research funding (SEK 715 million) from the Swedish government to lead and develop world-leading research in nine different areas over a period of five years.

However, the role of LUIS is not without its critics. Both its contribution and its output have been questioned. People have argued that too few ideas pass through LUIS. In the interviews conducted in a previous research project (Wigren-Kristoferson *et al.*, 2011) it was found that the researchers considered the current innovation system confusing and complicated, with too many actors providing different innovation service provisions in the region. Researchers at Lund University showed knowledge of the existence of LUIS, but limited interaction and interest in bringing their research to LUIS. It was found that researchers often preferred to seek advice on technology transfer from their existing social network – through spin-off firms from the research environments, or colleagues who had been successful in technology commercialization. Those organizations and individuals had become "brokers on the boundaries" – closer to the scientific arena, compared to a central commercialization support unit that was more distanced from daily research activities.

When the technology transfer office was launched at the beginning of 2000, it was decided that the work should not be conducted by external consultants; instead Lund University employed new staff for the positions, many of whom had PhDs. The consultants who previously had been hired to scout for ideas were employed by other support organizations in the region. These support organizations, having similar missions, were therefore seen as both competitors and collaborators.

In the autumn of 2008, the new Research and Innovation Bill reinforced the function of some of the university TTOs as regional technology transfer centers; consequently LUIS now serves as the regional technology transfer center, not just for Lund University, but for the south of Sweden, including Malmö University College, Kristianstad University College, and Blekinge University College.

Entrepreneurship education

Since the early 2000s, Lund University has systematically built an education platform in entrepreneurship. Today this platform includes a large number of courses and involves a lot of students and different faculties within the university. The number of faculty members working at the business school with entrepreneurship has increased from two in 2005 to 19 in 2012. In the academic year 2012/2013, a total of 538 students were involved in over 25 individual courses. True to the broad mission of the university, entrepreneurship is provided to several different departments, ranging from humanities to engineering. A detailed overview of these numbers can be reviewed in Table 7.2.

The development of a more systematic interest in entrepreneurship and innovation gained momentum at the end of the 1990s. The university received two donations for the creation of two endowed chairs, one in entrepreneurship and another in innovation. The donations could be regarded as the starting point for a more systematic work on innovation and entrepreneurship research and education at the university. In 2003 the first achievement was made to create a research program on innovation and entrepreneurship that later became the basis for the creation of the Center for Innovation, Research, and Competence in the Learning Economy (CIRCLE). Today, CIRCLE employs around 40 researchers and is regarded as one of the leading research centers in Europe. Their research could be defined as innovation studies on a more macro level of analysis, for example, with regard to global, national, and regional innovation systems.

In 2004 a request came from the university to design and implement a platform for innovation and entrepreneurship education at the university. Thus, innovation and entrepreneurship education were initiated from the top level of university management, i.e. the Vice-Chancellor and the university director. In retrospect we can observe that entrepreneurship education has always been highly supported by this Vice-Chancellor and the management of the university, as they have been instrumental in promoting and building a strong entrepreneurship education platform at Lund University.

The organizational affiliation of entrepreneurship education became the Lund University School of Economics and Management (LUSEM). LUSEM did have a track record with regards to entrepreneurship education, with moderate success. As early as the 1970s some courses were developed for new entrepreneurs and small business managers, using the industrial network around the Department of Business Administration and the Faculty of Engineering (LTH). However, these achievements never received strong internal commitments either from the department or from LTH, and after a few years the educational initiative vanished.

Another attempt was made at the end of the 1980s when workshops on entrepreneurship were organized twice a month for one year at the Department of Business Administration, a project financed by the National Swedish Board for Technical Development (STU). The idea received industry support but neither internal support nor long-term financing – and once more entrepreneurial education was set aside.

Table 7.2 Course offerings in entrepreneurship at Lund University

Undergraduate courses	Faculty	ECTS points	No. of students
Entrepreneurship and project management in film production (FMPM03)	Humanities	15	21
Project management and entrepreneurship (HTXH01)	Humanities	15	13
Entrepreneurship and business development – From idea to market (EXTP05)	Engineering	6	26
Entrepreneurship and environment (EEMF01)	Engineering	9	95
Entrepreneurship and business creation (GEMA40)	Engineering	7.5	27
Business development and entrepreneurship (FEKG40)	Business	9	95
Entrepreneurship (FEKH91)	Business	7.5	40
Innovation management (FEKH92)	Business	7.5	27
Entrepreneurship and project management (ENTA70)	All	15	20
Master's program			
Entrepreneurship: New Venture Creation (NVCR)	All	60 (6 courses)	40
Entrepreneurship: Corporate Entrepreneurship and Innovation (CEIN)	All	60 (6 courses)	33
Master's courses			
Economic Growth over Time and Space (EKHM22)	Social sci.	7.5	35
Small Business Economics, Regional Development and Entrepreneurship (EKHM23)	Social sci.	7.5	24
PhD courses			
Entrepreneurship – commercialize your research	All	7.5	20

A third attempt was made at the end of the 1990s when the program "Business Administration for Entrepreneurs" was created for managers of small businesses. The idea was to give existing entrepreneurs a short version of the traditional business education program at the department. However, it was difficult to attract entrepreneurs who could dedicate their time for a long-term program in business administration, so this attempt to create entrepreneurship education was also terminated.

One may conclude that there have always been individual scholars at the LUSEM who have shown an interest in entrepreneurship and there has been an interest from the industry in the region, but it has been difficult to raise a more internal commitment within the university which had made entrepreneurship invisible and new venture issues have been channelled in other ways, for example, through batchelor's theses and student mentors.

Based on a new initiative at the university in the early 2000s, the first course in entrepreneurship was launched in 2005. Since then the number of courses in entrepreneurship has increased steadily and fairly fast. For example, over the first few years, several courses in entrepreneurship were launched at different faculties within Lund University, as well as cross-faculty courses that involved students with different disciplinary backgrounds. However, the real challenges in building a platform for entrepreneurship education at Lund University came with the creation of a master's program in entrepreneurship in 2007. The idea behind the program was to create a one-year program based on an action-oriented pedagogical approach, where the student would learn through the building of their own venture.[1] The program became a success. In only the first year (2007) the program attracted 464 applicants for the 27 seats in the program (note that, at that time, higher education in Sweden was still free from fees for non-European students).

In 2009 the Higher Education Authority in Sweden announced a call to develop two master's programs in entrepreneurship at Swedish universities that could model excellence and have the potential to become world-leading programs. Together with 11 other universities in Sweden, Lund University applied; the master's program in entrepreneurship was the basis for the application. The evaluation was a success and the master's program was one of two programs that received extra funding for developing an existing program into a leading program in entrepreneurship. (Chalmers Institute of Technology in collaboration with Gothenburg University was the other program that received funding). The increased number of courses in entrepreneurship at Lund University, together with more resources, created a need to recruit more scholars into the field. In 2004, two courses were given and four scholars were involved in entrepreneurship teaching and research. In 2009 the numbers increased to nine courses and eight scholars. Today the entrepreneurship staff includes 19 scholars (including two professors) and nearly 15 scholars from other disciplines who assist in entrepreneurship teaching and research.

The crowning achievement in the entrepreneurship education platform is the one-year master's degree program, which is divided into two paths: New Venture Creation and Corporate Entrepreneurship and Innovation. It is one of the master's programs at Lund University with the highest application rates, and has regularly received the highest number of applicants of all entrepreneurship master's programs in Sweden. As can be seen in Table 7.3, the program is highly international, admitting students from almost 30 different countries; as well as being multi-disciplinary in its character in regards to the disciplinary background of the students; we find students predominantly with management/business degrees, but also economics and engineering, as well as social sciences philosophy, psychology, etc.

The staff was heavily teaching-oriented in the beginning, and little time could be devoted for research. Feeling a need to balance teaching with research in entrepreneurship, recent years have been heavily devoted to finding appropriate facilities for both research and education. In the fall of 2011, the industrialist Sten K. Johnson donated a large sum of money for the creation of a center for entrepreneurship, and in January 2012, the Sten K. Johnson Centre for Entrepreneurship was inaugurated. Today, it is a balanced department, where most of its staff are involved in teaching as well as research in entrepreneurship. Teaching in entrepreneurship requires a specific pedagogic approach, and Lund University's pedagogy is mainly based on Kolb's experiential learning theory (Kolb, 1984).

Table 7.3 Master's program in entrepreneurship: student statistics

Parameter	
Number of applications to the program	496
Number of students, of which	42
Venture Creation	24
Corporate Entrepreneurship	18
Share of women students	32%
Nationalities (based on admission numbers) (%)	
Sweden	9
Rest of Europe	50
USA	11
China	4
Rest of the world	28
Disciplinary background of the students (%)	
Management	54
Economics	12.5
Engineering	8
Other	30
Fee-paying students (non-EU students)	20%
Average age	27 years
Average work experience	4 years

The basic idea in the entrepreneurship education at Lund University is the combination of theory, action, and reflection. The students are encouraged to act, but in seeking an academic education, it is important that the students also have the opportunity to make academic reflections about what they have done, see Figure 7.2.

Role models and social networks are particularly important in entrepreneurship education, so the students are located in an entrepreneurial environment. When working with their venture projects, students have project offices at Ideon Science Park in Lund; in this way they can learn from other, more experienced entrepreneurs, while creating their own social networks.

Conclusions

Lund University has gone through substantial changes in its entrepreneurial environment. As described above, these changes are reflected primarily in the developments of the Ideon Science Park, the Lund University Innovation System, and the Entrepreneurship Education platform at Lund University. This chapter has focused on these three organizations that contribute to a robust entrepreneurial ecosystem. They have all three become institutionalized in their own right – that is to say, none of the three settings relies heavily on project money, but they are all incorporated into the university structure and are, in that sense, sustainable. Thereby, they are well established to play important roles in the ecosystem for the foreseeable future.

The structural changes in the late 1970s mounted sufficient support to create Ideon Science Park, the first cornerstone of the ecosystem. While some steps were taken to create a wider entrepreneurial ecosystem in the

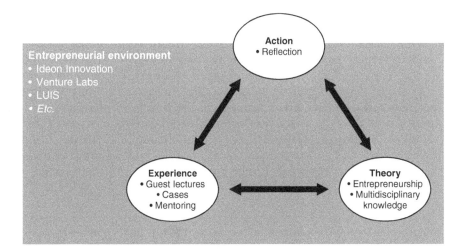

Figure 7.2 Pedagogical approach.

1980s, the system then did not seem to have the institutional support to meet this change. However, large companies, such as Ericsson Mobile came to dominate the science park in the late 1980s and early 1990s which helped to maintain Ideon, as if in waiting to meet its greater purpose. In the late 1990s, when the legislation about universities' third mission was passed, the entrepreneurial ecosystem took another development step as the university decided to support the tech transfer office at the university and to fund two research chairs – one in entrepreneurship and one in innovation. As a consequence, significant research funding in the field of entrepreneurship and innovation was attracted to the university. An entrepreneurship education platform was established in 2005, and a full master's degree program in entrepreneurship was established in 2007. In the mid-2000s Lund University Innovation System was funded as an official technology transfer office, with a quite broad agenda.

Since 2005, the Lund entrepreneurial ecosystem has developed rapidly and experienced strong support from Lund University, not least from the Vice-Chancellor of the university. While entering recently into the arena of entrepreneurship education, Lund University is one of the top providers of entrepreneurship education in Sweden. The master's program in entrepreneurship enjoys among the highest application pressure of any master's program in Sweden.

The description presented in this chapter offers one interpretation of the history and current situation of the, admittedly complex, entrepreneurial ecosystem at Lund University. We have selected to look specifically at three key and somewhat complementary actors in the entrepreneurial ecosystem. This is not a comprehensive review of Lund University entrepreneurial ecosystem, as much more could be said and discussed. The strong basic science elements of the university will continue to play an important role in the ecosystem, facilitating entrepreneurship based on innovative research. An overall key to understanding Lund University is the acknowledgement of valuing basic science and applied sciences. Currently, Lund University dedicates much focus to basic science and its related infrastructural investments – investments that may result in new breakthroughs in the future. At the same time, Lund University encourages the entrepreneurial ecosystem to grow significantly, supporting many different organizations and actors – and through them, to be close to external actors. The motto from the seventeenth century, *Ad utrumque*, "to be prepared for both," remains apt.

Note

1 Experience from other universities has shown that it is difficult to get entrepreneurship students to engage in two-year programs.

References

Acs, Z.J., Braunerhjelm, P., Audretsch, D.B., and Carlsson, B. (2009). The knowledge spillover theory of entrepreneurship. *Small Business Economics*, 32(1), 15–30.

Benneworth, P., Coenen, L., Moodysson, J., and Asheim, B. (2009). Exploring the multiple roles of Lund University in strengthening Scania's regional innovation system: Towards institutional learning? *European Planning Studies*, 17(11), 1645–1664.

Foss, L. and Gibson, D.V. (2014). Institutional perspectives in innovation ecosystem development. In T. Kliewe and T. Kesting (eds), *Moderne Konzepte des organisationalen Marketing* (pp. 61–76). Munster: Springer Gabler.

Hallencreutz, D. and Bjerkesjö, P. (2009). *Skånes regional innovation system: En funktionsanalys*. Region Skåne, Malmö.

Jonsson, O. (2002). Innovation processes and proximity: The case of IDEON firms in Lund, Sweden, *European Planning Studies*, 10(6), 705–722.

Kolb, D.A. (1984). *Experiential learning: Experience as the source of learning and development*. Englewood Cliffs, NJ: Prentice-Hall.

Löwegren, M. (2003). *New technology-based firms in science parks: A study of resources and absorptive capacity*. Lund: Lund Business Press.

Melander, F. (2006). *Lokal Forskningspolitik: Institutionell dynamic och organisatorisk omvandling vid Lunds universitet 1980–2005*. Lund: Statsvetenskapliga instititionen.

Times Higher Education (2012). *The Times Higher Education world university rankings (2012–2013)*. www.timeshighereducation.co.uk/world-university-rankings/2012–13/world-ranking.

Westling, H. (2001). *Idén om Ideon – en forskningsby blir till (The idea about Ideon – The creation of a science park), Årsbok 2001*. Lund: Lunds universitetshistoriska sällskap.

Wigren-Kristoferson, C., Kitagawa, F., and Gabrielsson, J. (2011). Mind the gap and bridge the gap: Knowledge production, enterprise and public dissemination at Swedish "strong research environments." *Science and Public Policy*, 38(6), 481–492.

8 Entrepreneurial Aalto

Where science and art meet technology and business

Steffen Farny and Paula Kyrö

Introduction

Finland, a small, scarcely populated country at the arctic boundaries of Europe, is yet ranked among the top countries in several cross-country studies. Most recognized has been a leading position in education (OECD, 2009) and in anti-corruption practices (Transparency International, 2012). The World Economic Forum assigns Finland a top-3 position for global competitiveness (Schwab, 2012); and Hausmann *et al.* (2011), a top-6 position for industrial competitiveness. Both of these studies are static measures and provide an indication for success that overlooks the complex nature of obstacles in a nation. For instance, a surge in lay-offs due to the Nokia struggle, since 2011, is now reflected in the country's trade deficit for the first time in 20 years. The country's challenge is not only to create new jobs and to return to economic growth, but also to improve its business competitiveness. More dynamic cross-country studies pinpoint that Finland needs to catch up with its entrepreneurial aspirations and product competitiveness (IMD, 2012; Stenholm *et al.*, 2013). Despite holding the world-leading position in per capita R&D investments, the *Global Entrepreneurship Monitor* displays Finland as the third lowest in entrepreneurial aspirations of all innovation-driven economies, much behind its northern European neighbours. While many citizens feel they possess required competencies, they often lack a willingness to exploit them. With only 6 per cent of adults intending to start a business, the country ranks last in that category, far behind its Scandinavian peers. Autio (2009) proposes that explanations are to be found in the entrepreneurial culture, industrial traditions, and systemic experience in growth enterprises.

As a response to these societal needs and socio-economic developments, the government of Finland has started a small revolution in its higher education system. Finland's history shows a tendency to solve socio-economic challenges through an institutional response and integration into educational curricula. A successful past of institutional transitions has built political and societal support to address the aforementioned challenges via public institutions. The current university transition aspires to create multidisciplinary teaching and research. Entrepreneurial capabilities further enable active citizenship and societal development. The government emphasizes the role of entrepreneurship education, which has entered all stages of the educational ladder, starting at the primary school level. Yet, expectation resides within a transformation of the higher education sector aiming to support its innovation capacity.

In practice, the education reforms have led to merging institutions of compatible scientific fields. Whether understood as an entrepreneurial university (Etzkowitz, 2004) or a third generation university (Wissema, 2009), Aalto University is among the first resulting institutions to align national social development and a university mission. The first Finnish "innovation university" is a merger of the Helsinki School of Economics (founded 1904), Helsinki University of Technology (founded 1849), and the University of Art and Design Helsinki (founded 1871): three nationally leading institutions in their respective fields. Three hundred years of combined experience and its tripartite nature are viewed as an excellent opportunity for Aalto University to spearhead the European university transition. Regarding the national innovation capacity and competitiveness, Aalto University is expected to be a major local hub for the metropolitan region of Helsinki that connects public, private, and educational initiatives.

Entrepreneurial Aalto addresses entrepreneurship as a culture and mindset shift, beyond the traditional connotation of small business creation. Adopting purely a managerial view on the entrepreneurial, in its strict sense, refers to the activities of technology commercialization (Hjorth, 2003), which could be detrimental to the original cause (Dreisler *et al.*, 2003). This view is supported by the university principles. The target goes beyond start-up or venture creation and focuses on individuals acting entrepreneurially, taking initiative, creating new openings, renewing, and grasping opportunities (Hjorth, 2003). The entrepreneurial resonates in play, anomaly, and movement (Hjorth, 2005), portrayed by an ecosystem of initiatives and stakeholders connected to the university. Aalto is a national forerunner that integrates a mission of societal and economic development to foster active citizenship and democracy. In the following section, we will present the current internal elements and development process of entrepreneurial Aalto.

The start of Aalto University: history of the merger

The initiation of Aalto University is a deliberate move of the Finnish government to improve global competitiveness of the higher education system (Ministry of Education Finland, 2007). The Ministry of Education emphasizes the need to increase the university's autonomy, international competitiveness, quality research, and teaching (*ibid.*). Ratified by a charter endorsed in June 2008, the foundation for initiating an entrepreneurial university ecosystem was laid. "Whilst proud of its heritage, Aalto

University is not resting on its laurels but sees its tripartite nature as an excellent opportunity to redefine the role and functioning of modern European universities" (Aalto, 2013a). Each of the three schools converted from a separate government-run institution into a larger diversified foundation-based university. Since January 2010, the three former universities have officially operated as one institution. The current transition occurs nationwide and supports autonomy and accountability of the universities, partly a response to suggestions of the Organisation for Economic Co-operation and Development (OECD). As Kyrö and Mattila (2012) present, the OECD report recognizes (particularly in the Finnish context) the new role of universities as financial actors that yield returns on public money, which requires greater institutional autonomy in order to enable entrepreneurial behaviour. This maxim has been picked up by the government and is a guiding principle behind the nationwide transition.

Aalto is designed to be the world's first innovation university, initially conceived for cross-disciplinary collaboration of Finland's leading faculties, researchers, and their students (Louko and Cardwell, 2012). It pursues contribution to societal and economic development through world-class research, interdisciplinary collaboration, and pioneering education. The intention is to align the national mission with its institutional aims. As depicted in Figure 8.1, five key values guide the efforts: *passion* for exploration; *courage* to influence and excel; *freedom* to be creative and critical; *responsibility* to accept, care, and inspire; and *integrity*: openness and equality. These values contribute to a focus on innovation-based entrepreneurship that has a global impact for a better world. To pursue a societal impact, Aalto University has a high priority for entrepreneurship and sustainable development. Possessing a pioneering position in Finland, Aalto is expected to cultivate an innovation-based entrepreneurship culture across the nation.

The relationship between entrepreneurship and the university evolution has two central reasons. First, greater institutional competition requires active marketing, and attractive educational packages to pull talented students towards a university. The international tendency towards a monetization of education has no roots in Finnish education. Since education has been free of any fees, its institutional role has been to contribute to society through education of its citizens. In the past, sufficient talents were retained, but due to international trends, providing free access no longer suffices. Second, and related, to secure future funding from public and recently also private sources, a return on investment mentality has entered the sourcing discussion. Novel in the Finnish education context, the new requirements have been addressed through greater institutional autonomy believed to advance entrepreneurial practices inside the university. While initial suspicion about the creation of such an extensive organizational reform has been dominant, the first years show signs of a successful merger

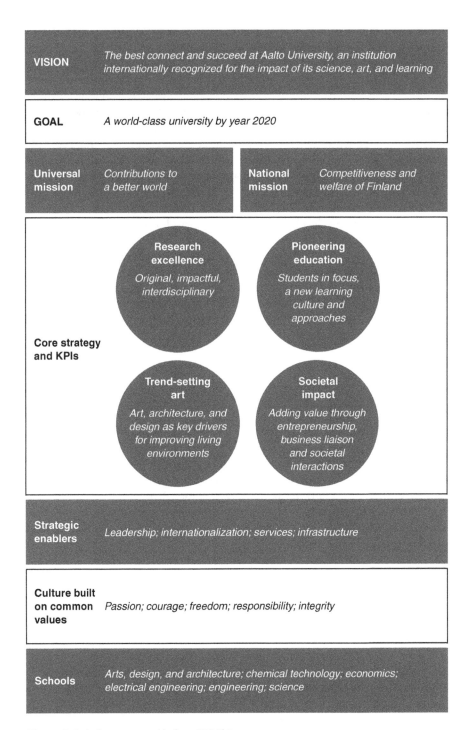

Figure 8.1 Aalto strategy (Aalto, 2013b).

due to its *organizational* change occurring in parallel with an *institutional* transition of a similar extent (Granqvist and Gustafson, 2013).

Immediately after the first president, Tuula Teeri, was chosen, an expert group formed to identify entrepreneurial activities and benchmark them against world leaders. Entrepreneurship has been raised from a programme level to the university level. This decision is rooted in the 1994 decision of the Finnish government to introduce entrepreneurship as a topic and competence at all educational levels. As an outcome, a generation that has been cultivated (since its entry to the educational system) to be more open towards entrepreneurship and entrepreneurial values have now entered the higher education landscape. Before the university merger, predominantly the entrepreneurship unit at the School of Business had been conducting master's and doctoral level education and research on the topic. Otherwise, entrepreneurship had played a minor role and had not been addressed in a sustained manner. Since the merger, entrepreneurial activities have been gathered under one umbrella, and entrepreneurship has been raised as a key strategic dimension at all six schools: arts, design, and architecture; chemical technology; business; electrical engineering; engineering; and science. Hence, the university portrays values of societal responsibility that are invigorated through a culture of innovation-based entrepreneurship.

The entrepreneurial ecosystem of Aalto University

A student-driven (r)evolution at the university

> Aalto started out with, what I like to call, the co-immersion model, where the university is very much out and engaged with the entrepreneurial community, and, that's already hard enough, but having the entrepreneurial community immersed in the entrepreneurial ecosystem as well, that's really hard to do for a lot of other places.... This is probably the strongest of all these schools being student driven, that the students are doing the vast amount of the work, providing the strategic vision and direction.
>
> (Norris Kruger, interviewed 22 October 2012)

To understand the dynamics of entrepreneurship in the ecosystem, one cannot neglect the central role organized student associations have played in the Finnish higher education sector for centuries. Upon joining a Finnish university, each student automatically becomes part of the school's student association. The academic year is plastered with a series of events, rituals, and symbols that strengthen a deeper identity with one's peers and establish a lifelong connection with the institution. Major associations such as Aalto University's student association AYY, own several facilities and have a respected bargaining position for securing sponsorship, attractive both to companies and students. In Finland, the student associations are a sign of equality, egalitarianism, and democratic empowerment of the student body.

Concerning entrepreneurial Aalto, the reason behind a fruitful implementation of most ideas is a simultaneous student movement aiming for similar goals. This fortunate circumstance opens up a variety of possibilities that would otherwise be hard to achieve. As an outside observer one could argue that an institutional resistance to change is partly circumvented by a parallel call from students to intensify entrepreneurial activities. Thus, the implementation of strategic plans to build the entrepreneurial ecosystem is significantly shaped by student engagement. At the centre of the student movement is Aalto Entrepreneurship Society.

Aalto Entrepreneurship Society (AES or AaltoES)

It all started when Kristo Ovaska returned from a trip to the Massachusetts Institute for Technology (MIT). Fuelled with inspiration, he decided not to wait for university formalities and, instead, initiated an informal student organization. Established in 2008, the Aalto Entrepreneurship Society is a completely independent association, founded and led by students, to promote and catalyse entrepreneurship. The idea was to create something new and radical that would inspire students, an element often missing at the university.

> AaltoES started with grassroots events, which are still the most valuable part of our activity. AaltoES gave people opportunities to build their very own team, pitch their ideas, get feedback from experienced entrepreneurs, and build professional network. In Twitter, #aaltoes became quickly the most popular hashtag in Finland.
>
> (AaltoES, 2013)

Avid response continues to show that the founder unveiled a desire shared by many students. AaltoES's declared primary objective was to change the university culture and thereby to contribute to building a thriving ecosystem for growth entrepreneurship in Finland. Following Peter Drucker's slogan "culture eats strategy for breakfast", they aim to foster entrepreneurial action among the students that contributes to an entrepreneurial culture. AaltoES encourages design-driven hi-tech and scalable entrepreneurship, and provides a tight-knit start-up community stretching from Finland across northern Europe (Louko and Cardwell, 2012). While growing organizations often become institutionalized, AaltoES holds open annual elections and, with the help of experienced mentors, lets the new cohort determine events and activities in the coming 12 months. Thereby they remain open for new students to enter, and entrepreneurial in spirit and practice.

AaltoES's young history is one filled with successes. In 2011 they attracted 9,000 participants to 45 organized events. National Failure Day, initiated on 13 October, became the most discussed news in Finnish media that day, and is now celebrated annually. Similarly, what began as an understated gala in 2010 snowballed into a nationwide phenomenon in autumn 2011 (Louko and Cardwell, 2012). For a panel discussion on post-welfare Finland, AES found political support to use Helsinki's national convention hall and drew distinguished Finnish opinion leaders Jorma Ollila, Björn Walhroos, and Risto Siilasmaa.[1] In a similar attempt to promote entrepreneurship, Steve Blank and Donna Novitsky were flown in from Silicon Valley. Remaining a student-run society, AES has positioned the student as a key actor in the entrepreneurial ecosystem. They run the biggest national seed accelerator programme, Startup Sauna, and northern Europe's biggest start-up event Slush (The Next Web, 2013), where, in 2013, Prime Minister Katainen has reaffirmed the value of the burgeoning start-up scene for Finland (*Wall Street Journal*, 2013).

The dynamics and elements of the ecosystem

Entrepreneurship is emphasized as a key enabler for future growth in Europe, which is why it has received increased attention and is to be included in educational settings. Yet, to adopt entrepreneurship in university transitions, one should seek an understanding of institutional and structural changes and the interplay of strategy, curriculum, pedagogy, and teaching (Kyrö and Mattila, 2012). While the university is young in institutional existence, we would like to argue that the current flux in programmes and facilities is designed to constantly renew itself, an inherent characteristic of an entrepreneurial university. Designed as such, processes

Student-driven milestone events	Year	University-driven milestone events
Aalto Entrepreneurship Society • established Venture Garage •	2009	
First Summer of Start-ups programme • 13 October, National Failure Day •	2010	• Aalto University established • EIT ICT labs • Service Factory • Media Factory • Aalto Centre for Entrepreneurship evolves
Start-up Life internship programme •	2011	• Three-year Stanford Partnership • Aalto Intrapreneurial Society
13 October, National Failure Day most • discussed event in Finnish media Venture Garage transformed into • Startup Sauna	2012	• AppCampus with Nokia and Microsoft • Health Factory • Aalto Ventures Program
Slush became biggest start-up • event in Nordics	2013	• MBA Entrepreneurship at Executive School

Figure 8.2 Aalto University and AaltoES timeline.

of renewal are expected to be the norm rather than the exception. To contribute to understanding the dynamics in the ecosystem, we distinguish between elements oriented towards high-growth entrepreneurship and those aimed toward direct social impact. While this distinction is not clearcut for all elements we present, it helps us to apprehend the dominating mind-set and practices of the distinct organizations, facilities, spaces, and programmes (see Appendix 8.1 for an extensive list).

Practice-oriented high-growth entrepreneurship

A dominating presence of technology- and science-oriented students has created an emphasis on *high-growth* entrepreneurship at Aalto's main campus in Espoo. Supporting efforts are shared among a number of entities within the university. Simultaneously, the strategic direction stresses the need for *social* entrepreneurial activities due to a symbiotic relationship between the two that enables transformational innovations. Ultimately, high-impact and high-growth entrepreneurship was the ambition of the resources invested through the merger. Even though a clear categorization of each entity or activity is not easy to draw, we continue by presenting the most impactful elements for growth entrepreneurship.

Aalto Center for Entrepreneurship (ACE): The Aalto Center of Entrepreneurship is an umbrella organization that coordinates Aalto activities related to technology transfer, intellectual property management, start-up company formation, and acceleration. Additionally ACE serves as a partner and provides resources for teaching and research activities at all six Aalto schools. For the entrepreneurial community ACE provides services to activities developed by the student community. It oversees the support and funding of Aalto Venture Garage, Startup Sauna, Summer of Startups, and Startup Life operations.

Further ACE houses all functions traditionally conducted by a technology transfer office. For university employees and researchers, commercialization of research occurs in line with ACE services. From a historical perspective, these activities have not been successfully performed at Finnish universities; meaningful research commercialization in Finland happened in cooperation with third parties, on contract-based research. Streamlining its services, ACE likewise welcomes student applications for creating university spin-offs. Regarding traditional technology commercialization efforts in Finland, ACE has taken a radical step benchmarking practices from successful US counterparts. First, a professional staff with years of experience in high-growth enterprises has been hired. Second, applications are no longer evaluated from an IP and technology perspective, but from a market perspective. Third, resources are strengthened for a smaller number of high-potential cases. Overall, a process model has been built to support technology spin-outs instead of licensing out technologies.

ACE is able to financially support potential technologies through the point of commercial project validation. Optimally, Aalto-based ventures are fully financed for 12 to 18 months and then spun out with a strong go-to-market plan and team. ACE services further have the objective to contribute to the VC environment and attract international resources.

AppCampus (corporate collaboration): an example of ACE services: One successful outcome of ACE's services is the corporate collaboration with Microsoft and Nokia. The multinationals have chosen to collaborate with Aalto to co-develop the world's leading mobile application development ecosystem. A report for the ministry by Louko and Cardwell (2012) claims the reasons for this choice are related to a tradition of strong research at the previous Aalto schools as well as the increased efforts of technology commercialization services provided by ACE. A total of US$24 million has been provided for a three-year build-up process. The majority of funds are reserved for direct team financing. The goal of AppCampus is to strengthen the creation of an application-developer ecosystem in Finland. The university serves as the hub for this focused student-researcher-industry collaboration. The three-year program is designed to develop the ecosystem to reach a level of self-sustaining dynamics that will convert to market driven development.

Aalto Ventures Program (AVP): Co-developed with Stanford Technology Ventures Program, Aalto Ventures Program is dedicated to research and education on scalable ventures and the practice of venturing. While it is formally hosted at the School of Science, it includes researchers from various departments, collaboration with the AaltoES and ACE. AVP's main task is to develop entrepreneurial interventions in all curriculums and to build strong internal relationships with other faculty and schools, which is claimed to be one key success factor for building successful ecosystems at universities (Rice *et al.*, 2010). On the educational side, the programme offers an Aalto-wide minor programme for all master's-level students. Its objective is to foster an entrepreneurial culture, with an emphasis on technology-driven growth entrepreneurship (including research on the subject matter).

Startup Sauna is an initiative of AaltoES to contribute towards the internationality of the entrepreneurial ecosystem. As a registered association it addresses aspiring entrepreneurs in Finland, Russia, and the Baltics; it organizes an accelerator programme and internships, and provides co-working spaces. The attractiveness of the co-working space is that users encounter different people every day (coaches, entrepreneurs, students), creating an opportunity for instant feedback and support on projects. Startup Sauna has gathered a pool of close to 100 coaches that enable the running of the acceleration programme. Coaches include some of the most successful entrepreneurs of northern Europe, such as Mårten Mickos (MySQL, Eucalyptus), Peter Vesterbacka (Rovio), and Sami Inkinen (Trulia). Following the open-source tradition common in Finland, all mentors work on a *pro bono* basis.

The Startup Sauna acceleration programme comprises two phases. First, a warm-up day is organized in cities in northern Europe and Russia. These one-day coaching events aim to scan the pool for high-potential start-ups. Second, a six-week programme trains 15 selected teams for the next development phase of their ventures. At the end of the programme, the best teams are flown to Silicon Valley to network with a pool of investors. During a demo day the teams present their ventures to the public in Helsinki.

A study of Startup Sauna was commissioned in 2011, to poll participants in two sessions from 2010 and one session in 2011. Louko and Cardwell (2012) summarize the key findings: more than 500 applicants and 250 teams were coached in the various warm-up events; 38 teams graduated; 82 per cent were still active while 18 per cent had discontinued activities; 29 teams (76 per cent of the alumni) had launched their product or service; ten teams (26 per cent of the alumni) had realized revenue that totalled more than €420,000 per year; alumni teams raised more than €9 million in funds as of 2012, an increase of more than 339 per cent over pre-camp team funding.

For earlier stage ventures, the Summer of Startups programme provides a crash course into the world of entrepreneurship. A ten-week summer programme allows teams to work on a full-time basis with the coaches of Startup Sauna to develop the idea and test the concept in the market. Even though this is hosted on the Aalto Campus participants are not required to be students of the university. The programme can be seen as a preparation for the more advanced Startup Sauna programme.

Startup Life: Another programme organized by AaltoES is an internship position offered in a global start-up hub through Startup Life. The internship programme lasts from three months to one year; during that time some of the most talented Aalto students are given a position in fast-growing start-ups in New York and Silicon Valley. This programme has grown rapidly from six students sent in 2011, to 100 sent in 2012. Accepted applicants receive a regular salary and work full time at the venture. Through Startup Life, Helsinki-based ventures also find a good venue to attract interns. Startup Life is an important element in the entrepreneurial architecture as it introduces students to high-level ventures, their culture, and speed of execution. It is further a marketing venue for AaltoES due to the high capacity of outbound students. In only the second year of the programme, several Silicon Valley-based enterprises sought talent in Helsinki, and some opened offices in Finland.

Research-driven entrepreneurship for sustainable development

Identifying Aalto's elements that emphasize entrepreneurship's societal and sustainable impact, we stress the research-driven elements, layers, and their interplay. Research, educational programmes, and student initiatives share facilities, co-exist, and have a constant impact on society. These entrepreneurial activities are more scattered than for high-growth purposes, which are streamlined with a limited number of building blocks. Entrepreneurial culture and practices focusing on a wider societal impact and dissemination can be seen as a constant, intertwined process. Here we present some of these distinctive influential elements.

Entrepreneurship discipline at the School of Business: Entrepreneurship and small business research and education began at the School of Business in the early 1990s. As a first entrepreneurship discipline programme in Finland, it has offered master's- and doctoral-level education for almost 20 years. In 2013, the current international venture-based process master's format is running its fourth cohort – and enhances a great variety of student ventures, from local cupcake baking (Cupcake Goddess) and social business (JerryBag), to scalable growth ventures (TAEL, Sportsetter, Polar Glucan). With an emphasis on entrepreneurship education, a national and European-wide research community exists on this topic. Entrepreneurship education research in Finland has produced approximately 25 PhDs and its findings promote entrepreneurship education at Aalto and beyond. The programme actively collaborates with international universities with similar venture programmes, e.g. "Entrepreneurship Capacity Building" between the Faculty of Commerce, Cairo University, and Aalto University School of Economics (May 2011 through December 2012). The research profile of the Aalto faculty prevails in opportunity processes and business modelling, with an emphasis on entrepreneurship for sustainable development, which is a core topic at the Department of Management and International Business in general.

Design Factory: The Design Factory is a 3,000 square metre co-working space equipped with tools required for prototyping work, such as metal- and wood-processing rooms, knitting equipment, and electrical engineering spaces. All spaces can be modified and rearranged for various purposes in order to allow flexible use, free interaction, and prototyping. Design thinking is a method and philosophy incorporated in all the activities of the Design Factory. Design Factory hosts a community of students, researchers, and companies, sharing a working ethos of collaboration and participation. Renewal of rooms and working elements is perpetual. A major part of the yearly activities hosted in the Design Factory occurs in collaboration with companies that financially support the operations. Due to its unique formula, Aalto Design Factory has received vast international attention and similar facilities have opened in Shanghai, Melbourne, and Santiago de Chile.

Small Business Center (SBC): Helsinki's most established organization disseminating knowledge to the wider professional business environment and thereby of substantial influence on the entrepreneurial ecosystem is Aalto's Small Business Center. Formed in 1997 in collaboration with the city of Helsinki and the European Union, the centre provides educational outreach and incubator activities beyond Aalto's staff and students. SBC provides courses to externals and enables continued education (a basic Finnish principle). As a local host of the national Protomo concept, SBC provides office space, professional mentoring, education and training programmes, and access to broad networks. At the same time, its incubator centre, the Startup Center, serves some 50 growth-minded companies at early stages. The concept has proven successful in the Finnish context, and the centre has supported the initial growth of companies such as Rovio and Supercell.

Figure 8.3 depicts the overall structure of Aalto's entrepreneurial architecture – an entrepreneurial culture based on passion, courage, freedom, responsibility, and integrity. While this is a vision shared between the

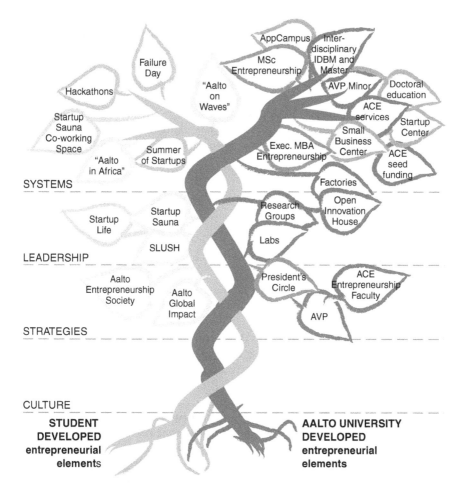

Figure 8.3 Aalto entrepreneurial university architecture as proposed by Nelles and Vorley (2010).

students and the university, they have separate leadership, systems, and structures in place. On the left is shown the Aalto students' leadership as driven by the schools' student association AYY and two groups, Aalto Entrepreneurship Society and Aalto Global Impact. These groups have set up various systems, such as Startup Life, Startup Sauna, and Slush, through which they run programmes, activate students, and integrate with the broader society. Structures are the most flexible element in this view, which are constantly adapted according to the needs. This entrepreneurial architecture is mirrored in the leadership of the university's presidential circle, Center for Entrepreneurship, and Aalto Ventures Program. They have set up research groups, various labs and factories, and an open innovation house; these link departments and function as communication bridges between interest groups.

Both the students' and university's principles share a strategic vision of emphasizing practice-oriented and multidisciplinary education. However, this view is limited and constrained to the internal architecture of an entrepreneurial university. It is precisely the fact that Aalto's vision is to lead the transition towards digital societies, human-centred living environments, and a sustainable use of energy and natural resources that is not portrayed here. Reducing complexity and complication, and disregarding dynamics can introduce the danger of losing definition. Therefore we describe a broader picture of the Aalto entrepreneurial ecosystem.

Aalto's entrepreneurial ecosystem and its future expectations

Building an entrepreneurial ecosystem in Helsinki with Aalto University serving as an innovation hub has been a strategic and deliberate move initiated by the central government. At the same time, a student movement aiming to change the regional mind-set and working culture spurred the rapidly developing ecosystem. Finland's current challenges related to the entrepreneurial culture, industry practices, and experience with growth companies, are addressed through ethical responsibility. Aiming to be a world-class innovation-based university, Aalto applies a broad perspective on entrepreneurship across diverse contexts. It is the university's ambition – through multidisciplinary research and education – to combine high-growth and socially equitable development (two sometimes opposing goals) to achieve complementary synergies.

Following Tansley's (1935) original idea of ecosystems, entrepreneurial Aalto consists of a strong local ecosystem that is connected and integrated globally with other ecosystems on various continents. Depicted in Figure 8.4, strategic level collaboration with global innovation hubs as well as students' proactive participation in other ecosystems forms the basis for global integration, which constantly changes in form and intensity. The ecosystem portrays values of openness instead of control.

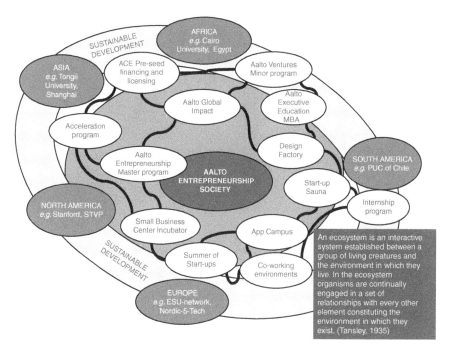

Figure 8.4 The dynamic entrepreneurial ecosystem at Aalto.

Through openness, the axiological domain that Aalto highlights in its philosophy becomes credible. Aalto's chosen path is to contribute not merely to growth and technological advancement, but also to equitable and ecologically sustainable development globally. The coming years will show whether the current ecosystem will continue to develop in the same accountable and socially conscious direction.

Currently high-growth entrepreneurship receives increased attention in Finland due to the need to fill the employment gap. In the future, we expect to see an emphasis of entrepreneurship as a driver towards active citizenship and democratic empowerment. Those countries with a strong tradition in welfare and equality provide a fertile breeding ground for a different path for growth and growth enterprises. It is within this frame that Aalto University follows the objective towards globally responsible practice and at the same time enhancing high-growth companies. Probably the unique element that makes science and art meet technology and business is the high student involvement in creating an entrepreneurial university.

Appendix 8.1

Table 8.A1 The internal organizations, facilities, innovation spaces, and programmes that form Aalto's ecosystem

Organization/ad hoc teams	Programmes	Facilities	Innovation spaces	Category
Aalto Entrepreneurship Society	Startup Sauna Accelerator Summer-of-Startups Startup Life Internship Slush startup conference	Startup Sauna (formerly Aalto Venture Garage)	Startup Sauna Co-working Space Startup Sauna Office Park	Student initiative
Aalto Global Impact	Aalto on Waves Aalto on Tracks Aalto in Africa			Student initiative
Rails Girls				Student initiative
Super Sisters				Student initiative
AYY		Several buildings across the city		Student association
Aalto Center for Entrepreneurship (ACE)	Innovation Funding tools ("TUTL") Startup Services	ACE Building	ACE Co-Working Space	University Initiative
AppCampus	AppCampus Funding AppCademy Acceleration	Open Innovation House	AppSpace	Industry Collaboration
Urban Mill		Urban Mill Co-working facility		City collaboration
EIT ICT Labs Helsinki Node	International masters and doctoral programs Startup Services	Open Innovation House	EIT ICT Labs Co-Location Center	International University and Industry Collaboration
Aalto Small Business Center	Protomo Incubator	Protomo Aalto Startup Center	Protomo Startup offices	Start-up services

Note

1 Jorma Ollila is the former CEO of Nokia and a Finnish opinion leader. In October 2013 Ollila published his memoirs, which have become a hotly discussed book. Björn Wahlroos is the former CEO of Sampo, northern Europe's largest insurance company. Wahlroos has repeatedly expressed his political opinion and engaged with national politics. Risto Siilasmaa is the founder of F-Secure and currently the CEO of Nokia.

References

Aalto University (2013a). *History of Alto University.* www.aalto.fi/en/about/history/ (accessed on 10 April 2013).

Aalto University (2013b). *Aalto University School of Business handbook.* Helsinki: Aalto University.

Aalto Entrepreneurship Society (AaltoES) (2013). *Aalto entrepreneurship history.* http://aaltoes.com/about-us/ (accessed on 10 April 2013).

Autio, E. (2009). *The Finnish paradox: The curious absence of high-growth entrepreneurship in Finland.* Helsinki: Research Institute of the Finnish Economy (ETLA) discussion paper No. 1197.

Dreisler, P., Blenker, P., and Nielsen, K. (2003). Promoting entrepreneurship: Changing attitudes or behaviour? *Journal of Small Business and Enterprise Development,* 10(4), 383–392.

Etzkowitz, H. (2004). The evolution of the entrepreneurial university. *International Journal of Technology and Globalisation,* 1(1), 64–77.

Granqvist, N. and Gustafsson, R. (2013). Fluidity in institutional embedding of proto-institutions. *Academy of Management Proceedings,* 2013(1), 15692.

Hausmann, R., Hidalgo, C., Bustos, S., Coscia, M., Chung, S., Jimenez, J., and Yildirim, M. (2011). *The atlas of economic complexity.* Cambridge, MA: Puritan Press.

Hjorth, D. (2003). In the tribe of Sisyphus: Rethinking management education from an entrepreneurial perspective. *Journal of Management Education,* 27(6), 637–653.

Hjorth, D. (2005). Organizational entrepreneurship: With de Certeau on creating heterotopias (or spaces for play). *Journal of Management Inquiry,* 14, 386–397.

IMD (2012). *World competitiveness yearbook 2012.* Lausanne: Internationall Institute for Management Development.

Kyrö, P. and Mattila, J. (2012). Towards future university by integrating entrepreneurial and the third generation university concepts: Case Aalto University from Finland. Presentation at the 17th Nordic Conference on Small Business Research, Helsinki, Finland.

Louko, P. and Cardwell, W. (2012). Accelerating innovation-based entrepreneurship at Aalto. Unpublished manuscript, Ministry of Employment and the Economy, Finland.

Ministry of Education, Finland (2007). *New university in the field of technology, business studies and art and design (Teknillisen korkeakoulun, Helsingin kauppakorkeakoulun ja Taideteollisen korkeakoulun yhdistyminen uudeksi yliopistoksi).* Reports of the Ministry of Education, Finland, 2007, 16.

Nelles, J. and Vorley, T. (2010). Constructing an entrepreneurial architecture: An emergent framework for studying the contemporary university beyond the entrepreneurial turn. *Innovative Higher Education,* 35(3), 161–176.

Organisation for Economic Co-operation and Development (OECD) (2009). *Pisa Database*. dx.doi.org/10.1787/888932343342.

Rice, M.P., Fetters, M. and Greene, P.G. (2010). University-based entrepreneurship ecosystems: Key success factors and recommendations, in M. Fetters, P.G. Greene, and M.P. Rice (eds), *The development of university-based entrepreneurship ecosystems: Global practices* (pp. 177–196). Cheltenham, UK: Edward Elgar.

Schwab, K. (2012). *The global competitiveness report 2012–2013*. Geneva: World Economic Forum.

Stenholm, P., Kovalainen, A., Heinonen, J., and Pukkinen, T. (2013). *Global entrepreneurship monitor: Finnish 2012 report*. Turku: GEM.

Tansley, A.G. (1935). The use and abuse of vegetational concepts and terms. *Ecology*, 16(3), 284–307.

The Next Web (2013). *Slush 2013: The trends and standout companies at northern Europe's biggest start-up event* http://thenextweb.com/insider/2013/11/19/slush-2013-trends-standout-companies-northern-europes-biggest-startup-event/ accessed 20 November 2013.

Transparency International (2012). *Corruption perception index 2012*. www.transparency.org/cpi2012/results accessed 10 April 2013.

Wall Street Journal (2013). *Finland's Prime Minister looks up to startups* http://online.wsj.com/news/articles/SB10001424052702303289904579197803449054732. Accessed 20 November 2013.

Wissema, J.G. (2009). *Towards the third generation university: Managing the university in transition*. Cheltenham, UK: Edward Elgar.

9 Kymenlaakso University of Applied Sciences, Finland

In search of university-wide entrepreneurial action

Ari Lindeman

This case tells the story of how a university of applied sciences in a relatively small and economically hard hit region has succeeded and struggled to become an adaptive partner in an innovation-generating ecosystem and a provider of a more creative and entrepreneurial class across disciplines and professions. It is a story of a genuine but winding pursuit to break out from deep-seated educational, professional, and disciplinary traditions; of benefiting from new funding opportunities; of searching for appropriate approaches for leadership, and of developing curricular models and organizational structure as well as operating systems that would allow entrepreneurial action to emerge among students and personnel without sacrificing steady production of quality degrees.

Regional setting

Kymenlaakso is one of 19 regions in Finland, located in the southeast of Finland about 100 kilometres from the nation's capital, Helsinki. The region borders with Russia, and St Petersburg can be reached by train in just two hours. The population of the region is small, with 181,000 inhabitants. Kymenlaakso (literally Valley of Kymi) is intersected by the Kymi River, one of the grandest rivers in Finland. In several occasions in history, long before Finland's independence as a nation, the Kymi River marked the border between Sweden and Russia. The river has also been the natural birthplace and location of the oldest and greatest Finnish paper and board mills which today are operated by world leaders in the paper industry including UPM and StoraEnso, to name the largest. The Kymi River enters the Baltic Sea at the Gulf of Finland, in Kotka where one may find the Port of HaminaKotka, Finland's largest cargo port.

Due to large-scale paper industry operations, Kymenlaakso has been economically strong for the latter half of the twentieth century. GDP per capita has been for long among the top three of the regions in Finland. Average salaries of workers have also been high due to secure and high-paying jobs at paper factories. Public sector spending and growth was steady and high as both income and corporate tax payments remained high, decade on decade. This regional prosperity changed drastically with the first large paper factory closure in 2006 in the north of Kymenlaakso, in Voikkaa. Since then several paper lines have been shut down by major players, and one paper company, Myllykoski Oy, closed its operations in Kymenlaakso altogether after being bought by UPM. Overall some 6,000 jobs have disappeared. From 2000 to 2010 (and essentially from 2006 to 2010), Kymenlaakso dropped from second place of GDP per capita to 11th among 19 regions in Finland. (Official Statistics Finland) No other region has suffered such a drastic relative loss of fortunes in such a short time.

The following case tells the story of how a small university of applied sciences in a relatively small region has transformed itself from a provider of skilled labour to big industry and public sector authorities to an innovation-generating ecosystem and a provider of a more creative and entrepreneurial class across disciplines and professions. The case also presents a unique story of how this particular university continues to evolve as a stronger partner for small- and medium-sized companies across a wide spectrum of research, development, and innovation activities – while offering students degrees that distinguish them wherever their careers take them.

Kymenlaakso University of Applied Sciences (in Finnish, Kymenlaakson ammattikorkeakoulu, hereafter Kyamk) offers a uniquely rich micro-level description of the evolution of entrepreneurial architecture in a Finnish university of applied sciences. The significance of the case stems also from being the first in-depth description of the evolution of the entrepreneurial outlook across the first 16 years of university's existence. The case shows how a typical – in terms of size, multidisciplinarity, and multi-location structure – regional university of applied sciences both succeeds at and struggles with becoming more entrepreneurial. It is a story of a genuine but winding pursuit to break out from deep-seated educational, professional, and disciplinary cultures; of benefitting from new funding opportunities; of searching for appropriate approaches for leadership; and of developing curricular structure and operating systems that allow entrepreneurial action to emerge among students and personnel without sacrificing the steady production of quality degrees.

Institutional background

Formation of Kymenlaakso University of Applied Sciences

Kyamk was formed in 1996 from several vocational colleges with nine locations in the Kymenlaakso region, with the farthest distance between units about 60 kilometres. There had been attempts to create two separate universities of applied sciences, one in the south, in the city of Kotka, and one in the north, in the city region of Kouvola. These separate initiatives were, however, combined by governmental order to create one higher education institution with greater critical mass. The formation of Kyamk was part of a nationwide institutional reform to create a system of universities of applied sciences across Finland.

The approximately 4,200 students of the new institution studied in departments of engineering, maritime, forestry, business, nursing, social services, and design and media. The university had a total of 28 batchelor's degree programmes, each 3.5 to 4.5 years in length. The same structure was in place until the first major reorganization in 2004/5. Across time, a few add-on research units had been attached to departments and funded by external project funding. On the one hand, these somewhat separate research units served the need to demonstrate academic credibility, and on the other hand, they were ways to tap into EU, national, and regional funding that gave the opportunity for staff development without changes in curricular practices.

Through changes in leadership to reorganization and a networked team-based institution

The beginnings of reorganization coincided with changes in leadership. After the first transitory rectorship under the previous technical vocational college rector, the second rector, with an academic background in the social sciences, led the university until 2004. The third rector, coming from another humanistic university of applied sciences, was appointed in fall 2004. His term lasted only six months. The attempt to fast-track consultant-driven reorganization and major faculties' rejection of radical team teaching ideas resulted in turmoil and forced the rector to step down.

After a brief interim period with the vice-rector, the fourth rector, this time coming from industry, was appointed in fall 2005. Under his term, 2005–2011, it became apparent that the reorganization was supported by more convincing leadership which was enhanced by a more consistent support by the board of directors to end the wheeling and dealing in the organization (Lindeman 2006).

The fourth rectorship ended with the rector's return to the corporate world. Frustrated with the pace and painfulness of change, at lunch during one of his last days on campus he expressed doubt that he had achieved meaningful results. But indeed he had, and it is during this term (2005 to 2011) that our story really begins.

In 2006, the various departments were merged into three sectors. Engineering, logistics, maritime, and forestry were brought together to form the technology sector. Nursing and social services merged. The third sector was formed from business, media and communications, and design. Several degree programmes were closed, particularly in forestry and some in engineering.

The number of locations was reduced from nine to three, with one campus in Kouvola and two in Kotka (including plans to have just one campus in

Kotka, which was eventually realized in 2014). Over €20 million were invested in strengthening the Kouvola Kasarminmäki campus with construction of the modern PAJA Design Studio building to contrast the historic buildings of the former 1912 army base that now served as a locale of learning. The overall attractiveness of the university increased the number of applicants by about 30 per cent. Moreover, a new strategic partnership was struck between Kyamk and Mikkeli University of Applied Sciences (Mamk) in line with the new developments in national higher education policy and with a view to international competition.

These are the hard facts about the reorganization during the fourth rector's term. Some people blamed the rector for having focused too much on organizational restructuring and financial matters. Short-term costs of reorganization were offset by unexpected positive results together with expected healthier finances. Positive things started to happen on the pedagogical side of the university when the same integrity that was used to manage "the hard side" was carried over to "the soft side" as consistent strategic support for pedagogical renewal.

After the fourth rector, there followed another interim period under another vice-rector from spring 2011 to spring 2012. During this time, the new structure was in operation but the system waited for new leadership to breathe life into its new, still tacit, networks and relationships. The fifth rector, having an academic and professional background in the arts as well as in research and development, was well poised to provide inspirational drive into internal and external networks of the institution. He and the board of directors went further with the reorganization to support real changes at the operative teaching level. Departments were dismantled; a new vice-rector was named, along with directors of education, and a director of research and development; and the faculty and staff under five directors was divided into 14 teams and three university-wide coordinating teams. This ambitious team-based structure was in place by spring 2013, just a year into the rector's term.

Figure 9.1 shows three main phases of Kyamk's organizational restructuring. The first structure on the left describes the university consisting of seven fairly independent departments with their own budgets and curricula. The real development of curricula, or development of anything, in fact, was very dependent on the respective department head and resulted in wide variance of development between departments. In the second (middle) phase, two departments were assumed inside one sector which was given a new name and a director. The aim was to create more cooperation and common development activities between at least those two departments. This new form of organization also included the establishment of the university-wide language department. Previously, language teachers had been part of professional departments' faculties in business, design and media, and social services and healthcare, whereas the engineering and maritime departments were serviced by a separate language

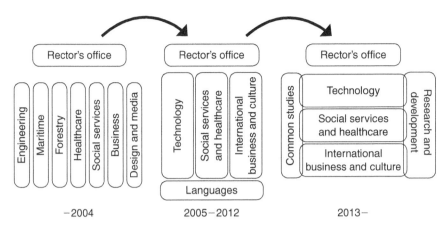

Figure 9.1 Schematic depiction of the transformation of Kyamk's organization structure.

department operating only in Kotka. A slow pace of integration between departments within each sector with respect to curriculum development, for instance, was to be expected since departments and the majority of old department heads remained in place despite the addition of a new organization level of sector directors. The schematic organization structure to the right in the Figure 9.1 describes the latest phase. Old sectors are still in place (though with new directors of education as they are now called) and departments replaced by 17 teams of 8 to 16 faculty members. New university-wide functions have been also added, including coordinating teams for common studies in leadership and entrepreneurship and in methodological studies, in addition to the previous language department being divided into two teams, one in Kouvola and one in Kotka. On the research and development side, the latest structure has three research officers in newly established strategic fields with a director of research as the head of these matrix operations.

   Despite its slow pace, the reorganization provided fuel for important developments towards reinventing the university. It legitimized and strengthened cross-disciplinary collaboration between active and open-minded individuals from different corners of the university working on special initiatives and projects concerning entrepreneurial activities and new models of learning and learning infrastructure, from different learning approaches and learning environments to innovation ecosystems. A new kind of collaboration was evident in an extensive multiparty process to develop an overall university strategy for 2010 to 2015. This latest move towards team-based organization marks an attempt to realize the promises of the new strategy in practice.

Towards entrepreneurial culture

Entrepreneurship through traditional business disciplines

The predecessor institutions of Kyamk had some experience with student projects with and for the regional business community and working life. Apart from traditional company visits, this kind of activity was more or less forbidden fruit in the 1980s but by the early 1990s vocational colleges were given more freedom in their engagement with businesses. Yet grey areas still remain regarding charging money for the projects and compensating teachers for the possible extra work involved, as well as how to handle arrangements in which a teacher's own company is a party in a project (Pelli, 2012).

In the curriculum, "entrepreneurship education" was discussed but it was not conceived as what we consider entrepreneurship education today. The promotion of entrepreneurial activity was gaining importance but it was seen as a question of including traditional business subjects (marketing, accounting, finance, business planning, etc.) into the curricula of non-business programmes. There were three to six ECTS credits (about 2 per cent of any one programme) for business-related subjects in other than business programmes, and that was considered sufficient to teach students about entrepreneurship (Pekkalin, 2012).

Interestingly enough, in the business department, the general view was that there was no need to add or change anything in the business curriculum or in ways of teaching due to the entrepreneurial pressures. By definition, the business department taught business subjects and also informed about entrepreneurs and their work. Thus, the department was considered to promote enterprises all along. The attitude and approach to what we now call entrepreneurship education was partly supported and sustained by the academic drift. There were many who were lured by the newly acquired higher institutional status, who wanted to compare themselves with traditional universities in which the lecturers themselves had been educated. The academic drift was perhaps most evident with respect to thesis evaluation criteria, and even more so in thesis supervision and evaluation practices. There was very little experience of, or searching for, other evaluation criteria of theses and thesis work though official guidelines and discussions did exist. It seemed as if meddling with thesis practices towards a more practice- and action-oriented direction would water down the whole idea of a quality higher education degree. Rigor had only one meaning – academic. Indeed, academic drift may explain much of the hidden or culturally deep-rooted opposition across all the departments towards bringing entrepreneurship ideology into the university. Small wonder, therefore, that entrepreneurship started to surge first where academic culture was perhaps most distant and practice the king, that is, in the culture, design, and communications department.

There was relatively little room for entrepreneurial action overall in the university from 1995 to 1998. Most of the departments (technology, maritime, forestry, business, healthcare, and social services) cooperated with large private and public organizations. On the private side there were large paper and forest industry corporations with their supplier networks, and on the public side, cities, hospitals, and similar authorities. Outside pressure to nurture business venturing hardly existed at all. Indeed, the department for culture, design, and communications was perhaps the department most engaged with small- and medium-sized enterprises as well as having the highest entrepreneurial spirit through its focus on craftsmanship (Pelli, 2012).

Experimenting with entrepreneurship as a discipline

However, small streams of entrepreneurial activity were emerging. This was partly due to the fact that the balance of society started to expect entrepreneurship to be taught, especially in the universities of applied sciences, and also that some students should be appropriately competent to take up an entrepreneurial career. In addition, some lecturers were interested in alternative pedagogies and experimentation began. Not to be ignored was a certain kind of enthusiasm among lecturers about the new possibilities in the newly formed university either. This was seen, for instance, in the business department in Kotka, in the vibrant atmosphere in which its curriculum was developed and international activities were carried out (even if some mistakes were made). Curriculum and teaching were developed together with colleagues, and lecturers often gathered to the workplace even on weekends to prepare for the coming week. This enthusiasm in some corners of the university was supported by good financial support for the universities of applied sciences in their build-up phase. This allowed lecturers to be compensated appropriately for extra work. Some students moved on outside university into regional incubators (Roslund, 2012).

Around the turn of the millennium, two lines of development took hold in the university. On the one hand, the new pedagogical strategies and internal training emphasized that one should move from lecture-based teaching towards more student-centred learning that could be achieved through cooperative learning techniques – problem-based and team-based learning – together with a call for more authentic engagement with working life through project-based learning (Pelli, 2012). On the other hand, the turn of the millennium saw the rise of academic entrepreneurship education research together with the first professorship in entrepreneurship education in Finland.

Five lecturers and project managers, two from business, two from media and design, and one from training services joined entrepreneurship professor Paula Kyrö's research team. Their aim was to complete compulsory doctoral study courses, and eventually PhD dissertations on entrepreneurship education. They were excited about the opportunity and bonded well around questions of entrepreneurship. Entrepreneurship education assumed a whole new meaning for these lecturers through their work in the research group (Pekkalin, 2012).

The change of perspective on entrepreneurship education – from teaching business subjects to all, towards fostering entrepreneurial behaviors in all activities related to the studies and in the university at large – was remarkable. This was a vital realization for the organization's holistic path towards entrepreneurial culture. Around the same time, Business Academy (BA) was founded in the Business Department in Kotka with the support of EU funding. Lecturers involved in entrepreneurship research got a perfect practice ground to turn what they had learned in the research group into a truly student-centred entrepreneurial curriculum. An unfortunate and unintended consequence of getting hands-on entrepreneurship education in the BA was that none of the original Kyamk members of the entrepreneurship research team have so far completed their dissertations. However, and most importantly, the impact of their enthusiasm, newly gained insights, studies, and hard work can be seen in university practice, embedded in entrepreneurial culture, rather than in research papers (Ala-Uotila, 2012; Pekkalin, 2012; Roslund, 2012).

Business Academy started in 2002 and ended in the reshuffling of study places between Kotka and Kouvola in 2008. In that time, about 100 students graduated as BBAs through the BA, or Specialization in Service Entrepreneurship of the Business Programme as it was officially called. Each year 15 students from the ordinary business programme in Kotka were selected for the BA on the basis of their interests, achievements, and an interview with the BA lecturers/coaches. Selection was made during the second semester and students completed their studies (2.5 years out of 3.5 year studies) in the BA. Each BA cohort formed a completely student-owned and -led company. The legal form of the company had to be cooperative, and separate from the school. Student cooperatives functioned in school premises in the city centre outside the campus. One lecturer acted as a coach for each cooperative. Other lecturers were brought in on demand according to their expertise. There were three active cooperatives when the programme was at full operation (Ala-Uotila, 2012; Pekkalin, 2012; Roslund, 2012).

The BA curriculum was based on three pillars: team work, projects, and self-study readings, and included a few compulsory courses (English and Swedish languages and economics) with the ordinary business programme. The cooperative was responsible for all matters of founding, handling accounting and finances, operating, identity building, marketing, selling, and executing projects, all the way through to the eventual profit-sharing among the members of the cooperative and dissolving of the company. Profits from the 2.5 years of operation ranged from €10,000 to €45,000 per cooperative ((Ala-Uotila, 2012; Pekkalin, 2012; Roslund, 2012)).

Business Academy took entrepreneurship education to a whole new level in Kyamk. BA's learning environment and pedagogical principles truly activated and challenged students. Students were made highly responsible for their studies, for the cooperation between students, as well as for their projects and client relationships. These were all intended consequences. If some students experienced an initial academic culture shock, they soon seemed ready to take advantage of their new liberties without too often forgetting the accompanying responsibilities. Programme lecturers soon became convinced that this new methodology was essential if entrepreneurship was to be promoted for real-world results. Companies in the southern part of the region in which BA mainly operated became highly attracted to the student cooperatives, and quickly learned to ask for services from them. Companies also showed interest in developing more innovative service and event management ideas with the students. Of course, there were economic reasons for business success in that student co-ops were highly competitive in certain kind of projects but companies valued flexibility and fresh ideas, too (Ala-Uotila, 2012).

There were also problems with BA's type of entrepreneurship education. First, some students found the responsibility overwhelming and they had difficulties in making meaningful contributions toward their co-op team. This led to occasional infighting and lower-than-expected achievement both in business and in learning terms. Of course, those most involved understood that this was one of the main aims of this learning model – to learn to cope with the uncertainties and risks inherent in enterprise. Second, projects started to resemble each other. Once the demand for a certain kind of project had risen, it was difficult to find new projects for both one particular co-op and the next year's co-op that would satisfy the progressive learning objectives of the curriculum. It was easier for students to meet the demand for those projects that were offered to them, ready-made, rather than developing their business further. Third, there was the somewhat problematic relationship with the rest of the business programme and university administration. Tensions rose between ordinary programme lecturers and BA lecturers. The longer BA lecturers worked in BA the more they viewed the practices of the ordinary business programme as actually holding students back from entrepreneurial action. The administration, on the other hand, raised concerns about the accrual of credits and graduation rate of BA students, not to mention their worry about the costs of the city centre premises and other special arrangements, particularly after EU funding for BA operations ran out (Ala-Uotila, 2012; Pekkalin, 2012; Pelli, 2012).

Alongside BA activities, individual students and small groups from various programmes (i.e. engineering, business, and design) were involved in active experimentation with interdisciplinary creative product development processes and incubation activities. This experimentation was supported by another EU-funded project to innovatively integrate students, small- and medium-sized companies, and their product development needs (Jaskari, 2012). In some ways, one can see these two lines of activities – BA and small cross-departmental project team experiments – augmenting each other and providing cross-fertilization and reflection on entrepreneurial action. The visibility of these activities in the whole university remained small, however, touching fewer than 5 per cent of the student population.

Promoting entrepreneurship through the designated research director

In 2004, the pressure to promote entrepreneurial activities around the region and entrepreneurial education within the university had risen, and a research director in the field of entrepreneurship was appointed for the fixed term of five years. He was to serve the whole university, though administratively the appointment was attached to the business department. The new appointment was made possible by external funding from regional and municipal authorities.

The new research director in entrepreneurship brought new dialogue about the global entrepreneurial mind-set. Success stories from global players were presented, and e-commerce was cited as the way forward in globalization of business activities with connections to world famous IT-hubs. Some students were attracted to participate in high profile national and international Venture Cup competitions. But only a few students, faculty members, and SME owners in the region were responding to this message and related initiatives very enthusiastically. It seemed as if people in the university and the region lived in an altogether different world from the one the research director was envisioning. With respect to entrepreneurship education "proper," the problem persisted that none of the research director's initiatives found its way into the curricula except as optional or free-choice. While the research director went on with his mission, unfortunately with limited success, the reorganization of 2006 and simultaneous reshuffling of study places between Kotka and Kouvola meant that BA would not continue after 2008. So, despite aspirations to the contrary, entrepreneurship education became an endangered species of education.

At this point, it became clear that the entrepreneurship research director's contract would not be extended, and he left for a top business research institution in Helsinki. There he found a better match with his global ideas in an equally globally connected university and business environment. It was decided that BA operations in Kotka were to be closed by 2008. It remained to be seen what form entrepreneurship education would take both in terms of organization and learning infrastructure and its place in the curriculum.

There was obvious sadness and disappointment among BA pioneers. It could be argued that the not-so-smooth transition from Business Academy type of advanced entrepreneurship education to what followed with the

Learning and Competence Creating Ecosystem model (see below) wasted three to five years of progressive development of entrepreneurial action. (Or is this just the way things evolve in real life?) There were also many non-BA lecturers who were worried about the future of entrepreneurial spirit and activities in and around the university.

Yet, despite the controversial closing of the BA, there were new interdisciplinary forces taking the entrepreneurial education and action forward. Growing awareness of possibilities for something new and entrepreneurial was especially present in the integrated sector of international business and culture which started to move to one campus in Kasarminmäki, Kouvola, in 2008 with its magnificent €20 million PAJA Design Studio building.

Reinventing the context of entrepreneurship education

A contextual rationale for a new perspective to entrepreneurial education

Two developments steered entrepreneurship education to the next level in a way that would impact the whole university. First there was the decision to apply for the national status of Centre of Excellence of Universities of Applied Sciences with the Learning and Competence Creating Ecosystem (LCCE) model, the development of which started in 2007/8. The second development was prompted by the EU-funded project geared to the development of an entrepreneurship curriculum, a path that any student could take regardless of discipline or department.

Unlike when the entrepreneurship research director started, the time was ripe for these developments to take hold in the organization. The rationale for the research director's global entrepreneurial message was slashed onto the region's face and into people's hearts when the first massive paper mill closure hit the UPM paper mill in Voikkaa, Kouvola, in 2006. Subsequently, there were major closures in the south of the region, including StoraEnso mill in Summa, Hamina, and smaller but painful cuts in its mill in Kotka, with negative consequences for port operators. In Kouvola, the second devastating announcement of paper mill closure came from Myllykoski Paper in 2010. Altogether, these restructurings meant immediate cuts in employment for about 6,000 people, a substantial proportion of the gradually declining working-age population in the small region.

Through these regional economic changes it became evident that it is very difficult if not impossible to compete with bulk production from Finland. This transit region – traditionally led by administrations (be it government, local, or municipal) and dominated by large corporations – now required entrepreneurship, innovation, and marketing for future prosperity. This message was enforced by the Ministry of Education's strategic development plan for 2006 to 2012, the Finnish Incubator Network's (FINPIN) recommendations within the university of applied sciences system (Auvinen *et al.*, 2010), and by the influential paper on higher education and innovations in the knowledge society by the Rectors' Conference of Finnish Universities of Applied Sciences (Laine *et al.*, 2008). The Rectors' Conference urged each higher education institution "to create their own model in their own context".

Let us now look closely at the response of Kyamk to the situation with the development of, first, the LCCE model and then, establishing an entrepreneurial path into all curricula. The story of these developments will then merge with the strategic reorientation manifested in the university's overall strategy for 2010 to 2015.

Creating a more holistic model of learning and competence development: the LCCE model

A major precursor to the development of the LCCE model was the Innolab project in 2006 and 2007. It was the first attempt to systematize tacit and explicit knowledge from various pedagogical experiments across the university. The Innolab project looked at pedagogical renewal from the point of view of learning environments. The aim of the project was to find common ground for learning environment development in the whole university and thus support overall pedagogic strategy work and infrastructure development. By the end of 2007, the project culminated in the publication, *From learning environments to an ecosystem of innovations*, available only in Finnish (Ala-Uotila, *et al.*, 2007).

The book described eight cases of learning environments and pedagogic development. There were cases from all departments written by the lecturers involved in each case. The cases offered accounts of:

- Business Academy;
- Kymi Design and Business unit;
- Software Academy;
- Dynamo, an entrepreneurial environment for social services students;
- Venelab (BoatLab);
- MuTeMa, a cross-disciplinary project development by design and engineering and marketing students;
- engineering office; and
- a description of a problem-based learning environment for nursing students.

In addition to these cases, the book included commentaries by six leading experts:

- Pasi Tulkki, docent, sociologist, on work-based learning environments;
- Esa Poikela, professor in education, on work process oriented curriculum;
- Kari Hakkarainen and Pirita Seitamaa-Hakkarainen, professors in education, on networked expertise;

- Kari Ristimäki, principal lecturer, on innovation and entrepreneurship;
- Paula Kyrö, professor, on the development of entrepreneurial learning environments; and
- Antti Hautamäki, philosopher, on ecosystem of innovations.

The first agreed commentary was the one by philosopher Hautamäki, who at that time had recently been at the University of California, Berkeley, developing his thinking on innovations in terms of ecosystems. He produced an account of the Kymenlaakso region as an ecosystem of innovations and envisioned Kyamk's role in this context (Hautamäki, 2007). It became obvious that the ecosystem perspective could not be ignored as the guiding principle in the development of learning environments in Kyamk, as was manifested in the title of the book, *From learning environments to an ecosystem of innovations*. The title acknowledged that in order to rise to a completely new level of global learning and international connectedness, the university would need to move on from small-scale experimentation in various pockets of the university to a networked host and facilitator of international and global knowledge streams in, out, and through the region.

At the time of publishing *From learning environments to an ecosystem of innovation* (Ala-Uotila *et al.*, 2007), the top management team of the university made an important decision to apply for the National Centre of Excellence award for the Kymi Design and Business (KD&B) unit in the faculty of International Business and Culture. The choice of the unit was based on the unit's ability to develop the region by connecting businesses and working life with the curriculum, i.e. students and lecturers, through a great number of authentic projects (about 200 annually). The decision to apply for the award was supported in fall 2007 and spring 2008 by consultations facilitated by Professor Esa Poikela from the University of Lapland. The focus of these consultations was the theoretical rationale and operating model of the KD&B unit.

These sessions included all programme heads of International Business and Culture and KD&B personnel as they tried to connect KD&B practices with work process oriented learning theories. The aim was to design a unique model that would capture what was already being done through the KD&B. It was believed that the modeling of these practices with the help of advanced learning theories, would weigh favorably in the Centre of Excellence application, as well as help leverage the operating model throughout the faculty. A team of four – director of the faculty, one lecturer from business, one principal lecturer from design, and the research director of the faculty – was formed to document the model and write the application for the Centre of Excellence award.

After the consultations and initial drafts of the operating model for the activities of the KD&B unit, it was realized that the activities of KD&B could not be meaningfully separated from the work of the rest of the faculty. Neither seemed there to exist a rationale to create separate structures comparable to technology transfer offices or incubators of larger universities. It appeared, under closer scrutiny, that KD&B was not actually a separate unit any more but rather the multipurpose glue of the operating model itself through its internal and external networks. KD&B was the manifestation of the collaboration between businesses, students, lecturers, curriculum, and the management of the university. This realization led, in early 2009, to a new decision by the management team of the university to apply for the Centre of Excellence award not for the KD&B unit but for the entire faculty of International Business and Culture. The model was also named at this point as the Learning and Competence Creating Ecosystem – LCCE model (Pelli and Mäkelä-Marttinen, 2009). The name sprang up quite naturally from Professor Poikela's consultations and the core team's deliberations – to capture the model's cognitive and reflective aspects of learning together with working life oriented competence development in an open and dynamic web of relationships between a multiplicity of actors in and particularly outside the university. Moreover, the rector decided that in the future the LCCE model would be applied in all of the other faculties as well.

The core team of four worked through 2009 to produce the Centre of Excellence application. Much of the work involved conceptual fine-tuning of the LCCE model, and gathering evidence from inside and outside the organization to support the model. This meant collecting details of the projects done between students, companies, and other working life partners, obtaining and summarizing feedback from different parties of the educational process, and working on the curriculum to accurately reflect the LCCE model. As the research director Pasi Tulkki put it, "It was time to show what we had been doing all along – nothing more, and nothing less."

Development of the university's entrepreneurial education model was thus geared solely towards the Centre of Excellence application, which meant that other educational development activities among staff were minimal during 2009. Eventually, the application process proceeded to internal and external stakeholder interviews, followed by the selection committee's deliberation. The joy was great among all involved when the faculty of International Business and Culture with its LCCE model was nominated as one of eight Centres of Excellence 2010 to 2012 from among 28 universities of applied sciences in Finland. Naturally, there was also joy among the management for the €500,000 that came with the nomination.

Subsequent development of the award-winning model took two main directions. First, ten internal LCCE agents were selected from among the faculty, tasked as consulting lecturers on how to develop and apply student-centred process evaluation methods and how to integrate working life into the educational practices within each 15-credit module. LCCE agents were also assigned to document their work with the lecturers with a view to writing articles for the second LCCE book due in 2011.

Second, direction of development dealt with further refining the curriculum. This coincided with the structural development of the university as it struck a strategic alliance with Mamk, a similar university of applied sciences in the neighbouring region. All courses were adjusted to five credits, and more importantly, in the spirit of the LCCE model, emphasis was put on the 15 to 30 credits modules rather than individual courses. The idea was that the larger modules would allow for more varied connections between subjects and more meaningful collaborations with working life partners. The success of this curricular refinement did (and does) hinge on the team-teaching abilities of the lecturers as well as on lecturers' perception of their available resources, i.e. their capacity to change their teaching habits instead of seeing the LCCE element as an add-on to their traditional way of teaching. Thus it was a test of the entrepreneurial capacity of lecturers. In addition, it was a test of how the culture and structures of the faculty supported entrepreneurial action within a study module in which students, lecturers, and working life partners were supposed to meet on an equal footing in order to form a microcosm of learning and competence creating ecosystem.

Unlike in the BA, where students created their own entrepreneurial learning environment with their own co-ops, in this phase of the LCCE model, the power remained in the hands of lecturers who were largely responsible for planning and executing the study modules. The faculty's collaboration platform, KD&B, was offering projects and facilitating connections to the regional and national business partners. Some lecturers tapped into these resources to make the ecosystem breathe but some did not. And even when the collaborative arrangement was formed between the three parties, a student, a lecturer, and an ecosystem partner, the challenge remained to integrate the teaching of several lecturers in the module if it happened that the skills and will for team teaching and facilitation were missing. It may look as if some lecturers were to blame for not changing their habits fast enough, but this is not the whole truth. After winning the Centre of Excellence Award the situation was also new for the faculty management. While well equipped to design the LCCE model, faculty management was not equally fluent in implementing the model across a fairly new and diverse faculty including culture (communications, design, and restoration) and business – both with quite different basic values and ways of working.

The director of the faculty who had led the campaign for the award with such determination and skill acknowledged the challenge:

> We have the model. How to make it work throughout the faculty?...
> The school doesn't change if teachers won't change. It doesn't matter what the model is if the change does not penetrate into the interaction between the teacher and the student.
>
> (Pelli, 2012)

While this is true, ultimately a new mode of executing change would be needed – with a new approach to leadership– to make the LCCE model work in practice, as envisioned by the creators of the model.

Leveraging the learning and competence-creating ecosystem thinking university-wide

The above describes the main developments with the LCCE model within the faculty of International Business and Culture. Leveraging the LCCE model more widely across the university started in 2009 and 2010 with several external expert lectures. Speakers included a prominent philosopher, a few professors in education, and faculty members and managers from exemplary universities of applied sciences in Finland. These events were organized in large lecture theaters for the entire staff of 400 people, with compulsory attendance. If the LCCE model was created as a model to support collaboration and entrepreneurial action in and around the university, these events functioned to the contrary. As these events were associated with leveraging the LCCE model, the model got a fairly unwelcoming reception in the faculties of Social Services and Healthcare and Technology. The mode of leveraging the LCCE model was quite opposite to the spirit of LCCE.

This uneasy start to integrate the LCCE model was rectified in the next phase. Top management decided that three open LCCE seminars would be organized, with each faculty responsible for planning one event as they saw fit. International Business and Culture started in spring 2011, Social Services and Healthcare came second in spring 2012, and Technology's turn was in spring 2013. This approach took the adoption of the LCCE model university-wide to a new level as each faculty interpreted the model against their own practices and in their own language. As a result, wider buy-in of department managers to the LCCE model was achieved. Furthermore, it showed that in some departments, especially Social Services, exemplary curricular and team-teaching practices together with long-term collaboration with working-life partners had been a programme-wide practice for several years. These best practices would need to be bench-learned by others. To this end, the Finnish Higher Education Evaluation Council's quality audit decision of August 27, 2012, nominated the Social Services batchelor's programme as the best-developed programme in the university, and in particular, as the best matching the ideals of the university-wide LCCE model (Virtanen *et al.*, 2012). Interestingly enough, the best application of the LCCE model was found outside the faculty which originally won the Centre of Excellence Award for the LCCE model.[1]

This strongly supports the earlier point that a new phase of development was needed in the International Business and Culture faculty – without diminishing its vital pioneering role in developing the university-wide model to reinvent Kyamk as part of the ecosystem of innovations. In sum, with the LCCE model the university regained a recognizable pedagogic direction that can be seen in the revival of pedagogic discussion over the financial concerns that dominated all discussions during the years of reorganization.

Reforming entrepreneurial education across curricula within the LCCE model

One may inquire how this intensive work on the LCCE model affected the entrepreneurial spirit and action across the university. One stream of the LCCE model development is today called the LCCE entrepreneurship process which can be seen as the most recent phase in institutional development towards entrepreneurial culture, as shown in Figure 9.2.

As indicated earlier, from a micro perspective the development of the LCCE model and dismantling of some entrepreneurial learning environments such as BA caused short-term damage to entrepreneurial culture within the university. On the other hand, the key developers of the LCCE model had an equally genuine vision: to promote more entrepreneurial practices throughout the faculty of International Business and Culture and eventually across all the faculties. The challenge was: How to give more than just 15 students per year a chance to reach their full potential through entrepreneurial action as part of their degree studies? This kind of aim is evident in the first LCCE book from 2009. Of the six theoretical articles of the LCCE model one deals explicitly with entrepreneurial learning from an action perspective (Pelli and Mäkelä-Marttinen 2009).

By the release of the second LCCE book in 2011, the entrepreneurship discourse had been immersed into the ecosystem discourse (Pelli and Ruohonen, 2011; see also Pelli and Ruohonen, 2012). On the one hand, a more strategic perspective had been taken on the university's role in the ecosystem of innovations. It seems that entrepreneurs, entrepreneurial skills, and entrepreneurial culture are so inherent in the ecosystem thinking that they did not need to be emphasized in this context. On the other hand,

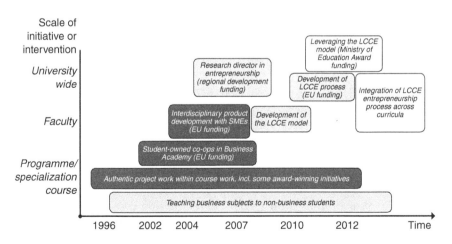

Figure 9.2 Timeline of selected initiatives and projects leading towards entrepreneurial culture.

the development of entrepreneurship education had taken a new start within the LCCE discourse. It found its place somewhat separately but still as an integral and important development under the title of LCCE entrepreneurship process. The latter development activities were again supported by an EU project in 2010 to 2013. The aim was to design an entrepreneurial path, or a tailored curriculum, that any student regardless of the discipline could follow to obtain a degree. The development of this curricular path was another initiative which coincided with the beginning of the strategic alliance with Mamk. As it happened, the entrepreneurial path development was quickly assumed by both strategic partners.

The LCCE entrepreneurial process was ready at the beginning of 2012 and it was applied in all curricula from fall 2012 onwards. Before that, most parts of the process had been implemented as optional courses. The whole LCCE entrepreneurial process consists of four levels. On the first level, two compulsory courses are offered in all curricula (except healthcare and maritime, with their own adaptations): "From idea to innovation" and "Entrepreneurship and small business marketing." On the second level, students may choose an innovation-driven module or a module geared more to a business start-up type of activities. The student may also combine elements from both modules. It is supposed that about 50 per cent of students take some of the level 2 courses. On level 3, students may enroll in multidisciplinary business sparring teams. It is estimated that about 10–20 per cent of students will opt for this more individual and intensive coaching process. Lastly, on level 4, students with a business to develop (a prerequisite) can enroll for business incubation activities. It is targeted boldly that 5–10 per cent of students will take advantage of level 4 immediately following graduation (Jaskari *et al.*, 2012).

It is too early to determine how many students become entrepreneurs through the LCCE entrepreneurial process. The process has been experimented with on levels 1 to 3. The level 1 course "From idea to innovation" seems especially promising to show first-year students their creative potential in a multidisciplinary setting and by genuinely exposing them to the possibilities of new ventures. The first year of full operation of level 1, spring and fall 2013, saw over 300 first-year students participating in about 65 teams in three large group course deliveries of "From idea to innovation" in Kouvola campus alone. In 2014, altogether 400 students did the same, including 100 students who attended online versions of level 1 courses, enabling level 1 to be kick-started also in Kotka campus before its full operation there in the academic year 2015–2016. In 2014, 70–80 students in about 25 teams attended workshops, summer start-up processes and venture camps on levels 2 and 3 in addition to about 60 students in other level 2 courses. As these numbers are based mainly on students from one campus, it is expected that, with Kotka campus fully engaged in the LCCE entrepreneurial process, there will be at least 200 new students taking level 2 and 3 entrepreneurial activities annually, which would make it reasonable to expect 50–80 students from among about a 900 annual intake of students to experiment with founding their own business (level 4) by 2017–2018.

If we compare this against the BA model – which, in effect, placed students onto level 4 education in the LCCE entrepreneurship process immediately after their freshman year – then we can appreciate the challenge that the university and its students are facing. Instead of 15 students from the business department (or one co-op a year) it is expected that from three to six times more students from different disciplines may complete part of their studies by setting up and running their own, or partly owned, business. They have more than the freshman year to prepare themselves for this real-world engagement, but such success would be staggering compared to the normal rate of 2–3 per cent of students becoming entrepreneurs from traditional universities and universities of applied sciences in Finland. If we take seriously the facts surrounding restructuring of the regional economy, the diminishing population, and global competitive forces, this is what is needed: entrepreneurship as a natural career for higher education graduates, i.e. more academic entrepreneurship.

Recreating the identity of the Kymenlaakso University of Applied Sciences

The case study points towards the reinvented identity of Kyamk. It shows how the discourse on entrepreneurship has changed from a disciplinary discussion to a conversation about how to deliver higher education with an entrepreneurial twist regardless of discipline. The storyline integrates other disciplines to reinvent one's own discipline. In the wicked world, the renewal of one discipline is only possible through critical and reflective engagement with other disciplines. The role of outside partnerships becomes crucial to university's educational mission. They are portrayed in the new light as integral contributors to the learning processes of students and staff alike. Learning is not owned by the university but by the community of practitioners in and around the university. The ecosystem partner enters into the heart of the university, and the university enters into the heart of its working life partner. Thus different professional and disciplinary learning cultures may merge and recreate one with another, rather than collide.

The case also tells about the beginnings of a journey towards Kyamk's reinvented position in the region as the creator of new opportunities for those engaged with learning and competence development. The university no longer sees itself just as a producer of graduates into existing jobs but as a co-educator of graduates to create improvements, innovations, businesses, and jobs. This reinvented identity includes also networked collaboration across institutional hierarchies of education. Kyamk recreates itself in active collaboration with vocational training schools and traditional universities, both nationally and internationally. It integrates the advantages of the different levels of education for the benefit of its learning and competence creating ecosystem. Collaboration among traditional universities serves to reflect its own knowledge, competence, and action from a wider perspective, even while keeping in touch with the realities of workplaces and work processes with its partners in the vocational training sphere.

Many forces have supported the Kyamk to find its own way. The new pedagogic direction has been established. The current environment – both regional business environment, and government measures to restructure and economize the university system, as well as global influence – is so complex and dynamic that one is forced to rethink one's role at all times. And despite the declining population and challenging economic situation around Kyamk, the region's treasure remains its intercultural location between Helsinki, Finland, and St Petersburg, Russia. The region's location is particularly amiable for entrepreneurial action as long as the entrepreneurial spirit is restored and openness to new ideas and people is maintained.

The strategic alliance with with Mamk provides provides credibility and muscle in national educational competition as well as international research and development partnerships. The common entrepreneurial strategy of the alliance also supports the continuous infiltration of entrepreneurial action in all curricula. Kyamk provides, as the case study shows, a rich body of experiences from experimenting with new modes and models of learning and entrepreneurship education. (See also Mäkelä-Marttinen and Hartikainen, 2013.)

The new leadership is tasked to execute continuous change and to transform challenges into strengths. This includes engaging the faculty members to become ever more responsible for the change itself by reinventing their roles in collaborative settings within the various networks of the ecosystem of innovations. The focus in the future is a student pedagogy through which students get the chance to reinvent themselves as reflective members of the community of practitioners, developers, and entrepreneurs. There is work still to be done to improve the facilities and learning infrastructure for ease of communication and collaboration. Mobile learning presents the new leadership with true challenges. At the same time, the curricular infrastructure is taking shape. Persistent development of entrepreneurial architecture is beginning to pay off. Finland's most influential business weekly ranked Kyamk the third as the producer of young entrepreneurs among nation's 25 universities of applied sciences (*Talouselämä*, 2013). It is now a matter of asking the right questions and listening to students, staff, and partners to help them to create effective learning environments and encounters for life. The fifth rector provided the Kymenlaakso University of Applied Sciences with the inspirational and entrepreneurial leadership that, at a crucial time, facilitated the formation of its long-sought entrepreneurial identity. From February 2015 onwards, Kyamk is poised to leverage its entrepreneurial journey under the sixth rector appointed as the common leader of the South-East of Finland University of Applied Sciences consisting of Kyamk and Mamk, and to be a fully merged new higher education entity by the end of 2016.

Appendix 9.1

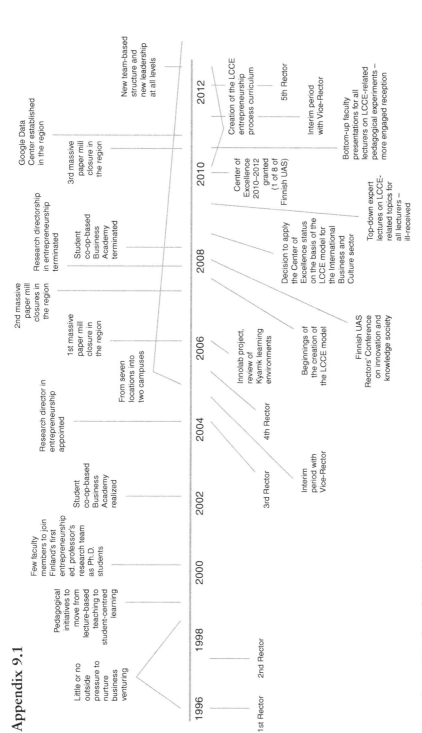

Figure 9.A1 Timeline of Kyamk's case.

Note

1 It should be noted that not all the programmes were evaluated in the audit.

References

Ala-Uotila, H. (2012, 6 August). Personal interview.

Ala-Uotila, H., Frilander-Paavilainen, E.-L., Lindeman, A., and Tulkki, P. (eds) (2007). *Oppimisympäristöistä innovaatioiden ekosysteemiin (From learning environments to an innovation ecosystem)*. Kymenlaakso University of Applied Sciences publications, B Series No. 46.

Auvinen, P., Kauppi, A., Kotila, H., Loikkanen, A., Markus A., Peltokangas, N., Holm, K., and Kajaste, M. (2010). *Ammattikorkeakoulujen koulutuksen laatuyksiköt 2010–2012 (Centres of excellence in universities of applied sciences 2010–2012)* Tampere: Korkeakoujen arviointineuvosto (Finnish Higher Education Evaluation Council).

Hautamäki, A. (2007) KyAMK Kymenlaakson innovaatioiden ekosysteemissä (KyUAS in Kymenlaakso's ecosystem of innovations), in Ala-Uotila, H., Frilander-Paavilainen, E-L., Lindeman, A. and Tulkki, P. (eds). *Oppimisympäristöistä innovaatioiden ekosysteemiin (From learning environments to an ecosystem of innovations)*. Kymenlaakso University of Applied Sciences publications, B Series No: 46 (only in Finnish).

Jaskari, P. (2012, 8 August). Personal interview.

Jaskari, P., Pienimäki, A., Vihavainen, O. (eds) (2012) *KIPINÄ Tarinoita yrittäjyydestä LCCE®-yrittäjyysprosessi (SPARK Stories about entrepreneurship LCCE® entrepreneurship process)*. Kouvola: Kymenlaakso University of Applied Sciences Publications, A Series No. 37.

Laine, K., van der Sijde, P., Lähdeniemi, M., and Tarkkanen, J. (eds) 2008. *Higher education institutions and innovation in the knowledge society*. Helsinki: Rector's Conference of Finnish Universities of Applied Sciences.

Lindeman, A. (2006). Unpublished development project report on organizational and pedagogical change process in Kymenlaakso University of Applied Sciences 2003–2005. As part of the professional teacher training in the vocational teacher training programme at Haaga-Helia University of Applied Sciences.

Mäkelä-Marttinen, L. and Hartikainen, N. (eds) (2013) *Kasvun voimaa Oppimisen ja osaamisen ekosysteemissä LCCE (Empowering growth in Learning and Competence Ecosystem LCCE)*. Kouvola: Publications of Kymenlaakso University of Applied Sciences. Series A. No. 42.

Official Statistics of Finland. GDP/capita by regions 2000–2010 (in Finnish). Available at: http://archive.today/tplsT (accessed 10 July, 2014).

Pekkalin, S (2012, 6 August). Personal interview.

Pelli, R. (2012, 2 August). Personal interview.

Pelli, R. and Mäkelä-Marttinen, L. (eds) (2009). *Kohti oppimisen ja osaamisen ekosysteemiä (Towards learning and competence creating ecosystem – LCCE)*. Kotka: Publications of Kymenlaakso University of Applied Sciences. Series A. No. 24.

Pelli, R. and Ruohonen, S. (eds) (2011). *Oppimisen ja osaamisen ekosysteemi (Learning and competence creating ecosystem – LCCE)*. Kotka: Publications of Kymenlaakso University of Applied Sciences. Series A. No. 32.

Pelli, R. and Ruohonen, S. (eds) 2012). *Learning and competence creating ecosystem – LCCE.* Kotka: Publications of Kymenlaakso University of Applied Sciences. Series A. No. 33.

Roslund, M. (2012, 6 August). Email and telephone interview.

Talouselämä (2013). AMK ammattikorkeakoulut 2013 (UAS Universities of Applied Sciences 2013). 33/2013, 29–35.

Virtanen, A., Keränen, H., Murtovuori, J., Rutanen, J., Yanar, A., Hiltunen, K., and Saarilammi, M.-L. (2012). *Kymenlaakson ammattikorkeakoulun auditointi 2012. (Audit of Kymenlaakso University of Applied Sciences 2012).* The Finnish Higher Education Evaluation Council FINHEEC.

10 UiT The Arctic University of Norway

Challenges at the Arctic crossroads

Elin Oftedal and Lene Foss

Tromsø is the capital of the Arctic.
(Secretary of State H.R. Clinton, 1 June 2012)

Research has shown that, theoretically and empirically, one can argue that innovations occurs more readily in large and densely populated areas where there are specialized market inputs conducive to innovation (Orlando, 2004). Further, innovative performance are often explained by a geographical concentration of similar firms and of research institutes. A key element in the concept of agglomeration economies are localized knowledge spillovers, which reflect the advantages that firms enjoy in accessing knowledge that, intentionally or unintentionally, "spills over" from other firms and research institutes. In such a geographical concentration, universities are important sources of localized knowledge (Ponds *et al.*, 2010). This chapter describes how the establishment of the University of Tromsø, The Arctic University of Norway (UiT Arctic, or simply UiT), has transformed its challenged and remote starting-point into a centre of localized knowledge. As the Arctic north has currently gained more national and international interest because of petroleum and mining resources, the UiT is pivotal in furthering a sustainable development of the north. In addition, the UiT Arctic has developed academic spin-outs and been instrumental in spurring industrial development where there was none. UiT has therefore been an engine for economic development led to increased knowledge about the northern areas of the world. However, the city of Tromsø still faces challenges as a remote region, as there is a lack of financial resources, distant markets, organizational and competency thinness – and thus high vulnerability for new and fledgling businesses (as for established industry). These are challenges which UiT must be instrumental in meeting. This chapter, therefore, is an attempt to give insight into the journey that Tromsø started when their university was created and in understanding the current challenges of the city region.

Developing a regional university in the Arctic: a history of strategy and leadership

Historically, it was not a given that Tromsø would achieve any economic or political significance. The establishment of the University of Tromsø[1] (UiT) was a political decision to achieve economic development in the remote and less developed northern regions of Norway. The north was also facing depopulation due to migration to the south, because of a lack of job opportunities. The political goal of establishing a university to give the northern youth improved educational opportunities and to attract professionals to the region was a heavily criticized idea (cf. Fulsås and Bråstad, 1998). The opposition assumed that the Arctic climate and remoteness would hinder a potential university from attracting the quality and talent desired to develop as a recognized educational institution. It was an intense political debate led by leaders and political visionaries, who argued against the opposition's claim that an Arctic university would not succeed and that there had to be special salary incentives for the faculty and staff relocating to the area (Fulsås and Bråstad, 1998). The Rector of UiT from 2001 to 2013 claimed:

> It was argued that it was perfectly possible to read biochemistry and physiology at remote Arctic locations if you had good textbooks. That argument won and we got a brand new School of Medicine. It was further argued that we should have an entire university. Out of almost nothing, a fully operational university was opened by the Norwegian king on September 1st, 1972. UiT was well funded from the beginning and attracted top academics primarily from Oslo. They wanted to use the new university as a career springboard.
>
> (Jarle Åarbakke, former Rector UiT, interview data)

The Norwegian government was aware of the difficulties a new university in the north would encounter and provided necessary funding to reduce the risk of failure (Fulsås and Bråstad, 1998). Thus, UiT became a part of "building the nation", an important political project after World War II (Simonsen, 2012).[2] Professor Peter F. Hjort, the first Rector of the university and an active leader in the creation of the ideological fundament for the new university, stressed:

> The UiT should be the flagship of regional policy – to educate and enhance the standard of living in northern Norway. The university should serve the people, not only science. The curriculum should be relevant for the region.
>
> (Fulsås and Bråstad, 1998)

From the beginning, the university's location made it a natural venue for the development of international competences with regard to the Arctic environment, culture, and society. The university's strategy was, in that respect, different from the main universities in Oslo, Bergen, and Trondheim in its multifaceted geographical focus. New programmes were continuously developed: the Law School was established in 1987, and the following year the College for Fisheries Science was established as a permanent scientific institution at UiT. In 1991 the Medicine and Health Sciences building was raised, along with the establishment of the Regional Hospital of Northern Norway. Further centres of excellence (CoE) and other targeted research centres were created, such as the Centre for Advanced Study in Theoretical Linguistics (CASTL);[3] the Centre for Theoretical and Computational Chemistry (CTCC);[4] and the Centre for Arctic Gas Hydrate, Environment and Climate (CAGE).[5] Other focus areas for UiT are Aurora Borealis research, space science, fishery science, biotechnology, linguistics, multicultural societies, Saami culture, telemedicine, epidemiology, and a wide spectrum of Arctic research projects. Thus, since 1971, the academic robustness has grown as 1,452 individuals have obtained their PhD degrees at the UiT.

Several initiatives have helped to shape Tromsø into a centre for state-of-the-art Arctic research. In 1984, Forut was created as a research institute for UiT (the research foundation for the University of Tromsø). Forut became Norut on 27 February 1992; the Norut group continued to develop new subsidiaries, but was restructured in 2007.[6] The current structure consist of Norut Alta, Norut Tromsø, Norut Narvik, and Norinnova, and has 130 employees.[7]

Further, the High North Research Centre for Climate and the Environment (FRAM Centre) was established in 2010 and contributes to Norway's management of the environment and natural resources in the High North. The FRAM Centre is an important arena nationally as well as internationally and consists of about 500 scientists from 20 institutions involved in interdisciplinary research in the fields of natural science, technology, and social sciences. The centre communicates science and research-based knowledge to authorities, business communities and the general public. Moreover, the close vicinity of the Norwegian Polar Institute, the Norwegian Institute of Marine Research, and the Polar Environmental Centre gives Tromsø added weight and importance as an international hub for Arctic studies.[8]

One may argue that the decision to create UiT in 1968 proved significant in developing the city by bringing relevant skills to the area. Moreover, the development of UiT has also had more unexpected side benefits. With a growing international recognition of the High North; (e.g. climate change, the opening of the North-East Passage due to ice melting, and petroleum resources), sustainable development in the north is no longer seen as just a regional policy aim, but rather as being of strategic national and international importance. Therefore, the Norwegian government formulated their High North strategy in 2009. The main purpose was to assess how the Arctic regions of Norway could be developed. A working group where UiT was present was established:

> An inter-ministerial committee, headed by the Minister of Foreign Affairs, has coordinated the work on the strategy. Additional expertise has been provided by an external committee of experts chaired by the Rector of the UiT, Jarle Åarbakke, who has drawn on the knowledge and experience to be found in the High North. We have also maintained close contact with a large number of groups and institutions in the High North, and with regional authorities and the Sami Parliament.
>
> (Government Strategy of the High North, 2006)

Both nationally and internationally there is an increased focus on the Arctic areas – and as former Rector Jarle Åarbakke states, the UiT has been a strategic important tool for exploring the north.

> For me the UiT comes before the High North strategy. In addition, just so you know, if the university had not been here, there had been no adequate apparatus for the government to do what they have done.
>
> (interview data)

To continue being a strong regional actor, the university has merged with other institutions in the north. The UiT and the Tromsø College (HiTø) merged in January 2009. HiTø had about 3,000 students and 300 employees (2006 figures). Through the merger, UiT saw an opportunity to establish Tromsø University School of Business and Economics (HHT). UiT was strongly represented in economics, whereas HiTø had a complementary strength in accounting. Furthermore, the private business school, BI Norwegian Business School closed their branch in Tromsø, leaving an opening to exploit the demand for corporate business education. In 2009, HHT opened with and currently offers study programmes at bachelor's, master's, and doctorate levels in economics, business administration, marketing and strategy, management, innovation, and entrepreneurship in addition to an executive MBA programme.

The process of growth through mergers continued: in 2013, the UiT merged with the Finnmark University College, located in Finnmark, the northernmost county of Norway. The new name of the merged institution is UiT The Arctic University of Norway (hereby called UiT Arctic), and it is now the largest research institution in northern Norway.[9] The UiT Arctic hosts 12,000 students on four campuses in the counties of Tromsø and Finnmark: Tromsø in Troms and Alta, Hammerfest, and Kirkenes in Finnmark. HHT has noticed a rapid growth due to the merging processes. In 2009, there were only 17 professional staff and about 300 students at the Business School. Today HHT has 34 permanent academic staff and 1,000 students in Tromsø. In addition, HHT has 12 scientific staff and 400 students in Alta. However, the growth is not just a result of merging processes. In 2014 the applications from students with first priority for the UiT Arctic increased by 30 per cent.

The current strategy of merging denotes the university's specific role in developing and educating the wider region. Further, this role also underlines and drives an incentive to embrace the third mission as stated in the strategy plan document of UiT:

> UiT Arctic shall be a driving force for innovation and economic development in the north ... and UiT Arctic shall stimulate the development of commercially viable ideas and build research that are robust and innovative through collaboration with applied research, innovation, and business environment.
>
> (UiT Arctic strategy document)

The strategy plan was endorsed by the new rector from 2013, Anne Husebekk, who is committed to developing strategies for employing the third mission.

> Traditionally, discussion of the role of universities is very much related to production of graduates. I consider the idea to be extended to knowledge production, research, and bringing research to business. Then, innovation and business development is inherent in the university's third mission. In addition, we are responsible for knowledge transfer to the public sector. We are interested in collaboration at any level of the university's education chain. We invite private and public sector representatives to come to campus. We aim to develop a partnership that can generate cooperation between the public sector, industry, and the university.
>
> (Anne Husebekk, current Rector of UiT Arctic, interview data)

The growth of UiT Arctic is a result of leadership on a national and local political level, but also of strong actors from the different scientific fields. Both tenured professors and the university leadership have played strong roles in the establishment of the university. UiT Arctic is also an example of a political decision in 1968 with an explicit third-stream mission, 30 years before the third mission was introduced in the university entrepreneurship literature. The third mission of UiT Arctic was thus mainly built on education and research for the public sector of the region. In retrospect, few would disagree that the UiT Arctic has been a success. Some lessons can be drawn from the UiT Arctic example: (1) the essence of local leadership to understand and cultivate the potential of a region; (2) the essence of developing unique competence based on an area's natural resources. Table 10.1 presents an overview of the milestones that have shaped UiT's Arctic entrepreneurial education and programmes.

The context of the north: challenges of a peripheral region

Tromsø, with its more than 70,000 inhabitants, is northern Norway's largest city and the administrative centre in Troms County. Historically, UiT Arctic has educated employees for the public sector, as the city has developed into an administrative and academic centre (Fulsås and Bråstad, 1998). Currently, the public sector accounts for about 45 per cent of employment in Troms County and the private sector is small and fledgling. Most of the employment is in public organizations such as the university, the hospital and health sector, and in local government. The centre of gravity in Tromsø revolves around the two main knowledge-based institutions: (1) the University Hospital of Northern Norway (UNN), the city's largest employer with 6,000 employees; and (2) UiT Arctic with 2,500 employees. More than 10 per cent of the citizens of Tromsø work in these institutions. Over the past 20 years, northern Norway has had a far weaker population growth than the rest of the country (2.1 per cent compared to 17.5 per cent at national level). In 2014 there were 479,256 inhabitants in northern Norway, representing only 9.4 per cent of the population in Norway, while the northern counties constituted more than 30 per cent of the land area of the country. The north also has far lower job creation than rest of the country. In ten years, employment has grown by 7.7 per cent in the north, to 236,000 people, compared to 12.6 per cent nationally in the same period. The number of enterprises has grown to 22 per cent in the north, compared with 39 per cent for Norway in the same period. Growth of new firms is thus weaker in northern Norway than in the country overall. Further, generally in the north, businesses only generate 15 per cent of total R&D investment, compared to 44 per cent nationally. Northern Norway has a relatively larger share of the added value of seafood, tourism, and renewable energy. However, adjusted for the industrial structure, investments from the northern Norwegian business sector still remain 42 per cent lower than the national average. Moreover, the proportion of companies with revenues from new products is lower than nationwide in almost all industries, and only 20 per cent of companies are characterized as process and innovation-oriented, compared with 25 per cent nationally (BCG report, 2014). The current rector recognized this issue in the following statement

> We live in a region where companies are relatively small. Many of them do not see the importance of research and development, they cannot afford it, and they are not linked to the university. For example, Finnmark is not used to having a university in the region, so

Table 10.1 Timeline of UiT Arctic entrepreneurial milestones

Spin-outs	Year	Milestone event
	1966	• Application for university
	1968	• University of Tromsø established
	1972	• Opening of UiT, with fisheries programme
	1973	• Medical programme
	1974	• Auroral lights programme
Biotec	1984	• FORUT
Pharmacon	1987	• The research foundation for the University of Tromsø
		• Law School
		• Engineering School
	1990	• Forskningsparken i Tromsø AS (FPT) established, NOK 25 million (US$4 million) seed fund
	1991	• Psychology programme
		• University Hospital
	1992	• FORUT becomes NORUT: NORUT Gruppen AS established with subsidiaries: Fisheries AS, NORUT AS, NORUT Social Research AS, NORUT Technology AS. ~200 employees
	1993	• Norwegian Centre for Telemedicine
Biohenk	1998	
Orthogenics ConTra	1999	• Nord Invest AS established NOK 30 million in a seed money fund
Probio	2000	• Såkorn Invest Nord AS (SINAS) established, merged with Nord Invest. Gen. 1 seed-funding, NOK 75 million (US$12.5 million)
Eximo Trofi	2001	

	Year	
Olivita Calanus	2002	• Centre for Advanced Study in Theoretical Linguistics (CASTL)
BioSea Mgmt Lytix Biopharma	2003	• FPT becomes Norinnova; receives NOK 60 million funding (US$10m)
	2004	• Dentistry programme
	2005	• TTO Nord • NOFIMA
	2007	• Norinnova Invest AS established with NOK 272 million (US$45 million) 2nd generation seed-funding Norinnova Forvalting AS established to manage Norinnova Fond (NOK 60 million), SINAS (NOK 75 million), Norinnova Invest (NOK 272 million) • Centre for Theoretical and Computational Chemistry (CTCC) • Mabcent: Centre for Research-based Innovation established by RCN; hosted by UiT • Merger UiT/Tromsø University College
Stella Polaris Prophylix Pharma	2008	• BCE programme
Globesar	2010	• Tromsø University Business School established
D'Liver Procelo	2011	• Norinnova Technology Transfer
	2012	• Design Thinking Lab • Centre for Arctic Gas Hydrate, Environment and Climate (CAGE)
Optisys AS	2013	• UiT merger with Finnmark University College • Optisys developing a new system for sorting waste in areas with optical sorting • The Research Centre for ARCtic Petroleum Exploration (ARCEx) is a national centre, with national and international partners, hosted at the Dept. of Geology, UiT
	2014	• Chondro Engineering AS should be able to produce cartilage *in vitro* from patients' own cells

they are reluctant. We have therefore appeared at industry conferences and given presentations about the university, attempting to describe the opportunities we provide. We need to interact.

(Anne Husebekk, current Rector, UiT, interview data)

The work of social scientist Ottar Brox has long influenced the northern region. While the central government made plans based on economic efficiency for the development of the north, Ottar Brox presented through his main work that the social context of the north was based on generations of experience and tacit knowledge. The planned policy decisions would compromise the order of life that prevailed in the north, rather than build it. He presented his finding in the book: *What happens in northern Norway* where he showed that the focus on pure economy and profit was erroneous for the north.[10] His work had serious impact and changed the way policymakers looked at the north. His views had resonance in more socialistic movements, where he himself enrolled politically. He had several followers in northern Norway. Although Ottar Brox's contribution was important and welcome in the debate about northern Norway, his engagement might have left a scepticism about commercial activities. At UiT, the main economic focus was resource economics at the Faculty of Fisheries. When UiT Arctic was asked to establish a business school, they first said no. There was also only very little cooperation between industry and academia as the following quote illustrates:

When we first started saying we were going to commercialise research, I was basically chased with a stick down the halls. The scepticism has gone now, however we still struggle with access to capital.

(Karl Johan Jakola, CEO Norinnova Fund Management, interview data)

As the quote indicates, a big challenge for the north is access to capital. Early-phase funding is crucial and in many ways as important as the idea itself. Private capital is needed to unlock public funds, but the north has very limited private capital. Investors with experience within these sectors understand the industry more and become more willing to take risks. Individual wealth has historically been scarce in general in Norway because of the focus on equality and a social profile, but this trend is strengthened in the north. Investments in new businesses require competent capital, which is limited as investors turn to well-known industries such as fisheries, fish farming, real estate, and retail. Investors have scarce experience in the emerging technology sectors in Tromsø, which increases risk averseness. Larger actors that could have helped to meet entrepreneur's needs for capital in Tromsø, such as local banks and the local power company, have had bad experiences in investing in new companies and have become risk averse. The need for public funds is therefore well known and the challenge is strong. In Tromsø, seed funding has dried up, and although there are several ideas that are ready to be commercialized, only one new company was funded in 2014. Further, the investments are smaller than they ideally should be.

There are, however, positive developments in the north: recent reports suggest that Tromsø is becoming more entrepreneurial (Vareide, 2010–2014). Productivity, and thus robustness, is much higher now than it was ten years ago. Overall, companies in the north have shown great adaptability and willingness to invest in the last ten years. The north has been in a unique position compared to the growth shown in governments' financial statements (Konjunkturbarometer for Nord, 2013). The financial turmoil in Europe has had far less impact in the north than for the economy of Norway overall.[11] At the same time as revenue in the north has doubled (in the last ten years), the turnover in Norway has grown less. Thus, northern Norway has the strongest growth in GDP, although still contributing slightly less than the average (93 per cent) (Konjunktur-barometer for Nord, 2013).

Despite varying reports on the dimension of oil reserves in the Barents Sea, petroleum activity is expected to provide even greater impetus to growth in the Arctic. Developments in the oil and gas sectors in the region are expected to be a major impetus to develop more hi-tech businesses, particularly within the supplier industry (Government strategy of the High North, 2006). Other growth sectors such as marine biotechnology, satellite technology, and other areas where the region has special advantages with major natural resources, are potential investment areas.

From science to industry: developing structures for academic entrepreneurship

The entrepreneurial role of a university deals with active commercializa-tion, including strategic and organizational dimensions. According to Ras-mussen and Rice (2012) active support for commercialization of research-based ventures may come through technology transfer office (TTO) activities aiming to actively place resources at the new venture's dis-posal. Furthermore, passive support involves providing an environment where resources are freely available for firms to access – including research, knowledge, and demand for services, complementary firms, and human capital.

At the national level, creating support and incentives to build TTOs, incubators, and science parks followed advice from research. In Tromsø, the UiT Arctic and Norut created Norinnova in 1990 as the tool to com-mercialize research.[12] It has multiple functions, one of which is operating an incubator service located in the science park. In 2005, TTO Nord AS was established as a tool to work with research-based ideas. In 2007 Norinnova was divided in two entities: Norinnova Fund Management

(NFM) and Norinnova AS. Norinnova AS became a development company for research-based start-ups, while NFM became a management company for seed funds. Further, Norinnova and TTO Nord merged in 2010 with the new name Norinnova Technology Transfer (NTT).[13]

NTT focuses on research-based ideas. They act as the tech transfer office for UiT, and aim to be the most preferred innovation partner for R&D groups in northern Norway. The company is a partner for the scientific community in developing research-based innovation, and hosts a business incubator for start-ups. NTT has strategic expertise in marine biotechnology, marine resources, remote sensing technology, and e-health applications. However, taking research-based ideas to commercialization has proven to be a hard job over many years for NTT:

> The scientists are mostly not interested in commercialisation. Thus, it is necessary to make it more lucrative for researchers to pursue their ideas. If we only can get them to submit their ideas and disseminate innovation.... We work with researchers and professors. Most of them are interested in teaching and publishing, which is what they are measured on in their environment. Unfortunately, no system gives them recognition for patents or driving innovative business, so this is a political issue. Obviously, they have some small incentives of getting financial rewards sometime in the future, since the invention might yield returns. In the short term, there are no incentives for encouraging them to commercialise their ideas and thus provide society with innovations. This is a fundamental problem.
>
> (Bård Hall, former director of NTT, interview data)

Generally, Norinnova has established an extensive competence in creating research-based businesses in the north. According to the former director, one of their challenges is to obtain enough capital for start-up companies. A lack of private investors in the region has resulted in small scale start-ups. In their experience, small establishments have proved less successful than larger ones and they find that investments must be a minimum of NOK 4 million in order to increase the survival rate. Another challenge is to find industry partners for their projects with both capital and competences. These partners are especially rare in Tromsø, where the few cases of individuals with market success have been in real estate, retail, or fisheries. A partner should ideally provide the needed market competence and access, as well as industry knowledge. Further, the relevant markets are often far away from Tromsø, indicating a need for international industry knowledge. Finally, there has been a lack of business competence as the public sector has dominated in regional employment. There is a large need for senior business developers with extensive knowledge of the specific markets Norinnova is targeting. Other TTOs are facing similar issues as Norinnova – however, these issues are more pronounced in the north than in more industrial, popu-lous, and central regions.

The Norinnova system has been structured around three seed funds that are now fully occupied beyond reserved funds for follow-up investments.[14] The situation becomes even more critical, because private capital is almost non-existent. The government is in the process of establishing two new nationwide seed funds, to be managed from Bergen and northern Norway. Each fund will be at least 300 million NOK, and companies will need to match government investments with private investments (each 50 per cent). Innovation Norway will administer the state's interest in the funds. Norin-nova has invested a total of NOK 87 million since its inception with a present-day value of NOK 804 million. NTT has contributed to the estab-lishment of 81 companies of which 43 are still active companies, 12 have been acquired, ten fall into a category of infrastructure (i.e. seed capital funds or other support structures), and 16 are bankrupt or have undergone solvent liquidation. That has so far resulted in 600 new workplaces based on technological or market-based opportunities. This leaves NTT with a success rate of 80 per cent, most of which is commercialization of research.

The next section will present three areas of academic entrepreneurship which have been promising in Tromsø, to describe some of the unique experiences connected to each of them.

Tromsø: a "hot spot for cold biotech"

In Tromsø, the biotechnology field was first initiated in 1986 by Dr Jan Raa, a professor who discovered that beta glucan added to fish feed protected the fish against a lethal salmon bacteria (*vibrio salmonicida*). This was the start of Biotec Pharmacon ASA, which was established in 1990, headed by Dr Raa and his student Gunnar Rørstad. Other companies also emerged that were based on the biodiversity in the Arctic marine territories. Among them was a company that initially was looking at extracting enzymes for molecular biology applications in waste streams of the shrimp industry.

Tromsø's biotechnology community is organized within the biotech cluster "Biotech North", a triple helix research and innovation cluster, focusing on research and commercialization of marine bioactive com-pounds from the Arctic. Approximately 500 researchers are engaged in bio-marine sciences at the university and eight other R&D institutions. Biotech North is a cluster of young biotech enterprises and R&D organiza-tions, which cooperate closely with regional funding and development actors (triple helix). The majority of Biotech North's enterprises are active within life-science applications and markets. To date the cluster contains around 30 organizations from both the private and public sector and is receiving support from both public and private organizations; it is funded through an ARENA programme grant from Innovation Norway relying on co-funding from the participant matching public support.[15]

A number of biotechnology companies operate in and around Tromsø in the fields of health and nutrition, medical devices, and molecular diagnostics. Highly skilled personnel from all over the world find their way to this region to explore exciting opportunities within research and industry. This position as an internationally leading region for marine biotechnology, has in turn, resulted in an emerging industry comprising of a range of biotechnology companies with state-of-the-art facilities. Companies in the region are mainly based on marine bioactive compounds from the Arctic and originated either as spin-offs from the UiT, Tromsø's University Hospital, or from the traditional fishery and harvesting industries. There are around 25 biotech companies in the Tromsø region with about 500 employees. These biotech companies develop and produce products applied within nutraceuticals, cosmeceuticals, medical devices and applications, drug discovery, molecular diagnostics, analytic services, consultancy services, and aquaculture.

Several institutions have been established to support the biotech industry. For example, the MabCent-SFI, based in Tromsø, is one of 14 research-based innovation centres initiated by the Research Council of Norway. Through its interaction with the interdisciplinary expertise at the UiT Arctic and other academic partners, the MabCent initiative helps stimulate research, innovation, and the creation of standards for future marine-based discovery and development within marine bio prospecting and biotechnology.

> We came up with the idea of a marine national biobank, it was quite pioneering thinking and the basis for today's MabCent.... That was the sort of elite commitment.
>
> (Jarle Åarbakke, former Rector, interview data)

Another example is Marbank, the national marine biobank coordinating a network of marine collections in Norway. The mission of Marbank and the network is to provide national and international academia and industry with easy access to marine biodiversity, its associated data, and extractable products. There is a special focus on marine bio-prospecting (i.e. the systematic search for interesting and unique genes, molecules, and organisms from the marine environment with features that could be useful to society or have potential for commercial development).

Tromsø's biotechnology actors benefit from well-developed infrastructure for both research and industry that includes the Barents Biocentre (third construction stage at the Research Park in Tromsø), offering state-of-the-art laboratories and office facilities for rent. In addition, NAMAB, a new biotech industry-park, was established in August 2014 with 1,000 square metres of pilot facilities for process development, up-scaling studies, and small-scale production.

Marine bio-prospecting deals with mapping the biodiversity marine species both at the genetic (DNA) and physiological level (compounds). Marine bioprocessing involves the extraction of interesting target compounds from the environment taking a step further so that the research results in new products. The new plant will be able to assist the companies with this. This bioprocessing pilot plant will be marketed to industrial players not only nationally, but also internationally.

(Even Stenberg, interview data)

Interesting examples of companies have emerged from biotech investments in Tromsø. One example is Prophylix Pharma, headquartered in Tromsø, with a subsidiary in New York. It was founded in 2008 by a Norwegian research team, NTT, and the University Hospital of North Norway. Prophylix Pharma AS aims to develop plasma-derived, first-in-class diagnostics for the prevention of life-threatening bleeding in foetuses and new-borns caused by a depletion of blood platelets.

Another example is Lytix Biopharma, a company that claims to have solved the cancer mystery with a technology that activates the patient's own immune system based on nature's defence mechanism. The company now has positive results from initial testing and will do a larger study on human patients. Lytix Biopharma has now relocated its headquarter activities to Oslo, for infrastructure reasons, as the recruitment and competence base became too narrow in Tromsø.

Barentzymes is the latest biotech undertaking in Tromsø. This is a new venture headquartered in Tromsø, based on one of the largest biotech investments in northern Norway, setting up operations with initially 12 employees in Tromsø and Copenhagen. The company focuses on the development of new enzymes for the industrial biotech market using rational bioinformatics tools and new approaches to fast-track enzyme development.

While Karlsen *et al.* (2011) uses the word "meagre" to describe the region's results in the biotechnology industry, they attribute this scarcity to (1) the lack of variety in the region's industry; (2) little knowledge to commercialize research results; (3) lack of inter-firm knowledge and knowledge spillover between local biotechnology companies.[16]

Despite these challenges, the region's biotechnology community continues to grow. In October 2014, UiT Arctic signed an agreement with German Lead Discovery Center, GmbH (LDC), which is part of the Max Planck organization ranked as one of the world's top five research institutions. The collaboration targets new drug development based on the Arctic Ocean's biodiversity and special environment.

LDC is considered to be an important partner for the Arctic BioDiscovery Centre that opened in February 2015. This new centre gathers expertise and infrastructure for bioprospecting and marine biotechnology from UiT, Nofima, SINTEF, IMR, Norut, and UNN in a strategic and organizational superstructure. The centre is being initiated as a project at UiT, but

204 E. Oftedal and L. Foss

the goal is to develop the Arctic BioDiversity Centre as an independent economic entity. These recent developments illustrate the long-term commitment of cooperation among the research institutes, industry, and public authorities of the region, in the support of growth in the biotechnology sector, and the realization of its potential for value creation.

Satellite technology

A small but growing arena in which UiT Arctic takes a leading role is that of satellite technology and earth observation. The companies K-Sat and Spacetec are leading in this field. They have R&D competence from NORUT and the university. The companies take data from different satellites at ground stations from the South Pole to Svalbard, and send data further on to different parts of the world. Other, smaller companies are Dualog and Globesar. Dualog is one of the world's leading independent providers of ship-to-shore data communication services and delivers IT services to ships and electronic reporting systems to fishing vessels. Globesar AS is a Norwegian earth observation company with its head offices located in Tromsø. By processing radar satellite (SAR) images, they are able to map and monitor potential surface movements/settlements of large areas of natural terrain and urban areas. However, this sector also suffers from Tromsø's remoteness from markets and industries. Globesar has created an Oslo office to be nearer to the market and potential partners.

Telemedicine – a challenged promise

Another unique area pioneered by UiT Arctic, founded in the remoteness and isolation of many north Norwegian villages and settlements, is that of telemedicine. With a scattered population, severe weather conditions in the wintertime, and specialist healthcare service in two regional centres only, telemedicine services had a natural basis to grow. The vision of working with remote solutions in healthcare started in 1987, when a telemedicine department of Telecom's research unit in Tromsø was established in collaboration with the University Hospital of Tromsø (UNN), Norut IT, Kirkenes Hospital, and Troms Military Hospital. In 1993, the Norwegian Centre for Telemedicine was established, as a department of the University Hospital in Tromsø.

The Norwegian Centre of Telemedicine (NST) is a national skills service for telemedicine, and one of the world's leading centres for research on telemedicine and e-health. The service has high-level multidisciplinary expertise. In 2002, the NST was designated as the first collaborating centre in telemedicine by the World Health Organization (WHO). In 2006, the NST was designated by the Research Council of Norway as a "centre for research-based innovation" (SFI), and Tromsø Telemedicine Laboratory was established as a research project with the University Hospital of North

Norway, through the NST, as its host institution. The centre has more than 200 employees with strong academic backgrounds.

However, the telemedicine area has received harsh criticism as it has been argued that 25 years of telemedicine has not made Norway a country where such solutions are common practice in healthcare. Furthermore, some feel that, apart from the NST which has managed to commercialize only a few good solutions, there are few telemedicine solutions in use in Norway. The solutions developed at NST have been hard to commercialize outside of northern Norway. One reason for this may be that telemedicine focuses on preventive measures and the private market does not have a larger customer base for such initiatives. There is a hope that new regulation may enable municipalities to be potential customers and thus improve the market situation. A recent master's thesis concludes that there has been a lack of awareness of strategy at NST, and that projects are picked according to academic competence. Business competence is a weakness in the organisation (Ahlkvist, 2014).

It is apparent that Tromsø manages to develop unique knowledge and solutions for important world challenges. However, according to Karlsen *et al.* (2011), the environments are too focused on the academic and less on industrial, market-based applications. A recent paper by Fitjar and Pose (2014) shows that industry networks outside of the local sphere are important for start-ups. The following section describes how Tromsø is developing arenas for networks

Designing the systems – conferences and arenas for networks

University contact is important for supporting research-based innovation (Di Gregorio and Shane, 2003; Powers and McDougall, 2005; Van Looy *et al.* 2011). This may come through a strong network of industrial partners, such as the presence of companies co-located with the university (i.e. in technology centres or science parks) and other industrial linkages. A report by Bye *et al.* (2010), stated that there were too few venues for networking in Tromsø, and that the research sector is not enough involved in industry activities. In order to build unique competence, there is a need for common arenas to discuss current issues and important questions. In recent years, UiT Arctic has created or co-created several arenas and venues for cooperation on issues concerning transfer of knowledge between the university sector and the private sector.

One strategic tool is the Tromsø High North Cluster (THiNC), a strategic alliance of seven research institutions in Tromsø.[17] THiNC is a forum for discussion, information exchange, and strategic cooperation for Arctic-related research. Its ambition is to strengthen Tromsø's position as a knowledge city and as "capital of the north", both nationally and internationally. The participants in the network take active responsibility in the knowledge-based development of the northern regions. This task requires close cooperation between research institutions in the north and coordination of efforts. Furthermore, it creates and arena for establishing national and international projects and conferences that are relevant to the High North. This work also involves strengthening basic and applied High North profile research through cooperation between the partners. Collaboration on recruiting talented students and researchers, as well as developing research training, is gaining emphasis.

An important international arena addressing development throughout the Arctic is the Arctic Frontiers conference. The rationale behind Arctic Frontiers is that increased human activity in the Arctic will have significant economic, political, and social implications for Arctic nations, and will influence Arctic ecosystems. The conference presents a platform to discuss how such opportunities and challenges may be handled to ensure viable economic growth and societal and environmental sustainability. Arctic Frontiers has received recognition as setting the agenda for development in Arctic Norway; therefore the conference attracts an annual attendance of more than 1,000 high-level participants from 25 Arctic and non-Arctic countries, representing science, business, politics, press, and civil society.

One important participant at the Arctic Frontiers, which is also called the secret tool of the UiT, is the High North Academy (HNA), located at the Faculty of Fishery Science at UiT. It aims to educate future researchers and build the competence of current and future researchers. HNA aims develop and coordinate research training courses in transferable skills that, while not necessarily academic at the core, are important in the interface between academia and industry. The overall aim is to increase the quality of research training in the High North and to improve recruitment to High North research.

Another conference that is especially important for marine biotechnology is the biannual Bioprosp conference. It is an international conference on marine biotechnology in Tromsø, and is considered one of the leading conferences in the area after more than ten years' history. The objectives of the conference are to illustrate applications and industry utility of discoveries based on marine bio-prospecting.

In Tromsø, students have also been important in creating arenas for knowledge exchange and networking. A very popular initiative is Håp i Havet (Hope in the Sea). This conference is student driven, originating from the Faculty of Fishery Science. Its focus is fisheries, economy, and marine bioscience. The arrangement has become an important arena where industry and students meet. The conference was first arranged in 2000, but due to its success, it has been a yearly tradition since 2006. The conference has touched upon subjects like value creation and cooperation concerning marine resources. Håp i Havet has grown each year since it started, and the number of participants has reached more than 500.

The circumpolar conference

On a smaller note, in 2012 the Tromsø School of Business and Economics (HHT) arranged a conference focusing on economic development, innovation, and entrepreneurship in Arctic regions. This was the first time HHT arranged an international conference and several students were involved as well as faculty members. The conference provided a unique arena for allowing the industry-research cooperation to influence the public. Speakers were invited from the circumpolar region and from other international and national cooperating partners to showcase expertise within economic development, mining and minerals, energy-related topics, investment and finance, and policy. Industry representatives were present and participated in thematic workshops to create a greater consciousness of the imperative to create good liaisons between industry and university.

   Such network arenas provide a basis for developing relations across different organizations, scientific fields, and disciplines, as well as between academia, industry, and government. An example may be drawn from a series of activities that emerged following the circumpolar conference. A new course was created at HHT: the course was Innovation to Market, in which innovation was related to certain industrial developments in the Arctic. Furthermore, it resulted in a closer cooperation between UiT Arctic's biotech programme (education), the business school and Norinnova, and Artic Frontiers, regarding the basis for a new project application – leading to the employment of a PhD student at HHT in innovation in the mining and mineral sector by autumn 2014.

Towards an entrepreneurial culture through structures

> It is fantastic to have access to young people who actually want to lead start-ups.
>
>   (Bård Hall, former CEO, Norinnova, interview data)

Because of the concentration of the public sector in Tromsø, the relationship between academia and the industry in Tromsø does not have long traditions. This lack of relationship has also made regional industry very slow to recognize the value of the university. Furthermore, local industry was small, mostly based on natural resources with little effort on development – and, as such, saw no need for scientific research. Bye *et al.* (2010) report that current industries do see a need for cooperation; but fear that it is costly and that suitable venues for cooperation do not exist. Although this relationship has improved over the years, industry in Tromsø often complains that UiT Arctic is too detached from the daily needs of local industry. However, the university is constant in its efforts to increase industry interactions. The following quote from the UiT Arctic strategy document describes how the university is expected to work collaboratively with different institutes.

> Commercially exploitable ideas and research results should be developed in collaboration with (the innovation system) Norut, TTO Nord, Norinnova, Nofima, the Norwegian Centre for Telemedicine, institutes such as the Polar Environmental Centre, Energy Campus North, and other communities in the region and the Barents Region. The goal is commercial reorganization and renewal.
>
> (UiT Arctic strategy document)

Inspired by the achievements developed at Chalmers University of Technology, Sweden, UiT Arctic established the Master's of Science in Business Creation and Entrepreneurship (BCE) programme at HHT in 2008.

> The story is: Foreign Minister Jonas Gahr Støre invited his colleague Carl Bildt and 100 Swedish business leaders with Marcus Wallenberg to meet in northern Norway from the 10th to the 12th of June 2007 to challenge the Swedish mentality (and facilitate sales). I chaired a meeting with a big crowd on campus on June 11; in the audience and [speaking] was Boo Edgars Chalmers, and Göteborg University and I agreed that we went for a variation of their BCE, as it was presented for the first time in Norway. The project got financial support from RDA and Innovation Norway and together with Boo Edgar in Chalmers HHT started the first BCE cohort, three students, who had their first term in Chalmers, as it took time to develop the portfolio of courses at the Business School.
>
> (Jarle Åarbakke, former Rector, UiT Arctic, interview data)

As the new business school had faculty in macroeconomics, accounting, and marketing, there were no faculty with an interest in launching an educational programme in business creation. Thus, HHT takes particular responsibility for developing the third mission, as pronounced in their strategy:

> Today's knowledge economy challenges the relationships between universities and industry and today it is expected that universities fulfil their "third mission" by contributing to regional innovation. One way to do this is to commercialise academic knowledge, which the University of Tromsø has a long history in the over 50 spin-offs since 1980 in foods, satellite surveillance, biopharmaceutical, marine bio-prospecting, fisheries and aquaculture, physics, and telemedicine. HHT has established the first international Master's program in Business Creation and Entrepreneurship (BCE) where students with professional knowledge in

the commercialisation of research ideas and then to establish a business based on the idea. HHT will help UiT to become an entrepreneurial university and develop knowledge of the factors that influences UiT his role in the commercialisation of academic research.

(HHT strategy document, unpublished)

The first academic responsible for the new BCE programme was an associate professor in marketing who had practical experience with start-ups and investments, and then an associate professor from organizational sciences. In the first years of the programme, the BCE faculty collaborated extensively with colleagues at Chalmers University to develop the curriculum and to incorporate Chalmers faculty as adjunct professors at HHT. The work to establish a course curriculum was immense, and there was skepticism at HHT. Finally, UiT Arctic saw the need for a chair and a programme director for the BCE, and thus granted a professorship in entrepreneurship and innovation with designated responsibility for the programme in 2010. The faculty director welcomed the demand for strengthening the focus in these areas and funded one associate professorship and two lecturer positions; in this way a strong faculty base was formed. The faculty developed a collaboration model with actors in the research-based ecosystem as shown in Figure 10.1.

An evaluation of the programme was performed in 2012. Courses and industry collaboration have been increasingly enhanced, often with solid input from students. Students are represented on the BCE board; they have been funded to visit student bodies at Chalmers. Many of the students have prior entrepreneurial experience, several with bachelor's or master's level education and varied international experience.

The BCE master's thesis is required to be a solid analytic work assessing the innovation and the market challenges in commercializing research-based

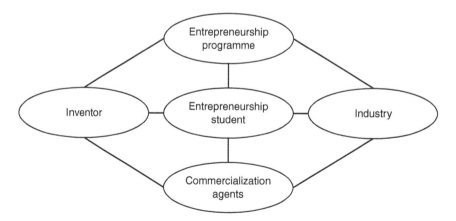

Figure 10.1 The BCE Cooperation Model (source: Foss, 2013).

ideas, typically provided by a UiT Arctic or UNN researcher. The thesis has to contain an umbrella introduction to position the thesis in the academic entrepreneurship literature, and to conclude with a business plan. A team of two or three students works with a professor through the project and receives supervision from BCE faculty and NTT.

BCE students ideally work directly with researchers who have invented new ideas; while professors often do not think in market terms, their purpose is to mentor the students in understanding the technology. The work in assessing commercialization is left for the students to perform. Thus the students gain first-hand experience in dealing with the different knowledge bases in academia and in industry.

> The BCE program trains employees for the portfolio companies. In a way, BCE trains managers and CEOs for these companies. Ideally, we are talking about a subset of ideas in which the inventor has no interest in pursuing the idea professionally. The researcher wants to stay in academia, and there is no one to lead, or take management of the idea further. Ideally, BCE should train candidates to fulfil that role.... In that respect the BCE program is ideal because it perfectly complements their interests.
>
> (BCE student, interview data)

Making an impact – the early results of BCE alumni

The early impact on commercialization from BCE alumni who have entered the labour market can be documented in various ways. Table 10.2 shows that within the first four cohorts (2008–2011) four businesses have been founded, two candidates have secured jobs as business developers in research-based companies and at NTT, and several international students have moved back to their home countries and started businesses. Several master's theses have been productive for establishing companies within NTT. Secondly, several master's theses have been used as input for NTT to help further develop projects such as the Yellow Binder, Procelo and Call-me-Smart.

Table 10.3 shows the companies where BCE students have been employed. Two BCE students have pursued a PhD at HHT and one at NTNU. Companies have employed BCE alumni as business developers. One example is Scandiderma, which develops and markets unique ingredients for high-end cosmeceutical products. Ingredients are based on bioactive compounds from the Arctic, discovered in close cooperation with research institutions such as Bioforsk. Another example is Ramsalt Lab, a web agency specializing in Drupal, a market-leading open source content management system. Ramsalt's clients include universities, online newspapers, and banks – with a global range that includes Chile to the south and Russia to the north. Fourth, and finally, there are two examples of

Table 10.2 BCE project status

Project	Cohort	Industry	Status
Globesar	2010	Satellite technology	Started with student as CEO. Second round financing completed.
D'liver	2011	Biotechnology	Started and sold. Student as CEO. Has now resigned.
Procelo	2011	Biotechnology	The inventor started without students.
Few Touch	2011	IT technology	Not started
Medication Assistance for Elderly Patients	2012	E-health	Not started
Synchronized Media Presentation	2012	E-health	Not started
Edmire Pickups	2012	Music technology	Not started
CallmeSmart	2013	E-technology	Not mature for start-up when students finished their thesis. Students later offered job.
Praqo Logging System	2013	Film technology	Not started. Student got job as intern in NTT and works now as communication officer at Barentzymes.
Fleksee Hygiene Bag	2013	Medical care technology	Not started
Arctic Terra Preta	2014	Agriculture	Testing procedures due before start-up
Chondro	2014	Medical technology	Must reach proof of concept.
UArctic Student Portal	2014	IT technology	Development project, already up and running. Student is employed.
Ramsalt Lab	2014	IT technology	Development project in existing company.
Arctic Bio Plants	2014	Nutraceutical	Will start. Student offered CEO position, but too late.
Kystens Mathus	2014	Retail	Already established project.
Turismeprosjekter	2014	Tourism	Student's own idea
Kildeboksen	2014	Waste removal	Already established project.

Table 10.3 Employment of BCE students

Company	Year established	Sector
Vijaya Development Resource Centre	1979	Non profit
Norinnova	1993	Business development
Taco Scientific	2009	Information technology
Scandiderma	2010	Cosmeceuticals
Globesar	2010	Information technology
Ramsalt Lab	2010	Information technology
D'liver	2011	Biotechnology
Kvalvik/Polybait	2011	Biotechnology
Moose on the Loose	2011	Retail
PhD candidate in International Entrepreneurship at NTNU	2013	Academia
PhD candidate in Innovation and Entrepreneurship in the Energy Sector at UiT	2013	Academia
PhD candidate in Academic Entrepreneurship at UiT	2013	Academia
Barentzymes	2013	Biotechnology
Lab for Design Thinkers	2013	Business development
ShapeClub24	2013	Nutraceutical
Pre-incubation Start UP	2013	Information technology
Hammerfest Kommune	2013	Community development

BCE students who, based on their theses, were offered CEO positions in a start-up company.

The BCE programme has developed through the years based on input from students and businesses, and close cooperation with NTT. While it is too early to judge the impact of the programme on regional innovation, it is apparent that it has been fruitful in educating a new type of candidate from UiT Arctic with commercialization skills. The BCE programme forms business developers who contribute to a more entrepreneurial culture in Tromsø by their active participation in regional industries.

> There have, however, been challenges in matching the expectations of the inventor to the expectations of the industry: the main challenge is to connect the business role with the scientific role. It is hard to understand both – it is hard to make inventors believe the information you have been provided from the business point of view, and you have to listen. We had an issue with competitors. It would be impossible for there to be no competitors, but it was hard for inventors to believe.
>
> (BCE student, interview data)

The BCE programme faces another big challenge in effective interaction and communication between all the relevant parties involved. There needs to be chemistry between the student team and the inventor that leads to trust to take the chance to develop a company. Further, there should be good communication between the inventor and NTT to have the proper financial support in place. Additionally, the students are inexperienced – and to be a manager of a technology start-up often involves a steep learning curve.

> What we are seeing is that we have ideas that are very complex and it takes quite some time to familiarize oneself with the technology and the market. Even if the students are brilliant or knowledgeable for their age, they are still young and immature. They cannot take the lead to begin with, and they can seldom create contacts of high importance. It takes a lot of effort to support the student groups, but this is a task we can do – if we are talking about the market risk. However, if we are talking about technology risk, that is something that the researchers must do themselves.
>
> (Bård Hall, former CEO, NTT, interview data)

Furthermore, it is challenging to balance highly practical work with academic competence. The students are often practically oriented and focused on entrepreneurship. Several of them wish to have more time to focus on developing their own ideas. The thesis, on the other hand, should be of high enough academic quality that students can later apply for PhD positions.

One experience from working with this programme is that Tromsø is surrounded by a larger region with small businesses that are resource-based, rather than knowledge- or technology-based. The region is based on natural resources and has fewer skilled technology jobs than other regions. One may argue that the industries have weak absorptive capacity that currently do not allow for hiring BCE candidates. This is due to the business structure in the north, but also the to the fact that BCE is an international programme – and that highly capable foreign workers with limited Norwegian language skills have trouble becoming employed. Furthermore, entrepreneurship education at HHT started late and is still in its nascent phase. The immediate reactions from UiT and management are positive – but it will take time for the region to create the capacity to absorb the new type of competence.

However a development is that more student-based initiatives are emerging from the BCE programme. Examples are: a dinner-sharing service, "purple dinner"; a social network for students, employ.me; and the co-working space Flow, created by Andreas Nilsen, BCE alumni and founder of Moose on the Loose. Flow is, in addition to being a co-working space, a facilitator for several network arrangements and is becoming an important element in the entrepreneurial landscape in Tromsø.

Signals from the management of the programme, and from students and partners is that BCE will benefit from a closer cooperation with other faculties, in order to recruit students in biotechnology, IT, petroleum, geology, etc. Northern Norway needs to expand in terms of commercialization competence. Another enhancement would be to couple PhDs in biotech, IT, technology, and geology as idea providers for the students, as a supplement to the ideas from NTT. The reason for this is two-fold. First, PhDs may be more willing than established scientists to have a commercialization team of master's students helping them. Second, the CEO of NTT is quite clear that the maximum number of research ideas from the university/research institutions is three or four per year. Thus, widening the variety of idea providers may give BCE students a larger pool of ideas to work on. Currently the BCE is developing into three tracks. (1) business development, where students work with a challenge in an established company; (2) innovation, where students work with the commercialization of a technological innovation; and (3) entrepreneurship, where the idea may be very creative although less technological.

Getting the creativity out through innovative structures: the Lab for Design Thinkers

In January 2013, faculty from UiT Arctic School of Business opened the Lab for Design Thinkers (DT Lab), a hub for hands-on co-creation and innovation through design thinking.[18] A kick-off event was held that screened an introductory movie on design thinking to150 people. Shortly after, the DT Lab attracted a group of 13 culturally and professionally diverse students to work voluntarily to develop the Lab further. The main driver behind the establishment of the new invention was lecturer Federico Lozano, a graduate from Stanford University.

> As a lecturer in practical entrepreneurship at UiT, I realized early on that there was a significant opportunity to increase the link between the classroom and the business world. Students were increasingly requesting more real-world experiences, and companies were in search of fresh talent and ideas. Having been exposed to design thinking during graduate school, I knew this methodology would serve as the glue, if you will, *between* the private sector and academia in Tromsø.
>
> (Federico Lozano, UiT, interview data)

The DT Lab was offered a seed grant from the BFE faculty during the first month of operations, and the necessary space to launch the initiative. In September of 2013, the DT Lab was also granted a significant amount of funding from Innovation Norway. This grant, in addition to UiT Arctic funding, allowed the DT Lab to hire two recently graduated master's students from the School of Business and Economics to run the daily operations of the Lab full time. Finally, the Lab was able to garner significant revenues from sales to the private sector, through creativity and innovation workshops. Today, the DT Lab works with companies, organizations, and students to increase innovation and creativity in the northern region of Norway. The DT Lab offers a great variety of services including workshops, innovation project consultancy, pre-incubation, and lecturing. Throughout the first 11 months of operations, the DT Lab has collaborated to different extents with more than 30 local companies, and more than 600 students have been exposed to design thinking through lectures and student workshops. Furthermore, 12 student internships and/or jobs have originated from student–company collaborations in the DT Lab.

Companies approach the Lab with a variety of issues. Drytech AS, a local company that produces dried food for both the private and military market, approached the Lab after one of their managers had attended a design thinking introduction workshop. Drytech's challenge was to gain more insights into the thought-processes of their current customers. For example, Drytech currently uses significant resources on producing products that have a shelf life of more than five years, but they were unsure whether this feature is really valued by their customers. By empathizing and learning more about their customers, Drytech hopes to spend their resources more efficiently in the future.

The DT Lab collaborates with companies in the oil industry, the IT sector, and biotechnology, amongst others. Common to these companies is a dedication to improvement and change through innovation. Through workshops and design challenges, the DT Lab helps these companies approach their business challenges. The DT Lab helps company employees understand the value of adopting a user-centric perspective, and of prototyping and iterating often and quickly. Many companies in Norway tend to be well structured and organized – yet they lack a sense of exploration, flexibility, and play. The Lab helps these companies and their employees identify their creative inner selves through workshops and engagements. The pool of companies interested in working with the DT Lab has grown steadily, and the university administration – at the highest levels – has shown increasing interest in expanding the DT Lab's reach. Research has documented that creating positive attitudes and norms toward third stream activities is a long and arduous process (Jacob *et al.*, 2003; Siegel *et al.*, 2004).

The latest development of the DT Lab is the "social innovation bunker" which will focus on solving societal needs through innovative methods.

New initiatives for student entrepreneurship

"The Young Entrepreneur Initiative", a regional collaboration for spurring the entrepreneurial competence and culture within the north, saw its first day in 2010. HHT, together with Harstad University College and Narvik University College, based on the BCE experience, was granted a two-year project from Innovation Norway. This project included establishing a case-pool of firms and a mentor network, funding an excursion to learn about entrepreneurial programmes at Chalmers, and organizing a large student workshop, "Idegnisten", during which students spent two days solving problems for local entrepreneurs. The project led to closer cooperation and a focus on student entrepreneurship activities between the partnering institutions.

The funding from the Young Entrepreneur Initiative sparked the first local START team at UiT Arctic in 2010. START is an international student organization with a strong presence in Norway. Their main event is the Venture Cup, during which student entrepreneurs compete to win funding for their venture. In the national Venture Cup finals in 2011, a BCE alumni team won second place. Furthermore, the 2012 local winner in Venture Cup became a working case for a team of current BCE students. Thus, a combination of researchers' project initiatives, the national awareness of the School of Business and Economics, and the following local start-up at UiT Arctic, shaped local platforms for students and would-be entrepreneurs to explore their entrepreneurial interests.

Venture Cup has also been transferred into a part of business students' curriculum in a subject called "Commercialization." Here students develop their own ideas and write a formal business plan, which gives students credit points in addition to participation in the Venture Cup competition. Twenty-four ideas were formed, and six were picked for the local finals. From that, two ideas were formally registered and four teams are considering moving on with their project. A trend here is that the teams that were picked to compete in Venture Cup have shown the most interest in continuing their project. The results of creating a competition element within the entrepreneurship programme are therefore promising.

A further development will be to gather the entrepreneurship and innovation activities in a separate centre, which will also host a student incubator. In this way, the focus on entrepreneurship and innovation gathers momentum within the whole university.

The future

The case of UiT Arctic is important in showing the crucial role a university may fill in creating activity in a remote city or region, and in understanding how it may be developed further. The UiT Arctic was controversial when it was established, but it soon put critics to shame. Although it initially started small and focused on the public sector, the university has since focused on developing unique competence based on its location in an Arctic environment. Furthermore, the university has captured and codified new knowledge that may be academically significant, in addition to having commercialization potential. In an era defined by a knowledge-based economy, UiT Arctic has become central in the national university landscape. In its 40 years of existence, UiT Arctic has developed from a regional university in the periphery to a sophisticated global centre for Arctic research.

Through the influence of government policy and larger academic institutions, the city of Tromsø has developed, which in turn has attracted other public and private sector institutions. Tromsø's location and infrastructure, with a good seaport and airport, have been important for its development. Nevertheless, the city's future growth depends on increasing innovation capacity in the private sector and the ability to recruit and retain professionals. One can argue that the former Rector Åarbakke started a pro-industry policy at the university which has helped to accomplish the third mission. The leader of the business school has also read the market well and supported entrepreneurship programmes such as the BCE. With the BCE programme, one sees that graduates pursue entrepreneurial opportunities and slowly change the landscape. Students are important in changing the culture and it may be wise to support students' activities. Further, the Design Thinking Lab is an example that has created enormous interest, as every company is welcome. The business school of Tromsø welcomed the BCE and gave it much support, despite early scepticism. Entrepreneurship and commercialization do not necessarily resonate in a classic economic environment at a university that has been directed toward the public. Furthermore, HHT is a business school and focuses on market needs and programmes that are economically defendable. The BCE programme is vulnerable in that it is small, and perhaps the expectations have been higher than the programme has delivered so far.

While UiT Arctic has made significant contributions, the challenges it faces remain strong. The Arctic still struggles with remoteness and isolation. Companies with intentions to grow still relocate to the Oslo area. The region also loses talent to the southern regions, where career opportunities are more plentiful. However, it may seem like both the university and the northern region are in a transition phase. The university is experiencing an institutional shift towards a large array of new faculties performing research and education relevant for the economy and well-being in the Arctic. The northern region itself is transforming through new developments of natural resources and through competence accumulated over the years. The University therefore has an important role in converting resource-rich northern Norway into an attractive place to live and for business to flourish.

Notes

1 Later: University of the Arctic.
2 The majority of cities in northern Norway was burned to the ground when German troops withdrew from the area in the late stages of World War II.
3 CASTL is a Norwegian Centre of Excellence in theoretical linguistics with a lively graduate school and research atmosphere.
4 CAGE is a world leader in gas hydrate research studying how methane release affects the marine environment and climate system. Read more at: https://cage.uit.no/.

5 The Centre for Theoretical and Computational Chemistry (CTCC) is a Norwegian Centre of Excellence (CoE) shared between the Universities of Tromsø and Oslo, established by the Research Council of Norway for a ten-year period in 2007. Led by ten principal scientists, the CTCC comprises about 60 members, in addition to visiting researchers from all over the world. Read more at www.ctcc.no/.

6 Norut consisted of Fiskeriforskning AS, Norut Informasjonsteknologi AS, Norut Samfunnsforskning AS, and Norut Teknologi AS.

7 Norut AS and Norut Gruppen AS merged into one company on 4 December 2007; Northern Research Institute Tromsø AS. All the Norut companies got new names and logos. The new companies are (short name in parentheses): Northern Research Institute Tromsø (Norut Tromsø), Northern Research Institute Narvik (Norut Narvik), Northern Research Institute Alta (Norut Alta).

8 The Arctic Council (1996) was established as a forum for the circumpolar collaboration in the whole Artic, and Tromsø received the administrative seat of this forum in 2013.

9 In comparison, the University of Nordland (UiN) has about 6000 students.

10 Brox (1966).

11 Strong economic growth in China has stimulated demand for metal and raw material production in northern Norway, and growing demand for fish has given the region the basis for a very successful aquaculture industry with tremendous growth over the past ten years.

12 Structure of ownership: Northern Research Institute (Norut) 50.6 per cent; SIVA Selskapet for industrivekst SF 22.8 per cent; Statoil Technology Invest AS 9.4 per cent; Sparebank 1 Nord-Norge Invest S 3.7 per cent; Troms Kraft Invest AS 3.5 per cent; Gjensidige Forsikring ASA 3.5 per cent; Fondet ved Universitetet i Tromsø 2.9 per cent; Universitetssykehuset Nord-Norge 2.2 per cent; Helse-Nord RHF 0.8 per cent; Hurtigruten Group ASA 0.8 per cent.

13 It is one of four national TTOs; in addition to serving the university, they collaborate with Norinnova AS to assist in commercializing ideas and research results. They are part of the national innovation system administered by the Industrial Development Corporation of Norway, which is a national cooperation owned by Norwegian Ministry of Trade and Industry. Their ambition is to "develop strong regional and local industrial clusters through ownership in infrastructure, investment and knowledge networks as well as innovation centers".

14 The first generation of seed funds was created when Norinvest was set up with approximately NOK 30 million in 1998; it was merged into Såkorninvest Nord in 2000 when the Såkorninvest Nord capitalized at NOK 75 million; Såkorninvest Nord was discontinued on 1 January 2014. In 2007, the Norinnova Investment Fund was established with NOK 272 million. These are the second-generation seed capital funds in Norway.

15 It has received Arena status and is funded through the Arena Programme. Previously the cluster secretariat was administrated by the Troms Chamber of Commerce and partly financed by the regional development fund RDA – Tromsø.

16 As the publication was based on data from 2008, a future task would be to do a follow up and test the growth of the marine biotech industry.

17 University of Tromsø, Norsk Polarinstitutt, Norut, Institute of Marine Research, Nofima, Akvaplan Niva, Tromsø University Hospital

18 Design Thinking is an innovation process which originated in Stanford University in California. The methodology is often used in the creation of new products, services, or processes, and companies such as Apple, Deutsche Bank, Phillips, and Procter & Gamble actively use design thinking in their operations. Design thinking as a methodology differs from other and more traditional innovation processes by its extreme focus on user empathy, prototyping, and testing.

References

Ahlkvist, C.E. (2014). Forvaltning av innovasjonsoppdrag gjennom strategisk arbeid Med utgangspunkt i telemedisinindustrien (Master's thesis, University of Tromsø).

BCG report (2014). http://sikt2014.no/files/SIKT_Rapport_Final_22.09.14.pdf

Brox, O. (1966). *Hva skjer i Nord-Norge? En studie i norsk utkantpolitikk (What happens in northern Norway?)* Oslo: Pax.

Bye, G.; Olsen, T.H., Gunnarson, D., Bæck, U.D.K., Moilanen, M. and Olsen, F. (eds) (2010). *Vi vil, vi vil, men får vi det til?* VRI rapport. Norut Tromsø/Høgskolen i Harstad.

Di Gregorio, D. and Shane, S. (2003). Why do some universities generate more start-ups than others? *Research Policy*, 32(2), 209–227.

Fitjar R. and Pose, A.R. (2014). The geographical dimension of innovation collaboration: Networking and innovation in Norway. *Urban Studies*, 51(12), 2572–2595.

Foss, L. (2013). Innovasjon gjennom akademisk entreprenørskap: Nye samarbeidsmodeller for utdanning av entreprenører (Innovation through academic entrepreneurship: New models of collaboration for the education of entrepreneurs). In H. Garmann Johnsen and O. Pålshaugen (eds), *Hva er innovasjon? Perspektiver i norsk innovasjonsforskning* (pp. 215–238), Oslo: Cappelen Damm Akademisk.

Fulsås, N. and Bråstad, E. (1998). *Et Kort Tilbakeblikk tarbeidet av Kortversjon av boka Universitetet i Tromsø av Narve Fulsås.* University of Tromsø.

Government strategy of the High North (Regjeringens nordområdestrategi) (2006). www.regjeringen.no/globalassets/upload/kilde/ud/pla/2006/0006/ddd/pdfv/302927-nstrategi06.pdf

Jacob, M., Lundqvist, M., and Hellsmark, H. (2003). Entrepreneurial transformations in the Swedish university system: The case of Chalmers University of Technology. *Research Policy*, 32(9), 1555–1568.

Karlsen, J., Isaksen, A., and Spilling, O.R. (2011). The challenge of constructing regional advantages in peripheral areas: The case of marine biotechnology in Tromso, Norway. *Entrepreneurship and Regional Development*, 23, 235.

Konjunkturbarometer for Nord (2013). www.kbnn.no/#/.

Orlando, M.J. (2004). Measuring spillovers from industrial R&D: On the importance of geographic and technological proximity. *Rand Journal of Economics*, 35(4), 777–786.

Ponds, R., Van Oort, F., and Frenken, K. (2010). Innovation, spillovers and university–industry collaboration: An extended knowledge production function approach. *Journal of Economic Geography*, 10, 231–255.

Powers, J.B. and McDougall, P.P. (2005). University start-up formation and technology licensing with firms that go public: A resource-based view of academic entrepreneurship. *Journal of Business Venturing*, 20, 291–311.

Rasmussen, E. and Rice, M.P. (2012). A framework for government support mechanisms aimed at enhancing university technology transfer: The Norwegian case. *International Journal of Technology Transfer and Commercialisation*, 11(1/2), 1–25.

Siegel, D.S., Waldman, D.A., Atwater, L.E., and Link, A.N. (2004), Toward a model of the effective transfer of scientific knowledge from academicians to practitioners:

Qualitative evidence from the commercialization of university technologies. *Journal of Engineering and Technology Management*, 21(1/2), 115–142

Simonsen, G.L. (2012) Medisinutdanning ved Universitetet i Tromsø som redskap for regional endring i Nord-Norge. Masterprogram i region og regionalisering, Universitetet i Bergen

UiT Arctic strategy document (n.d.). http://en.uit.no/om/art?p_document_id=377752&dim=179033.

Van Looy, B., Landoni, P., Callaert, J., van Pottelsberghe, B., Sapsalis, E., and Debackere, K. (2011). Entrepreneurial effectiveness of European universities: An empirical assessment of antecedents and trade-offs. *Research Policy*, 40(4), 553–564.

Vareide, K. (2010). Nærings NM. NHO Rapport Nett: www.nho.no/kommunekaringer.

Vareide, K. (2011). Nærings NM. NHO Rapport Nett: www.nho.no/kommunekaringer.

Vareide, K. (2012). Nærings NM. NHO Rapport Nett: www.nho.no/kommunekaringer.

Vareide, K. (2013). Nærings NM. NHO Rapport Nett: www.nho.no/kommunekaringer.

11 Stavanger

From petroleum focus to diversified competence through crisis and consensus

Elin Oftedal and Tatiana Iakovleva

Stavanger: entrepreneurial past – academic future?

Mounting interest in the university's economic development role is typically stimulated by high-profile examples of successful regional economies in which the university contribution to the industry is identified (Lester, 2005). Stavanger provides a different story, in which industry has fuelled university growth. The idea of establishing a university in Stavanger was introduced in 1965. Yet in spite of strong internal support, it took a long struggle – academically, politically, and financially – to realize the university's launch in 2005.

Since the university has a rising role in Stavanger's innovation ecosystem, it is important to understand its history and context in one of the most expansive regions in Norway (NHO, 2013). The Stavanger region is internationally oriented, and has traditionally prided itself on its entrepreneurial culture. At the same time, it has remained a main agricultural region, measured by production output, as well as an important region for aquaculture. The city of Stavanger is the centre of the Norwegian oil and gas industry, an industry with a growing dynamism. Yet, the present situation is a result of earlier struggles, crises, and defeat. In the 1800s, the city of Stavanger had a strong economy based on the herring and shipbuilding industries. As the herring industry ended in 1870, the canning industry emerged; this, and shipbuilding, were the town's main industries. In the early 1960s, the canning industry suffered decline, and the city was in need of another economic driver. Local politicians looked towards academia and articulated the need to build a regional university. However, there was little enthusiasm outside the region to establish a university in Stavanger, as the nation's attention was largely focused on the Arctic.

The city of Tromsø had benefited from a new university, leaving only minor funds for academic development in Stavanger. Yet, these events took a dramatic change in 1973 with the discovery of oil in the North Sea Basin and the announcement of the first licensing round. The oil sector became the city's new economic platform, and the need for new competence contributed to the formation of a new academic environment built around the petroleum sector. In 1986 the Rogaland University Center was established, which included Regional College and Stavanger Engineering College. Almost the same years, 1988, a Stavanger College of Nursing was established, which included Sanitar Union Nursing School and Red Cross Nursing School.

Stavanger University College (HiS), the forerunner to the university, was established in 1994 through the merger of six public colleges and one private college in Stavanger, including Rogaland University Centre, Norwegian School of Hotel Management, Stavanger Teacher College Conservatory of Music, Social Stavanger College, Stavanger College of Nursing, and the Norwegian Church Congregation College.

HiS continued to pursue its goal to attain university status, and in August 2004 a commission announced that HiS was approved as a university. In January 2005, 40 years after the initiative had begun, the University of Stavanger (UiS) was launched by the king of Norway.

University leadership, at that point, wanted the university to be known for a focus on entrepreneurship and innovation. However, local economic pressure steered the focus towards the energy industry; and while the Stavanger economy is strong, an underpinning concern is whether an "oil-infused" regional economy can foster and maintain a viable entrepreneurial spirit and activity. This chapter therefore focuses on how Stavanger's competence as petroleum hub has spurred university development, which is now laying a foundation for diversified business development.

The first section describes key institutions in Stavanger and how the petroleum industry influenced the formation of the university, with a focus on current regional activities. This introduction to the University of Stavanger and other educational institutions will thus give an overview of regional academic and entrepreneurial initiatives.

The petroleum era impact on university as a regional goal

Making Stavanger the Norwegian base of petroleum activity was an act of civic entrepreneurship from the city administration and business leaders. Stavanger had paved the way for the international exploration companies, with base areas and infrastructure. Thus the oil service industry in Stavanger got its start even before the first commercial discovery was made in 1973 (Ministry of Petroleum and Energy, 2013). International offshore oil exploration companies needed a base area for their onshore support operations. At this same time, Stavanger's local businesses and politicians led by Mayor Arne Rettedal were searching for new economic activities. These regional leaders created a strategy to stimulate foreign oil companies to base their Norwegian business activities (including homes and schools), in Stavanger which helped win the competition over alternative regions in Norway. Between the 1960s and 1970s, Stavanger's population grew by more than 50 per cent.[1] Industrial workplaces were created as multinational oil production and service companies established themselves in the region. Stavanger became the global headquarters for Statoil, the Norwegian national oil company responsible for the main source of national income. Statoil also played an important role in stimulating local industrial innovation and the development of innovative supplier firms. Several international oil companies located in the region, including Phillips, which placed its largest non-US unit in Stavanger, making the city an important global arena for petroleum-based industry.

However, despite early economic growth, the petroleum industry showed itself volatile and vulnerable to challenges. In 1998, petroleum prices were at a historic low of $8 a barrel. Nationally and locally, there was a deep concern about the region's (and indeed the nation's) economic future. This crisis led to strong cooperation between the municipalities in the Stavanger region, and an initiative called the ARNE Project that was established in 1999. The idea was to develop a platform for diversification in the region through creating systems and networks for entrepreneurial activity.

This project involved cooperation among major leaders and stake-holders in the region – and committees and workgroups developed a consensus among the major partners. The ARNE Project established working groups across the region, aided by the Stavanger Chamber of Commerce. Several cross-company networks were created which served as arenas to discuss common challenges and to develop a consensus on controversial issues. The project was successful in creating a sense for a common direction within the region as politicians managed to identify common interests, mutual goals, and appropriate strategies. ARNE's success resulted in the project being expanded to include 11 municipalities – and thus became the Greater Stavanger Economic Development (GS) organization, which today acts as a catalyst for regional economic development.

The most tangible outcome from this process was a strategic plan for the region: Strategisk Næringsplan (SNP). Greater Stavanger's SNP included both short- and long-term goals and suggested an implementation plan across three strategic sectors: (1) food production, including development of culinary expertise, (2) culture, and (3) energy, mainly focused on oil and gas. Common among all three strategic sectors was that they should be knowledge based, and so the goal was articulated to establish a fully fledged university in Stavanger. It was also determined that the university, in addition to educating the talent base to support these sectors, would facilitate networks and support local initiatives concurrent with the strategic plan. There were already several educational institutions with limited offerings, in and around Stavanger, prior to 1965. Established in 1969, Rogaland Regional College focused on an engineering programme that, since 1984, has served the petroleum industry. In 2000, it was decided that a university should be established, and to implement this goal the University Foundation was originated. Monetary support of NOK 100 million from a large municipality-owned energy company, Lyse Kraft, was injected into the University Foundation with the aim that the University College of Stavanger would receive full university status. An application for full university status was submitted 2003 to the NOKUT,[2] which is the controlling authority for educational activity at all Norwegian universities. The application was accepted in 2005.

The current challenge: fostering a strong academic platform

The establishment of the University of Stavanger in 2005 was a milestone in the region's competence as well as its cultural, social, and economic life. Ten years after its establishment, the university has 10,100 students and 1,350 administration, faculty, and service staff that serve three faculties: the Faculty of Social Sciences (FSS), the Faculty of Science and Technology (FST), and the Faculty of Arts and Education (FAE). The university's structure is depicted in Appendix 11.1. University programmes include 34 batchelor's, 28 master's, as well as eight PhD programmes. UiS's links to industry are strong, and its educational programmes have been targeted to meet industry needs for special competences. For employers, the demand for a quality workforce led to continuous competition for competence in the public and the private sector, making it crucial for industry and university to cooperate. This translates into regional career opportunities and university students find jobs with relative ease. A study from 2011 (TNS Gallup) shows that 94 per cent of UiS students found relevant work within six months. This is important for local industry, and UiS (as an important supplier of a competent labour force in the region) has a recruiting effect. Further, UiS has built strong links towards external institutions such as the International Research Institute of Stavanger (IRIS) and Stavanger University Hospital (SUS) for both research and commercialization purposes.

Nevertheless, a main challenge for the University of Stavanger is financing of research, which is typically awarded according to established research and publishing points. Not having accumulated strong research communities, newer universities like UiS are in a weaker position in comparison to older, traditional universities. The development of UiS has been accomplished with limited financial aid from the government – and while their strategy prioritizes research alongside education and commercialization, the lack of funding is underscored as a serious challenge for fostering research activities and their associated innovations.

Strategic areas of development and collaboration for research

The University of Stavanger established three main strategic areas for research and development: (1) energy, technology, and environment; (2) security and management of risk – locally and globally; and (3) professional areas such as science of education, health-related areas, and tourism.

The majority of externally financed research activities occur in cooperation with the research institute that is partly owned by UiS: International Research Institute of Stavanger (IRIS). Established in 1973 and renewed in 2006, IRIS remains an independent research institute, with research and related activities in petroleum, new energy, marine environment, biotechnology, the social sciences, and business development. IRIS employs 210 employees of 25 different nationalities, who are teamed with UiS scientific personnel, on an individual basis.

Another main research partner is the University Hospital (SUS), which employs 7,300 people, including 100 staff with doctoral degrees, 25 of these being professors. Thirty-six SUS employees work partly for the university. Fifteen PhD defences are juried annually and 140 scientific articles were published in international journals by SUS employees in 2011. UiS also works on occasion with other regional institutions and colleges such as Business School BI Stavanger, the Norwegian School of Veterinary Science, and Diakonhjemmet Collegde Rogaland (described in Appendix 11.2).

UiS emphasizes the combination between education, research, and innovation through the Centre for Innovation Research. Viewing research on innovation as a driver for value creation and the development of welfare in a global economy, the Centre for Innovation Research has developed unique competences in entrepreneurship and in innovation processes at the national, regional, and firm level. The centre contributes to a greater interaction between researchers at UiS and IRIS, which elevates the quality of this research.

Several other UiS entities also have centres for innovation within their organizational structure, including ICT (CIPSI), oil recovery (COREC), energy (Cense), and integrated operations (CIAM). UiS is committed to innovation in non-technology sectors such as food. The Centre for Reading Research also promotes innovation in UiS. These varied research centres contribute to the development of cutting-edge research in diverse disciplines and foster innovation across UiS. This widespread pursuit of innovation has helped the University of Stavanger become the only Norwegian member of the European Consortium of Innovative Universities (ECIU). An overview of UiS innovation centres including their research focuses, ownership, and year of establishment, can be found in Appendix 11.3.

Industry

While the national government discounted Stavanger as a university city, the presence of strong industry provided a dynamic force in the development of targeted education, as well as research in crucial industry themes. In fact, it is a common understanding that without this strong industry, UiS would not have been established – a view reflected in the following quote by the former university president.

The private sector – and in particular the business community in the region – has been exceptionally important for the university. The private sector has had the role of a midwife for the establishment of the University of Stavanger and has great expectations for future development. The private sector is also a source of future growth, as UiS become increasingly dependent on external funding from industry.

(Per Ramvi, former UiS President, 2013)

The Rogaland region has more than 250,000 employed people, and is a mixed manufacturing and service region. This city is the petrocapital of Norway with most of the oil/gas industry (55 per cent of the national employment) and a large share of the maritime and metal industries. Currently, there is a total of 338 active companies and the number of persons employed in the oil industry in the Stavanger region has increased since 2006 from 19,000 to 29,000, representing a compound annual growth rate of 7.1 per cent (Ministry of Energy, 2013). The region also has a very strong manufacturing base (22 per cent of all employment), specialized in oil/gas and maritime manufacturing, hi-tech manufacturing, agriculture, and partly in consulting industries. The strong economy has led to the lowest unemployment rate in the country at 1.8 per cent in 2013 (SSB). The companies' total revenues from oil and gas activities in the region was nearly NOK 90 billion in 2012. This makes Stavanger Norway's largest region within the petroleum sector in terms of income. The image of Stavanger as Norway's largest oil region is strengthened when considering that a full 15 per cent of the region's employees work in the oil industry.

However, not only petroleum-based energy has been important for Stavanger. One of the regions' emerging sectors is based on hydro power. Lyse is a Norwegian industrial group in energy and fibre-based broadband. The group started operations on 1 January 1999, but has roots going back more than 100 years. The Lyse Group is owned by 16 municipalities in the Greater Stavanger region. It was originally based on hydro power from waterfalls, the construction of hydroelectric power stations, and the grid network that came to the region as a whole. The Lyse Group has developed into a major national player in renewable energy. With experience from the construction and operation of infrastructure, the group has established itself as the national leader in fibre-optic broadband. In recent years, Lyse developed a gas network in South Rogaland and operates a liquefied natural gas business in the Nordic market.

Another essential industry in Rogaland is food. This industry is of national importance. Being one of the largest food clusters in the country with focus on meat production, dairy, and animal feed, the area is the strongest agricultural sector in Norway. Stavanger has a viable restaurant scene – grown out of the needs of the oil industry – that has been nationally and internationally successful. Within agriculture, the region is leading with over 20 per cent of the country's livestock, as well as significant production of greenhouse industry. The aquaculture industry is growing and attracts leading researchers. The creation of NCE Culinology and Culinary House has given the region the opportunity to strengthen its role as a national centre of expertise. In addition, food festivals and excellent chefs have helped to build Rogaland's reputation as a "food county".

An important emerging industry that has grown out of the oil industry is the financial sector. Over the last 20 years, several leading finance companies have based themselves in Stavanger to create the second largest fund management community after Oslo with a capital base of more than NOK 105 billion (US$15 billion). On top of that, private equity companies here have accumulated NOK 10 billion dedicated towards seed, venture capital, and buy-out opportunities. It is argued that the financial industry is responsible for the strongest increase in wealth creation in Norway following oil, according to the report from Fafo Institute for Labour and Social Research (2008), Rogaland employs 3,100 people within the financial sector. The driving force behind this has been Norway's immense oil and gas wealth, as the following quote illustrates:

> If you look back on our history dating back to 1839, banks were founded on the fishing industry, which was then our most valuable raw material.... The second raw material was oil and gas and has given us much more than fish. The third is the money as a result of the oil and gas.
>
> (Executive Vice-President, SR-Bank, Nortrade, 2009)[3]

The finance community in Stavanger has been cooperating with the university. The largest fund managers raised NOK 20 million for a master's degree programme in applied finance, which started in the autumn of 2008. The university matched this amount over a five-year period. The initiators of this educational component compare the finance industry to the petroleum industry as the quote below reveals:

> Today the finance industry is where the petroleum industry was in the 1970s. This industry has great potential. When the oil has been pumped out of the North Sea and converted into cash, it has become another raw material to be husbanded. The key to it all is competence which we can contribute to maintaining the prosperity that has been created in this region.
>
> (Sveinung Hestnes, CIO, at Sparebank 1 SR-Bank,
> Nortrade, 2009)

Petroleum funds have also been re-invested in cultural activities. As a balance towards capital intensive industries, it was important for the Stavanger region to leverage focus on cultural activities. Becoming a cultural capital in 2008 highlighted this effort. The Stavanger region served, together with Liverpool, as a European Capital of Culture in 2008. Stavanger was, however, in a unique position to attract culture for culture's sake (Fitjar *et al.*, 2013). The emphasis on culture was a part of the strategy in Stavanger to diversify the concentration on industry and create a more attractive place to live. According to Fitjar *et al.* (2013), the majority of cultural capital was engaged in order to increase tourism. However, Stavanger "had a different aim – that of opening up minds and imaginations". Stavanger had the luxury of being able to focus almost entirely on culture. The university has also worked together with the cultural sector to develop a first-class music conservatory. In short, there has been an effort to create cultural-based industry within the Stavanger region.

Developing the innovation ecosystem

The creation of a support infrastructure for commercialization activities, such as technology transfer offices (TTOs) and incubators, has been highly prioritized in Stavanger which established a research park in 1993. The current innovation ecosystem in Stavanger is oriented around the research park (Ipark) and the TTO (Prekubator) and has become more institutionalized. However, entrepreneurship in the region traditionally came from practical solution-oriented ideas of individuals and was not typically the product of systematic, coordinated academic research (see Figure 11.1).

Fitjar and Rodriguez-Pose (2013) claim that Stavanger is among the Norwegian city regions with the lowest rates of R&D expenditure per inhabitant, yet in the same time period the Stavanger region had the highest number of registered patents per capita of all Norwegian city regions. Further, general education has been lower than in the rest of the country. As an example, Fitjar and Rodriguez-Pose (2013) show that in

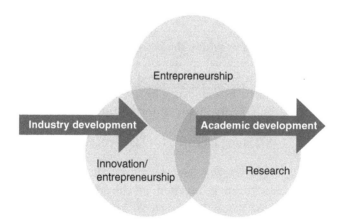

Figure 11.1 The dynamics of entrepreneurship ecosystem in Stavanger.

2005, 23.1 per cent of people in southwest Norway had a university degree, compared with 34.0 per cent in Oslo and a national average of 24.8 per cent. The quote below shows the low standing of academia in the region:

> I would say most ideas in general have come from industry; many people have highlighted the Stavanger area as the site of many good ideas. However, in this region, the concept of "getting things done" has enjoyed high status, while schools/education have traditionally had lower social status. I think this is about to change and that we come to expect that a higher proportion of good ideas will come from academia.
>
> (CEO TTO company, 2013)

Ipark, the incubator and Prekubator

Established in 1993, Innovation Park of Stavanger (Ipark) was Norway's first knowledge park and currently houses more than 150 different companies with over 800 employees. Owners of Ipark include Statoil, SIVA,[4] Rogaland County, and Rogaland Science Park Foundation. The goal is to leverage opportunities for business growth. Further, Ipark Eiendom is a major property manager and offers modern facilities and environment for innovative companies.

Ipark's tool for entrepreneurship and innovation revolves mainly around Prekubator (which is their TTO focusing on academic spin-offs) and the incubator working with knowledge-based companies from both industry and academia. As the name suggests, Prekubator deals with projects in a very early phase before graduating some of the projects to the incubator.

Prekubator: the TTO

> From being something individuals have been doing, entrepreneurship is now becoming systematized in academia, in industry, and in public management.
>
> (Anne Cathrin Østebø, CEO, Prekubator)

In 2003, new legislation passed by the Norwegian parliament came into effect, granting universities the right to commercially exploit intellectual property (IP) developed by their employees. This set a new national ambition to effectively bring more innovations to the market. Based on this legislation, the University of Stavanger and collaborative research institutions have committed to transferring innovative technologies faster and more successfully than before. The TTO had been established on behalf of the University College of Stavanger and research institutions as a joint function of innovation in 2002. The Prekubator TTO is owned by a consortium of organizations, with its main mission being to close the gap between science and industry by building a solid, sustainable bridge between inventors and industrial partners. A classical tech transfer model has been implemented, starting with discoveries by university researchers in their laboratories, and proceeding to disclosure by the inventors, patenting by the university and the inventor, and ultimately licensing of the technology, frequently to start-up or early stage technology-based enterprises founded by the inventors themselves.

Prekubator's primary TTO functions include encouraging the disclosure of new discoveries and ideas; establishing and maintaining a proper and supportive innovation culture; and identifying and managing new innovative projects and the research institutions' IP portfolio. Prekubator secures IP rights, closing the founding gap between the discovery of new ideas and the proof of concept and generating revenues for the inventors and the research institution. It develops and maintains strong collaboration with industry and commercial partners, enforcing commercial awareness and motivation among researchers and licensing technologies. TTO activities are closely connected to the FORNY Program of the Norwegian research council where Prekubator TTO has been a commercial partner since 2002. The company is situated at Ullandhaug[5] within Rogaland Innovation Park Stavanger (Ipark). Since its establishment in 2002, Prekubator has been involved in more than 180 commercialization projects. It has commercialized 50 start-ups or licences. Prekubator already realized more than NOK 9 million, and has a portfolio in start-ups valued at NOK 11.5 million. In addition, Prekubator raised more than NOK 330 million for its projects/start-ups. Prekubator has now established a patent portfolio consisting of more than 50 patents with priority dates. Prekubator has generated a 24 per cent profit of total turnover in the ten-year span.

> From the university we annually review about 50–60 ideas, of which 15 to 20 are projects, resulting in approximately five business ventures or licences. Prekubator is the tool to take ideas across to commercialization. One criterion for the quality of what we do is the ability to raise capital from the private sector to these establishments.
>
> (Per Ramvi, former UiS President, 2013)

Figure 11.2 shows the result from a comparative study of all the regional commercialization actors in the academic year 2011/12. It investigates status for organizations funded through FORNY[6] within the period 2006–2010. The numbers show the sum of the external capital in Norwegian krone (NOK) (i.e. seed funds, venture capital, business angels, public funds, industry, or other sources). Prekubator attributes its success to the long and extraordinary cooperation with industry and to the local entrepreneurial culture.

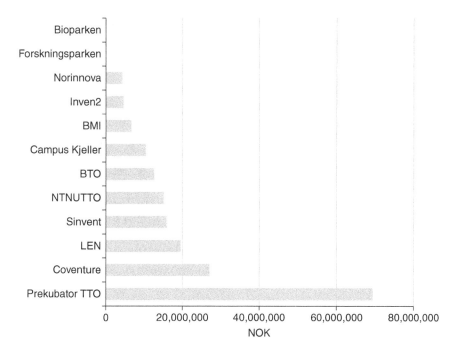

Figure 11.2 Comparison of TTOs in Norway, sum of external capital 2006–2010 (source: 2020 Norwegian Council).

The development of the incubator

While the Ipark itself serves larger, established knowledge-based companies, the aim of the Ipark incubator is to spur new business growth. The incubator works closely with Prekubator and in addition to physical facilities it focuses on bringing knowledge and networks to the fledgling businesses and in the further development of the company. Ipark also assists in raising capital, finding initial customers, partners, and alliances to develop potential businesses. The influence of petroleum activities, initially spurred entrepreneurship in the Stavanger region and several new companies focusing on services for the petroleum sector and oil tools companies were formed (i.e. Hitec, the IKM group, Åarbakke). According to the director of Innovation Norway:

> I think the Stavanger region has gotten a somewhat undeserved reputation as a region that floats too much on oil and are not thinking creatively in other fields. Rogaland takes 19 percent of the national pot of funding for industrial research and development through Innovation Norway. The pot was NOK 259 million in 2013. A

large part of this was the projects that were not associated with oil and gas. In establishing supplements we take 14 percent of the national pie: 83 million. This is in addition to regional funds. Innovation Norway gives money to small and large innovative ideas. In 2013, 440 applications from Stavanger were granted out of 550. Many of those projects were in ICT, maritime, energy, and the environment, as well as in agriculture and health.

(Director Marit Karlsen Bran Dahl, Innovation Norway, 18 February 2014,)

Following the ambitions of the strategic plan, the oil-related technology, petroleum, and energy sector was well represented in the Ipark and in the incubator. In 2004 Ipark began working with cultural incubators, which was followed by working with a food incubator. In 2013 this was merged into a joint model with additional specializations such as health, cleantech, ICT, and biotech. A company can also be admitted to the Incubator if it falls outside these categories. New experiences have been accumulated with these developments. An interesting aspect of the food incubator has been the increased participation of female entrepreneurs:

This year (2013) we will take in 20 new companies. When I started working in Ipark we had almost zero female entrepreneurs in the incubator. Then we started up with new programs related to food, and I think almost 50% were female.

(CEO, incubator)

Another finding was that the culture sector had very different concepts of what a business actually is.

We see that the mechanism we use in the incubator could work but we have to have a brand new language for this. We have to convert some of the words and business models that we use, as we can't use those for the culture. We need another language! We have to explain it in another way.

(Marit Hagland, Head of Ipark, 2013)

Ipark's incubator also serves as a source of funding for start-ups. The Ipark incubator is quite special in Norway – because it has been able to invest directly in their firms. The Ipark investment fund comprises about NOK 50–60 million, and was gained by the sale of some buildings owned by Ipark. Each year about NOK 6 million are invested in the new companies. Some firms allocated in Ipark's incubator can benefit from both obtaining a stipend from Innovation Norway (which cannot be more than 50 per cent of the project amount) and receiving matching funds from the incubator.

Funding resources

Another link between oil and money can be found in Stavanger's private equity community. The major private equity companies here were started by oil veterans and are focused on energy investments. Some have established offices in the other international petroleum capitals such as Houston and Aberdeen. For example Hitec Vision has its roots as an oil service company, but has grown to become the second largest private equity company in Norway with US$1.2 billion in committed capital.

> The private equity community in Stavanger is more internationally oriented than the Norwegian private equity industry in general.... This is a reflection of the international outlook of the local industry. That's what companies here do. They serve oil companies globally.
>
> (Pål Dahlberg, Hitec Vision CEO, 2013 Nortrade)

Energy Ventures is a venture capital company with NOK 2.3 billion in committed capital divided over three funds. The company targets mainly hi-tech oil service companies based in the North Sea or North America, but also considers environmental technology companies. Its latest fund, for example, recently invested in Energreen, a local company with a technology that generates clean energy from pressure drops in fluid process systems.

Other Stavanger private equity companies include Såkorninvest, the only seed fund (i.e. early funding which enables a project or idea to develop into a business); Procom Ventures, a "speed seed" fund; and Progressus, which operates within expansion and internationalization. The Norwegian Private Equity and Venture Capital Association (NVCA) estimates the Stavanger private equity industry has around NOK 10 billion in total committed capital. An overview of the venture funds can be found in Appendix 11.4.

External contributors to the innovation ecosystem

It is important to notice the external organizations working together with UiS in several arenas and contribute to the innovation ecosystem. These organizations have different roles that are complementary to that of the university, the TTO, and Ipark.

One of the oldest and most influential organizations in the region is Stavanger Chamber of Commerce. It has one of the country's highest member base and is important for network building and involvement in the strategic work. Within the Chamber of Commerce there is a division created several years ago that focuses on entrepreneurship and innovation in the region. It hosts seminars and talks on related topics and stimulates entrepreneurial initiatives in the county.

In 2002, a network named Innovasjon Rogaland has been initiated by Ipark as an arena for knowledge exchange between industry, academia, and public institutions. In addition, it also created arenas for tech transfer and triple helix based networks. This network is no longer very active.

The Greater Stavanger organization that came out of the ARNE project in 2006 facilitates relationships between industry, the public, and the knowledge sector. It is funded by one of the largest industry parks in the country, with additional financial aid from the participating municipalities. Greater Stavanger contributes to collaboration between different parties interested in networking, regional development, and research on innovation, entrepreneurship, and regional development. Their most important output is the strategic plan for the region.

Further, Stavanger Region has two international offices which are placed under the responsibility of the Greater Stavanger Economic Development. A European office in Brussels was created in 1993 as the first of the Norwegian regions, and a Houston office was established in 2005 because of the close relationship between the two petroleum based cities. It is also planned to open a third international office in St Petersburg, as Russia represents an attractive market for Norwegian export-oriented firms.

In 2006, as the ARNE Project transformed itself into Greater Stavanger Economic Development, a separate organization named Skape was created the same year. Skape is an association for entrepreneurs, which falls outside the established knowledge sector (UiS/Ipark). It was established as a partnership between state governments, municipalities, and the county of Rogaland, represented by Innovation Norway, Fylkesmannen in Rogaland,[7] and NAV,[8] to provide guidance and training to entrepreneurs.

In 2010 a new network named Nettverk Stavanger, was born. This dynamic network arranges arenas for young professionals to meet each other and potential mentors.

In summary, Greater Stavanger, Chamber of Commerce, Nettverk Stavanger and Skape facilitate a dynamic and vibrant environment that stimulates new ideas, projects, and entrepreneurship in the region.

Booming industry stimulating academic growth

Since the late 1960s, the Stavanger region wanted to have a fully fledged university, in hopes that it would stimulate economic growth. Instead, the oil industry was born during that period, yet it produced considerable growth of competence in both applied and geographic sciences. Thus, the story of Stavanger shows that burgeoning industry can be a locomotive for academic development and growth. The timeline seen in Table 11.1 shows the main events from the beginning of the oil era to the present.

Starting from civic entrepreneurship, the region has now developed through industry-driven economy. However, the entrepreneurial spirit is still present, as many small enterprises serve as a support belt around core industries. The university plays an important role – to foster entrepreneur-ial development through entrepreneurship education and spillover of knowledge through spin-offs.

Fostering entrepreneurship education

When UiS was established, it positioned itself as the "innovative/entrepre-neurial university" based on strong cooperation with industry. There was an aim that entrepreneurship education should be cross-disciplinary and, as such, be included in every discipline offered by the university. While the Norwegian government has named entrepreneurship education as an important university mission at the society level, it has been stated that there is little interest for entrepreneurship among UiS students.

> We had quite low interest among students in entrepreneurship courses. We see that students prefer to go into established companies when they graduate.
>   (Bjarte Ravndal, Head of Stavanger Business School in UiS)

However, in 2009, the Centre for Entrepreneurship was established to spread entrepreneurship education across departments and disciplines, to help students pursue entrepreneurship education, and to extend UiS educa-tional offerings in entrepreneurship. As of today, there is no bachelor's or master's programme in entrepreneurship at Stavanger University. Instead, about 12 courses take entrepreneurship as major or minor concentration across different faculties and institutions. Appendix 11.5 presents a table with short descriptions of these courses.

In 2012 the university decided to enhance entrepreneurship education considerably. In light of this, a new course in entrepreneurship was offered in 2013 for bachelor students at the UiS Business School. In 2014 a new master's level course was launched. There is also discussion about the establishment of a minor in entrepreneurship across two faculties. The pro-gramme will include a continuous set of subjects open for master's students in both divisions, so that over a two-year period students will acquire knowledge related to idea generation and creativity, business modelling, and business planning.

In addition to this set of courses, there are a number of events in the university or in the community to which university students and faculty, as well as the public, are invited to participate. The overview of these events is presented in Table 11.2.

Establishing a culture for entrepreneurship

Culture represents an important dimension of the entrepreneurial univer-sity. According to Kenney and Goe (2004), the cultural embeddedness of

Table 11.1 Timeline of Stavanger region milestone events for entrepreneurial architecture

1965	• The idea of establishing a university in Stavanger started
	• The first licensing round for petroleum announced
	• Four new petroleum-based companies located to Stavanger, one company established
1969	• First commercial petroleum discovery
1972	• Rogaland Regional College established (engineering programme serving petroleum industry)
	• Oljedirektoratet (Oil Directory) located to Stavanger
	• The Regional Hospital of Rogaland established
	• One new petroleum-based company established
1973	• Rogaland Research established
	• One new petroleum-based company located to Stavanger
1984	• ULLRIGG Drilling and Well Centre built with offshore drilling rig and access to seven wells
1986	• The College Centre in Rogaland (HSR) created
1988	• Stavanger College of Nursing
1993	• The Knowledge Park/incubator established (Ipark)
1994	• The University College of Stavanger (HiS) established (forerunner to the UiS, merged from six public and one private college in Stavanger)
1995	• One new petroleum-based company established
1998	• Crash in petroleum prices: historical lows at $8/barrel
1999	• The ARNE Project (Arena for Regional Economic Development and Entrepreneurship) established to stimulate new regional growth
	• Vision of university is reborn
2000	• The University Foundation established to finance university building
2001	• Two new petroleum-based companies established
2002	• Prekubator formed to support university's "third mission" in commercializing research-based ideas. Owned by UiS, IRIS, SUS and Ipark
	• CIAM (Centre for Industrial Asset Management) established
	• Innovation Rogaland network is started on behalf of Knowledge Ipark
	• One new petroleum-based company established

2003	• COREC (Centre for Oil Recovery) established
	• Two new petroleum-based companies established
2004	• Centre for Reading Research and Centre for Behavioural Research
	• CSSW (Centre for Smart and Safe Wells) established
	• Three new petroleum-based companies established
2005	• The University of Stavanger established
	• Two new petroleum-based companies established
	• IRIS established (technical restructuring of the ownership of Rogaland Research)
	• CORE Centre for Organelle Research established
	• TTO established (transformation of Prekubator)
	• Rogaland Kunnskapspark strengthens incubator and starts work to establish a cultural incubator, which was followed by a food incubator
	• The ARNE Project becomes Greater Stavanger Economic Development
2006–2007	• Six new petroleum-based companies established
	• Rogaland Knowledge Park changes name to Ipark
	• Norwegian Centre of Expertise (NCE) Culinology established
	• 12 new petroleum-based companies established
2008	• Stavanger and Liverpool are Cultural Capitals of Europe
	• Centre for Innovation Research (SIF) established
2009	• Centre for Sustainable Energy Solutions (CenSE) established
	• Centre for Risk Management and Societal Safety (SEROS) established
	• PreSenter established for labour renovation
	• Norwegian Centre for Offshore Wind Energy (NORCOWE) established
	• One new petroleum-based company established
2012	• CIPSI Centre for IP-based service innovation established
2013	• Incubator merges activities into a joint model with specializations i.e. health, cleantech, ICT, and biotech
	• National Centre for Learning and Behavioural Research established as restructuring of Centre for Reading Research and Centre for Behavioural Research

Table 11.2 Entrepreneurial events in the Stavanger community

Activity	Description
START	The START organization is established and run by local student teams. The main organization is located in Norway's Technical College (NTNU). They spread information about entrepreneurship and initiative several events, with the main one being Venture Cup.
Venture Cup	Scandinavian business plan competition, administered by the national student organization: START, NTNU, in which entrepreneurs with unique business ideas compete for investment capital. Run by non-profit organizations in Denmark, Finland, Norway, and Sweden.
Gründerskolen	Norwegian Entrepreneurship programme is a Norwegian academic cooperation programme involving all the universities and several university colleges in Norway (Oslo, Bergen, Stavanger, Trondheim, Tromsø, and Ås).
Startup Weekend	Startup Weekends, powered by the Kauffman Foundation, are specifically designed for entrepreneurs interested in receiving feedback on an idea, looking for a co-founder, or wanting to learn a new skill.
Grunder Trainee	The Grunder Trainee is a collaborative project between the University of Stavanger, Ipark, Innovation Norway, and Statoil. The project provides Ipark (their incubator businesses) the opportunity to hire a student from the university for 20% position, through a nine-month period.

entrepreneurial activity is a powerful predictor of individual attitudes towards commercialization activity in the relevant context. The people of the Stavanger region have always considered themselves entrepreneurial individualists with a "can do" attitude. Moreover, something happened in Stavanger through the work on the strategic plan when several groups were formed in cooperation with external partners, and both formal and informal networks were established. Fitjar and Rodriguez-Pose (2013) point to the high level of trust and openness towards international relations in the Stavanger region. The mix of local and international networks has facilitated openness and trust between partners. Certainly, these networks became important for cooperation, but moreover, they spurred a specific working culture in the Stavanger region referred to as a "consensus or harmony culture". This culture came out of the understanding that consensus around main regional decisions was imperative for successful implementation.

Therefore, cooperation through networks and project groups – with careful dialogue with all enrolled parties – continued until people found common solutions that the majority could agree on. This broad consensus was crucial for the Stavanger region to achieve important collective tasks as the quote below states:

> Consensus is important for achieving increased total momentum in the regions effort. The University of Stavanger (UiS) needs ambient competence, projects, and economic support. The same applies to industry and regional developmental actors, which look to UiS competence strengths to involve them in their development strategies. There is a common understanding that consensus is important, and it is a prerequisite to the development of the regions strong networks.
>
> (Per Ramvi, former UiS President, 2013)

An example of successful collaborative effort is the new initiative on welfare technology. The municipalities need new smart solutions for primary health services, and the hospital has corresponding needs for clarification as to its role vis-à-vis primary health services. Furthermore, suppliers and businesses deliver new smart solutions and technologies to these needs (including ICT), and academia contributes with competence, research, and research-based solutions. In January 2013, the mayor of Stavanger invited key stakeholders to a meeting – a group that now coordinates the region's commitment around this theme.

While such collaboration clearly can be beneficial for regional development in some fields, it also has a downside. While this critique is usually made in reference to political processes, one could also argue that a strong consensus culture might sometimes prove to be a hindrance for the free thought and action of the entrepreneur. Below is a quote from the media on the political debate discussing that exact culture in Stavanger:

It is a tradition and a pressure in this region that one should agree on things. Conflicts are hidden and the opposition is gagged. This means that some forces gets a freer leeway, such as certain businesses, builders, and people with capital who want something.

(*Stavanger Aftenblad*, 2014)[9]

Entrepreneurial cultures rest on private initiative and innovation – an ability to "think outside the box" – as well as tolerance to such diversity. For the future of the region, it is therefore of high importance that the Stavanger system avoid cultural rigidity. Open public dialogue represents a key element toward a needed cultural flexibility.

Industrial diversity is similarly vital. The continual pressure of today's oil economy can easily dominate regional investments of talent and capital. A more entrepreneurial choice would be to also place investments in targeted emerging industries, thereby ultimately enlarging the regional industry base toward cluster formation. While Stavanger's core industries, oil and maritime, will necessarily influence which new industries will emerge, it is important for the region to invest in supportive and complementary industries.

Until now oil has been a great blessing. In the future it may be well be a curse. I see a great danger in oil sector becomes too large compared to all other sectors. Especially in a time of high oil prices. The day the oil price is 60–70 dollars a barrel we will notice the curse-effect. To "move" the resources from the oil sector to other sectors is not done overnight.

(CEO of local technology company)

The region also exhibits some of Norway's lowest unemployment rates. The presence of the oil industry attracts an educated workforce, and the jobs are well paid. This results in a lower willingness to take the comparative risks associated with an entrepreneurial career.

It seems to me that people are more interested in secure, well-paid jobs than investing 10 years of hard work and little pay in something that just might be successful in the future. The most popular jobs for several years have been in major, established companies such as Statoil, Aker, KPMG, and others. Perhaps young people rather should be inspired to work for research companies and small technology companies.

(CEO of local technology company)

Another issue is that the petroleum industry introduces a rising cost structure that can hinder companies and entrepreneurs as they seek to become established in the region.

The largest challenge of being an entrepreneur in Stavanger I think is that the oil industry wages, pace, and terms of costs make it difficult to create a cost-conscious culture that builds stone by stone with reasonable salary expectation.

(CEO, local gazelle company)

Further, despite success, regional universities face challenges inherent to a culture for *academic* entrepreneurship. The challenge is to develop an environment that proliferates innovation and entrepreneurship. Whether as receivers, partners, or actors, firms typically have little experience, expertise, or insight into the nature of research and its requirement for time.

Businesses are often more concerned with quick solutions and answers to questions than research-based solutions. It will therefore rather use accumulated knowledge than developing new knowledge.

(Per Ramvi, 2013)

The challenge is to get industry and research parties to understand each other, and approach each other, to their joint and mutual benefit. The opportunities for both parties are large; firms can help researchers identify specific questions and contribute financially so that the researchers can immerse themselves in a topic to explore new solutions. Together they can apply for external funding from research councils, EU, and others – and thus increase their resources. But this is not an obvious path for local firms, and cooperative efforts between industry and research institutions are limited in Stavanger.

Conclusion

This chapter highlights the development of the Stavanger region from a petroleum-based economy toward a more balanced innovation ecosystem. The petroleum sector has opened a window of opportunity for the city, and civic entrepreneurs from the region have created a foundation, on which the city now rests.

Strong industry, and the region's position as an oil centre, influence the academic sector in Stavanger. The University of Stavanger and its surrounding industry are developing into a symbiotic structure that is mutually reinforcing. However, the ability of that sector to attract human and monetary resources on behalf of other sectors is well known and debated, and effort is required to develop new competencies. Also, in the case of entrepreneurship in Stavanger, success is often credited to the oil industry, not the regional initiatives. Yet the University of Stavanger may help the city gain its rightful position on the map through redistributing the knowledge and competence gained from the petroleum sector through strong academic programmes.

Today Stavanger University serves as the main source for a qualified workforce, whether for oil or other industries. The challenge of the University of Stavanger may be to strengthen its role towards industry and take the lead in promoting and developing the entrepreneurial and innovative culture of the region. Today university education follows a regional path and offers those professions that are most in demand, and entrepreneurship is not listed among them. Although some actors (i.e. Ipark and the UiS students' entrepreneurial organization) ask for strengthening educational offerings within entrepreneurship, there are still very limited educational offerings in UiS in that field. At the same time, it is important that desire for a more entrepreneurial university should emerge from a bottom-up approach, so that shared norms and values may be embedded across the university culture.

Further, the role of UiS as an academic entrepreneur also needs to be enhanced in order to transfer research-based innovations to the market. Today, in spite of all the governmental support and stimulus, only a modest part of university-born innovations are connected to the market. According to *Global Entrepreneurial Monitor Research* (2014), Norway has an innovation-based type of economy. In such economies, innovation is the driving force of economic development. Therefore, the university could play a considerable role in stimulating such economic development.

Stavanger is known to be a city where strong networks and the presence of supporting structures contribute to the development of the regional actors. Such structures as Greater Stavanger, Skape, the Chamber of Commerce, Innovation Norway, Prekubator TTO, and Innovation Park Stavanger foster the entrepreneurial spirit of the region. The structural framework positively influences both business development and start-up activities in the region and the region is known to have civic entrepreneurship culture, and to be the place where "things do happen".

This positive spirit for business has stimulated growth not only in the oil industry, but also in related fields, like maritime, ICT, and even culture and food. Stavanger is known for its strong collaboration culture, which was important to overcome regional challenges faced in the early 1990s. While this continues to be the way to find solutions when forces needs to be gathered to overcome challenges, in some situations consensus might be a barrier to new and different ideas, and in that way hinder the innovative spirit for which the region is known.

We conclude that the Stavanger region has several strengths, including its booming oil industry (with its munificent business climate), an infrastructure that is helpful for entrepreneurial activities, and the presence of the university. The university plays an important role in the regional ecosystem, particularly as a supplier of a qualified workforce. This role should be enhanced through offering educational initiatives related to the field of entrepreneurship and innovation, and through higher enrolment of the university into regional collaboration activities, which can be achieved by fostering academic entrepreneurship in the university.

Appendix 11.1.

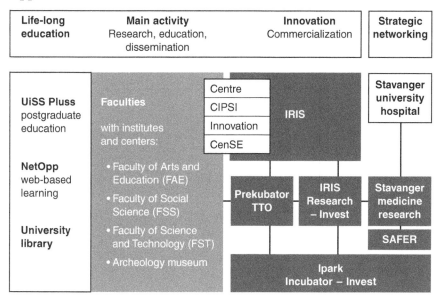

Figure 11.A1 Structure of UiS: 10,100 students, 1,350 staff.

Appendix 11.2.

Table 11.A2 Other UiS regional research partners

Research outside of UIS	Description
Business School BI Stavanger	BI Stavanger provides education to 573 bachelor full-time students and to over 200 part-time master's students. In addition BI Stavanger provides different courses to about 2,000 students, including 1,000 students from oil- and gas-related industries.
Norwegian School of Veterinary Science (NVH)	It is a part of HVH Institute for Animal Medication and has about 20 employees. The school provides education for veterinary students within limited areas.
School of Mission of Theology	A private university focusing on global perspectives of the church's mission as well as religious and cultural encounters. It has 350 students and 23 PhD students.

Appendix 11.3.

Table 11.A3 UiS research centres

Centre	Description
Centre for Industrial Asset Management (CIAM), 2002	The focus of CIAM is to make industrial production, manufacturing, and process assets more cost-effective through continued learning and innovation, and thereby contribute to increased value creation and reduced risk exposure for our industrial partners.
Centre for Increased Oil Recovery (COREC), 2003	The overall goal for COREC is to increase oil recovery from producing fields by understanding the reservoirs and the relevant methods and to become a leading IOR centre in an international network. COREC supports building and maintaining a strong national competence within improved oil recovery, through education and research. Centre owned by IRIS; UiS, ConocoPhillips.
Centre for Smart and Safe Wells (CSSW), 2004	CSSW aim is to increase national competence within drilling and to gather different kind of actors related to oil industry. Owned by UiS, IRIS, oil industry actors.
Centre for Reading Research and Centre for Behavioural Research, 2004	As part of the University of Stavanger, the Reading Centre activities relate to education and research in special education (reading and writing) and reading science (reading development and training). Reading Centre teachers coach at pre-school and primary education, continuing education, various master's and PhD programmes. The centre also collaborates with other academic departments at the university on research, research training, teaching, and guidance.
Centre for Organelle Research (CORE), 2006	The overall vision of CORE is to understand the biological function and complexity of organelles in eukaryotic cells.

Norwegian Centre of Expertise Culinology, 2007	Norwegian Centre of Expertise (NCE) Culinology. The food cluster in **Rogaland** has deep historic roots in the production of agricultural-based food and seafood.
Stavanger Centre for Innovation Research, 2008	Centre based on a donation from a local entrepreneur. It initiates and participates in international and national projects to achieve a greater understanding of innovation.
CenSE, 2009	The Centre for Sustainable Energy Solutions, CenSEis a result of a regional initiative in south-west Norway. The centre's main focus is innovations within renewable energy areas.
SEROS, 2009	**SEROS** research embraces the overall themes as well as the relationship between risk management and societal safety. Owned by UiS and IRIS.
PreSenter, 2009	PreSenter promotes cooperation between research, development, and new technologies within areas of labour renovation. Owned by AFI (Oslo), UiO, UiS, **IRIS**.
CIPSI, 2012	Established to strengthen applied ICT research within welfare technology. Established in cooperation with Lyse and IBM.
National Centre for Learning and Behavioural Research, 2013	The Learning Centre was formed from a merger between the Centre for Behavioural Research in Stavanger and Lillegården Resource Centre in Porsgrunn. Its work can be divided into three parts: outreach activities (among other programmes, projects, and courses aimed at schools, kindergartens, **PPT**); research and publication; and teaching and supervision at postgraduate level

Appendix 11.4.

Table 11.A4 Venture companies in Stavanger

Source	Description
Hitec Vision	Jon Gjedebo started Hitec in 1973 selling instrumentation to the petroleum industry in Stavanger. The first private equity fund was launched in 2002, solely to Norwegian investors. Its latest and largest fund, HitecVision V (2008), has a committed capital of US$816 million and attracted 52% participation among foreign investors. The fund targets control buyouts and growth capital investments in the international oil and gas sector.
Energy Venture	Independent venture capital firm dedicated to new upstream oil and gas technologies. Since Energy Venture's creation in 2002 the company have reviewed more than 2,500 deals, made 32 investments and successfully exited 12 companies. Energy Venture manages and advise four venture funds. Investments range from $5 to $30 million per company, with typical holding of 10 to 40% of equity.
Procom Venture	Norwegian based early-stage venture capital company focusing on promising technology companies in the petroleum, clean energy, and industrial biotechnology sectors. In May 2009 Procom Venture AS took over as manager for SåkorninVest AS and SåkorninVest II AS. SåkorninVest II AS has a capital base of NOK 340 million.
Portfolio Ipark AS	Ipark attracts between NOK 5 million and 10 million in growth industries as part of developing power. The focus is on expertise and technology companies. Investors who want involvement in this type of businesses are welcome to cooperate.

Appendix 11.5.

Table 11.A5 Courses within entrepreneurship offered in UiS

Course/programme	Faculty	Frequency	Season	No. of students	Type of students
Entrepreneurship and business plan	FSS	every year	autumn	60	Mixed (business, engineers, social sciences)
Operational management	FSS	every year	autumn or spring	30	Mixed (business, hotel business, engineering and maths students), mostly bachelor; master's students can also apwply, open for international students
Modelling a business process	FSS	every year	spring	20	Mixed (business, hotel business, engineering and maths), bachelor students
Innovation management	FSS	every year 1 semester	autumn	15	Business students, mostly master's students, some bachelor also accepted
Innovation management	FTS	every year 1 semester	autumn	15	Business students, mostly master's students, open for PhD students
Management	FSS	every year 1 semester	autumn	N/A	Business students, social sciences, master's students
Business ideology	FTS	every year 1 semester	spring	300	Bachelor of Engineering students
Entrepreneurship for technology ventures	FTS	every year 1 semester	autumn	10	Technical sciences, master's students
Work knowledge	FAE	Every year 1 semester	spring	17	Bachelor in Arts – Dance
Musical	FAE	Every year 1 semester	autumn	20	Bachelor in Arts – Music
Work ethics	FAE	Every year	autumn	N/A	Teacher education and pedagogics

Notes

1 ssb.no (Statistical Central Register of Norway).
2 NOKUT is Norwegian Agency for Quality Assurance in Education and is the controlling authority for educational activity at all Norwegian universities, special field universities, university colleges, and institutions with single accredited higher education programs.
3 Here and throughout the text, quotations are taken from interviews conducted with experts (company representatives, government officers, university representatives, etc.) by the authors in the period 2011–2013.
4 SIVA is the Industrial Development Corporation of Norway. IT is the governmental corporation and national instrument founded in 1968. SIVA is owned by the Norwegian Ministry of Trade and Industry. SIVA aims to develop strong regional and local industrial clusters through ownership in infrastructure, investment, and knowledge networks as well as innovation centres.
5 Ullandhaug is an area where organizations important for Stavanger innovation infrastructure are situated, including Oil Directorate, Innovation Park Stavanger, Innovation Norway, International Research Institute of Rogaland, Drilling and Well Centre, and University of Stavanger.
6 FORNY is a programme funded by the Norwegian Research Council aimed at supporting the commercialization of R&D results. It funds the Norwegian technology transfer offices (TTOs) and projects in need of proof-of-concept.
7 Fylkesmannen in Rogaland is the county of Rogaland's governor.
8 NAV is the Norwegian Labour and Welfare Administration.
9 *Stavanger Aftenblad* is a local newspaper: www.aftenbladet.no.

References

Fafo Institute for Labour and Social Research (2008). www.fafo.no.
Fitjar, R. and Rodriguez-Pose, A. (2013). The geographical dimension of innovation collaboration: Networking and innovation in Norway. *Urban Studies*, 0042098013510567.
Fitjar, R., Rommetvedt, H., and Berg, C. (2013). European Capitals of Culture: Elitism or inclusion? The case of Stavanger 2008. *International Journal of Cultural Policy*, 19(1): 68–83.
Global Entrepreneurial Monitor Research Report (2012). www.gemconsortium. org/docs/3165/gem-norway-2012-report.
Kenney, M. and Goe, W. (2004). The role of social embeddedness in professional entrepreneurship: A comparison of electrical engineering and computer science at UC Berkley and Stanford. *Research Policy*, 33(5), 691–707.
Lester, R.K. (2005). Universities, innovation, and the competitiveness of local economies: MIT Industrial Performance Center Working Paper 05–010, 13.12.2005, available at http://web.mit.edu/lis/papers/LIS05–010.pdf.
Ministry of Petroleum and Energy (2013). Facts 2013: The Norwegian petroleum sector. www.npd.no/en/Publications/Facts/Facts-2013/.
NHO (2013). NHOs Kommune NM2013. En rangering av kommuners og regioners vekstkrav og attraktivitet. Report. www.nho.no/siteassets/nhos-filer-og-bilder/filer-og-dokumenter/offentlig-sektor-og-naringslivet/nhos-kommunenm-2013.pdf.
TNS Gallup Report (2010). www.tns-gallup.no/.

12 The entrepreneurial university
Case analysis and implications

Lene Foss and David V. Gibson

Introduction

The ten case narratives provide rich and varied insights about university change toward the entrepreneurial turn in different regional and national environments. Adding to this variety, each case is presented by participant observers from their unique perspectives. Accordingly, the cases, as a group, provide insightful but highly diverse accounts of the development of entrepreneurial architectures in small and large, old and new, and in major to emerging research universities, in order to address the following research questions:

1   What actors and forces are important in motivating institutional change in the development of a university's entrepreneurial architecture?
2   How do universities interact with their institutional context in developing entrepreneurially?

Our objective in Chapter 12 is to analyse the case narratives at organizational and institutional levels focused on each of the five dimensions of entrepreneurial architecture. To this end, we begin with an overview of our research methodology and limitations followed by discussion and analyses of the five architectural dimensions. We conclude with our summary findings and research and policy implications.

Grounding the entrepreneurial architecture in an institutional perspective

The guiding premise of our case analyses is to discuss, in different regional and national settings, the relative importance of the architectural dimensions in a university's transition toward the third mission. The entrepreneurial university is, in our view, an emerging organizational form that in many instances has yet to be legitimized and institutionalized. As noted in Chapter 1, there are four main components of institutional theory that underpin our research methodology and discussion of the case narratives. First, each case emphasizes the importance of context, as the emphasis is on the importance of the "ground" or environment in which the university is embedded. Second, innovative actions are seen to arise from pre-existing activities while entering into new activities to which they must adjust. This perspective highlights the continuing impact of the old on the new and the existing on the becoming. In accord with institutional theory, the case narratives also emphasize "how things happen", in addition to "what" happened. Third, we recognize the important role played by ideas and symbolic elements in the functioning of organizations – in addition to material resources, technological drivers, and exchange/power processes. Fourth, our analysis supports the interdependence of factors operating at multiple levels to affect the outcomes of interest. In many of the cases we see the interplay of top-down and bottom-up processes as they affected the formation and sustainability of the entrepreneurial university. When placed in the context of an organizational field, there are forces at work between organizations and agencies that interact at the regional, national, and international levels, and together impact the entrepreneurial turn.

We suggest that it is helpful to study processes of forming and institutionalizing the entrepreneurial architecture at regulative, normative and cognitive-cultural levels of influence and control. Scott's (2014) three pillars of institutions direct attention to different levels of activity to influence change top-down and bottom-up both within and external to the university (Figure 12.1). In a top-down scenario, national regulations influence formal and informal rules within the university, which in turn influence formal and informal rules in the various academic departments, which in turn influence what is accepted, or resisted, by faculty, staff, and students depending on individual preferences, perspectives, and institutional settings. Bottom-up influence can occur when individual views and initiatives are sufficiently strong and represented that they influence academic departments and disciplines, university-level leadership, and administrators leading to normative and regulative change (Holand, 2014).

This methodology is supported by Grimaldi *et al.* (2011) who suggest, that in order to enhance entrepreneurial competency building, one should consider factors in terms of:

• system level (governmental, institutional, and local context specificities)
• university level; and
• individual scientist level.

The importance of the level of analysis issue is further supported by Rasmussen *et al.* (2014: 103) who observe that, even if national policy supports entrepreneurship at the university level, there may be challenges at the departmental level, where differences in performance can emerge:

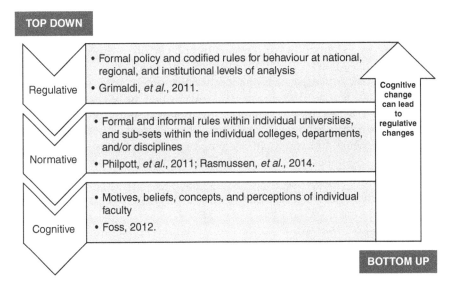

Figure 12.1 Levels of influence of the three pillars in impacting university's entrepreneurial architecture change efforts (source: Holand, 2014).

"Without the explicit support of the head of the department, the provision of slack resources, a key enabler of commercialization, was effectively constrained at the department level. The department and its faculty can act as a moderator of the degree or level of support towards spin-offs or as a gatekeeper to the university's entrepreneurial resources."

Accordingly there is "need for a shift in focus from the well-studied university level to the relatively neglected department level to help explain institutional differences in university entrepreneurship or spin-off activity" (Rasmussen *et al.*, 2014: 92)

Philpott *et al.* (2011: 165–166) found differences in attitudes towards "the entrepreneurial paradigm" among university informants representing a divide by discipline. Supporters were found in science, engineering, and medicine disciplines; while opponents were located in the arts and social sciences and business schools, especially those that targeted their graduates for employment in large established companies and consulting firms. There are also studies on faculty views and motivations on academy–industry relations and knowledge transfer, and on how the idea of the entrepreneurial university is reflected in researchers' collaborative forms of interaction (Owen-Smith and Powell, 2001; Bicknell *et al.*, 2010; D'Este and Perkmann, 2011). Such research leads us toward understanding how personal and professional predispositions may affect, at the individual level, how academics orient toward the third mission and view commercial opportunities.

The connectivity across regulative, normative, and cognitive levels of influence supports our emphasis on the importance of context in building entrepreneurship theory. Hackman (2003: 166) states that an understanding of context is important to frame entrepreneurship at lower and higher levels of analysis. West (2003: 55) observes, "It is clear that, in the domain of entrepreneurship, aspects of one level of phenomena have an impact and a bearing on aspects of other levels." According to Welter (2011: 68) context on a higher level of analysis (the political and economic system) interacts with the phenomenon on lower levels (opportunities identified by the entrepreneur) and results in a context-specific outcome. Accordingly, analyses of the importance of regional and national context need to consider top-down effects of regulative policy as well as bottom-up processes from the cognitive-cultural level.

Case analysis

Case analysis in the narrative tradition builds on an epistemological and ontological position that denies the possibility of a theory-neutral language. Consequently, insider bias is a part of creating a reality from the viewpoint of the author and is an output of human cognitive processes (Johnson and Duberley, 2000). This affects how the cases can be analysed and the strength of what can be concluded. The explorative character of this volume follows a theory-building approach (Eisenhardt and Graebner, 2007). As Tsoukas and Hatch (2001: 979) state, "The potential contribution of the narrative approach is to develop second-order thinking about organizational complexity." In advocating the need for complexity in studying the entrepreneurial university we are inspired by the following five properties of complexity science: complex systems are non-linear, fractal, exhibit recursive symmetries, are sensitive to initial conditions. and include feedback loops (Tsoukas and Hatch, 2001: 988). While the case narratives were written by participant observers from their unique perspectives, the authors also conducted interviews and used archival material to help them produce an accurate portrayal of their universities' entrepreneurial turn. The case analysis compares and contrasts examples selected from the narratives by the editors and chapter authors to analyse the five entrepreneurial architecture dimensions in terms of their contribution to a university's entrepreneurial turn while including the context in which the university is embedded. Guided by the two main research questions, individual and cross-case analyses present how different organizational fields shape, constrain, and empower the university as well as how these fields of concern are also influenced by the interests and activities of university participants.

Our chosen methodology is supported by the contention that institutional research needs to ensure that the setting examined has a wide applicability and includes investigations from multiple countries; otherwise it is difficult to be sure that institutional impact is applicable to a wide set of environments rather than merely representing an idiosyncratic result of the sample of a given country. However, our methodology is challenged as it is difficult to base research conclusions on selected insights of personal accounts of ten universities located in five nations. Despite this serious constraint, we endeavour to provide (1) new knowledge on actors and forces that motivate change in universities' entrepreneurial architecture, and (2) comparative analysis on select universities as they affect and are affected by institutional contexts and organizational fields of activity in their entrepreneurial development. Our challenge as we embrace the institutional perspective in this analysis is to put conditions on generalizations by operating at an "intermediate level" rather than seeking universal social laws or pure narrative descriptions.

Culture

Nelles and Vorley (2010a) identify the architecture dimension of culture at the university level in terms of institutional, departmental, and individual attitudes and norms. We define culture more broadly as "an object of orientation existing outside the individual" (DiMaggio and Powell, 1991: 17). However, in all the case narratives, culture is the least well identified and discussed dimension. Indeed, as the chapter authors are of, and in, the national, regional, and university cultures they write about, it is not surprising they are relatively immune to the impact of culture on their university's entrepreneurial activities and programs. As Scott (2014) suggests, "culture" is often the "elephant in the room" in that it is a dominant force that is often ignored in institutional studies. According to DiMaggio (1986: 337), "organization field has emerged as a critical unit bridging the organizational and the societal levels in the study of social community and change". As emphasized by DiMaggio, organizational field is the totality of both actors and organizations involved in an arena of social and cultural production and dynamic relationships (Bourdieu and Wacquant, 1992: 96).

While the case narratives may not specifically assess university, regional, and national cultural dimensions, they do emphasize the importance of the regional and national context in which universities are embedded. Thus, in our analyses we consider regional and national culture as one component of the university's context. Welter (2011) classifies the dimensions of context as business (industry, markets), social (networks), spatial (geographic environments), and institutional (culture, society, political, and economic systems). We suggest that important contextual and cultural differences do become apparent when comparing across regions and universities within the same country and across regions and universities in different countries. The culture dimension is presented as the first of the five architectural dimensions in our analyses because we consider that it is

indeed the most important determinant of the speed and success of a university's entrepreneurial turn. Furthermore, as noted earlier, the five architecture dimensions are highly interrelated and the examples below of the
cultural dimension clearly also present aspects of leadership, systems, and
strategies.

In the case studies there is a good representation of cultural diversity,
and discussion of the strengths and challenges this can bring to the entrepreneurial turn, as well as the effort that is needed to adjust a traditional
culture to accommodate different activities and different values relating to
innovation. In the case narratives we find examples of how university and
regional cultures support formal and informal networking and collaboration; a culture of inclusion and a "can do" attitude; cultures of celebrating
the entrepreneurs; and even examples of the importance of a culture of creative industries. All the case narratives provide instances where the university's institutional context motivated attitudes and institutional change
toward the entrepreneurial turn within the university. One common observation across all the cases is a combination of exceptional leaders or influences within or outside the university reacting to an initial impetus for
change that came from the university's context.

At Kingston University (KUL), extra-curricular programmes offer entrepreneurial opportunities that student feedback indicated was highly valued,
but its reach was limited since the university culture had not integrated
enterprise education into its wider thinking. Motivating a shift in 2010, Dr
Martha Mador, Head of Enterprise Education, raised the awareness of the
need for enterprise education not just in class modules labelled entrepreneurship, but across disciplines. In addition, KUL developed Enterprising
Business Awards and a virtual incubator to provide students and staff with
the opportunity to meet on a weekly basis and to learn new skills, find
mentors, and apply for funding. The Enterprise Education Unit is to
support academic enterprise and the development of knowledge transfer
across the university and manages regional growth programs for SMEs.

In addition to world-class research, two key normative characteristics
are seen to have helped shape the effectiveness of Cambridge's culture that
fostered the Cambridge Phenomenon. They are:

1   The enabling norm of "benign neglect" that permitted faculty to
    pursue interests external to their university roles, including exploiting
    their research findings, as long as they continued to pursue high-
    quality research, publications, and teaching at Cambridge.
2   Regularly scheduled college dinners that faculty were expected to
    attend and that facilitated cross-disciplinary communication, connec-
    tivity, and relationship building.

Gothenburg, Sweden's second largest city, has a 200-year history of large
and successful firms making it the nation's most R&D intense per capita.

A cultural challenge for Chalmers University lies in supporting researchers to commercialize intellectual assets and at the same time perform high-quality research and education. The context/culture of New York City has been an extremely important catalyst for New York University's transition as an entrepreneurial university. As the case narrative states, NYU, in keeping with the founder's vision, is "in and of the city" and draws inspiration from the city's international and entrepreneurial vitality. The financial crises of 2008 motivated the city's mayor and the NYU president to focus on entrepreneurship and innovation to diversify the city's economic base beyond Wall Street. In fairly rapid succession, the NYC Economic Development Corporation, a public–private partnership with NYU Poly, launched the Varick Street Incubator in 2009 followed by the NYC Accelerator, the DUMBO Incubator, and most recently the Clean Technology Entrepreneur Center.

The predecessor institutions of Kymenlaakso University of Applied Sciences had some experience with student projects with and for the regional business community, but apart from company visits this kind of activity was more or less forbidden fruit in the 1980s. By the early 1990s vocational colleges were given more freedom in their engagement with businesses; however, grey areas remain regarding charging money for projects and compensating teachers, including how to handle arrangements involving a faculty-owned company. As the promotion of entrepreneurial activity gained importance it was seen by many faculty and administrators as a question of including traditional business subjects (marketing, accounting, finance, business planning) into the curricula of non-business programmes. In the university's business department, the general view was that there was no need to add or change anything in curricula or in methods of teaching as it was thought that, by definition, the business department taught business subjects and also informed about entrepreneurs and their work. Rigour had only one meaning – academic –which may generally explain a culturally deep-rooted opposition towards bringing entrepreneurship ideology into the university.

Although "entrepreneurial fever" has recently and steadily grown across all university colleges of UT Austin, the broader Austin region was considered to be an important catalyst for the entrepreneurial turn of the university. And despite a significant decline of the state's financial support for the university and other emerging regional challenges, including a dramatically rising cost of living and traffic congestion, the Austin case suggests that two main cultural assets of Austin's DNA will continue to set the region apart as a "talent magnet" and recognized leader in creativity and innovation. One is the high level of open and accepting "live and let live" or "keep Austin weird" culture that the authors suggest is sustained by Austin's music, cultural, and creative environment. Austin's second defining asset is seen to be the cooperative "can do" attitude that key academic, business, and government influencers exhibit when coming together at important moments to implement regional action strategies or to assist civic, social, or technology entrepreneurship.

Public and private leaders at the regional level first championed the founding of the University of Stavanger in 1965; but this vision for higher education was not supported by Norway's national government which supported a new university in the far north in Tromsø. Despite the lack of national support, public and private leaders representing Stavanger's rapidly growing oil and gas industry pushed to found the University of Stavanger (UiS) in 2005. Stavanger is considered an entrepreneurial region where one can find a mixture of local and international networks symbolized by openness and trust. Such networks were important for fostering a "harmony culture" that came out of the understanding that consensus around key regional decisions was an imperative for successful implementation.

Despite Tromsø being identified as the "capital of the north", Tromsø University also faces difficult cultural challenges due to the university's lack of business school traditions, its inherently public sector and administrative environment, its geographical remoteness, and its arctic climate. Also, despite the region's research-based companies and growing industries within biotechnology and satellite industries, entrepreneurial traditions are weak and lack a culture of venture financing and investment capital. The experience with the Business Creativity Entrepreneurship (BCE) programme working with UiT faculty indicates that a culture change towards commercialization is beginning but still has a long way to go.

The case narratives strengthen our belief that the institutional, regional, and industrial context and culture in which a university is embedded are of huge importance for developing programmes and activities supportive of entrepreneurship and technology venturing. The "culture" component, as presented in the case narratives, emphasizes the importance of regulative, normative, and cognitive levels of influence and associated approaches to entrepreneurship, innovation, and regional economic development.

Leadership

Nelles and Vorley (2010a) emphasize the qualifications and orientation of key influencers including university administrators, boards of directors, department heads, and "star scientists" as important to the development of an entrepreneurial architecture. Formal and informal leadership is clearly exercised both inside and outside the academy in the governance processes through which the university determines its direction and contributions to the entrepreneurial turn. On the informal side, there is recognition of the roles key actors have, both inside and outside the university, as opinion leaders. This dimension also applies to the social and cultural (e.g. context) position universities often hold as leading institutions in their regions, especially as a source of educated talent, knowledge, and technology.

The Cambridge Phenomenon, launched in the 1960s, was motivated by an informal and influential "group of 25" local academic, business, and government influencers who represented all the agencies of a modern innovation ecosystem. Several of these individuals visited Silicon Valley, California; they formed a similar vision of Cambridge as a centre for hi-tech business; and they took personal responsibility to make this happen. At the regulative level, a key milestone in Cambridge's evolution was the 1969 Mott Committee Report that was a response to a 1964 national government initiative that urged UK universities to expand their contract with industry. The objective was to increase the return from the country's investment in basic research and higher education. One of the report's recommendations was to develop a science and technology (S&T) park to cluster technically advanced industry close to research.

NYU's emergence as a leading entrepreneurial university was championed by NYU's president, the governor of New York State and the mayor of New York City. Governor Andrew M. Cuomo launched START-UP NY to create tax-free zones to attract and grow new businesses across the state and to accelerate entrepreneurship and job creation. Mayor Michael Bloomberg emphasized the importance of the entrepreneurial economy in all five of NYC's boroughs. Similarly, key influencers from The University of Texas at Austin, state and city government, and regional business were critical to Austin's winning major national R&D consortia that catalysed the city's transformation from a university and state government town to a major technology centre.

An early and important catalyst for the entrepreneurial turn of The University of Texas was the appointment of a successful California-based entrepreneur, Dr George Kozmetsky as Dean of the university's College of Business in 1966. Dean Kozmetsky founded the IC^2 (Innovation, Creativity, and Capital) Institute, at UT Austin in 1977 and in 1989 secured university, city, and chamber of commerce financial and other support to launch the Austin Technology Incubator and the Texas Capital Network. Several of UT Austin's later developed entrepreneurial support structures were founded by students, such as Moot Corp, a well-recognized international graduate school of business entrepreneurship competition which is now called Venture Labs and is in its 30th year of operation. Nelles and Vorley (2010a) include "star scientists" as being important leaders in the entrepreneurial turn. The Austin case emphasizes the importance of endowed professorships in science and technology to attract high-quality faculty who can help win major competitive research funding and attract highly capable students, all of which were key to building world-class centres of research and education excellence.

Kingston University's recently appointed Vice-Chancellor motivated KUL to launch a new "Led by Learning" organizational strategy with the objective of building Kingston's entrepreneurial reputation across a range of domains. This strategy was designed to enable continuous learning by faculty, students, and staff, by pushing the boundaries of teaching, research, and professional practice to develop potential, transform lives, and improve the world. As a follow-on effort, in 2012/2013, the Vice-Chancellor initiated strategic changes that were targeted to reward academic enterprise activity and to inspire overall cultural change for KUL. For example, the Academic Progression and Promotion (AP&P) initiative for the first time, rewards academics with career progression through to a professorship on the basis of their international reputation and expertise including "enterprise and knowledge transfer".

Torkel Wallmark spent 14 years at RCA Laboratories in Princeton, New Jersey, where he was inspired by the emerging microelectronics revolution and the opportunities he envisioned for academic entrepreneurship in Sweden. In 1964 he was appointed professor at Chalmers University and in this capacity was a big supporter of innovation and entrepreneurship. As a result, the university was an early leader in having an innovation centre that provided advice and courses to professors and students who were interested in starting technology-based ventures. Continuing this effort, Wallmark's successor, Soren Sjolander, co-founded important entrepreneurial support structures, including the first Swedish US-type of venture capital firm in 1994; the school of entrepreneurship in 1997; starting the university's own seed investor fund in 1998; and launching an incubator in 1999.

From the perspective of Lund University Innovation System (LUIS) there had, for a long time, been an attitude at the university that cooperation with the surrounding society was not necessary. This has gradually changed and an important catalyst was when Per Eriksson took over as Vice-Chancellor in 2009. He came from being general director of VINNOVA, the Swedish governmental agency for innovation systems. He thought that Lund University should support innovation in areas important to society and that social scientists should dare to be involved in societal development and not just act as evaluating and critical scientists.

The Kymenlaakso case describes, on a personal level, the hard facts about university reorganization. As the author states, real development of curricula (or development of anything) in a university, is very dependent on the respective department heads, which results in wide variance in change attempts. He notes that the slow pace of integration between departments with respect to curriculum development, for instance, was to be expected since the majority of established department heads remained despite the addition of a new organization level of sector directors. New university-wide functions were added, including coordinating teams for common studies in leadership and entrepreneurship and methodological studies. The university's reorganization provided fuel for important university developments as it legitimized and strengthened cross-disciplinary collaboration among individuals from "different corners of the university" working on special initiatives and projects concerning entrepreneurial activities and new models of learning environments to innovation ecosystems.

The case narrative of UiT illustrates how a strong rectorship has been essential to define a sustainable strategy for the Arctic University. The third mission at UiT is understood in terms of social responsibility toward the region as well as commercialization and entrepreneurship education. Tromsø's orientation towards the public sector and the 2010 launch of the business school has motivated the university to secure its position as "the capital of the north". Derek Clark, Director of the Handelshøgskolen School of Business and Economics, played an important role in supporting the innovation and entrepreneurship research group within the larger faculty of biosciences, fisheries, and economics. As the Business Creativity and Entrepreneurship (BCE) programme, the Design Thinking (DT) lab, and a PhD course in academic entrepreneurship were established, the faculty began to see collaboration advantages with entrepreneurship and innovation.

While the above examples emphasize top-down leadership initiatives, the important role of students as champions for the entrepreneurial university is stressed in many of the case narratives and has also been discussed in the literature (Politis *et al.*, 2011). An example of a top-down initiative motivating greater student involvement is Finnish higher education, that encourages students to become members of entrepreneurial associations when enrolling in a Finnish university. The Aalto case provides a useful example of students of the Aalto Entrepreneurship Society being at the forefront in the university's entrepreneurial ecosystem where top-down strategies and student-driven push came together in the development of the university's Presidential Circle, Centre for Entrepreneurship, and Ventures Program. Aalto University students also manage StartupSauna, the largest national seed accelerator program, and northern Europe's largest start-up event, Slush. The Kymenlaakso case provides a detailed description of how two rectors initiated and carried through transformational leadership which led to institutional change promoting a networked and team-based institution. Effective leadership at the team level was the result of pushing power and responsibility downwards in the organization. Mid-level leadership by a small number of committed entrepreneurship lecturers and department managers sustained the effort along with leadership from the students which took form through the Patteri Entrepreneurship Society (a student-run organization at Kyamk which supports an entrepreneurial spirit and gives practical advice and support to students with entrepreneurial goals).

Stavanger University was born as an act of regional civic entrepreneurship in 2005. Currently there are several actors at UiS that are moving the university toward a more entrepreneurial path including the Centre for Entrepreneurship and the Centre for Innovation Research that have helped stimulate entrepreneurial development at UiS. Working with the Centre for Entrepreneurship, UiS students have launched a venture capital competition and other events related to entrepreneurship across the campus. The student organization START has played an important role in fostering entrepreneurship at the university by working with industry representatives to launch new entre-preneurship courses at the master's level. In addition START students interested in entrepreneurial activities are encouraged to get involved in entrepreneurial programmes in other Norwegian universities.

These findings support recent research on the premises of shared gov-ernance on Nordic universities, where leadership and leadership develop-ment were shown to be a key measure in strengthening governance capacity (Stensaker and Vabø, 2013). The authors state that the challenge with the dominance of entrepreneurial governance emphasizing leadership is that trust and engagement are more easily linked to the personal charac-teristics of leaders than to cultural characteristics and the identity of the institution. These researchers also observed that most universities seem to overlook the cultural and symbolic aspects of governance, a finding that was also supported in our cases.

Systems

The "systems" component emphasizes networks and linkages that apply within the university and between the university and the external environ-ment. Since third-mission activities require reaching outside the university by initiating networks and building relationships, there may be tension as to where to focus time and effort. Furthermore, linkages within the univer-sity can be a constraint when vertical rigidities of academic disciplines do not accommodate horizontal linkages across the university community or to the "outside" business community. External relationships require considerable effort to build and maintain, which can conflict with the mandate to focus time and resources on deep academic verticals. Research on university–industry interactions emphasize that it takes a strong com-mitment from the university at several levels of responsibility to enable effective engagement with industry and to enhance the dialogue between industry and researchers, while lowering transaction costs (Ranga *et al.*, 2008; Bruneel *et al.*, 2010).

Several of the cases reveal how public–private collaboration was requested through regulative action. In the case of Sweden, a 1992 national law motivated universities to cooperate with surrounding institutions while focusing on entrepreneurship and technology. This national regulation had central importance in the development of the Lund University Innovation System and a similar impact on Chalmers University. Kingston University (KUL) led the WestFocus Consortium that was founded as a nationally inspired collaboration among seven quite different universities to leverage their unique strengths. Overcoming many challenges, the consortium was successful in creating the business portal (WestFocus) that had four main activities to foster communication across the partner institutions: know-ledge and business development networks, business creation, University Talent, and the Entrepreneurship Centre. As the lead member of the

WestFocus consortium, KUL manages the organization's governance on behalf of members, and in developing entrepreneurship activities within and beyond the consortium. KLU's Entrepreneurship Centre was initially conceptualized as a means of supporting regional SMEs; however, once WestFocus began operating, this remit was quickly expanded to include developing new enterprises and, in particular, encouraging students to value their own ideas and develop them into enterprises. These examples illustrate policy initiated collaboration of heterogeneous institutions with the aim of facilitating knowledge transfer among academics, students, alumni, entrepreneurs, businesses, and community groups.

While the case narratives indicate that university–industry linkages and resulting relationships can be either formal or informal, and research suggests that both are important, in a recent study of university–industry collaboration and its effect on innovation, Howells *et al.* (2012) found that informal links were more important than formal ones in terms of innovative outcomes for firms. In support of this finding, Chalmers University (which ranks number three in the world of the 2013 Leiden Ranking regarding university–industry collaboration) emphasizes that regional and university entrepreneurship activities were developed without much organized effort from the university. Initially informal faculty networks with industry were facilitated, in the 1970s, by the Innovation Centre and Chalmers Industrial Technologies (CIT) that conducted commercial R&D. Over the years, faculty–industry interaction was increasingly supported by such initiatives as appointing Wallmark Professor of Innovation Engineering in 1982, by facilitating incubator seed investors, and launching a school of entrepreneurship in the late 1990s.

Chalmers third evolution of an entrepreneurial architecture was launched in 2005 and represents a heightened integration of research and innovation into a network model where research groups get support in dealing proactively with innovation in their research strategies and where students are expected to have hands-on learning throughout their education. Collaboration across academic institutions seems to be especially challenging regarding technology commercialization. While informal collaboration between Chalmers University and the University of Gothenburg initially seemed to be productive, opportunities from such consolidation have yet to be realized as complexities within each university made it questionable about the wisdom of cross-institutional structural consolidation.

Several of the cases exemplify how collaboration between university leadership and regional government can be beneficial to the entrepreneurial turn. New York University is a good example of how a university can be a regional asset for collaboration among diverse regional networks needed for the entrepreneurial turn where city-wide structural components are leveraged by university entrepreneurial programmes and activities. NYU's success in establishing the entrepreneurial turn was the result of a collaborative effort between city and state government leaders and the university chancellor.

The Tromsø case emphasizes that a strong Artic research base is a pre-requisite for building strong regional, national, and international networks and entrepreneurial programmes. Formal and informal networks have been formed around select academic disciplines linked to regional and industry needs. For example, the Business Creation and Entrepreneurship (BCE) programme has fostered student initiatives that have been important in creating an entrepreneurial culture across the university and within the region. BCE students, of which about 50 per cent are foreign, have launched ventures involving university research with the participation of local public–private sectors. In such a small town, individual actors become known and there is little distance between academics, business leaders, and policymakers. The common objectives are to strengthen Tromsø's position as a knowledge city and to establish platforms for ensuring economic growth and societal and environmental sustainability while promoting higher education in the north and research nationally and internationally.

Stavanger public–private committees and workshops established the ARNE Project with the Stavanger Chamber of Commerce that created a sense of common direction within the region which led to the formation of the Greater Stavanger Economic Development organization. However, the Stavanger case also illustrates that, while close and coordinated public–private collaboration can "get things done", there can also be perceptions of making it difficult to "think outside the box" when one group has too much influence. For example, due to the dominant success of the energy industry and its motivation to launch the University of Stavanger to educate needed talent and by providing excellent job and career opportunities for graduates, it has been a challenge for UiS to diversify its curriculum, to attract students to entrepreneurship, and to build the necessary momentum to develop an entrepreneurial culture that encourages risk-taking in creative and innovative arenas.

The Kymenlaakso case is an example of how faculty members, engaged by new leadership, became responsible for the entrepreneurial turn by rein-venting their roles in collaborative settings within the various networks and ecosystem of innovations. Outside partnerships were seen to con-tribute to the university's educational mission. This strategy was greatly helped by the Learning and Competence Creating Ecosystem (LCCE) model and accompanying corporate project liaison person on the univer-sity's campus, whose entrepreneurial drive knit companies tightly into courses and authentic interdisciplinary learning projects and processes through improved contracting of university–industry activities. This catalysed a "reinvented identity" in Kymenlaakso University from a disciplinary focus to more of a learning model, including a networked collaboration between institutional hierarchies of education.

To conclude, the system component is in many ways the glue, or con-nective tissue, of the entrepreneurial architecture within the university including regional and national contexts. As noted networks are inhabited by participants at multiple levels of influence, they span different organizations and milieus, and can be initiated by academic, business, or government actors at different levels of influence that are likely to change over time.

Strategies

The "strategies" component concerns institutional goals elaborated through planning documents, incentive structures, and policy (Nelles and Vorley, 2010a). Research has considered different university strategies for executing the third mission, including incentive structures and predictors of technology transfer performance (Henrekson and Rosenberg, 2001; Markman *et al.*, 2004; Powers and McDougall, 2005; and Nelles and Vorley, 2010a: 171). This book's case narratives highlight examples of strategy toward the entrepreneurial turn at the level of national, regional, and university policy.

The case narratives often highlight where key regional or national events have been the catalyst for policy initiatives that motivate university change toward the entrepreneurial turn. For example, while the Cambridge narrative emphasized the importance of regional public–private influencers, it is recognized that national policy was also important. As part of a competitiveness drive for British industry to harness new IT development, the CadCentre was launched in Cambridge in the 1960s as a national government initiative. And in an important strategic decision, the management of the centre was given to a private company rather than a research council so an industry perspective drove the selection of staff and the research agenda. This public–private initiative attracted relevant talent to the centre and to Cambridge which generated the first wave of regionally based hi-tech companies in the 1970s and helped create the needed businesses to attract additional business and entrepreneurial services to the region. A second important result of this strategic decision was to reinforce the linkage between the academic research community and emerging technology businesses as it was accepted that smart scientists could do interesting work in start-ups. An additional strategic change at Cambridge University involved the management of intellectual property. Historically the university allowed individual academics to use their research findings without reference to the UK legal position, but from 1970, with the founding of the Wolfson Industrial Liaison Office (WILO), a voluntary arrangement was instituted to help faculty who aspired to use IP from their work to find the right commercial outlet including licensing or spin-outs.

As with other case narratives, the larger context or institutional environment was the catalyst for KUL to develop a strategy that (1) responded to national government initiatives, and (2) would attract student applicants in London's extremely competitive higher education environment. To the first point, the Higher Education Funding Council for England (HEFCE) is responsible for university funding and in 2001, HEFCE announced a third-stream oriented funding programme, the Higher Education Innovation Fund (HEIF) "to support and develop a broad range of knowledge-based interactions between universities and colleges and the wider world, which result in economic and social benefit to the UK". KUL applied for and received funding from several HEIF grants that made possible KUL's efforts to develop an entrepreneurial architecture. To the second point, KUL strengthened and promoted its entrepreneurial programmes and activities to attract and retain students and to develop "the entrepreneurial person" as motivated by the potential and the need for enterprise education to address a wide range of skills, knowledge, attitudes, and capabilities.

Aalto University's entrepreneurship strategy was motivated by the desire to align national social development with the university's mission. The national government's directive was to merge the Helsinki School of Economics, Helsinki University of Technology, and the University of Art and Design in Helsinki. The expectations of the new institution include being a major hub for the Helsinki region while connecting public, private, and educational initiatives. The vision and strategy of Aalto University is to be the "world's best innovation university and to contribute to societal and economic development through world-class research, interdisciplinary collaboration, and pioneering education.

Due to large-scale paper industry operations, Kymenlaakso University was economically strong for the latter half of the twentieth century. Average salaries were high and public sector spending and growth were steady as both income and corporate tax payments were secure. However, the region's prosperity changed drastically with the closing of several large paper factories from 2000 to 2010. Kymenlaakso dropped from second place in GDP per capita to 11th among 19 regions in Finland. No other region had suffered such a drastic relative loss of fortunes in such a short time. Set in this rather dramatic context, the Kymenlaakso case tells the story of how a small university of applied sciences in a relatively small region transformed itself from being a provider of skilled labour to big industry and public sector authorities to an innovation-generating ecosystem and a provider of creativity and entrepreneurs across disciplines and professions.

Chalmers and Lund University (and other Swedish universities) have a somewhat unique strategy regarding commercializing university-based R&D. The Swedish model diffuses inventions through faculty offering patent ownership to industry partners and occasionally founding or co-founding ventures around their IP. Accordingly university licensing is almost non-existent and universities have almost no IP ownership role to play, other than when faculty voluntarily ask for such a link. Chalmers and Lund operate under such a "professor's privilege regime" which implies a bottom-up environment. While other universities worldwide have been focused on creating technology transfer offices (TTOs) and an IP and licensing model; Chalmers and Lund have focused on how innovation and entrepreneurship can be encouraged at the level of the individual professor rather than at the level of the institution.

The 1994 Swedish government transformation of Chalmers from a state university to a "private" foundation-based institution gave the university the freedom to operate and to form new structures and mechanisms for innovation and entrepreneurship. But it is still a work in progress concerning how to institutionalize the third mission along with the established missions of teaching and research. In a similar manner, based on its deep historical traditions in science and education, the Lund case demonstrates how a culture can be "produced" by a solid academic institution with an impressive heritage that has generated a normative pillar that sets the standard for activities the university will perform.

On the one hand, Lund University's strategy has stressed the importance of excellence in teaching, research, and collaboration while the subject of entrepreneurship has been largely defined as "outreach". On the other hand, Lund was the first Swedish university to establish a Professor of Entrepreneurship and the first to initiate a science park. In brief, these cases demonstrate that when strong values, expectations, and standards are infused into organizations, it may take considerable time and effort for them to change. It is interesting to note that, for both Chalmers and Lund, engagement in the entrepreneurial turn was supported by Sweden's Higher Education Act of 1997 that stated that, in addition to "producing scientific knowledge and raising the level of advanced knowledge among students", the university should also "collaborate and cooperate with the surrounding society and inform about its actions".

University of Tromsø's strategy was to become academically excellent in areas that were especially relevant for the arctic environment. Such a focus has proved to be extremely beneficial for the university and for the region. It has facilitated the development of research and teaching competence that fills important gaps in the national university structure and also facilitates regional development. From UiT's launch of third-mission activities and programmes the focus was on creating jobs and wealth in the high north. Successions of rectors have followed the path of addressing the value and strength of the northern region and have not tried to copy the strategy of other more established Norwegian universities and regions. In short, the UiT case demonstrates a synergistic relationship between strategy and leadership within a regional context.

Stavanger launched its entrepreneurial effort in 1993 by opening Norway's first knowledge park followed by the TTO Prekubator in 2003. Both of these regionally focused entrepreneurial activities proceeded the funding of the University of Stavanger (UiS) in 2005. The strategic push was for the university to be a main source for qualified employees in the rapidly growing oil, energy, and related industries. As a result, UiS's role in the regional economy is primarily associated with the supply side of a qualified workforce resulting in the university's engagement in the third mission being less pronounced. Recruiting student talent for the university's third mission has been a challenge and UiS has yet to develop a competence base to become a recognized regional leader in innovation and entrepreneurship.

Structures

Uyarra (2010: 1239–1240) states that a university's age is a factor in its regional engagement. She suggests that newer universities tend to give economic development a higher priority than older universities and present external mechanisms better suited for engagement with the region than older institutions (Charles and Conway, 2001; OECD, 2007). This is an interesting observation given our case descriptions if, for example, we contrast Cambridge (established 1209) or Lund University (established 1666) with more recently established universities. Each of our case studies emphasizes an "over time" perspective as it was the task of the authors to best determine what contextual and organizational change events to elaborate and at what level of analysis to best describe these events. Accordingly, our cases demonstrate various degrees of timing, process, width, and strength of building the structure component of the entrepreneurial architecture.

Kingston University's entrepreneurial strategy was considerably strengthened in 2004 with government's Higher Education Innovation Fund and was able to build needed entrepreneurial programmes to attract and train students. It would seem that radical or disruptive innovation is more likely to come from Cambridge while Kingston will contribute most through student-driven incremental entrepreneurial activities. Despite the vast differences in institutional age, heritage, mission, and resources, both activities are important to regional and national entrepreneurial development. Whereas Lund's early milestones were dedicated to the overall development of the university, the period after 1940 added a focus on commercialization and building the university's current entrepreneurial architecture which is underpinned by three main structures and associated activities: entrepreneurship education, Ideon Science Park, and the university's technology transfer office (TTO), as well as collaboration across these entities.

The first science park in Europe was launched in Cambridge in 1973 with the active support of key participants in the region's emerging entrepreneurial economy. Launched in 1977, the IC^2 Institute was and continues to be an effective catalyst for the entrepreneurial turn at UT Austin and within the greater Austin region. Stavanger's Prekubator was launched in 2002 to facilitate the commercialization of research three years before the founding of the university. The University of Tromsø's Business Creativity and Entrepreneurship (BCE) Program was launched in 2008. Such structures can, with the supporting university and regional involvement, catalyse interest to initiate related or supporting entrepreneurial oriented programs and activities. In this way, the cases reveal a dynamic between structure and agency. Theoretically this supports Organizational Process Theory where Hernes (2014: 93) talks about temporal agency and event formation: "The agency of events lies in their ability to redefine the meaning of the past and define the contents of future events." Scott elaborates that conceptualizing "over time" is a challenging task since institutional change is an unending process of learning about the imperfect enactment of social rules in interaction with a complex and unpredictable environment (Scott, 2014).

In terms of physical structures, the most successful example of science and technology park development is described in the Cambridge case where each of several parks is associated with a Cambridge college. It all started when members of the "Group of 25" visited Silicon Valley and Stanford Research Park in the 1960s. With the support of the government-sponsored Mott Committee Report, the Cambridge area science park model was launched in 1973 with Trinity Science Park. (As another example of the diffusion of the science park model, history suggests that in 1981 a Finnish chemistry professor, Sture Forsén, read an article about the first British science park established in Cambridge and started to lobby for the establishment of Ideon that was established in 1983.) Eight college-affiliated research and technology parks in Cambridge have followed including St John's Innovation Centre in 1987; Granta Park in 1997; and Peterhouse Technology Park in 1988, the home of ARM, a world leader in semi-conductor research for mobile devices. A second wave of development has focused on the emergence of biotechnology. In more of a top-down initiative, the UK government identified Cambridge as the preferred location for national competiveness investments in biotechnology. Resulting success stories include the Laboratory of Molecular Biology established in 1962, the Sanger Institute and the Genome Campus, the European Bioinformatics Institute, and the Babraham Research Campus and all these Cambridge structural initiatives benefitted from Cambridge long history for related Nobel Prize-winning research.

Chalmers (established 1829) is also an early leader in entrepreneurship, programmes, and activities that have evolved and changed over 40 years from primarily internal academic structures (departments and innovation centres) into the mid-1990s to a period focusing on incubators and seed-financing, and a school of entrepreneurship linking students and technology transfer activities. A significant boost in third-stream activities came to Chalmers in 2007 when the Swedish government named the university as one of five key GoINN actor projects supported by an eight-year budget. This was a main source of mobilization and transformation at Chalmers, as GoINN focused on early-stage innovation processes and the building of intellectual assets around ongoing research by engaging advisors and commercial actors to process innovations around specific disclosures and to build intellectual assets.

Historically, Lund University was generally resistant to participation in regional engagement outside the faculties of medicine and engineering. But beginning in the 1980s the university started to see itself as an important actor in society and it was emphasized that collaborations with business society should be developed. The change in attitude was also influenced by the establishment of Ideon in 1983 which made it possible to exploit knowledge from the university. In 1994 the Lund University Limited Company (LUAB) was established to support university innovations and to ensure that knowledge from the university was commercialized. In 2003, Lund University Innovation (LUI) was formed to further encourage staff members to commercially exploit their knowledge as it was determined that university research and resulting ventures should generate funds to strengthen education and research.

NYU, in cooperation with other regional universities, city business leaders, and city and state government officials has launched and sustained a range of entrepreneurial structures, activities, and support services. In many instances these were motivated by university leaders; in other instances they were motivated by city and state government leaders and include the Berkley Center for Entrepreneurship and Innovation at the Stern School of Business, the NYU Poly Tech Incubator, and NYU's office of industrial liaison (OIL). As NYU implemented university-wide policies to increase its commercialization footprint, an important challenge was networking and coordinating across all the relevant entities. In response to this challenge the university founded the Mark and Debra Leslie Entrepreneurs Lab in 2013 to facilitate university-wide collaboration and coordination of a range of entrepreneurial structures and initiatives.

UT Austin's Office of Technology Licensing (OTL) was founded in 1991 and was staffed by lawyers with the main objective of "protecting" UT Austin IP. In 2003 the office was renamed the Office of Technology Commercialization (OTC) with an emphasis on technology marketing and licensing. Since 2011 OTC has organized a university-wide Commercialization Series and an Inventor of the Year award to celebrate outstanding faculty who exemplify the link between excellent research, technology transfer, and commercialization. UT Austin President William Powers noted at the 2014 event, "If necessity is the mother of invention, then surely education is its father. When the two come together in a place like The University of Texas at Austin, magnificent things happen." As "entrepreneurial fever" grew across UT Austin, each college began to claim its own entrepreneurial identity, including launching courses, competitions, and business incubation. Like the NYU case, a challenge of such "entrepreneurial fever" is establishing effective collaboration and coordination across the university to maximize the benefits to faculty and students and third-mission activities and impacts for the region and beyond.

Structures are clearly an important and controversial dimension in the entrepreneurial turn of a university and the surrounding region. On the one hand, university and regional examples abound, where a highly promoted technology park or incubator is constructed with minimal or no university and regional participation, no attention given to capacity-building or training for staff, and no plan for sustainability. On the other hand, the case narratives provide positive examples of structures that were positive and successful catalysts for fostering entrepreneurship. It is our belief that, with effective academic, business and regional government collaboration and an effective business model, structures can be an important and sustainable catalyst for the entrepreneurial turn. However, developing such structures should not be independent of the attitudes and norms towards entrepreneurship at the university as well as the region embedding the university.

Conclusion

Despite being constrained by our small number of case examples, at the start of our analyses we tried grouping the ten universities by characteristics like age of the institution, number of faculty or students, research budgets, or whether the university was located in a rural or city environment. The rationale was that these factors might relate to specific university profiles (age and size of the university, research versus teaching universities or whether they were located in a small region or large city) and that these characteristics could influence the universities entrepreneurial development. For example, were the older universities freer from central control? Were younger universities more entrepreneurial? Did larger universities or research or teaching universities exhibit early activity and success toward the entrepreneurial turn? However such a clustering of the cases around common characteristics did not prove useful for describing differences in entrepreneurial programmes on any of the five architecture dimensions. We then tried constructing a matrix comparing and contrasting the universities in terms of the importance, or lack of importance, of any one, or combination, of the five entrepreneurial dimensions. Each case narrative presents numerous examples of the impact, toward the entrepreneurial turn, of a university's culture, leadership, systems, strategies, and structures. But defining these dimensions in a table proved difficult since each is difficult to compartmentalize or measure. For example, when comparing across cases what does "structure" mean, each case gives examples of entrepreneurially oriented structures; however, the entities presented in each case ranged from science parks to incubators, technology transfer offices, business portals, and more.

The main conclusion from all the case narratives is the importance and impact of the regional and national context in which the university is embedded for the launch, development, and sustainability of programmes and activities supporting the entrepreneurial turn. In this regard, we are in strong agreement with Nelles and Vorley (2010b) concerning the importance of regional and national context on how and at what speed a university employs an entrepreneurial architecture. As institutionalists stress the continuing impact of the old on the new and the existing on the becoming, all the case narratives provide examples of where innovative actions make use of pre-existing activities and enter into existing contexts which affect them and to which they must adjust. The case narratives also emphasize "how things happen" to uncover the sources of agency in the entrepreneurial university. Clearly all five dimensions are interrelated and recursive, supporting the notion of the university as a social system (cf. Tsoukas and Hatch, 2001).

In a second major conclusion, the case narratives presented examples where institutional change toward the entrepreneurial turn was effectively initiated "top down" and "bottom up" by formal and informal leaders reacting to regulative, normative, and cognitive influences at regional and national levels of analysis. While some universities represent change efforts more influenced by and influencing the national context of higher education, other more regionally oriented universities arguably had less opportunity to have such a national impact. In some cases change was catalysed by national policy while in other cases there is almost complete freedom within the university as to its support of the third mission, as the organization had a large degree of independence from national control. It seems that, both by necessity and ability, some universities were more constrained by their regional context. However, even in the cases which emphasized university autonomy, a national law or environmental jolt was often an important motivator or supporter for change toward the entrepreneurial turn.

Analysis of the cases seems to question the Nelles and Vorley (2010a: 169) contention that successful implementation of the third mission requires coordination among all five dimensions and that the absence of one dimension may contribute to weakness in the evolution and implementation of the third mission. From the cross-case analyses, the general picture emerges that there are different ways to accomplish third-mission activities and even specific entrepreneurial architecture dimensions may be employed in different ways and strengths. However, in all cases, there is general agreement that the dimensions interact both within the academy and with regional actors well representing the multi-dimensional nature of a university's role in the organizational field of activity. We also question the conclusion that "none of the architecture dimensions is more important than the others in the entrepreneurial turn". As we have concluded, context at macro and regional levels is an important determinant of the entrepreneurial turn; we follow this logic by suggesting that context impacts university culture, which impacts leaders and influences that are critical to the implementation of successful and sustainable entrepreneurial systems, strategies, and structures. However, as institutional theory states, in organizational fields of concern there are feedback, or recursive loops, and organizational learning throughout these processes (Figure 12.2).

Accordingly we suggest that building "a structure" first – without considering university and regional leaders, systems, and strategies – is not the most effective or efficient way to motivate the entrepreneurial turn. Our proposition is that the development of such structures benefits by being aware of and perhaps influenced by existing normative and cognitive attitudes towards entrepreneurship at key levels or sectors within the university, as well as the region in which the university is embedded. Worldwide, there are countless government supported structures (e.g. science parks, incubators, research centres) built as a visible and important commitment to a creative and innovative economy that do not contribute to the entrepreneurial turn in a meaningful and sustainable manner.

In conclusion, university entrepreneurship is inherently institutional in character, in that the framework elaborates how developing entrepreneurially is a complex task crossing levels of influence and control while being strongly influenced by external institutional and organizational environments. The case narratives reveal that different universities have a different "take" on the entrepreneurial architecture dimensions that reflects the context in which they are embedded. The speed and depth of development of the architecture dimensions are heavily influenced and constrained by the national and regional context in which the university is embedded.

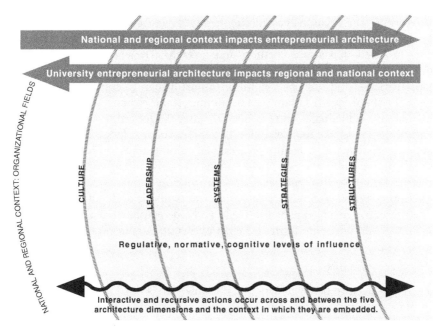

Figure 12.2 Interactive and recursive actions occur across the five architecture dimensions and the three pillars of influence as well as the context in which they are embedded.

Implications for future research

The architecture dimensions

The case narratives in this volume emphasize the authors' personal views of "their" university's entrepreneurial turn. This strategy resulted in insightful and rich narratives as well as highly personalized accounts. The architecture dimensions of culture, leadership, systems, strategies, and structures, while being useful frames of reference for the authors, were not well assessed in each of the cases. There is a need to better define and operationalize these dimensions so that their impact on the entrepreneurial turn can be specifically assessed. This is a challenging task as the case narratives show there is a broad range of styles, forms, programmes and activities that can be identified within the entrepreneurial turn. For example, the "culture" dimension as defined by Nelles and Vorley (2010a) includes institutional, departmental, and individual attitudes and norms. The case narratives did present interesting insights on these cultural dimensions and the cognitive-cultural pillar was presented as being important to consider, along with regulative and normative levels of influence, in institutional change. However, the cultural dimension was largely represented by an appreciation for the impact of regional and national context.

There is clearly a host of culturally themed issues to further explore in terms of the entrepreneurial turn. For example, are university and regional networking and relationship building highly structured, formalized, and vertical – or are they more informal, inclusive, and horizontal among participants involved in venture creation and growth? To what degree does the university value bottom-up communication for entrepreneurial initiatives? Does regional and university culture support a high tolerance for entrepreneurial risk-taking? Is failure seen as an important learning activity or as the end of an individual's entrepreneurial career? Does the regional culture encourage, reward, and celebrate entrepreneurship? Does the university, college, department, or faculty professional culture value and reward the economic and social impact of research or is the only important career success metric the number of published articles in select referred journals? In one interesting study, research indicates that the symbolic and cultural functions of governance arrangements are likely to be de-emphasized when entrepreneurial governance emphasizes leadership (Stensaker and Vabø, 2013).

The three missions

There is a need to better understand the university's third mission in relation to the academy's traditional emphasis on teaching and research. Some scholarship reports the potential for third-stream activities to detract from core university functions by prioritizing commercial imperatives and applied research over teaching and basic research (Nedeva, 2007; Naidoo, 2005). Other researchers find that there is sparse evidence that the third mission adversely affects teaching and/or basic research (Behrens and Gray, 2001; Geuna, 1999; Ziman, 1991), while still others assert that it has a positive impact on the core missions of the university (Martin and Etzkowitz, 2000). Vorley and Nelles (2008: 162) suggest that the integration of the entrepreneurial mission into teaching and research activities can reinforce a university's historically prominent missions. An important issue is the degree to which triangulating teaching, research, and third-stream activities reinforces the respective dynamics of each activity through recursive and reciprocal development. As stated by Vorley and Nelles (2008: 131) the third mission presents an opportunity for universities to redefine themselves as well as strengthen the core missions of teaching and research. An interesting and somewhat contrary research perspective is that the impetus for a university executing the third mission comes from the desire to be perceived as a legitimate or valued institution within society. According to this view, universities respond to regulative level by adapting or labelling structures and activities to legitimize their entrepreneurial role. The objective is to be perceived as an entrepreneurial university while at the same time protecting the core missions of teaching and research by decoupling third-mission activities and employing various types of buffers (DiMaggio and Powell, 1991; Meyer and Rowan, 1977; Erlingsdottir and Lindberg, 2005).

Organizational fields

All the case narratives emphasize the importance of national and regional context which impact and are impacted by the university, emphasizing the importance of "the ground" in which the university is embedded and which impacts the architecture dimensions. Future research should clarify and better define context in terms of organizational and institutional fields of concern. DiMaggio and Powell (1983: 148) define the organizational field as those organizations that, in the aggregate, constitute a recognized area of institutional life, such as key suppliers, resource and product consumers, regulatory agencies, and other organizations that produce similar products or services. According to Hoffman (1997: 352) "field" is formed around issues that become important to the interests and objectives of a specific collective of organizations. In our conceptualization, the organizational field of concern is defined by those organizations, agencies, programmes and activities and relationships that enhance or inhibit innovation-based economic development. While ecologists such as Hawley (1950), Warren (1967), and Astley (1983) employ the concept of inter-organizational community to focus on a geographically bounded collection of organizations rendered interdependent because of functional ties or shared localities, Scott and Meyer (1983: 132–133) point out that a limitation of the regionally based view is its tendency to focus more on colocation than on functional interdependence and the effect that important connections and exchanges have among organizations outside the spatial boundaries of the community at sectorial, societal, and trans-national levels. An important observation is that, while organizations may make claims about being, or not being, part of the field, their membership can be defined and measured through social interaction patterns. The relevant and important emerging research area of social physics, which applies the physics of complexity to the world of social science, is being used by scholars to measure structures and processes in the networked society (Urry, 2004; Butler and Stephens, 2014).

Organizational field is an intermediate unit between micro levels (individual actors and organizations) and macro levels of systems of societal and trans-societal actors. The focus is on the way higher- and lower-level actors and structures shape, reproduce, and change the contexts within which they operate. Research emphasizes interweaving of top-down and bottom-up processes as they combine to influence institutional phenomena (Barley and Tolbert, 1997). Our case narratives have given a host of instances where universities were penetrated by their environments and where they responded to these influence attempts creatively and strategically. As Scott emphasizes (2014), while organizations are creatures of their institutional environments, most modern organizations are constituted as active players not passive pawns. In short, there is a need to craft research designs on the entrepreneurial turn to more empirically examine the complex recursive processes by which universities and their surrounding contexts both shape and are shaped by organizational fields of activity and influence.

The diffusion and institutionalization of the entrepreneurial university

Universities are complex institutions on a range of dimensions; they have a long and distinguished history as exemplars of creative and innovative thinking and have been crucial to great advancements in science and deep analysis of humanities and the arts. Further, universities are often the champions of long-established traditions and ways of teaching and research. The literature presents a broad range of complex issues regarding the university's role in stimulating innovation and economic growth (Hughes and Kitson, 2012) and there is disagreement on how third stream activities should be defined and operationalized (Perkmann *et al.*, 2013). Universities are at a crossroads in terms of how students and society benefit most from scholarship, research, and teaching and how this knowledge might be best transferred, disseminated, used, and commercialized. In particular, science and technology commercialization has sparked research interest from institutional scholars studying institutional transformation (Powell *et al.*, 2007; Colyvas and Powell, 2006; Colyvas, 2007).

In "Gone shopping? Universities on their way to the market" (Czarniawska and Genell, 2002) present the emerging role of universities as moving from state-financed monopolies to self-financed participants within knowledge production markets. In "The rationalization of universities," Ramirez (2006: 244) concludes that the socially embedded university has become more prominent as the normative values of broad inclusiveness, social usefulness, and organizational flexibility become associated with recent democratization and marketization, making the traditional more restricted, distant, and timeless university less legitimate. This perspective builds on Scandinavian new institutionalists who embrace concepts of translation (Czarniawska and Joerges, 1996), imitation (Sevón, 1996), and editing (Sahlin-Andersson, 1996) as organizations are seen to become increasingly homogenous. On the one hand, Czarniawska and Sevón (2005) consider imitation as a central learning mechanism of universities in terms of the entrepreneurial turn. On the other hand, Scott (2014) emphasizes that there are differences among organizations in their response to the "same" environment, in that organizations learn from their own experience and the experience of others and while some practices or structures are adopted by some, they are not adopted by others in similar situations. Oliver (1991: 152) delineates five strategies that organizations/ universities can employ in responding to calls for institutional change: acquiescence or imitation and conformity; compromise; avoidance or concealment of efforts, including buffering parts of the organization, as exemplified in "loose-coupling" (Weick, 1976) or "myth and ceremony" (Meyer and Rowan (1977); defiance; and manipulation by attempting to co-opt influence or control the external pressure. Future research might consider these institutional perspectives in the diffusion and adoption of architecture dimensions of the entrepreneurial university.

Policy implications: capacity-building

There is great disparity among the cases as to the age of the university and its size in terms of faculty, students, and research budgets. On the one hand, newer universities in emerging regions have an important role to play in catalysing the entrepreneurial culture and activity of a region; however, they are generally in a weaker position than older more established universities, to successfully compete for national research funds and attitudes. On the other hand, older research universities often benefit from established research excellence, a track record of publications, and credibility to win competitive financial awards. Additionally, the financial value of knowledge transfer from universities is seen to vary with regional context. A main conclusion of the case analyses is that national and regional context impacts the speed and form of a university's development of an entrepreneurial architecture. Clearly, even within one university, there are important professional and cultural differences across and within colleges and research units in addition to levels of authority among faculty and administrators and students. Accordingly, policymakers at national and regional levels should appreciate that there is no "one best way" or "set of best practices" to legislate an entrepreneurial economy or entrepreneurial university and that policy directed at "the university" is often interpreted and employed differently across and within university colleges and departments. Accordingly, there is a challenge of how best to structure policy to fund research and capacity-building that recognizes and rewards established excellence as well as newer institutions or academic areas that do not have established and well-recognized research traditions. In short, how can policy initiatives encourage experimentation as well as capacity-building in newer universities as well as reward established centres of excellence toward the entrepreneurial turn? One suggested regional response is to build research excellence by pooling specific capacities of research excellence to build a critical mass of talent in areas that are seen to be of strategic importance (Kitagawa, 2010; Jessop, 2001, 2007).

References

Astley, G. and Van de Ven, A. (1983). Central perspectives and debates in organisation theory. *Administrative Science Quarterly*, 28, 245–273.

Barley, Stephen and Tolbert, P. (1997). Institutionalization and structuration: Studying the links between action and institution. *Organization Studies*, 18, 93–117.

Behrens, T.R. and Gray, D.O. (2001). Unintended consequences of cooperative research: Impact of industry sponsorship on climate for academic freedom and other graduate student outcome. *Research Policy*, 30(2), 179–199.

Bicknell, A., Francis-Smythe, J., and Arthur, J. (2010). Knowledge transfer: Deconstructing the entrepreneurial academic. *International Journal of Entrepreneurial Behaviour and Research*, 16(6), 485–501.

Bourdieu, P. and Wacquant, L.J. (1992). *An invitation to reflexive sociology*. Chicago: University of Chicago Press.

Butler, J.S. and Stephens, B. (2014). Reviving the theoretical tradition of social physics: The interdisciplinary impact of August Comte. Working paper, IC^2 Institute, The University of Texas at Austin.

Bruneel, J., D'Este, P., and Salter, A. (2010). Investigating the factors that diminish the barriers to university–industry collaboration. *Research Policy*, 39, 858–868.

Charles, D.R. and Conway, C.D. (2001). *Higher education–business interaction survey: A report to the UK HE Funding Bodies and the Office of Science and Technology*. Higher Education Funding Council for England.

Colyvas, J.A. (2007). From divergent meanings to common practices: The early institutionalization of technology transfer in the life sciences at Stanford University. *Research Policy*, 36(4), 456–476.

Colyvas, J.A. and Powell, W.W. (2006). Roads to institutionalization: The remaking of boundaries between public and private science. *Research in Organizational Behavior*, 27, 305–353.

Czarniawska, B. and Genell, K. (2002). Gone shopping? Universities on their way to the market. *Scandinavian Journal of Management*, 18(4), 455–474.

Czarniawska, B. and Joerges, B. (1996). Travels of ideas. In B. Czarniawska and G. Sevón (eds), *Translating Organizational Change* (pp. 13–48). Walter de Gruyter, New York.

Czarniawska, B. and Sevón, G. (2005). Translation is a vehicle, imitation its motor, and fashion sits at the wheel. In B. Czarniawska and G. Sevón (eds), *Global ideas: How ideas, objects and practices travel in the global economy* (pp. 7–12). Copenhagen: Liber and Copenhagen Business School Press.

D'Este, P. and Perkmann, M. (2011). Why do academics engage with industry? The entrepreneurial university and individual motivations. *Journal of Technological Transfer*, 36(3), 316–339.

DiMaggio, P. (1986). Structural analysis of organizational fields: A blockmodel approach. *Research in Organizational Behavior*, 8, 335–370

DiMaggio, P.J. and Powell, W.W. (1983). The iron cage revisited: Institutional isomorphism and collective rationality in organizational fields. *American Sociological Review*, 48(2), 147–160.

DiMaggio, P.J. and Powell, W.W. (eds) (1991). *The new institutionalism in organizational analysis* (Vol. 17). Chicago: University of Chicago Press.

Eisenhardt, K.M. and Graebner, M.E. (2007). Theory building from cases: Opportunities and challenges. *Academy of Management Journal*, 501(1), 25–32.

Erlingsdottír, G. and Lindberg, K. (2005). Isomorphism, isopraxism, and isonymism: Complementary or competing processes? In C. Barbara and S. Guje (eds), *Global ideas: How ideas, objects and practices travel in the global economy* (pp. 47–71). Malmö: Liber and Copenhagen Business School.

Foss, L. (2012) "The university–industry interface: A collaborative arena. In H.C.G. Johnsen, and R. Ennals (eds), *Creating collaborative advantage: Innovation and knowledge creation in regional economies* (pp. 209–221). Farnham: Gower.

Geuna, A. (1999). *The economics of knowledge production: Funding and the structure of university research*. Northampton, MA: Elgar.

Grimaldi, R., Kenney, M., Siegel, D.S., and Wright, M. (2011). 30 years after Bayh–Dole: Reassessing academic entrepreneurship. *Research Policy*, 40, 1045–1057.

Hackman, J.R. (2003). Learning more by crossing levels: Evidence from airplanes, hospitals, and orchestras. *Journal of Organizational Behavior*, 24(8), 905–922.

Hawley, A. (1950). *Human ecology*. New York: Ronald Press.

Henrekson, M., and Rosenberg, N. (2001). Designing efficient institutions for science-based entrepreneurship: Lesson from the US and Sweden. *Journal of Technology Transfer*, 26, 207–231.

Hernes, T. (2014). *A process theory of organization*. Oxford: Oxford University Press.

Hoffman, A. (1997). *From heresy to dogma: An institutional history of corporate environmentalism*. San Francisco: New Lexington Press.

Holand, A.M. (2014). Academic Entrepreneurship term paper for BED 8004, University of Tromsø, Norway.

Howells, J., Ramlogan, R., and Cheng, S.L. (2012). Innovation and university collaboration: paradox and complexity within the knowledge economy. *Cambridge Journal of Economics*, 36(3), 703–721.

Hughes, A. and Kitson, M. (2012). Pathways to impact and the strategic role of universities: New evidence on the breadth and depth of university knowledge exchange in the UK and the factors constraining its development. *Cambridge Journal of Economics*, 36(3), 723–750.

Jessop, B. (2001). Institutional re(turns) and the strategic-relational approach. *Environment and Planning A*, 33(7), 1213–1236.

Jessop, B. (2007). *State power, A strategic-relational approach*. Cambridge: Polity Press.

Johnson, P. and Duberley, J. (2000). *Understanding management research: An introduction to epistemology*. Thousand Oaks, CA: Sage.

Kitagawa, F. (2010). Pooling resources for excellence and relevance: An evolution of universities as multi-scalar network organisations. *Minerva*, 48, 169–187.

Markman, G.D., Gianiodis, P.T., Phan, P.H., and Balkin, D.B. (2004). Entrepreneurship from the ivory tower: Do incentive systems matter? *Journal of Technology Transfer*, 29(3–4), 353–364.

Martin, B. and Etzkowitz, K. (2000). The origin and evolution of university species, *VEST*, 13(3–4), 409–434.

Meyer, J.W. and Rowan, B. (1977). Institutionalized organizations: Formal structure as myth and ceremony. *American Journal of Sociology*, 83, 340–363.

Naidoo, R. (2005). Universities in the marketplace: The distortion of teaching and research. In R. Barnett (ed.), *Reshaping the university* (pp. 27–36). Maidenhead, UK: Open University Press/McGraw-Hill.

Nedeva, M. (2007). New tricks and old dogs? The "third mission" and the reproduction of the university". In *The world yearbook of education 2008: Geographies of Knowledge/Geometries of Power: Framing the Future of Higher Education* (pp. 85–105). New York: Routledge.

Nelles, J. and Vorley, T. (2010a). Constructing an entrepreneurial architecture: An emergent framework for studying the contemporary university beyond the entrepreneurial turn. *Innovation in Higher Education*, 35, 161–176.

Nelles, J. and Vorley, T. (2010b). From policy to practice: Engaging and embedding the third mission in contemporary universities. *International Journal of Sociology and Social Policy*, 30(7/8), 341–353.

Oliver, C. (1991). Strategic responses to institutional processes. *Academy of Management Review*, 16, 145–179.

Owen-Smith, J. and Powell, W.W. (2001). Careers and contradictions: Faculty responses to the transformation of knowledge and its uses in the life sciences. *Research in the Sociology of Work*, 10, 109–140.

Perkmann, M., Tartari, V., McKelvey, M., Autio, E., Broström, A., D'Este, P., Fini, R., Geuna, A., Grimaldi, R., Hughes, A., Krabel, S., Kitson, M., Llerena, P., Lissoni, F., Salter, A., and Sobrero, M. (2013). Academic engagement and commercialisation: A review of the literature on university–industry relations, *Research Policy*, 42, 423–442.

Philpott, K., Dooley, L., O'Reilly, C., and Lupton, G. (2011). The entrepreneurial university: Examining the underlying academic tensions. *Technovation*, 31(4), 161–170.

Politis, D., Winborg, J., and Dahlstrand, A. (2011). Exploring the resource logic of student entrepreneurs. *International Small Business Journal*, 30(4), 659–683.

Powell, W.W., Owen-Smith, J., and Colyvas, J.A. (2007). Innovaton and emulation: Lessons from American universities in selling private rights to public knowledge. *Minerva*, 45(2), 121–142.

Powers, J.B. and McDougall, P.P. (2005). University start-up and technology licensing with firms that go public: A resource-based view of academic entrepreneurship. *Journal of Business Venturing*, 20, 291–311.

Ramirez, F.O. (2006). The rationalization of universities. In M.-L. Djelic (ed.), *Transnational governance: Institutional dynamics of regulation* (p. 244). Cambridge: Cambridge University Press.

Ranga, L.M., Miedema, J., and Jorna, R. (2008). Enhancing the innovative capacity of small firm through triple helix interactions: Challenges and opportunities. *Technology Analysis and Strategic Management* 20(6), 69.

Rasmussen, E., Mosey, S., and Wright, M. (2014). The influence of university departments on the evolution of entrepreneurial competencies in spin-off ventures. *Research Policy*, 43, 92–106.

Sahlin-Andersson, K. (1996). Imitating by editing success: The construction of organizational fields. In B Czarniawska and G. Sevón (eds), *Translating organizational change* (pp. 69–92). Berlin: Walter de Gruyter.

Scott, W.R. (2014). *Institutions and organizations: Ideas, interests, and identities*. 4th edition. Sage.

Scott, W.R. and Meyer, J.W. (1983). The organization of societal actors. In J. Meyer and W.R. Scott (eds), *Organizational environments: Ritual and rationality* (pp. 132–133). Beverly Hills, CA: Sage.

Sevón, G. (1996). Organizational imitation in identity transformation. In B. Czarniawska and G. Sevón (eds), *Translating organizational change* (pp. 49–68). New York: de Gruyter.

Stensaker, B. and Vabø, A. (2013). Re-inventing shared governance: implications for organisational culture and institutional leadership. *Higher Education Quarterly*, 67(3), 256–274.

Streeck, W. (2010). Institutions in history: Bringing capitalism backing. In Glenn Morgan, John L. Campbell, Colin Crouch, Ove Kaj Pederson, and Richard Whitley (eds), *The Oxford handbook of contemporary institutional analysis* (pp. 659–686). Oxford: Oxford University Press.

Tsoukas, H. and Hatch, M.J. (2001). Complex thinking, complex practice: The case for a narrative approach to organizational complexity. *Human Relations*, 54(8), 979–1013.

Urry, J. (2004). Small worlds and the new "social physics." *Global Networks*, 4, 109–130.

Uyarra, E. (2010). Conceptualizing the regional roles of universities: Implications and contradictions. *European Planning Studies*, 8(8), 1227–1246.

Vorley, T. and Nelles, J. (2008). (Re)conceptualizing the academy: Institutional development of and beyond the third mission. *Higher Education Management and Policy*, 20(3), 1–17.

Warren, R. (1967). The interorganizational field as a focus for investigation. *Administrative Science Quarterly*, 12, 396–419.

Weick, K. (1976). Educational organizations as loosely coupled systems. *Administrative Science Quarterly*, 21, 1–19.

Welter, F. (2011). Contextualizing entrepreneurship: Conceptual challenges and ways forward. *Entrepreneurship Theory and Practice*, 35(1), 165–184.

West, G.P. (2003). Connecting levels of analysis in entrepreneurship research: A focus on information processing, asymmetric knowledge and networks. In C. Steyaert and D. Hjorth (eds), *New movements in entrepreneurship* (pp. 51–70). Northampton, MA: Edward Elgar.

Ziman, J. (1991). Academic science as a system of markets. *Higher Education Quarterly*, 45(1), 41–61.

Index

Please note that page numbers relating to notes will be denoted by the letter 'n' and note number following the note. Page references to figures will be in **bold**, while those for tables will be *italics*.